THE NATIONAL TRIBUNE Remembers the Atlanta Campaign

Battles, Skirmishes, Marches, and Camp Life as Recalled by the Union Veterans Themselves

edited by
STEPHEN DAVIS

SB
Savas Beatie
California

First edition, first printing

Library of Congress Cataloging-in-Publication Data

Names: Davis, Stephen, 1948- editor.
Title: The National Tribune Remembers the Atlanta Campaign: Battles, Skirmishes, Marches, and Camp Life as Recalled by the Union Veterans Themselves / edited by Stephen Davis.
Other titles: Battles, skirmishes, marches, and camp life as recalled by the Union veterans themselves
Description: El Dorado Hills, CA : Savas Beatie, [2025] | Selections from material published in the National Tribune between 1877 and 1911. | Includes bibliographical references and index. | Summary: "Edited by Stephen Davis, this offers 70 selections pertaining to the Atlanta Campaign. Our hope is that these entries advance the cause of Civil War scholarship by bringing back into print an array of some of the most important writing about the conflict penned by the men who fought in it"-- Provided by publisher.
Identifiers: LCCN 2024056318 | ISBN 9781611217278 (paperback) | ISBN 9781611217285 (ebook)
Subjects: LCSH: Atlanta Campaign, 1864--Personal narratives. | Atlanta Campaign, 1864--Press coverage. | Atlanta Campaign, 1864--Sources. | United States--History--Civil War, 1861-1865--Veterans. | National Tribune (Newspaper)
Classification: LCC E476.7 .N38 2025 | DDC 973.7/371--dc23/eng/20250203
LC record available at https://lccn.loc.gov/2024056318

SB
Savas Beatie
989 Governor Drive, Suite 101
El Dorado Hills, CA 95762
916-941-6896 / sales@savasbeatie.com / www.savasbeatie.com

All of our titles are available at special discount rates for bulk purchases in the United States. Contact us for information.

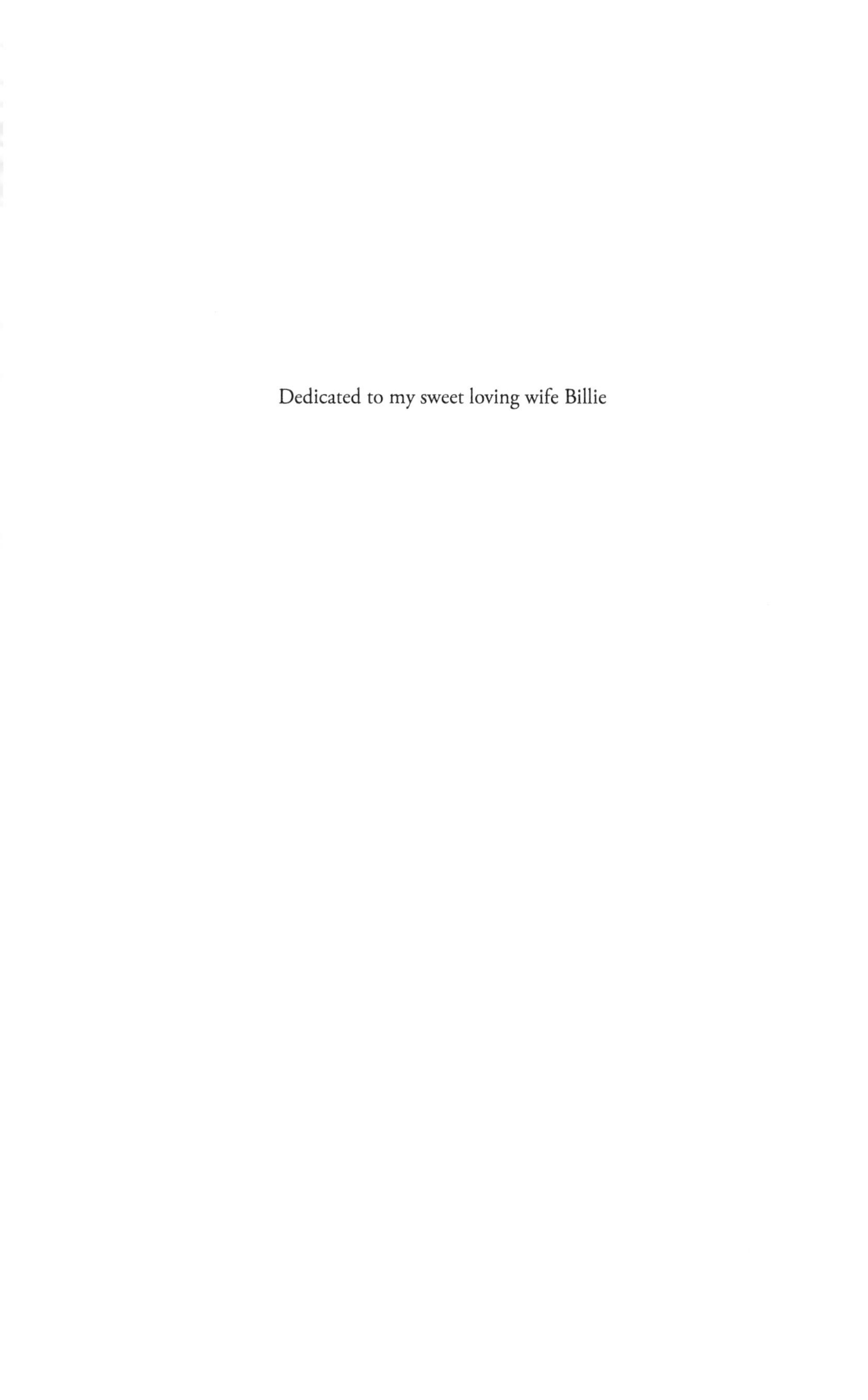

Dedicated to my sweet loving wife Billie

TABLE OF CONTENTS

TABLE OF CONTENTS (continued)

TABLE OF CONTENTS (continued)

Introduction

> Still, everyone who writes truthfully of what fell under his immediate observation at least adds something to history, and is therefore to be given due credit for what he contributes, so there is something to be gained even in thrashing over the straw.

So wrote First Lieutenant A. J. Gleason in an article published in the *National Tribune* of February 11, 1897. Writing about a couple of Northern comrades' recollections of the battle of Pickett's Mill, Georgia, fought on May 27, 1864, Gleason mildly chided two authors for getting the names of the battle wrong (both called it New Hope Church, which was fought two days earlier). But his point was a good one: "everyone who writes truthfully of what fell under his immediate observation at least adds something to history."[1] Lieutenant Gleason could not have better described the contents of the *National Tribune* or hinted at the importance of its articles to today's students and scholars of the Civil War.

Modern historian Richard A. Sauers proclaimed the *National Tribune* as "the premier newspaper published for Union veterans of the Civil War and their families." George E. Lemon, editor and proprietor, who was himself a veteran of the 125th New York Infantry, founded the newspaper in October 1877 in Washington, D.C., as a monthly, eight-page paper.[2] A year's subscription was modestly priced at $1 with Lemon urging readers to hand each copy around to other veterans whom he sought to build his subscriber base.[3]

1 A. J. Gleason, "Confusion as to Names: New Hope Church, Pickett's Mill, Dallas" (February 11, 1897), 3.

2 Richard A. Sauers, "Introduction" in Sauers, ed., *The National Tribune Civil War Index: A Guide to the Weekly Newspaper Dedicated to Civil War Veterans, 1877-1943*, 3 vols. (El Dorado Hills, CA: Savas Beatie, 2018), 1:vii.

3 "History of the Bounty Bill," "Twain's Tales," "Introductory," and "Terms to Subscribers" (October 1877), vol. 1, no. 1; James Marten, *Sing Not War: The Lives of Union & Confederate Veterans in Gilded Age America* (Chapel Hill: University of North Carolina Press, 2011), 147.

Its first issue demonstrated the purposes of Lemon's newspaper. The first page declared it to be "a monthly journal devoted to the interests of the soldiers and sailors of the late war, and all pensioners of the United States." Accordingly, volume 1, no. 1 carried long articles about Union soldiers' pensions. A Washington attorney, Lemon specialized in helping Union veterans secure their rightful compensation. Since *National Tribune* intended to educate as well as entertain, page two reprinted a story by Mark Twain that had appeared in the *Atlantic* that month.

"Is the Country Too Poor to Pay Its Soldiers?" headlined the paper's second issue in November 1877, reemphasizing Lemon's primary purpose with the *National Tribune.* The paper also offered such diversions as a poem entitled "An April Fool," an article on Abraham Lincoln as a duelist, and a subscription appeal to members of the Grand Army of the Republic, the principal postwar organization of Union veterans. As a further inducement, the editor announced in February 1878 that he was reducing his subscription rate from a dollar to fifty cents. "Soldiers stand by the *National Tribune*," he implored, "give us a circulation of 250,000, and we will put through the Pension and Bounty Bills, and will effect the needed reforms in the Pension Office. Do not delay. Decide fairly, frankly, and at once."[4]

Lemon was not above stoking wartime animus. The front page of his issue for February 1878 spotlighted the horrors of Andersonville, the notorious Confederate prison camp in southwest Georgia, complete with graphic woodcuts of emaciated inmates. One was of Private John Breinig, showing his frightened countenance, his unkempt beard and hair, and his skin-and-bones body lying helplessly in bed. Its caption read, "admitted April 18, 1864. Improved a little for two weeks, then gradually failed and died on the 12th instant." An accompanying article explained how the pictures had been obtained from the U.S. Committee on the Conduct of the War. In it was printed a letter, sent on behalf of the committee chairman, Ohio senator Benjamin F. Wade, harrowingly describing the condition of Breinig and other Andersonville prisoners. "No one, from these pictures, can form a true estimate of their condition then," it asserted; "not one in ten was able to stand alone; some of them so covered and eaten by vermin that they nearly resembled cases of small-pox and so emaciated that they were *really* living skeletons."[5]

As Lemon suggested in February 1879, the paper began catching on with the public. "Friends," the editor explained, "we are sorry to inform you we cannot

4 "Is the Country Too Poor to Pay Its Soldiers?", "An April Fool," "President Lincoln as a Duelist," "Grand Army of the Republic" (November 1877), vol. 1, no. 2; "Reduction of Subscription" and "Soldiers Stand by the *National Tribune*" (February 1878).

5 "Andersonville" and "Photographs of Prisoners of War, Showing Their Condition When They Reached the Union Lines" (February 1878), vol. 1, no. 5.

supply back numbers. We have had such a rush and demand for them, that we exhausted a large extra edition. You can have the January number, 1879, for free."[6]

The breakthrough came when the *National Tribune* began printing articles on war history. In January 1878, Lemon reprinted from the *Rochester* (NY) *Democrat and Chronicle* a veteran's article, "Reminiscences of Gettysburg." A few months later, it reprinted an additional piece from the *Harrisburg Telegraph* about Northern enlistments of 1861. A year later, in March 1879, the paper excerpted a letter received from G. N. Bachelor of Fitchburg, Michigan. It contained several anecdotes that he remembered from the war, including his service under Brigadier General Lovell Rousseau at Perryville. Then followed in April a piece entitled "An Iowa Mother Who Had Eleven Sons in the U.S. Army—Their Record" (three had died in the war). Two months later, the June issue featured "A Memory of the War: The Amputation of Gen. Rice's Limb" at Kennesaw Mountain.[7]

This is where we begin—the first article pertaining to the Atlanta Campaign, one of a hundred or so articles reprinted in this collection. We are not placing them in the order in which they appeared in the *National Tribune*; instead, we have arranged the articles in a chronological order of the campaign, adding editorial background or commentary.

Some three and a half years after its founding, the *National Tribune* was doing so well that on August 20, 1881, George Lemon turned his paper from a monthly into a weekly. Then, a few years later in 1884, Lemon hired John McElroy, another Union veteran, as managing editor. McElroy formerly edited the *Toledo Blade* and had written a sensational memoir of his wartime imprisonment, *Andersonville* (1879), which was said several decades later to have sold 600,000 copies. After Lemon's death in December 1896, McElroy bought the paper, serving as owner and editor until his death in October 1929. W. L. Mattocks then became editor.[8]

6 "Back Numbers" (February 1879), vol. 2, no. 2.

7 "Reminiscences of Gettysburg"(January 1878), vol. 1, no. 4; "The Truth of History" (April 1878), vol. 1, No. 7; "Soldier's Anecdotes" (March 1879), vol. 2, no. 3: "An Iowa Mother Who Had Eleven Sons in the U.S. Army—Their Records" (April 1879), vol. 2, no. 4; "A Memory of the War: The Amputation of Gen. Rice's Limb" (June 1879), vol. 2, no. 6.

8 Sauers, "Introduction," vii-viii, xi; John McElroy, *Andersonville: A Story of Rebel Military Prisons, Fifteen Months a Guest of the So-Called Southern Confederacy* (Toledo: D. R. Locke, 1879); "For Commander-in-Chief" (December 23, 1909), from McElroy's 600,000 copies. McElroy's prison expose was reprinted by the *National Tribune*'s Washington publishing company in 1899 (William Marvel, *Andersonville: The Last Depot* [Chapel Hill: University of North Carolina Press, 1994], 319). More recent editions are Roy Meredith, ed., *This Was Andersonville* (New York: McDowell, Obolensky, 1957) and Philip Van Doren Stern, ed., *Andersonville: A Story of Rebel Military Prisons* (Greenwich CT: Fawcett Publications, 1962).

Students of the *National Tribune* have generally not commented on McElroy's prodigious volume of writing for the newspaper, which contributed respectable scholarship on a wide range of topics from campaign histories to generals' biographies. Of his more than two dozen series in the *National Tribune,* those devoted to the last year of the war (118 articles), to General Grant (101), and to "leading Civil War battles" (98) were the longest.

Moreover, McElroy was remarkably consistent in his production of copy for the newspaper. In two years, spring 1897-spring 1899, only two issues appeared without an article bearing his name. Then he took a few years off, for there was no McElroy piece in the *National Tribune* from April 20, 1899 to November 17, 1904. Another huge spurt of work came from November 24, 1904 to July 18, 1912; only one week's issue appeared without a McElroy contribution. (For more than half of the year 1909, McElroy had *two* articles in each weekly issue.) Sometimes a few months would pass between the conclusion of one series and the start of another. Half of the paper's issues in 1921 carried no piece by the editor; another 33-week dearth occurred from November 6, 1924 to June 18, 1925.

When tallied, more than 1,000 articles appeared with McElroy's name in the *National Tribune* from March 11, 1897 to October 24, 1929. During this time, the paper put out 1,291 weekly issues, 87 percent of which during that 32 1/2 years span included an article by McElroy. Just as remarkably, he kept writing to the very end. At the time of his death on October 12, 1929, at the age of 83, he had just started yet another series of articles, "Most Critical Period of Civil War Days"; the first installment appeared on October 17 and the second a week later.

Over the decades, the *Tribune* published long series of articles by such famous Union officers as Maj. Gen. Oliver O. Howard. Just as notable, the paper published, in two dozen installments, excerpts from Confederate Gen. John Bell Hood's memoir *Advance and Retreat* (1880), Feb.-Aug. 1906. The *Tribune*'s printing company published books as well: not only McElroy's *The Struggle for Missouri* (1913) but works by other writers. For example, after the paper presented J. P. Cannon's "Inside Rebeldom: Life of a Private in the Confederate Army" in forty articles (Oct. 1897-Apr. 1898, it published Cannon's memoir of service in the 27th Alabama.[9]

The *National Tribune*'s last issue appeared on December 30, 1943. Sadly, in its last years the paper published more veterans' obituaries than it did expository

9 Allan Nevins, James I. Robertson, Jr., and Bell I., eds., *Civil War Books: A Critical Bibliography*, 2 vols. (Baton Rouge: 1967, 1969), 1:67. The paper announced it would publish excerpts of Confederates memoirs, including Hood's : "A good deal of attention will be paid to the stories of the other side. . . . [[It is] very entertaining, often, to hear the story of the fellow who was shooting at you" (October 26, 1905) 8.

articles on war history. Between its first article relating to the Atlanta Campaign, on the amputation of General Rice's leg (June 1879) to June 25, 1942 (a Northern shell exploding in Atlanta), the newspaper ran at least a thousand articles or letters on the contest between Sherman, Johnston and Hood. For reasons we explain in our commentary, we have selected 118 of them. Broadly speaking, they are almost entirely written by veterans, mostly Federals but occasionally by Confederates. As expository pieces on events that the writers witnessed or participated in, some of the best were printed in a regular section under the title, "Fighting Them Over. What Our Veterans Have to Say About Their Old Campaigns," which began in March 1883. Many articles are also conversational exchanges among ex-soldiers recalling the same incident; some allowed good-natured point-counterpoint as veterans read each other's recollections, remembered something different, and wrote the newspaper to "correct the record."

The *National Tribune* obviously fed on readers' written contributions. A lively weekly section entitled "Picket Shots" offered summaries of the many letters received from veterans, usually commenting on something they had read in the newspaper. In 1905, the newspaper began running a weekly series, "Recitals and Reminiscences. Stories Eminently Worth Telling of Experiences and Adventures in the Great National Struggle." It featured rather long articles (two to three long columns on page three) submitted by veterans with a good tale to tell.

Given the enormous number of articles about the Atlanta Campaign that appeared in the *National Tribune*, we have limited our selections to the period from 1877 to 1911. It was in the latter year (April 27) that the newspaper ceased to print Civil War-related articles on its front page. About that time, editor McElroy informed readers that he was changing the look of the paper to keep pace with the times. New sections such as "Woman and the Home" and "Farm and Garden" appeared. As a final demonstration of the aging of the *National Tribune*, its third and last editor, W. L. Mattocks, was not even a veteran of the Civil War but of the Spanish-American War.[10]

In our annotated commentary of our contributors' writings, we have not been uniform. For some tactical, more technical narratives, we have interspersed bracketed, italicized insertions. For others, we have posted italicized commentary either at the beginning or end of the *National Tribune* articles. (It is sort of how John McElroy edited his pieces.) As a final note, we do not correct archaic spellings or misspellings, especially of Georgia place-names (e.g., Chattahoochie).

With this we express hope that present and future scholars will more readily turn to the pages of this underappreciated historical resource.

10 Sauers, "Introduction," xi.

PHOTO GALLERY

Union Generals

Major General William T. Sherman

Library of Congress

Major General George H. Thomas

Library of Congress

Major General John M. Schofield

Library of Congress

Major General James B. McPherson

Library of Congress

Major General Joseph Hooker
Library of Congress

Major General John A. Logan
Library of Congress

Major General George Stoneman
Library of Congress

Major General Oliver O. Howard
Library of Congress

Brigadier General Judson Kilpatrick

Library of Congress

Confederate Generals

General Joseph E. Johnston

Library of Congress

Lieutenant General William J. Hardee

Library of Congress

Lieutenant General Leonidas Polk

Library of Congress

Lieutenant General John Bell Hood

Library of Congress

Lieutenant General A. P. Stewart

Library of Congress

Major General Benjamin F. Cheatham

Library of Congress

Major General Carter L. Stevenson
Library of Congress

Major General William H. T. Walker
Century Book

Major General Joseph Wheeler
Library of Congress

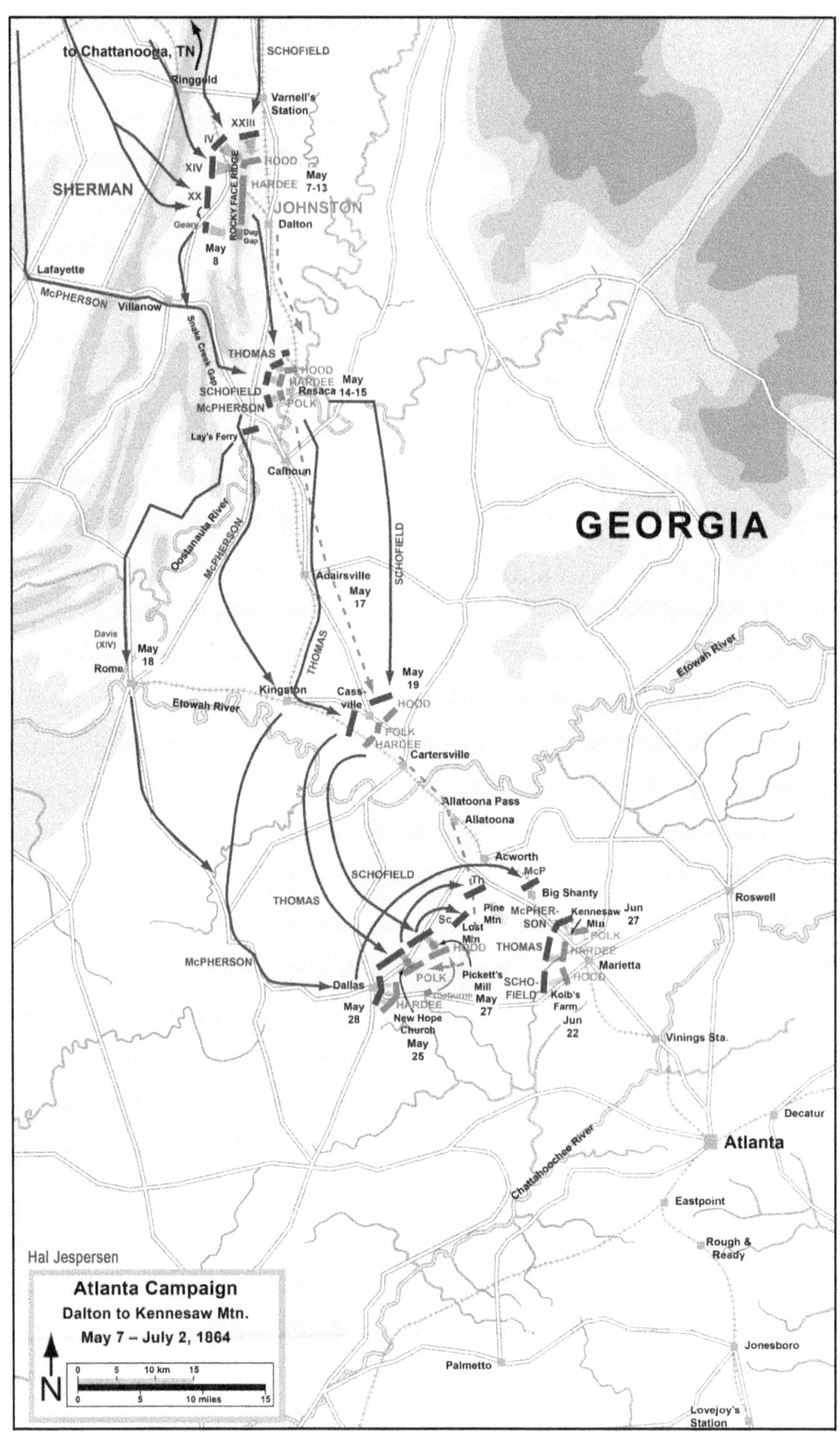

Hal Jespersen
Atlanta Campaign
Dalton to Kennesaw Mtn.
May 7 – July 2, 1864
GEORGIA
SHERMAN
JOHNSTON
to Chattanooga, TN
Ringgold
Varnell's Station
Dalton
Rocky Face Ridge
Lafayette
Villanow
Snake Creek Gap
Resaca
Lay's Ferry
Calhoun
Oostanaula River
Adairsville
Rome
Kingston
Cassville
Cartersville
Etowah River
Allatoona Pass
Allatoona
Acworth
Big Shanty
Pine Mtn
Lost Mtn
Kennesaw Mtn
Marietta
Kolb's Farm
Pickett's Mill
New Hope Church
Dallas
Roswell
Vinings Sta.
Decatur
Atlanta
Chattahoochee River
Eastpoint
Rough & Ready
Jonesboro
Palmetto
Lovejoy's Station

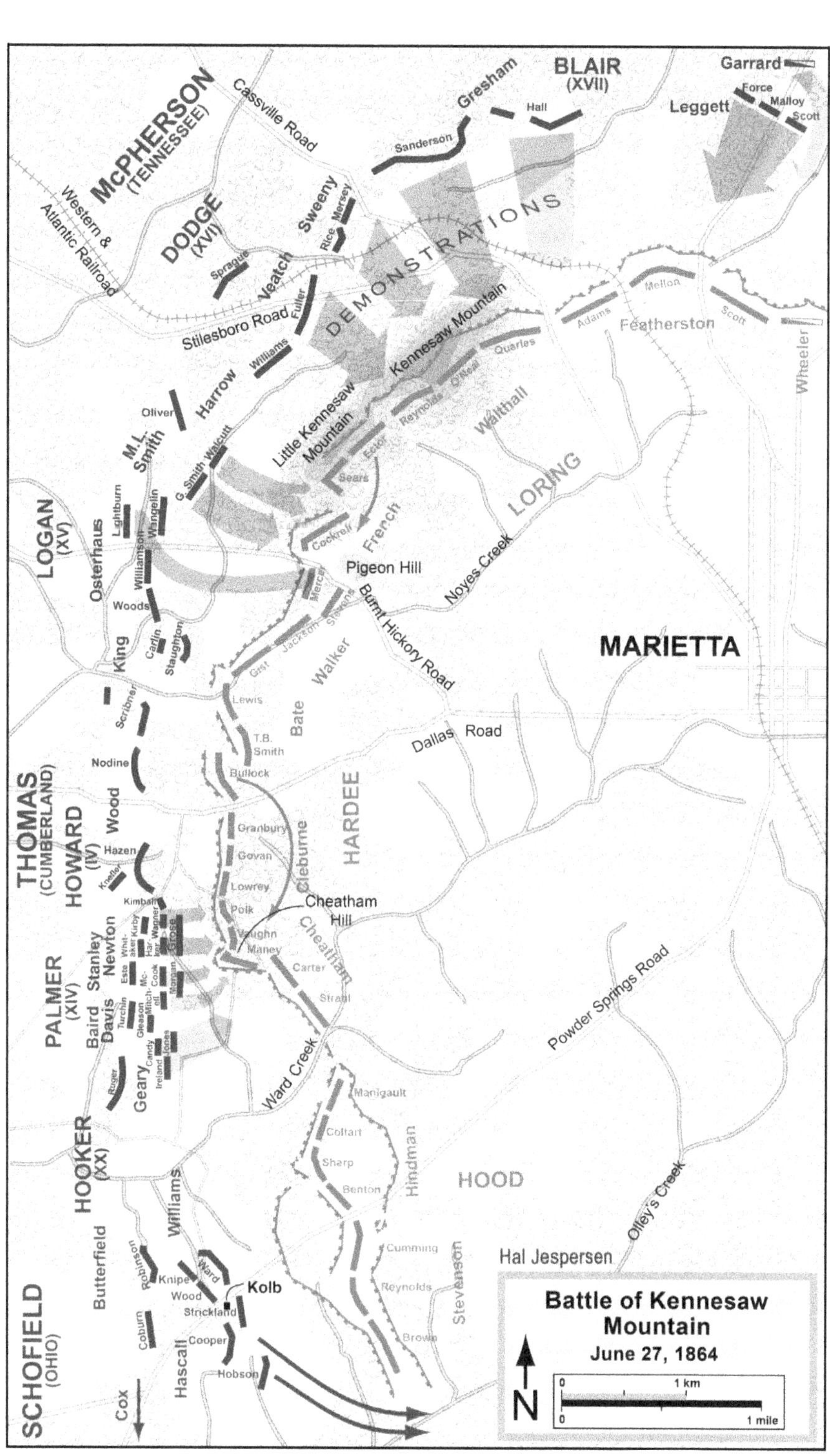
Battle of Kennesaw Mountain
June 27, 1864
Hal Jespersen
N
1 km
1 mile
McPHERSON (TENNESSEE)
BLAIR (XVII)
DODGE (XVI)
LOGAN (XV)
THOMAS (CUMBERLAND)
HOWARD (IV)
PALMER (XIV)
HOOKER (XX)
SCHOFIELD (OHIO)
LORING
FRENCH
WALKER
BATE
HARDEE
CLEBURNE
CHEATHAM
HINDMAN
HOOD
STEVENSON
MARIETTA
DEMONSTRATIONS
Kennesaw Mountain
Little Kennesaw Mountain
Pigeon Hill
Cheatham Hill
Kolb
Western & Atlantic Railroad
Cassville Road
Stilesboro Road
Burnt Hickory Road
Dallas Road
Powder Springs Road
Noyes Creek
Ward Creek
Olley's Creek
Garrard
Leggett
Force
Malloy
Scott
Gresham
Hall
Sanderson
Sweeny
Mersey
Rice
Sprague
Veatch
Fuller
Harrow
Williams
Oliver
M.L. Smith
G. Smith
Walcutt
Lightburn
Wangelin
Williamson
Osterhaus
Woods
Carlin
Staughton
King
Scribner
Nodine
Wood
Hazen
Knefler
Kimball
Stanley
Newton
Kirby
Whitaker
Wagner
Harker
Grose
Este
McCook
Morgan
Baird
Davis
Turchin
Mitchell
Gleason
Candy
Jones
Ireland
Geary
Ruger
Butterfield
Robinson
Knipe
Ward
Wood
Strickland
Coburn
Cooper
Hascall
Hobson
Cox
Wheeler
Featherston
Adams
Mellon
Scott
Quarles
O'Neal
Reynolds
Walthall
Ector
Sears
Cockrell
Mercer
Stevens
Jackson
Gist
Lewis
T.B. Smith
Bullock
Granbury
Govan
Lowrey
Polk
Vaughn
Maney
Carter
Strahl
Manigault
Coltart
Sharp
Benton
Cumming
Reynolds
Brown

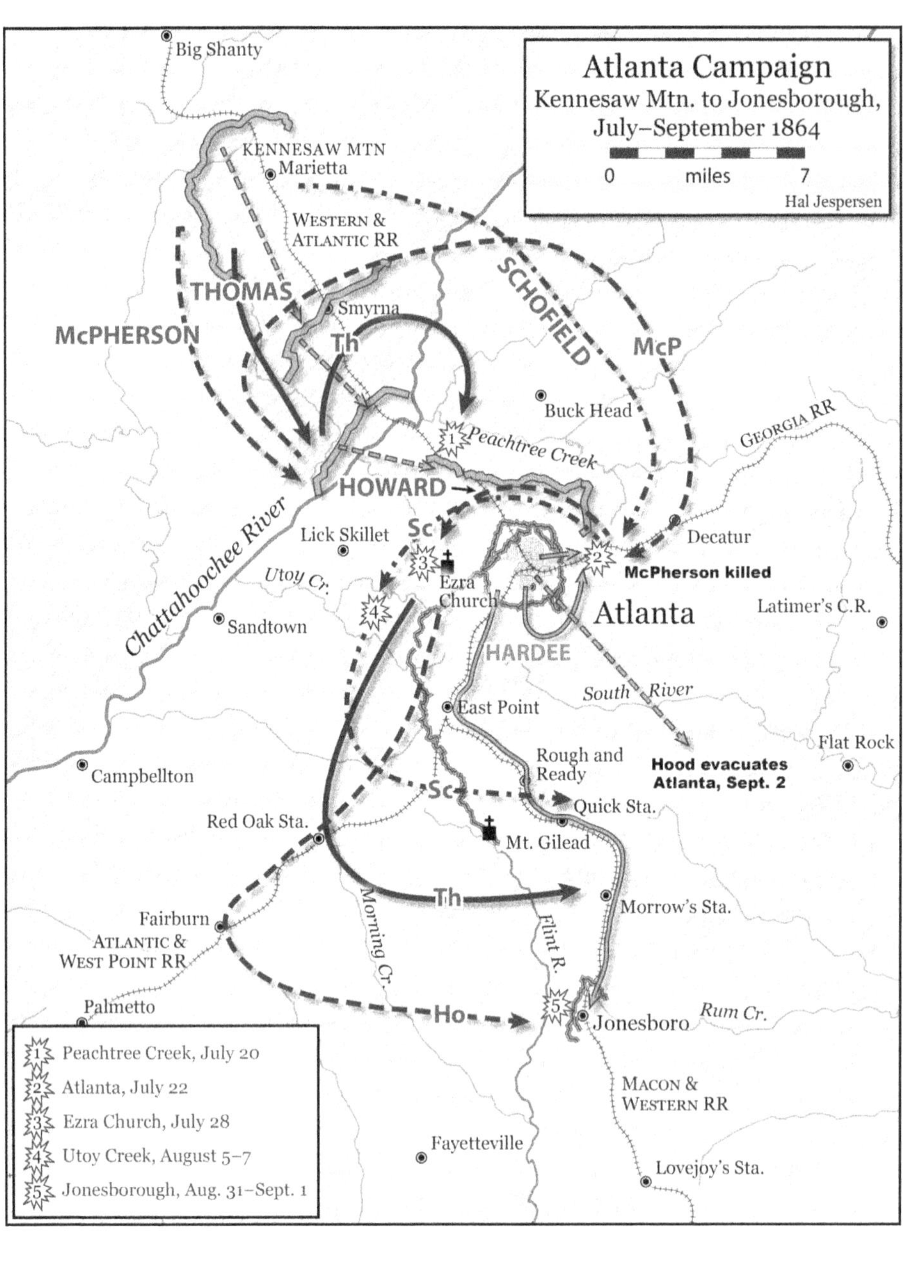

Atlanta Campaign
Kennesaw Mtn. to Jonesborough,
July–September 1864
0 miles 7
Hal Jespersen
Big Shanty
KENNESAW MTN
Marietta
Western & Atlantic RR
THOMAS
McPHERSON
SCHOFIELD
McP
Smyrna
Th
Buck Head
Peachtree Creek
Georgia RR
HOWARD
Chattahoochee River
Lick Skillet
Sc
Decatur
Utoy Cr.
Ezra Church
McPherson killed
Atlanta
Sandtown
Latimer's C.R.
HARDEE
South River
East Point
Flat Rock
Rough and Ready
Hood evacuates Atlanta, Sept. 2
Campbellton
Sc
Quick Sta.
Red Oak Sta.
Mt. Gilead
Th
Morrow's Sta.
Fairburn
Atlantic & West Point RR
Morning Cr.
Flint R.
Palmetto
Ho
Jonesboro
Rum Cr.
Macon & Western RR
Fayetteville
Lovejoy's Sta.
1 Peachtree Creek, July 20
2 Atlanta, July 22
3 Ezra Church, July 28
4 Utoy Creek, August 5–7
5 Jonesborough, Aug. 31–Sept. 1

1
Sherman Establishes His Supply System

John McElroy, "The Atlanta Campaign: Mighty Preparations"

(January 28, 1909, p. 2)

Most of the 27 articles written by John McElroy appeared weekly from January 21 to July 29, 1909. This second chapter is subtitled, "Sherman Strips His Army for Swift, Hard Work—Johnston Gathers His Army Behind the Granite Walls of Rocky Face Ridge." Here we have excerpted its first part regarding how Sherman assembled a logistical system to feed and supply his army's men and animals once the campaign began in north Georgia.

The Question of Supplies

Gen. Sherman's first and most intense thought was given to the all-important question of supplies. An active army of 100,000 men meant, with its necessary attendants and adjuncts, at least 125,000 men, besides a myriad of animals, all ravenous devourers of rations and forage. Chattanooga had to become an immense maw into which must flow constantly and without interruption a great Mississippi River of bread, meat, oats, corn and hay. All this had to be brought from Louisville, nearly 400 miles away. Between Nashville, 151 miles away, and Chattanooga ran a single-track railroad, never of the best and which had suffered immeasurably from destruction by the contending armies and the guerrillas. It ran a large portion of the way thru a very hilly country, with deep cuts, large fills and long, high bridges, all of which invited trouble to the working of the line and offered tempting opportunities to enemies. The first work was to put a great force of men at work under the able superintendence of Col. [*William W.*] Wright to put the roadbed between Nashville and Chattanooga in as good condition as possible to facilitate the rapid and uninterrupted movement of trains. This was followed by the erection of block houses at every bridge, culvert and tunnel. This protected them from dashes of the guerrillas. These block houses were something unique in the history of war, and were evolved, like many other valuable features of the science of warfare which were developed by the keenly active American soldiers, from the very necessity of the situation. The Army of the Cumberland was the only army in history that operated continuously along a line of railroad, and had to depend wholly upon the road for its supplies. The construction of these protections for the bridges had been commenced by Gen. [sic*: Col. George P.*] Buell's Engineers, who had constructed stockades in the shape of a Greek Cross, with each bastion the size of a Sibley tent. Each bastion was therefore made a home for a squad, with the Sibley tent for the roof. These did very well to resist infantry attacks, but a single piece of artillery would convert them into a slaughter pen by dropping in a shell. Col. W. [*William*] E. Merrill, Chief Engineer of the Army of the Cumberland, improved upon these by designing a rectangular block house strong enough to resist light artillery, and the [*1st*] Michigan Engineers, under Col. [*William P.*] Innes, did excellent work in erecting them. They were built up with heavy logs from below the surface of the ground, and roofed with a layer of logs laid side by side and covered with earth. On top of this was a roof of shingles or boards when they could be procured. Above this roof rose the tower, which afforded an excellent lookout, but was not strong enough to resist artillery, and was vacated if the attacking force had guns. Inside of the block house were the bunks and living rooms of the garrisons, with water tanks and cellars for supplies. These fortifications did magnificent service, and repeatedly beat off determined attacks of heavy forces. They were, in fact, the anchors of the army's safety, since they secured the maintenance of its cracker line. Many brilliant defenses by these little garrisons are on record, and one particularly, by 30 men of the 115th Ohio, commanded by Lieut. H. [*Henry*] H. Glosser, held for three weeks the block house protecting Overall's Creek, five miles north of Murfreesboro. It was repeatedly attacked by Bate's Division of infantry, with some cavalry and three 12-pound guns. These latter fired 72 shots at it, but the garrison maintained itself for the two critical weeks during Hood's siege of Nashville, and saved not only their block house, but the railroad bridge. Gen. Hood ruefully admits the strength of these defenses in his "Memoirs." After he had captured Dalton, in the Fall of 1864, he attempted to march thru Mill Creek Gap, but was stopped by the men in one of these block houses placed there to defend the bridge over Mill Creek. Hood's artillery cannonaded it savagely, but the plucky garrison held out, one of Hood's staff officers was severely wounded while trying to demonstrate how it could be taken, and Hood at last had to march 20 miles to get around it.

The railroad from Louisville to Nashville was helped out in transporting supplies by steamboats coming up the Cumberland River. They also came up the Tennessee River as far as Johnsonville, 30 miles from Nashville, from which their supplies were sent forward by rail to Nashville. From Nashville to Chattanooga, however, all the supplies had to come over the single track railroad referred to.

Other Demands Upon the Road

Not only had the 125,000 men and 35,000 animals gathered at Chattanooga to be supplied, but a large portion of the Armies of the Tennessee, Cumberland and Ohio operating near the railroad and the citizens of the country. The base of the Army of the Ohio was at Cincinnati, and a railroad ran from that city to Nicholasville, 18 miles beyond Lexington. From there to Knoxville, Tenn., is 250 miles over great mountain ranges and country of extreme ruggedness, with great mountain torrents, all unbridged, and the worst possible roads. Therefore, a great deal of the supplies needed by that portion of the Army of the Ohio in East Tennessee had to be sent up the river from Chattanooga to Knoxville and distributed there. Not only had the daily wants of this great host of men and animals to be provided for, but a stock sufficient for 30 days had to be accumulated in order to provide against any of the very likely interruptions of the railroad by the attacks of the enemy or, what was even more dreaded, the destruction of bridges and culverts by the severe storms of Winter.

General Sherman's able staff speedily worked out a system by which 135 carloads a day, each of 10 tons, should be delivered in Chattanooga. For this service 100 locomotives were secured and 1,000 cars, and every locomotive and car kept running night and day. The people of the country were denied the use of the road, the troops were required to march instead of riding on the cars, and immense herds of beef cattle were driven over the mountains. Sherman records with grim humor that in order to supply himself with engines and cars his men laid hands on everything that came within reach, and he made his reach very long. Establishing a car ferry at Louisville, he was enabled to catch trains from the Northern roads, and it was very amusing to see afterwards away down in Georgia cars and locomotives labeled Pittsburg & Fort Wayne, Delaware & Lackawanna, Baltimore & Ohio, and so on. He expressed some curiosity as to how the Northern railroads got their property back and accounted to the other railroads for its use.

McElroy pays appropriate attention to Sherman's masterful effort to keep his army supplied—the practice of logistics. A telling instance is the general's calculation that to build his supply base at Chattanooga he needed 130 train cars, each carrying ten tons, unloaded daily (Marlin G. Kime, "Sherman's Gordian Knot: Logistical Problems in the Atlanta Campaign," Georgia Historical Quarterly, *vol. 70, no. 1 [Spring 1986], 105). One further example is Sherman's attention to blockhouses as protection for railroad bridges against Rebel cavalry raids. Before his campaign began, 50 of these little forts were built on the Nashville & Chattanooga Railroad. Each was to be garrisoned by 20 to 25 men, supplied with food, water, and fuel to hold out until help arrived. As* *mentioned by McElroy, Union Lieutenant H. H. Glosser wrote on December 18, 1864, that he had been "hemmed in for thirteen days" by Confederates who had repeatedly called upon him to surrender but who finally gave up and rode off (*The War of the Rebellion: A Compilation of the Official Records of the Union and Confederate Armies, *128 vols. (Washington, D.C., 1880-1901), Series I, vol. 45, part 1, page 633, hereafter cited as* OR. *All references are to Series 1 unless otherwise noted.).*

Colonel Merrill describes his system of block houses in "Block-houses for Railroad Defense in the Department of the Cumberland" (Robert Hunter, ed., Sketches of War History 1861-1865: Papers Prepared for the Ohio Commandery of the Military Order of the Loyal Legion of the United States 1880-1890, *6 vols. [Cincinnati: Robert Clarke & Co., 1890], 3:389-421*).

*Hood in his memoirs acknowledges that Major Kinloch Falconer of his staff was severely wounded in the fight at the Mill Creek Gap blockhouse in mid-October 1864 (*Advance and Retreat, *262), but McElroy is incorrect stating that the blockhouse held out; it surrendered to Confederates in Hood's march into north Georgia, October 13 (Richard McMurry,* John Bell Hood and the War for Southern Independence *[Lexington: University Press of Kentucky, 1982], 161).*

Finally, in his Memoirs, *Sherman admits during his Atlanta campaign that he "was amused to see, away down in Georgia, cars marked 'Pittsburg & Fort Wayne,' 'Delaware & Lackawanna,' 'Baltimore & Ohio,' and indeed with the names of almost every railroad north of the Ohio River" (*Memoirs of General William T. Sherman. Written by Himself. Planning the Great Campaigns of 1864 *(February 11, 1897), 2:12).*

*General Sherman commends Colonel Wright in his campaign report: "Col. W. W. Wright, who has charge of the construction and repairs, is not only a most skillful, but a wonderfully ingenious, industrious, and zealous officer, and I can hardly do him justice" (*OR *38, pt. 1, 83).*

2

Thomas Discovers Snake Creek Gap

F. Phillips, "Snake Creek Gap: Gen. Thomas's Proposition to Take the Army of the Cumberland and Attack Johnston's"

(June 30, 1904, p. 3)

During the winter of 1863-64, Johnston strengthened his army's position around Dalton. To the west of town ran a tall north-south ridge called Rocky Face; along it, and running east into Crow Valley north of town, Confederate infantry was deployed for the attack that Johnston desired. All were well supported by artillery, with cavalry pickets out front and on the flanks. The main cut through Rocky Face was Mill Creek Gap, also called Buzzard Roost. Through it ran the Western & Atlantic Railroad and the main road to Chattanooga. About three and a half miles south of Mill Creek was Dug Gap; in several days of skirmishing there in late February, the Federals nearly broke through the Confederate lines before the Southerners frantically called for reinforcements.

From this encounter, Union Maj. Gen. George Thomas deduced that there were likely other gaps. He was right; the Northerners soon learned of Snake Creek Gap, five miles south of Dug Gap, affording a passageway through the steep ridge well south of the Rebel line.

Thomas then proposed to Sherman that while McPherson and Schofield held Johnston's attention with demonstrations against his Rocky Face line, Thomas would march his large army through the undefended gap. Once through, he could get into the rear of Johnston's army, and either engage it in battle, or cow it into a hasty retreat before he cut the Rebels' supply line, the Western & Atlantic Railroad to Atlanta. Sherman said no, preferring to send Maj. Gen. James B. McPherson's Army of the Tennessee. "Cump" Sherman genuinely liked McPherson, and had a higher regard for his army (which he had previously commanded) than Thomas's, which he generally thought moved too slowly.

Here a veteran learns of the story from Donn Piatt's General George H. Thomas *(1893)—an illustration of how readers of the* National Tribune *were keeping up with the developing literature.*

EDITOR NATIONAL TRIBUNE. In reading Donn Piatt's Life of Gen. George H. Thomas, I came across the statement that Gen. Thomas offered to take his army (the army of the Cumberland), numbering 60,000 effectives, and march through Snake Creek Gap, while the balance of the army, under Gen. Sherman, continued to make demonstrations in front of Rocky Face Ridge; Thomas by marching through the Gap would cut off Gen. Johnston's connection with his depots at Resaca and force him to give battle, or else to retreat toward the rear through a broken and barren country, where it would be very difficult to march or to maintain an army.

Col. Piatt states that when this plan was submitted to Sherman by Thomas he declined to let Thomas take the Army of the Cumberland, but, instead, after two or three days' delay, sent Gen. McPherson with 20,000 men through the Gap (Snake Creek), and that as he was not strong enough to fight Gen. Johnston's army he only hastened the falling back of the Confederate army from Rocky Face Ridge, when Johnston found that the Union army was getting too near his line of retreat.

Do any of the men who were there know whether such an offer was made by Thomas and declined by Sherman?

Again, is it certain that if the Army of the Cumberland had been sent on any such errand, they would have been able to defeat the rebel army themselves?

There must be many men still living who can give a good account of this proposed move.

Col. Piatt says that if the offer of Thomas had been accepted, in all probability there would have been no Atlanta Campaign, for the Confederate Army would have been beaten right there at Dalton by Thomas as it was afterward at Nashville.

I have not read Piatt's book before and he makes some rather strong statements as to the conduct of officers in the West in '63 and '64.

We have learned through the National Tribune what regiment it was that raised the first flag on Lookout Mountain at the time of the battle, and what part of the army captured those four guns at Resaca; also what battery it was that killed Polk. Now let us find out, if we can, why Gen. Sherman would not let Gen. Thomas make the move he wanted to at Rocky Face Ridge in May, 1864.—F. PHILLIPS, No. 770 Holton Street, Milwaukee, Wis.

3

Sherman, McPherson, and Snake Creek Gap, May 8-10

"Memoirs of General William T. Sherman. Written by Himself. Planning the Great Campaigns of 1864"

(February 11, 1897, pp. 1-2)

When the campaign opened in early May, Sherman stuck with his plan: Thomas and Schofield launching demonstrations against the Rebel line, May 8-9, while McPherson's Army of the Tennessee stealthily marched through Snake Creek Gap, heading east for the Western & Atlantic in Johnston's rear. If he could interpose his infantry on the railroad, Johnston's supply line would be blocked, and the Confederates would either have to retreat or attack McPherson. Sherman's plan worked well—at first. Johnston had left the gap virtually unguarded; on May 9, McPherson's troops marched through it and toward the railroad. But then, fearing a Confederate counterstrike, he halted his column and ordered it back into the gap (Stephen Davis, Texas Brigadier to the Fall of Atlanta: John Bell Hood *[Macon: Mercer University Press, 2019], 123).*

Sherman was disappointed, to say the least, as he expressed in his Memoirs, *which were published in 1875, a year after Johnston's* Narrative of Military Operations, *and five years before the posthumous publication in 1880 of John Bell Hood's* Advance and Retreat. *The* National Tribune *printed excerpts of Hood's memoir in its pages from February 22 to August 9, 1906. Editor McElroy apparently chose not to reprint portions of Johnston's' book in his newspaper.*

The National Tribune *published a long section of Sherman's* Memoirs *in 98 parts, April 12, 1896 to February 24, 1898. The portion pertaining to the Atlanta Campaign consisted of parts 44 to 51, from the advance on Dalton to the Federal occupation of Atlanta (February 11-April 1, 1897).*

Here, from the February 11, 1897, issue we read of Sherman's chagrin over McPherson at Snake Creek Gap.

. . . on the 9th McPherson's head of column entered and passed through Snake Creek, perfectly undefended, and accomplished a complete surprise to the enemy. At its farther *debouche* he met a cavalry brigade, easily driven, which retreated hastily north toward Dalton, artillery was to his rear and within a few miles of his railroad. I got a short note from McPherson that day (written at 2 p.m., when he was within a mile and a half of the railroad, above and near Resaca), and we all felt jubilant. I renewed orders to Thomas and Schofield to be ready for the instant pursuit of what I expected to be a broken and disordered army, forced to retreat by roads to the east of Resaca, which were known to be very rough and impracticable.

That night I received further notice from McPherson that he had found Resaca too strong for a surprise; that in consequence he had fallen back three miles to the mouth of Snake Creek Gap, and was there fortified. I wrote to him the next day the following letter, copies of which are in my letter book; but his to me were mere notes in pencil, not retained:

> GENERAL: I received by courier (in the night) yours of 5 and 6:30 p.m. of yesterday.
>
> You now have your 23,000 men, and Gen. Hooker is in close support, so that you can hold all of Jos. Johnston's army in check should he abandon Dalton. He cannot afford to abandon Dalton, for he has fixed it up on purpose to receive us, and he observes that we are close at hand, waiting for him to quit. He cannot afford a detachment strong enough to fight you, as his army will not admit of it.
>
> Strengthen your position; fight anything that comes, and threaten the safety of the railroad all the time. But to tell the truth, I would rather the enemy would stay in Dalton two more days, when he may find in his rear a larger party than he expects in an open field. At all events, we can then choose our own ground, and he will be forced to move out of his works. I do not intend to put a column into Buzzard Roost Gap at present.
>
> See that you are in heavy communication with me, and with all Headquarters. After to-day the supplies will be at Ringgold.

M'PHERSON HAD STARTLED JOHNSTON

in his fancied security, but had not done the full measure of his work. He had in hand 23,000 of the best men of the army, and would have walked into Resaca, then held only by a small brigade, or he could have placed his whole force astride the railroad above Resaca, and there have easily withstood the attack of all of Johnston's army, with the knowledge that Thomas and Schofield were on his heels. Had he done so, I am certain that Johnston would not have ventured to attack him in position, but would have retreated eastward by Spring Place, and we should have captured half his army and all his artillery and wagons at the beginning of the campaign.

Such an opportunity does not occur twice in a single life; but at the critical moment McPherson seems to have been a little cautious. Still, he was perfectly justified by his orders, and fell back and assumed an unassailable defensive position in Sugar Valley, on the Resaca side of Snake Creek Gap. As soon as informed of this I determined to pass the whole army through Snake Creek Gap, and to move on Resaca with the main army . . . on the 11th, perceiving signs of evacuation of Dalton, I gave all orders for the general movement . . . through Snake Creek Gap [and] during the 12th and 13th the bulk of Thomas's and Schofield's armies were got through, and deployed against Resaca, McPherson on the right, Thomas in the center and Schofield on the left. Johnston, as I anticipated, had abandoned all his well-prepared defenses at Dalton, and was found inside of Resaca with the bulk of his army, holding his divisions well in hand, acting purely on the defensive. . . .

Sherman understated his dismay in terming McPherson "a little cautious." In McPherson's defense, after getting through Snake Creek Gap, he was advancing east, pushing back a Confederate mounted brigade, but without cavalry of his own to warn of a Rebel counterattack as he approached the Western & Atlantic. Besides, as historian John R. Scales has charitably observed, this was McPherson's first test as commander of the Army of the Tennessee; he had been promoted from XV Corps command just a month and a half before.

John R. Scales, Sherman Invades Georgia: Planning the North Georgia Campaign Using a Modern Perspective *(Annapolis: Naval Institute Press, 2006), 163.*

4

"It makes me hot under the collar"

Henry H. Cook, "Defends McPherson"

(October 14, 1909, p. 7)

> For once in his brilliant career McPherson failed to comprehend the spirit of his orders. He reconnoitered the works around Resaca, found them alarmingly strong and seemingly well garrisoned. He hesitated before making an assault which would have been costly in life and possibly not successful. He was ignorant of the country around him, and did not know what force Johnston might have near at hand to throw upon his flank. He therefore made the crowning mistake of his career in listening to the voice of prudence, and in withdrawing his men to the strong position at the foot of the gap.

So wrote John McElroy in an installment of his "Atlanta Campaign" series that appeared on February 4, 1909. It prompted the following comment from a reader.

Editor National Tribune: I read your history of the campaigns and battles of the civil war with great interest. They put together the fragments I gathered as an actual participant in the heat of the conflict, or near enough to know something about the moves on the field of action, which extended from the Mississippi River to the Atlantic Ocean and to the final surrender of the so-called Southern Confederacy. In your history of the Atlanta campaign you repeat the story of Gen. McPherson's timidity when he passed thru Snake Creek Gap and advanced toward Resaca. I was one in the front on that move, with Battery H, 1st Mo. L.A., Third Division, Sixteenth Corps. When night came on we were on the west side of Camp Creek, about two miles from Resaca, or the railroad, tangled up in the brush, hills and swamps so well described by Gen. Logan when he charged over the same ground. To the west black and threatening clouds gave forth peals of thunder, with the heavens apparently on fire with flashes of forked lightning, all warning the traveler to seek cover. Gen. McPherson had certainly learned enough about the ground in front to know he could advance no farther that night, his force was in no position to receive the enemy, who was well acquainted with the lay of the land and every road and bypath. Gen. McPherson did what he was compelled to do under the circumstances—fell back where he could put his army in a position for defense. About dark the rain came on, and it rained all night, as hard as it can in that country—as if the heavens were sending down the waters of a Niagara. The battery unhitched and fed the horses, hitched up, and with everything ready for action the men trod around the guns in the storm all that long and dreadful night. Camp Creek, which was in our immediate front when we fell back, was bank full, and more, the next morning. Suppose Gen. McPherson or any other commander had struggled on and attempted to reach the railroad that night? The historian of that campaign would have called him crazy, as it now calls McPherson too timid. Gen. Sherman was disappointed, and so he was many times when circumstances came in the way of his plans, and it makes me hot under the collar to hear Gen. McPherson criticized as he has been for his action on this occasion.—Henry H. Cook, Sergeant, Co. H, 1st Mo. L. A., Ottawa, Kan.

5
Who Took Snake Creek Gap?

[F. H. Wagner], "Snake Creek Gap"

(August 14, 1902, p. 3)

*"On May 8 the Army of the Tennessee entered the western end of Snake Creek Gap and encamped in the three-mile-long valley," writes Steven E. Woodworth (*Nothing But Victory: The Army of the Tennessee 1861-1865 *[New York: Alfred A. Knopf, 2005], 493).*

Historians know that Brig. Gen. Thomas W. Sweeny's Second Division of Maj. Gen. Grenville M. Dodge's XVI Corps was at the head of the marching column on May 8-9 (Albert Castel, Decision in the West: The Atlanta Campaign of 1864 *[Lawrence: University Press of Kansas, 1992], 135). Which regiment, though, could claim credit for this important tactical achievement? As one sees in the following two letters published in 1902, decades after the war, readers of the* National Tribune*—often, the veteran participants themselves—liked to duke it out in the pages of the newspaper.*

The first, by F. H. Wagner, is a bit murky as to time; Dodge's advance entered Snake Creek Gap on the afternoon of May 8 and by the end of the day had gained control of it.

When Gen. Sherman started on his Atlanta campaign, the necessity for seizing Snake Creek Gap became evident, and the 9th Ill., under Col. [*Lt. Col. Jesse J.*] Phillips, was assigned to the duty. F. H. Wagner, Co. D, 9th Ill., now living at Warrensburg, Mo., writes of the expedition: "We made a night march, and our trusted guide led us to the entrance of the gap, through which ran a small rivulet of clear water. One short hour of rest for man and beast was given. I was Sergeant-Major of the regiment, and I received the order to detail 16 men and a Sergeant to take the advance into the dark and frowning gap. Serg't Mueller and 16 picked men went forward; only five returned. At the western mouth of the gap the rebel pickets were completely surprised and their horses seized, with a shot being fired. When half way through the gap we met a relief party, and our advance made a dash at them and followed closely on their heels into a large rebel camp. In the fight which followed our men drove the rebels from their camp into an open space of about 20 acres, and over this open space the 9th Ill. charged, driving the rebels into the woods at the other side. The Johnnies took shelter behind trees and huge rocks. We dismounted and held the rebels until we were reinforced by the 50th Ill. This regiment coming up made a dash, gaining an advanced position, which they at once began to fortify. This fight secured for us Snake Creek Gap. Col. Phillips received a saber wound and was shot through the right leg."

[*The 9th Illinois was a regiment of mounted infantry, and the only horsemen McPherson had to spearhead his advance; it was part of the Second Brigade of Sweeny's division. The 50th Illinois Infantry belonged to the division's Third Brigade.*]

EDITOR NATIONAL TRIBUNE: In the issue of August 14 F. H. Wagner, of Co. D, 9th Ill., gives an account of the taking and holding of Snake Creek Gap. Ga. He says: "We made a night march to the entrance of the gap. . . . We dismounted and held them until we were reinforced by the 50th Ill."

Now, nearly all of this differs from what I think are the facts. While Sherman was engaging the enemy at Tunnel Hill and Buzzard Roost, Gen. McPherson took two divisions of the Sixteenth Corps and marched for Snake Creek Gap, some 16 or 18 miles south of Tunnel Hill. On May 9 [sic *May 8*] the 39th Iowa, of the Third Brigade, Second Division, was in advance. We arrived at the mouth of the gap about 4 p.m., where we came to a halt. While we were there Gens. McPherson and Dodge came up, and sat down on the ground and took out a map. They seemed to be talking over the situation. They were not 50 or 75 feet from our company, and we could understand a little of what they said. It seemed that they had not fully determined whether it was best to try to reach Resaca, some seven or eight miles away, that night. After remaining there about one hour, we were ordered to fall in, and marched through the gap, the 39th Iowa in advance. When we reached the east end of the gap it was nearly sundown. We went into camp for the night, with the remainder of the brigade camped along through the gap in our rear, including the 50th Ill. The 39th Iowa was in front, with two companies of the 9th Ill., as we understood it, still in our advance, perhaps a half-mile or more.

The next morning [*May 9*], between daylight and sunrise, the 9th Ill. was attacked by the rebel cavalry. Hearing the guns, the 39th Iowa fell in line at once and marched to their relief. We had marched out perhaps a half-mile, when we met the 9th Ill. falling back, closely followed by the rebels. The Confederates did not seem to realize that there was any infantry near them until they ran into our lines, where a number were killed and captured.

This ended all the fighting at the mouth of Snake Creek Gap, and it was done by, I think, only two companies of the 9th Ill. and the 39th Iowa, and not by the 50th Ill. I do not wish to take anything from the record of the 50th Ill., as it was as grand an old regiment as ever went into the service, but these honors belonged to the 39th Iowa, and not to the 50th Ill. We understood at the time that there were only two companies of the 9th Ill. with us in taking possession of the gap, and I think so yet, though in this I may be mistaken.

Now, all of this night marching and fighting through the gap is certainly not correct. As we arrived at the gap, at 3 or 4 o'clock in the afternoon, the two companies of the 9th Ill. being in advance of the 39th, might have arrived an hour or two earlier. We marched through the gap in the daytime, without a shot being fired.

After driving the cavalry force back two or three miles we ran into a large cavalry force, and perhaps infantry. We then fell back to a hill or two, and threw up strong breastworks across the valley from hill to hill, and held them until Sherman came up with nearly all of his army.—CHAS. VAN GORDER, Co. B, 39th Iowa, Audubon, Iowa.

Van Gorder's account is substantiated by Maj. Gen. Grenville Dodge's campaign report: "May 8, the command, Second Division in advance, moved . . . to Snake Creek Gap, which was occupied, and the command bivouacked therein—the Ninth Illinois Mounted Infantry, supported by the Thirty-ninth Iowa Infantry, being pushed forward . . . to hold the eastern outlet of the gap."

Late on the 8th, the Rebels driven from the gap by the 9th Illinois Mounted spread the alarm, and a Confederate cavalry brigade under Colonel J. Warren Grigsby was sent on a night march to Snake Creek. About dawn of May 9, Grigsby's troopers approached the gap and engaged the Federals. (Van Gorder is correct in surmising that Grigsby's men were probably surprised to run into enemy infantry; the previous night's report would have only mentioned mounted Federals.)

*General Dodge further corroborates: "At daylight in the morning (May 9) the advance, consisting of the Ninth Illinois Mounted Infantry and Thirty-ninth Iowa Infantry, was attacked by Ferguson's [*Grigsby's*] brigade, of the enemy's cavalry. The Second Brigade of the Second Division was immediately ordered up, and, moving forward, promptly drove and routed the enemy. In this engagement the gallant Lieut. Col. Jesse J. Phillips, commanding Ninth Illinois Mounted Infantry, was severely wounded."*

6

Thomas and Schofield Demonstrate, May 8-9

John McElroy, "The Atlanta Campaign. Resaca"

(February 11, 1909, p. 2)

While McPherson conducted his Snake Creek Gap march, May 8-9, Sherman had Thomas and Schofield move against the Rebel lines to hold Johnston's attention. Here is another excerpt from McElroy's narrative in which he summarizes the push of Howard's IV Corps north of Mill Creek Gap, with an emphasis on Col. Emerson Opdycke's 125th Ohio.

The Fight Around Buzzard's Roost

On Monday, May 8, while McPherson was making his way toward Resaca, the Armies of the Cumberland and the Ohio were keeping Johnston's attention very closely. On the extreme right Hooker's Twentieth Corps was making a strong demonstration of renewing its attempt to force Dug Gap and other depressions. Palmer's Fourteenth Corps maintained its close advance to the palisades on either side of Mill Creek, and the enemy from the secure heights above kept up their volley of great stones and boulders sent plunging over the edge of the crest. Howard's Fourth Corps made a most determined effort to advance along the crest of the ridge north of the gap. Harker's Brigade of Newton's Division of the Fourth Corps, with Col. Opdycke's 125th Ohio in advance, became involved in a regular battle in attempting to push on down the ridge toward the gap. Col. Opdycke made a skilful effort to get a foothold on the crest. He first made a feint as if to go down on the eastern side of the ridge, which was from 500 to 600 feet high, and, leaving a portion of his men to keep up skirmishing, he started with the rest obliquely up the western side, hoping to get to the crest before the enemy discovered the movement. About 8:30 he was on the crest and moving south, when he encountered a heavy force which stood its ground obstinately. The fire from both sides was heavy, but the rocks afforded good shelter equally to both. Finally Opdycke found that he could form a company front, when he massed his regiment, and, making a determined push, drove the enemy one-third of a mile to the shelter of heavy stone fortifications which he saw at once could not be forced. He halted there under orders, the 15th Wis. was sent to his assistance and afterward the 65th Ohio. The position gained was a fine point of observation, and a signal station was at once established to communicate with headquarters on Tunnel Hill. From this point a full view was had of the enemy's works and batteries and also of the town of Dalton. In this movement Opdycke lost eight killed and mortally wounded and 17 wounded. The next day, May 9, Opdycke maintained heavy skirmishing until 5:30, when a determined assault was made, preceded by the 79th Ill. as skirmishers. These were followed by the 64th Ohio, 3d Ky. and 125th Ohio. The ground was so precipitous that many men were injured by falling over the cliffs. The enemy's position was found to be too strong to be forced, and the attack was discontinued after a considerable loss in each of the regiments.

The Army of the Ohio

Gen. Schofield did the best that he could to assist the Fourth Corps in carrying the north end of the ridge. [*Brig. Gen. Henry M.*] Judah's Division of the Army of the Ohio advanced as far as possible in support of the Fourth Corps, while [*Brig. Gen. Jacob D.*] Cox's and [*Brig. Gen. Alvin P.*] Hovey's Divisions, still further to the east, pushed down the more open valley for nearly two miles until they came to a heavy fortification along the ridge north of Dalton. These works were at once seen to be too strong to assault with any hope of success, and the day was spent in demonstrations which were to be converted into real attacks should the assault upon the ridge be successful and turn the left flank of the works.

The fight on the ridge was in full sight of Schofield's men, and was a most thrilling spectacle. The long line of blue could be traced up the ridge, and the men on the crest stood out in strong relief against the western sky. They could be seen to gallantly charge, meeting a storm of fire which nothing could resist. They would fall back, reorganize and renew the assault with the same ill fortune. Their splendid courage and determination were admired by the thousands of spectators, but the uselessness was plain to all. Night closed with the troops along the entire length of Johnston's front, in full touch with the enemy and ready to take instant advantage of what Sherman was so much hoping for, a rapid and confused evacuation of the stronghold. Sherman waited all day of the 10th for Johnston to begin the retreat, which would follow the discovery of McPherson's threatening of his rear, but the wily Confederate General showed that wonderful deliberation and full knowledge of the possibilities which distinguished his conduct during the whole campaign. He realized that he had to leave, but he was resolved to take his own time about it, and make one of those skilful retreats which marked the history of the campaign and which excited the admiration of even his enemies.

[*With McPherson still at Snake Creek Gap, Sherman ordered him to push toward Resaca; Thomas and Schofield were to follow him. Learning of the Federal movement, Johnston began withdrawing from Dalton to Resaca on May 11-12. The Confederate army occupied defensive works there on the 12th and waited for Sherman to come up.*]

Sherman also waited for the arrival of Stoneman's and Garrard's cavalry. He wanted all his horsemen in hand, so as to take full advantage of Johnston's condition when he began to fall back. On May 10 Sherman began to move Hooker's Corps down to support McPherson, and the next day he left the Fourth Corps and Stoneman's Cavalry to watch Buzzard Roost Gap, while the rest of the army marched over the rough, tortuous roads for Snake Creek Gap and Resaca. The passage was exceedingly difficult for such a mass of men and trains, and May 12 and 13 were occupied in making it and in getting the army into position around Resaca, whither Johnston had retreated in good order. Seeing the impossibility of getting all his men thru over one rough road, Sherman had other roads and paths cut out. Signboards were put on the trees indicating the course that different bodies should take, and at night torches and fires lighted the way. Johnston put his whole force into the works there to cover the passage of his trains across the Oostanaula. He calculated exactly the time it would require Sherman's army to pass thru Snake Creek Gap and get into position, so that he did not leave Dalton until May 13, when his smaller army marched by direct roads into the position which he had previously selected for them.

[*McElroy is being generous to General Johnston, who wrote in his memoirs, "We had examined the country very minutely; and learned its character thoroughly. We could calculate with sufficient accuracy, therefore, the time that would be required for the march of so great an army from Tunnel Hill to Resaca, through the long defile of Snake Creek Gap, and by the single road beyond that pass. We knew also how many hours our comparatively small force, moving without baggage-trains and in three columns, on roads made good by us, would reach the same point from Dalton" (Johnston,* Narrative of Military Operations *[New York: D. Appleton and Company, 1874], 316).*

By this strained rhetoric, Johnston sought to escape blame for having allowed McPherson's army to march through Snake Creek Gap and threaten his rear. Some historians had derided this pretzel-twisting as ludicrous; most conclude that Johnston was ignorant of the gap. Atlanta historian Wilbur G. Kurtz has likened it to "the good man of the house who, knowing that thieves are abroad, bars the front door and all the windows, but leaves the back door open, reassured by the knowledge that he is only a dozen paces from the open portal." (Unpublished typescript, Wilbur G. Kurtz, "Why Was Snake Creek Gap Left Unguarded?" ca. 1935, Kurtz Collection, Atlanta History Center, Atlanta, GA., MSS 130, box 49, folder 14, 21.)]

During May 14 Sherman had his whole army again well in hand before the works, which were found strong at every point and strongly manned. Again Schofield with the Army of the Ohio was on the extreme left, Thomas with the Army of the Cumberland in the center, and McPherson on the right. . . .

While the prestige of the opening of the campaign was strongly with the Union army, yet both Sherman and Johnston had been much disappointed, Sherman in his hope of catching Johnston at a disadvantage, and Johnston in his expectation that at some point on his line there would be a determined assault made which he could repulse in a way to more or less cripple his antagonist.

After the war, Johnston argued that he had not been outsmarted by Sherman's Snake Creek Gap maneuver, and that he had been able to (as he wrote in his memoir of 1874) "calculated with sufficient accuracy . . . the time that would be required for the march through the long defile of Snake Creek Gap."

John McElroy took him at his word.

7

"Well, Mac, you have missed the great opportunity of your life."

Willard Warner, postwar letter to Ellen Sherman

(January 27, 1898, p. 2)

When Sherman encountered McPherson on May 12, he was still fuming over the latter's hesitance to advance after successfully passing through Snake Creek Gap. "Well, Mac, you have missed the great opportunity of your life," he is said to have snapped.

The line has worked its way into the literature. Albert Castel quotes it in Decision in the West: The Atlanta Campaign of 1864 *(Lawrence: University Press of Kansas, 1992), 150. So does William R. Scaife,* The Campaign for Atlanta *(Saline MI: McNaughton and Gunn, 1993), 23. Both cite as their source the paper read by Capt. Rowland Cox before the New York Commandery, Military Order of the Loyal Legion of the United States (MOLLUS) on December 2, 1891, and printed in 1897. Scaife cites the latter source; Castel cites Captain Cox's address, reprinted in Sydney C. Kerksis,* The Atlanta Papers *(Dayton OH: Press of Morningside Bookshop, 1980), 341.*

But how did Cox get this memorable anecdote? In his Memoir, *Sherman writes, "Such an opportunity does not appear twice in a single life"—the line is repeated in his editions of 1876 and 1886 (Sherman died in 1891). As will be seen in the article, after reading General Sherman's* Memoir *(1875), Lt. Col. Willard Warner—who had served as Sherman's Inspector-General—on February 22, 1876, wrote Mrs. Sherman (though why he did not write the general himself, we can't tell). In his letter, he tells of hearing Sherman deliver the rebuke to McPherson. Warner's 1876 letter may be the source of the published famous line, but as the* National Tribune *did not print Warner's letter until its issue of January 27, 1898, it remains unclear how Captain Cox was able to quote it more than six years before.*

In addition, there is Lieutenant Colonel Warner's recollection that even before he had begun his campaign for Atlanta, Sherman was already thinking of a march through Georgia to the Atlantic coast ("salt water"). In his Sherman's March *(New York: Random House, 1980), Burke Davis writes that "at the opening of the spring campaign, Sherman's inspector general had asked what was to be done after the capture of Atlanta. Sherman whacked ashes and sparks from his cigar and said brusquely, 'Salt water. Salt water,'"—but in his bibliography, Davis does not cite Warner's letter from the* National Tribune.

For both of these reasons, Willard Warner's letter to Mrs. Sherman of February 1876, a score of years later, deserves more citation than it has received in the hands of campaign historians.

Under date of Feb. 22, 1876, Willard Warner, Brigadier-General of Volunteers, and former United States Senator from Alabama, wrote Mrs. Sherman, relative to various incidents of the great march. His letter follows:

MY DEAR MADAM: I have read with great interest Gen. Sherman's Memoirs, and some of the criticisms made, and venture to give my testimony in regard to some of the disputed points falling within my personal knowledge, as of interest possibly to some of my comrades-in-arms, if not to the general public and history.

On the 5th of May, 1864, I reported to Gen. Sherman at Ringgold, Ga., for duty as Inspector-General on his staff. The General, with his map before him, explained the general course of his proposed campaign against Gen. Johnston, ending with the capture of Atlanta. I remember that he had his coat and hat off, and his slippers on. When he had done his explanations, he began walking the floor of the room, smoking a cigar.

I said to him that when he got to Atlanta he would be 450 miles from his real base of supplies, with one railroad as his only means of transportation, and every mile of that liable to be broken by the enemy, and that it would absorb the whole of his army to hold Atlanta and protect the road, and asked him what he proposed after the capture of Atlanta.

Stopping short in his walk, and snapping the ashes of his cigar in a quick, nervous way, he replied in two words—"Salt water." I did not comprehend his meaning, but after a little further examination of the map I asked him if he meant Savannah or Charleston, and he said, "Yes."

Again, soon after the capture of Atlanta, he called Col. Beckwith, his Chief Commissary, and myself, into his room in Judge Lyon's house in Atlanta, and, locking the door, laid his map on the floor, and indicated his proposed march to Savannah. Col. Beckwith's first question naturally was, "How about supplies?" The General replied that there were 1,000,000 people in Georgia, and that where they could live his army would not starve.

SNAKE CREEK GAP

Before and during the movements against Gen. Johnston, at Rocky Face, Gen. Sherman explained to me and others of his staff that the demonstrations on Johnston's front and right were feints to cover and hide the real movement of attack by Gen. McPherson through Snake Creek Gap. In speaking of the danger that Johnston might fall on McPherson with his whole force, and crush him before help could be got to him, he said that the 23,000 muskets of the Army of the Tennessee could not "be run over by anybody in a hurry," and that the moment Johnston let go of Rocky Face, Thomas and Schofield would be in his rear, and thus place him between two fires, when ruin would be sure.

On the night of May 9, as we were at supper at the brick house by the spring near Tunnel Hill Station, a letter was brought to the General. Reading it, he instantly left the table, and bade me to follow him. When he had got a little way from the house, he stopped short, and, with a vehement gesture of his right hand, clinched, said:

"I have got Joe Johnston dead. This letter is from McPherson. At 1 o'clock to-day he was within one and a half mile of the railroad. He must be on it now. I want to go over to see 'Tom'"—meaning Gen. Thomas.

On his way he said that Johnston would be compelled to abandon the railroad and most of his artillery and trains, and retreat to the east through the mountains (Pigeon Mountains, I think they were called); that we would follow the railroad and beat Johnston to Atlanta.

Arriving at Gen. Thomas's Headquarters, we found him at supper, and Gen. Sherman repeated to him the same expressions he used to me. Gen. Thomas was also greatly pleased, and my recollection is that he said he thought Johnston would fortify and defend the gap.

Sherman and Thomas agreed that Johnston must now let go Rocky Face, and that Thomas and Schofield must push him hard in the morning to crush him and prevent his crushing McPherson. This understanding had, we returned to Headquarters, Gen. Sherman being in high spirits.

Late that night word came from McPherson that he had failed to seize the railroad, and had fallen back to the mouth of the gap and fortified. I think that all the members of the staff will remember how disappointed and excited the General was on receipt of this news, and how cross he was the next day, and that we all thought he might relieve McPherson of his command, though the General gave no intimation of such intent—to me, at least. We simply inferred it from McPherson's failure to execute the work expected of him.

I was present when Gen. Sherman and McPherson first met after this, and well remember that Gen. Sherman's manner toward McPherson was one of sadness rather than anger, and that his first remark was:

"Well, Mac, you have missed the great opportunity of your life."

Gen. Adkins and Col. Hickenlooper, both of whom were in good position to know the truth, express, I think, he general judgment of the Army of the Tennessee—that if certain other division commanders had been in the lead, the railroad would have been seized and held, and Johnston ruined.

That the failure to do this was by far the most grievous disappointment which Gen. Sherman met with during the Atlanta Campaign, will, I think, be admitted by all who participated in it, and were familiar with its history.

Willard Warner's claim that Sherman may have contemplated relieving McPherson after Snake Creek Gap cannot be substantiated, but it is enough that his staff officers believed, if only briefly, that he might is important in itself.

8

Charles Coffin Summarizes the Battle of Resaca

"Carleton," "The Battle of Resaca"

(October 21, 1886, pp. 1-2)

Born in New Hampshire in 1823, Charles Carleton Coffin was prevented by a prewar ankle injury from serving in the Union army. When war broke out, he started writing about it for the Boston Globe, *covering events in the eastern theater.*

After the war, he wrote several books about his experiences, as well as biographies of Presidents Lincoln and Garfield.

Between December 6, 1883 and March 15, 1888, the National Tribune *ran nearly a hundred articles by Coffin ("Carleton") under the title, "Saving the Nation: The Story of the War Retold for Our Boys and Girls." The very first installment began thus:*

To the boys and girls of the United States:

You all know that there was a great war between the Southern and Northern sections of the United States, which began April, 1861, and lasted four years; that terrible battles were fought; about half a million men were killed and wounded or died of disease. The war ended before you were born, or when you were so young that you have no remembrance of soldiers in blue uniforms going to or returning from the war. It was one of the greatest wars in the world's history—waged not for conquest, nor for fame or glory; it was a conflict of ideas and institutions affecting not only the United States, but other countries.

[*In subsequent articles, "Carleton" told the boys and girls of America a really long narrative of the war's big battles and important campaigns. Usually, the narrative appeared on the front page of the paper, bleeding over onto a second. The author focused on both the eastern and western theaters. Notable, too, was his attention to black folk; occasional columns discussed "contrabands" and Lincoln's journey toward abolition as a war aim.*

Coffin knew he was taking his readers, presumably youngsters with short attention spans, through an extensive story. At one point, regarding Burnside's approach to Fredericksburg, he admits, "this chapter is not very interesting, but it is needful to a comprehension of the campaign."

Altogether, the 96 articles form a lengthy history of the war that was apparently never reprinted in book form. Chapter LXXXIV, "Resaca," reviews events from Snake Creek Gap to Cassville. Here we will reprint most of it, a text that notably quotes the memoir of "a Confederate soldier." The work is Sam R. Watkins's reminiscence, Co. "Aytch": or, a Side Show of the Big Show. *The book had just appeared in 1882; "Carleton's" excerpts, appearing four years later, could possibly be the first in reprint. Since then,* Co. "Aytch" *has been quoted so many times as to become a staple in the literature of the Army of Tennessee, although our author refers twice only to "a Confederate soldier" as its author.*]

To the Boys and Girls of the United States:

Gen. Joseph E. Johnston had brought the Confederate army up to a high state of efficiency. He was severe in discipline. Seventeen men were shot at Tunnel Hill and a whole company at Rocky Face Ridge. Instead of the whipping-post he established the pillory. Men who committed petty crimes wore barrel shirts, and it was laughable to see what was called the barrel-shirt brigade. A Confederate soldier gives this picture of an execution: "The snow was on the ground and the boys were hard at it snowballing. While I was standing looking on a file of soldiers marched by me with a poor fellow on his way to be shot. He was blindfolded and set upon a stump, and the detail was formed. The command, 'Ready—aim, fire.' was given, the volley discharged, and the prisoner fell off the stump. He had not been killed. It was the Sergeant's duty to give the coup de grace, should not the prisoner be slain. The Sergeant ran up and placed the muzzle of his gun at the head of the poor, pleading and entreating wretch, his gun was discharged, and the wretched man only powder-burned, the gun being one that had been loaded with powder only. The whole affair had to be gone over again. The soldiers had to reload and form and fire. The culprit was killed stone dead this time. He had no sooner been taken up and carried off to be buried than the soldiers were throwing snowballs as hard as ever, as if nothing had happened."

M'PHERSON'S OVER-CAUTION

At 2 in the afternoon of May 9 McPherson is through Snake Creek Gap. It is startling news which Johnston hears, that the Union troops are moving toward Resaca on the road from Sugar Valley Postoffice. While he had been watching his front and right, Sherman has been turning his left and is moving to seize the railroad at Resaca.

There are only a few troops at Resaca to hold McPherson in check. Just how many were there cannot be ascertained. Johnston says there were two brigades, other accounts say there was but one brigade. Dr. Johnson, who is still living at Resaca, who was at home on that afternoon, says that there was only a part of a brigade in the village. It is quite probable that when the skirmishers of McPherson appeared, coming through the woods west of the railroad, there were but a handful of Confederates at the station, guarding the road and bridge over the Oostanaula. Others soon came from the fort on the hill east of the village. They were under Gen. Canty [*Brig. Gen. James Cantey*]. They go upon the run out through the meadow west of the railroad. Some rush up the hill northwest of the village and open fire upon McPherson's advance. They string out in a long line and make all the racket possible. McPherson's troops, instead of rushing on with a hurrah, as they might have done, come to a halt in the edge of the woods west of Mr. Hill's house. They are only a third of a mile from the railroad and the bridge which spans the Oostenaula. Let them rush on and seize them, and there will be consternation in Johnston's army. All communication with Atlanta will be cut off. No more supplies can be brought up. Let them but rush on, and to-morrow's morn will see Johnston doing one of two things—either bringing a large part of his army from Buzzard's Roost to attack McPherson, or his whole army in flight eastward along the country roads, attempting to reach Atlanta. On that afternoon a great opportunity has come to the Union army—one which will never come again. Why does not McPherson improve it? Why does he hesitate? He has 23,000 men, and Hooker is not far away with 11,000 more. His right flank rests on the Oostenaula and cannot be turned. He can be attacked only on his left. That is what he fears. He is brave and able, but he has been placed in command of the Army of the Tennessee, and feels the great responsibility. He must not endanger the army. He does not know how great is the force in front of him. Were not night coming on he might venture to bring on a battle. He has been cautioned in his orders not to endanger that army. Caution holds him when he should move his divisions forward.

Says Sherman: "McPherson found the gap undefended and accomplished a complete surprise to the enemy. At its farther debouche he met a cavalry brigade, which was easily driven and which retreated hastily toward Dalton and doubtless carried to Johnston the first intimation that a heavy force of artillery and infantry was in his rear and within a few miles of the railroad. I got a note from McPherson that day, written at 2 p.m., when he was within one and a half miles of the railroad, above and near Resaca. I renewed orders to Thomas and Schofield to be ready for instant pursuit of what I expected to be a beaten and disordered army, forced to retreat by roads to the east of Resaca which were known to be very rough and impracticable."

WAS THE COUNTRY READY?

A few weeks later McPherson gave up his life, and we shall never know just what considerations turned him back when he was so near the coveted prize. Shall we say that the time had not come? It is Gen. Sherman's view that the country was not ready for breaking up the rebellion. We are to remember that the Confederate Government had taken great offense at the enlistment of negroes as soldiers; that they would not recognize them in exchange of prisoners. Throughout the North were men bitterly hostile to the proclamation of President Lincoln giving freedom to the slaves as a war measure, and were denouncing the war as unrighteous and wicked. If Johnston's army had been annihilated at the outset of the campaign, with such animosity against the colored race, would the measure of freedom [have] been what it is to-day? Would the negroes have become citizens of the Republic? Under an all-wise Providence, which sees through from the beginning to the end, which guides the Nation to its mighty destiny, McPherson turned back. There must still be the outpouring of the precious wine of life, the agony of the battlefield, the hospital, the endurance of the prison, the lengthening trenches and ghastly scenes of Andersonville, the sacrifices of thousands of lives, before the government of the people could be established on an enduring basis, with the full measure of freedom to every man, irrespective of race or color, before the United States could take the exalted place of leader and teacher of all the Nations in their march toward freedom.

Although McPherson had gained his left flank and threatened his rear, Johnston, finding that he had fallen back, made all haste to hold Resaca till he could withdraw the army from Dalton. Sherman was in no hurry to compel his departure. He was planning a larger movement. We see him withdrawing Schofield, sending Williams's Division of Hooker's Corps to support McPherson, and waiting for Stoneman's Division of Cavalry which was coming to join him. He issues orders to Schofield to go through Snake Creek Gap and join McPherson. His whole army is in motion toward Resaca. So quietly was all done that not till the main part of the army had passed through the gap does Johnston discover the movement.

THE RETREAT FROM DALTON

There was a sudden packing of wagons at Dalton on the afternoon of May 12, 1864. The Confederate artillery went down the road, the horses upon the gallop and the infantry upon the run, toward Resaca. Maj.-Gen. Polk's [*sic: Lt. Gen. Leonidas Polk's*] Corps was in the advance moving to head off the Union troops under McPherson, which were west of Resaca. The left of the Confederate line rested on the Oostenaula. During the night [*of May 12-13*] the Confederates were hard at work with their shovels, throwing up breastworks on the swell of ground by the house of Mr. Hill and on the ridge northwest of the railroad. When morning dawned [*on the 13th*] McPherson beheld long lines of embankments in front of him. A little stream comes down from the north, Camp Creek, and empties into the Oostenaula a half mile west of the railroad. The ridge of ground along which Johnston was throwing up his defense lies between the creek and the railroad. Next to Polk we see Hardee with his corps, then Hood. Polk and Hardee face west, while Hood faces north.

The long lines of wagons belonging to the Union army are parked at the lower end of Snake Creek Gap, guarded by [*Brig. Gen. Alvin P.*] Hovey's Division of the Army of the Ohio. Gen. McPherson advances, with Logan's Corps on is right, and the cavalry, under Kilpatrick, swinging out through the woods and fields southwest, while the other divisions move along the road and north of it toward Resaca. Gen. Thomas comes in from the west toward the house of Mr. Moore, with Hooker opposite the house of Mr. Ruckert, which the Confederates are tearing down to obtain lumber for their breastworks. Gen. Schofield, with the divisions of Gens. [*Henry M.*] Judah and [*Jacob D.*] Cox, moves in rear of Thomas, crosses the field near the house of Mr. Wright and the meadows at the head of Camp Creek, turns south and faces the Confederates under Gen. Hood. Gen. Howard, with the Fourth Corps, is on the march from Dalton along the railroad, picking up straggling Confederates who have dropped behind in retreat. Gen. Sherman receives word that the Fourth Corps is close at hand, that all the troops are in position, and orders an advance of the entire line.

SHERMAN FOLLOWS HARD AFTER

It is about noon when Gen. Sherman rides up to the point on the line east of Mr. Wright's house, where the Army of the Ohio joins the Army of the Cumberland. Gen. Schofield and Gen. Thomas are both there and together they watch the movement. There are several little streams to cross, fences which must be torn down and thick brambles which impede their way. The artillery finds it difficult to get across the miry meadow, and the advance is quite slow. Schofield's two divisions move south. Gen. Cox on the east side of the Dalton road, Gen. Judah west of it. The artillery begins the battle [*on May 14*]. A little later a line of skirmishers in blue pick their way along the fences across the meadow, and the musketry begins. The Confederate skirmishers east of the road are driven across the little creek, but those behind the fences and in a thicket by the bridge keep up a sharp fire and hold the ground a while, but are driven at last, and then the whole Army of the Ohio crosses the creek. The battle opens fiercely east of the road, where Cox's Brigades rush upon the Confederates and drive them from their breastworks. The Confederates fall back to a second line of works. Cox can advance no farther, and the men lie down behind the breastworks which they have captured, holding them until Gen. Howard brings up Wood's and Newton's Divisions to support him. The division under Gen. Judah has a harder task to perform and is less fortunate. The ground over which the troops march is broken and there are tangled thickets through which the troops must charge up a steep hill swept by a cross-fire from the Confederate batteries. There are three brigades which move steadily forward. Shells explode among them and a pitiless storm beats upon them from the veteran Confederate soldiers under Hood, which have been in a score of battles, and the Union men are repulsed with heavy loss.

Gen. Johnston discovers that Gen. Stanley's Division of Gen. Howard's Corps, east of the Dalton road in rear of Gen. Wood's Division, has no support and lays his plans to strike a heavy blow. Hood sends two of his divisions, Gen. Stewart's and Gen. Stevenson's, directing them to come round upon Stanley's left flank and crush it. Very fortunately at the same moment Gen. Sherman, finding that there is not sufficient room to deploy all of Thomas' troops, sends Hooker eastward toward the Dalton road, the troops marching in rear of the Army of the Ohio. Johnston, to conceal his movement and to prevent Sherman from sending supports to Stanley, orders the Confederate artillery to open all along the line. He does not know that Hooker is on his way toward Stanley's position. The Confederates under Stewart and Stevenson come upon Stanley, making a fierce attack, but soon find themselves confronted by a superior force. Williams's Division of Hooker's Corps is in advance and arrives just at the moment when Stanley needs him. The Confederates are repulsed with great loss and the Union troops hold the ground.

LOGAN TAKES A HAND

Going down now to the Army of the Tennessee [*on the Union right*], we find Gen. Osterhaus with a division of Logan's Corps on the road which leads west from Resaca to Sugar Valley Postoffice. The Confederate troops at this point are west of Camp Creek. There is a bridge across the creek, which they hold. There are thick woods along the valley, and the Confederate skirmishers are sheltering themselves behind the trees. The 12th Mo., of Osterhaus's command, is on the skirmish-line, and the soldiers leap across the creek, gaining the rear of the Confederates, who abandon the west bank and flee across the bridge. Gen. Logan orders Gen. Giles A. Smith and Gen. C. R. Woods with their brigades, supported by Veatch's Division, to advance. They cross the creek, drive the rebels, secure a strong position, and throw up intrenchments. The artillery hastens forward, comes into position, and sends shells crashing into the railroad station and the bridge spanning the Oostenaula.

Gen. Polk makes an attempt to drive them from the position [*on the afternoon of May 14*], but his troops are repulsed. From the moment that Logan secured this position Gen. Johnston saw that he must sooner or later retreat. No railroad trains could bring him supplies across the bridge. He set his bridge builders to work, constructing one bridge near the railroad crossing and another around the bend a mile east of the railroad bridge, beyond the reach of the Union artillery.

ANOTHER FLANK MOVEMENT

While the cannon are thundering at Resaca Gen. Sherman is executing another important move. He has no intention of attacking Johnston behind his breastworks, but hopes to gain his rear, intercept his line of communication with Atlanta, and compel him to fight a battle in the open field. The course of the Oostenaula is southwest. The railroad runs nearly south, and he sends Kilpatrick's Division of Cavalry and Sweeny's Division of Infantry down the west bank of the river 10 miles to Lay's Ferry, with a pontoon train, with orders to cross the river, lay the pontoons and secure a position on the east [*south*] bank. If this can be successfully done, if he can march his army across the river at that point and seize the railroad near the town of Calhoun, he will compel Johnston either to fight him or retreat across the country toward Kennesaw Mountain. The cavalry reach the river, drive the Confederate pickets across the stream, and push out on all the roads. Capt. [*Chauncy B.*] Reese, McPherson's Chief Engineer, has the pontoons in place in a very short time. One of Sweeny's Brigades crosses the Oostenaula. A messenger comes down the road informing Sweeny that the Confederates are crossing the river above him to gain his rear and cut off his retreat. The troops which have crossed the river go back upon the run, and Sweeny hastens back a mile and a half before he learns that it is a false report.

Gen. Johnston learns that Gen. Sherman's troops are crossing at Lay's Ferry, and sends Martin's Cavalry and Walker's Division of Infantry to Calhoun to hold the railroad. Had not Sweeny hastened back, but pushed on to the railroad, he might possibly have seized it, but it is doubtful if he could have held it. Had he done so it is certain that there would have been a sudden commotion in Johnston's center at Resaca. On the evening [sic: morning] of the 15th of May we see Sweeny once more crossing the Oostanaula and moving towards Calhoun, but he is not now strong enough to take possession of the railroad.

At sunrise the following morning [*May 15*] the skirmishers are firing all along the line. Gen. Sherman is intending to make a vigorous demonstration [*against the Confederate right, Hood's sector*]. During the night the Fourteenth Corps has moved to the ground occupied by Schofield, who in turn has moved east, thus strengthening the line. Johnston sees what is going on and withdraws a portion of Hardee's and Polk's troops to reinforce Hood.

It is past noon before the demonstration begins. Butterfield's Division of Hooker's Corps and Stevenson's of Hood's are the first to clash. Instead of a demonstration it soon becomes a furious battle. Stevenson brings forward a battery to a knoll, from which he will hurl a storm of shells upon the Union army, but the sharpshooters in blue pick off the gunners, who abandon their cannon. Through the afternoon the uproar goes on, the Union men gaining inch by inch, driving Stevenson, who is not able to withdraw the cannon. Col. [*Lt. Col. Robert*] Kilpatrick, of the 5th Ohio, watches his opportunity. His men leap up the hill, seize the pieces and make the air ring with their hurrahs. There is a vigorous cannonade all along the line, with severe fighting on the part of the infantry here and there. Night closes over the scene, and the Union soldiers go to work with axes and shovels, making their lines very strong. Gen. Sherman intends to make them so strong that a few troops will be able to hold them while he withdraws the remainder of the army for the movement to Lay's Ferry to gain Johnston's rear.

JOHNSTON MOVES AGAIN TO THE REAR

Commanders of armies are often obliged to do things that are exceedingly distasteful. Gen. Johnston had been compelled to give up his strong position at Dalton because he left a door open at Snake Creek Gap, by which Sherman outflanked him. There were no mountain passes around him at Resaca, but the Oostenaula was at his back, too deep to be forded. The Union army was moving to get in his rear, and there was but one course to pursue. He must retreat before Sherman can transfer his troops across the Oostenaula at Lay's Ferry. He must be quick about it. He must abandon all the lines of breastworks which have been thrown up and find another position. He issues his orders accordingly. Before the sun goes down [*on May 15*] the wagon trains are ready to move. As soon as it is dark the troops begin to withdraw, Polk's Corps crossing the railroad bridge, Hardee's Corps the bridge immediately above it, and Hood's Corps the bridge beyond the bend. Morning [*of the 16th*] dawns, but no Confederate troops are at Resaca; all have gone.

The newspapers of the South said that Johnston was falling back to get Sherman away from his supplies, that he might utterly crush him in a great battle that would soon be fought; that Sherman would have fewer troops the farther he advanced, because he would be obliged to detach a large force to guard the railroad. Johnston, on the other hand, would be getting nearer his base of supplies, while his army would be growing stronger day by day. Gov. Brown, of Georgia, had called out the militia, which would guard the railroad, while the Regular troops could all be employed against Sherman. A Confederate soldier gives this picture of affairs:

"We had stacked our arms and gone into camp, and had started to build fires to cook supper. I saw our cavalry falling back, I thought, rather hurriedly. I ran to the road and asked them what was the matter? They answered, 'Matter enough; yonder are the Yankees, are you infantry fellows going to make a stand here?' I told Col. Field what had been told to me, and he hooted at the idea; but balls that had shucks tied to their tails were passing over, and our regiment was in the rear of the whole army. I could hardly draw anyone's attention to the fact that the cavalry had passed us, and that we were on the outpost of the whole army, when an order came for our regiment to go forward as rapidly as possible and occupy an octagon house in our immediate front. The Yankees were about a hundred yards from the house on one side and we about a hundred yards on the other. The race commenced as to which side would get to the house first. We reached it, and had barely gotten in, when they were bursting down the paling of the yard on the opposite side. The house was a fine brick, octagon in shape, and as perfect a fort as could be desired. We ran to the windows, up-stairs, down-stairs and in the cellar. The Yankees cheered and charged, and our boys got happy. Colonel Field told us he had orders to hold it until every man was killed, and never to surrender the house. It was a forlorn hope.

"We felt we were 'gone fawn skins,' sure enough. At every discharge of our guns, we would hear a Yankee squall. The boys raised a tune—

"I'se gwine to jine the rebel band,
A fighting for my home"—

as they loaded and shot their guns. Then the tune of—

"Cheer, boys, cheer, we are marching on to battle!
Cheer, boys, cheer, for our sweethearts and our wives!
Cheer, boys, cheer, we'll nobly do our duty,
And give to the South our hearts, our arms, our lives."

"Our cartridges were almost gone, and Lieut. Joe Carney, Joe Sewell, and Billy Carr volunteered to go and bring a box of 1,000 cartridges. They got out of the back window, and through that hail of iron and lead, made their way back with the box of cartridges. Our ammunition being renewed, the fight raged on. Capt. Joe P. Lee touched me on the shoulder and said: "Sam, please let me have your gun for one shot." He raised it to his shoulder and pulled down on a fine-dressed cavalry officer, and I saw that Yankee tumble. He handed it back to me to reload. About 12 o'clock, midnight, the 15th [*sic: 154th*] Tennessee, commanded by Col. McGevney [Michael Magevney], came to our relief.

The firing had ceased, and we abandoned the octagon house. Our dead and wounded were there, 30 of them, in strange contrast with the furniture of the house—fine chairs, sofas, settees, pianos and brussels carpeting being made the death-bed of brave and noble boys, all saturated with blood; fine lace and damask curtains, all blackened by the smoke of battle; fine bureaus and looking-glasses and furniture being riddled by the rude missiles of war; beautiful pictures in gilt frames, and a library of valuable books, all shot and torn by musket and cannon balls. Such is war."

One doesn't have to read too far to discern that this long article, ostensibly written for "Our Boys and Girls," is a detailed tactical account of the Atlanta Campaign's opening—suggesting either that America's youth of the 1880s was a fairly sophisticated and inquisitive readership, or that "Carleton" was giving himself leeway to write in an informal or conversational style—as opposed to the technical military terminology that was already beginning to be seen (think of Battles and Leaders*).*

Coffin's article, written two decades after the war, demonstrates the task facing an early war historian. Volume 38 of the Official Records, *those treating the Atlanta Campaign, had yet to be published (1891). "Carleton's" knowledge of the terrain around Resaca, and mention of several residences there, suggests that he had visited the area. He quotes Sherman with a text closely resembling that seen in his* Memoirs *(1875).*

At this early date, Coffin presages the main courses of the historical literature about Resaca: the terrific opportunity that Snake Creek Gap provided Sherman, McPherson's hesitancy, and Johnston's good fortune resulting from it. He also mentions Johnston's retreat from Dalton, May 11-12, and describes how the opposing forces took up positions west and north of Resaca on the 12th and 13th.

It is in some details that "Carleton" falters. The statement regarding McPherson that "his right flank rests on the Oostanaula and cannot be turned" is puzzling; McPherson's infantry was marching through Snake Creek Gap, almost ten miles north of the river. His column was advancing without cavalry, and he thus succumbed to fears that he would be assailed by Rebels pushing south of Dalton. The author is correct in emphasizing McPherson's concerns for his troops' safety. He had just been appointed commander of the Army of the Tennessee a month and a half before, and this was his first field operation in that capacity.

"Carleton" chronicles the five phases of the battle of Resaca, May 14-15: 1) Federal attack on the Confederate center-right; 2) Confederate assault on the Federal left; 3) Federal advance on the Confederate left (Polk's sector) getting within artillery range of the vital railroad bridge; 4) Federal attack on the Confederate right held by Hood's Corps; and 5) Confederate counterattack on the Federal left.

During all this fighting, the author rightly focuses on Sherman's main gambit: throwing Brig. Gen. Thomas Sweeny's division across the Oostanaula at Lay's Ferry, well downstream of Johnston's position. On the afternoon of May 14, Sweeny crossed some of his infantry, but, fearing attack, ordered them back to the north bank. At this point "Carleton" was a bit muddled as to further events. Sweeny's infantry recrossed the river on the morning of May 15 and a pontoon bridge was laid for more to cross. Confederate Maj. Gen. William H. T. Walker's division, hustled down by Johnston, attacked but could not drive off Sweeny's bridgehead.

Meanwhile, Hood's sector, fighting on the other side of Johnston's line, involved a four-gun battery being pushed ahead of the Confederate entrenchments. As Coffin states, Federal assaults forced the Southern artillerists back, leaving their cannon out in the field. But he errs as to how the Federals captured the four guns of Capt. Maximilian Van Den Corput's Cherokee Battery: during the night of May 15-16, men of the 5th Ohio stealthily approached, dug through the Rebels' parapet, and dragged them away with ropes.

They were aided by the fact that Johnston, knowing that the enemy was across the river and threatening his rear, had ordered his army to retreat again, which it did that night.

The incident Private Watkins refers to at the end of Coffin's article occurred on May 17 near Adairsville, a dozen miles south of Resaca. Major General Benjamin Franklin Cheatham's division of Hardee's Corps marched as the rearguard in the Confederate army's retreat. Near Adairsville, it formed a defensive line against the pursuing Federals; the 1st/27th Tennessee, Watkins's regiment, occupied all three stories of a tall octagon-shaped house and fired from its windows.

Incidentally, the "Cheer, boys, cheer" lyrics are from Henry Russell's song published in Nashville and Memphis in 1861. Also called "The Song of Southern Boys," the chorus runs, "Cheer, boys, cheer, for country, mother country/Cheer, boys, cheer, the willing strong right hand,/Cheer, boys, cheer, there's wealth for honest labor,/Cheer, boys, cheer, for the new and happy land!" (E. Lawrence Abel, Confederate Sheet Music *[Jefferson NC: McFarland, 2004], 38-39).*

As for "I'se gwine to jine the Rebel band," Watkins writes, "Now, reader, the above is all I can remember of that beautiful and soul-stirring air" (Ruth Hill Fulton McAllister, ed., Co. "Aytch" First Tennessee Regiment or a Side Show of the Big Show *[Franklin TN: Providence House Publishers, 2007], 66-67).*

9

Federals Drive Polk Back, Afternoon of May 14

Alex C. Harter, "Wood's Brigade at Resaca"

(February 10, 1910, p. 7)

By dawn on May 13, Johnston's army had taken up a new line on ground west and north of Resaca. Both flanks rested on rivers: the Confederate left on the Oostanaula, the right on the Conasauga. Behind the position ran the Western & Atlantic and the rail and wagon bridges.

In front of Johnston's left (to the west), now held by Lt. Gen. Leonidas Polk's corps (just arrived from Mississippi), ran Camp Creek. Between it and Polk's main line rose a hill on which Confederate skirmishers had entrenched. This became the target of a Federal attack on the afternoon of the 14th, as Alex Harter relates here.

Editor National Tribune: It was with great pleasure that I followed Comrade McElroy's history of the Atlanta campaign. He has the main facts down to the letter, but there are some important details lacking. Take his description of the battle of Resaca, which is based on the report of Gen. Logan. While this report is correct as far as it goes, it says nothing of the peculiar situation which his First Division, and especially the First Brigade under Gen. Wood [*Brig. Gen. Charles R. Woods, commander of First Brigade, First Division, Major General John A. Logan's Fifteenth Corps*] had got themselves into.

It was only by the stubborn, reckless fighting of those seasoned veterans that they saved themselves from disaster, and certainly saved Sherman from a mortifying reverse.

There were two hills running parallel with Camp Creek, north and south, the first extending from near the Oostenaula River northeast to within 75 yards of the wagon road running west from Resaca; the second hill was a little farther east and not quite so long.

We of Wood's Brigade were ordered to take and hold the first hill, but thru the excitement of the advance never even halted, but kept on over the hill and on to the second one, 100 yards or so farther on, right, you might say, into the arms of the enemy.

[*Around 5:30 p.m., Wood's and Giles Smith's brigade advanced across the creek and drove the Southerners from their advanced hill position. At 7:30 p.m., with the sun going down, Polk ordered counterattacks to retake the hill. They failed, and Wood's troops hung on. During the night Polk ordered a withdrawal a half-mile eastward to a new line almost upon the railroad.*]

Then came the real tug of war. After firing our guns we had not time to re-load (the enemy, either, for that matter), so we went at each other with bayonet and saber or with clubbed guns. Finally, as Gen. Logan says, "The enemy retreated," and the respite gave us time to gather together our wits and reload our guns.

Owing to the fact that our brigade had advanced farther than it was ordered, our right flank was unprotected. Gen. Giles A. Smith, with his brigade of the Second Division, was to have come up with us; but owing to his way having been rougher and with a marsh of considerable extent to get thru, he could not keep up with Wood's Brigade, who had somewhat fairer ground to pass over. When Smith did get thru the tangle and arrived at the hill, he stopped where he was ordered to, and this left us in a bad fix.

The enemy rallied and came at us again. The air was a hissing, shrieking, seething inferno of shot and shell. It seemed for a space of two hours and a half that no living thing could survive that horrible carnival.

Poor Gillispie was struck fair in the face by a cannon ball and his head cut clear off his body. Sam Cooper and I were knocked over by the concussion of a bursting shell, and crawled to our feet, looking for all the world like two whipped puppies.

But they came again and again, gathering strength by numbers from other parts of the battlefield, hurling themselves against that living wall of devoted heroes, until at last the regiment on our extreme right, an Iowa regiment that had lost in killed and wounded all but a pitiful handful of men, could stand it no longer, and as the enemy made what was by mercy its last but most vicious advance upon us, began slowly to give ground. They had reached the hollow between the hills, and in another moment would have been in full retreat, and our regiment, the 27th Mo., being next to them, on the left, the 76th Ohio on our left, would have to either bear the brunt of a flank movement and an enfilading fire or else retreat, too. It was a critical moment for all concerned. Realizing our situation, and knowing that our great chief, Sherman, was watching the outcome of the battle from the west side of Camp Creek while surrounded by Gens. McPherson, Logan, Hooker and Sickles and their Aids, some one called out: "Come on; the Johnnies are retreating!"

Their officers took up the word, and finally got the men (who were not at all panic-stricken, but were as tho they had been thrust underwater and were endeavoring to get their heads above so as to get a breath of fresh air) to turn back.

We called out to them to load, and as they came scrambling up the hill every one of them had managed, somehow, to shove a load into his gun. When they arrived at the top of the hill they ran right into the enemy, and it was a good thing that they had their guns loaded. They poured a deadly fire into the enemy. In the meantime the rest of us were not idle. We had no time to watch those brave Iowans struggle back up the hill. I assure you we had all we could do to hold our place on the firing line.

At this juncture Smith's brigade and another brigade commanded by Gen. [*Joseph*] Lightburn arrived on the ground, and that settled the question with the Johnnies. They did retreat in earnest, and that was the last we saw of them in close proximity that day. They kept up desultory firing till long into the night, but that finally ceased, and in the morning Johnston had his army on the south side of the Oostenaula River [*Not correct; Johnston held his lines throughout May 15, and retreated during the night of the 15th-16th after Sweeny's division got across the river that morning.*]

I cannot help mentioning an incident or two during the battle. One is that of a drummer boy of about 13 years, who had thrown his drum away and took up a gun. He had crouched down behind a large pine stump and was blazing away at the enemy with all the energy he could command, when a solid shot struck the stump, bursting it and sending the boy several feet away; but he scrambled up, and, grabbing his gun, loaded it and went back to his dilapidated stump and began firing away at the enemy again.

Another thing noticed by us was a little dog which was between the two armies. After the enemy had advanced and retreated he would jump and skip about in the small brush and grass, barking all the time, and springing up as high as he could, as you have seen dogs do that have started a rabbit and have lost sight of it. He rushed back and forth and seemed to enjoy the game. So far as we knew he passed thru the battle unhurt.

Our loss, according to Logan's report in McElroy's history, in killed and wounded was 628.—Alex C. Harter, Co. A, 27th Mo., 2003 Richard street, Dayton, O.

10

Resaca—Capture of a Rebel Battery

W. H. H. Minot, "At Resaca. The Capture of the 4-Gun Battery—Some Interesting Incidents"

(December 16, 1886, p. 3)

EDITOR NATIONAL TRIBUNE: James H. Goff, 129th Ill., must not claim wholly for his brigade the honor of capturing the 4-gun battery at Resaca, for the Second Brigade, Third Division, Twentieth Corps, took a very prominent part in that capture. I belonged to that brigade and have a very distinct recollection of being present on that occasion—Sunday, May 15, 1864. They maneuvered us around in such shape among the grubs and hills that I could not tell where we came from or where we were going. We could not see three rods in any direction. At last they got us into shape and ordered us to charge. There were three or four lines ahead of us, and when we came to the edge of the woods the lines in front of us lay down and we ran right over them.

Of course, I cannot speak knowingly of anything but what happened in my immediate vicinity, but I think that Weaver F. Shoening, of Co. B, 22d Wis., was the one that led that charge; for when we came to the road we were in plain sight of the Johnnies, and as soon as we saw them Shoening shouted: "Here they are boys, come on."

He started for them as fast as he could run, and Co. B right after him, away in advance of anything on the line. That 4-gun battery was playing on us as fast as it could fire, and did some frightfully wicked work.

We did not capture that battery, neither did the brigade to which Goff belonged. We drove the men from the guns and the works, but our men could not stay there a moment, as the Johnnies had other works that commanded the fort, and we could not get in to haul off the guns. They were hauled out after dark by some of the men of the Third Division, Twentieth Corps. There were, however, three or four men, of whom Silas Wright, of Co. B, 22d Wis., was one, who crawled into the fort and lay around in the corners and acted as sharpshooters the balance of the day, and did very effective work.

After we had driven the Johnnies from the battery we took a position on a ridge to the left of the fort, from which the Johnnies tried to drive us by repeated charges. Gen. Ben [*Col. Benjamin*] Harrison's command was the line in the rear of us. Ben was sick that day and it was a great effort for him to give a command; but the Johnnies were charging us, and he was going to fix for them. Holding onto a sapling for support, he said:

"Seventy-fifth Ind., attention! Fix bayonets! If they come through the first line give them the cold steel. Do you understand?"

Lieut. Mosley, of our company, who was by my side, had just taken a big chew of tobacco. He munched it about twice, then turned around to the General, and said:

"They are not coming through, General."

There was so much force to Mosley's remark that the boys began to cheer, and a look of determination settled down on all of them. The 75th Ind. did not have to use the bayonet.

About that time a red-headed Lieutenant (I won't say what regiment he belonged to) came tearing back through the lines, clawing off his shoulder-straps, and getting to the rear as fast as he could go. Although men were dropping in our own ranks, the boys just yelled and laughed to see that Lieutenant run.

Gen. Joe Hooker was right by our company a part of the time, and his utter disregard for rebel lead gave pluck and courage to a good many of our boys.—W. H. H. MINOT, Co. B, 22d Wis., Second Brigade, Third Division, Twentieth Corps, Marshall, Mich.

Veterans of Maj. Gen. Joseph Hooker's XX Corps wrote voluminously in the National Tribune *about the capture of a Confederate battery during the battle of Resaca.*

On the morning of May 15, Lt. Gen. John B. Hood, in charge of the Confederate right, ordered Maj. Gen. Carter Stevenson to place a battery on high ground some 20 yards in front of his infantry's entrenched line—the position would allow the guns to counter fire from annoying enemy artillery. The cannon, four Napoleons of Capt. Maximilian Van Den Corput's "Cherokee Battery," were advanced into an earthen lunette built by the infantry. They had scarcely taken position when they were attacked by two brigades, Brig. Gen. William Ward's First and Col. John Coburn's Second, of Maj. Gen. Daniel Butterfield's Third Division, XX Corps (Stephen Davis, "Sherman in North Georgia: The Battle of Resaca," Blue & Gray, *vol. 31, issue 4 [Summer 2015], 45-46).*

Minot refers to an earlier article in the National Tribune *by James H. Gaff (not "Goff"), in which Gaff argues that Ward's First Brigade "captured the guns and took them off the field after dark" (May 31, 1883). Here Minot contends that his unit (Coburn's Second Brigade) assisted in the feat. Both Minot and Gaff correctly state that while Butterfield's troops overran the battery and drove the gunners back into Stevenson's trenches, they could not retrieve the four cannon under gunfire.*

The next day General Butterfield issued a congratulatory order that gives more credit to the First Brigade than to the Second, as the two authors state (J. W. Hogue, "Disputed Actions of the Twentieth Corps," National Tribune, *May 31, 1883). Yet Minot, Gaff, and Butterfield miss the point that it was men of Brig. Gen. John W. Geary's Second Division, XX Corps (not Butterfield's troops) who, during the night of May 15-16, crawled to the Rebel earthwork, dug through it, and pulled by rope each of Van Den Corput's cannon (Albert Castel,* Decision in the West: The Atlanta Campaign of 1864 *[Lawrence, KS, 1992], 179-180).*

Once again—not to diminish their contributions—writers to the National Tribune *are found faulty in some of their details. Benjamin Harrison, for example, did not rise above the rank of colonel during the war.*

11

General Sweeny Writes of Crossing the Oostanaula

William M. Sweeny, "Active Service of Gen T. W. Sweeny"

(October 10, 1895, p.1)

Among the little-known treasures in the National Tribune's *coverage of the Atlanta Campaign are the writings of Union Brig. Gen. Thomas W. Sweeny, division commander in the XVI Corps, as edited by his son, William M. Sweeny. So far as I know, this is their first appearance in the literature.*

In ten articles appearing from August to October 1895 (three years after General Sweeny's death), his war record is presented, from service in Missouri in 1861 to his relief of command in July 1864 following a fistfight with his superior officer, Maj. Gen. Grenville M. Dodge.

"In the following narrative are letters, the portion of a series written by Brig.-Gen. T. W. Sweeny, U.S.A.," the younger Sweeny begins in his first article (August 8, 1895). "They were not originally intended for publication," he continues; "their chief interest is in the fact that they were written by an active participant in the events narrated, while the occurrences were fresh in his memory—frequently, while they were actually happening."

William proceeds with a summary of his father's pre-Civil War service with the U.S. Army in Mexico (including the battle of Churubusco, August 1847, when he lost his right arm). Then followed frontier service out West and recruiting duty in New York City (doubtless among the city's Irishmen; Sweeny was born in Cork, 1820). At the start of the war, Captain Sweeny was stationed at St. Louis, serving under Brig. Gen. Nathaniel Lyon.

The series' second installment continues to summarize Sweeny's Missouri activity. In its course, the editor includes text of a letter Sweeny had written in early July to a friend named Bodge (whom William does not identify). In addition to this correspondence, the son also had his father's diary ("In a diary of events kept by Sweeny at the time he says . . .").

In the third article, published on August 22, Sweeny again writes Bodge from Springfield, Mo., July 24, 1861. Two weeks later, the battle of Springfield was fought; the captain's diary is quoted at length regarding the engagement in which Lyon was killed and Sweeny was shot in the leg.

Personal diary entries and letters to Bodge, knitted into William Sweeny's narrative, continue Capt. Sweeny's service in successive articles through promotion to colonel (January 1862), assignment to regimental command, and transfer to Grant's Army of the Tennessee (August 29); Shiloh (September 5); Corinth and brigade command (September 26, with letters to Bodge and to his daughter); as well as promotion to brigadier general and command of the Second Division, Sixteenth Corps (October 3).

The "Active Service of Gen. T. W. Sweeny" carries the subject and his division, part of McPherson's Army of the Tennessee, to the beginning of the Atlanta Campaign. This article includes several important letters from Sweeny to Bodge that describe his activity in the field from the opening of the campaign, through Snake Creek Gap, across the Oostanaula near Resaca, across the Etowah, and through the battle of Dallas, May 28.

Sweeny addresses Bodge when near Kingston, Ga., May 21:

"We left Pulaski [*Tennessee*] on the 29th ult. [*April 29, 1864*], and reached Chattanooga, via Huntsville [*Alabama*], on the 4th. Left Chattanooga on the 5th, and encamped on the battlefield of Chickamauga same evening, where I met Hooker [*commander of the 20th Corps in George Thomas' Army of the Cumberland*] and Sickles. The former I had not seen since 1850, but he remembered me at once; the latter I met for the first time since he lost his leg. [*Maj. Gen. Daniel Sickles had a leg amputated after a cannon round struck him on the second afternoon of Gettysburg. Continuing in active service but not in the field, Sickles was probably visiting Joe Hooker, his old friend from his days with the Army of the Potomac.*]

"My division was ordered forward to take Snake Creek Gap, which it did on the 8th. On the following morning the enemy attempted to drive us out, but did not succeed, and we moved on Resaca, with the intention of destroying the railroad bridge, etc., cutting off Johnston's communications with Atlanta. We found the place too strong, however, and fell back on Snake Creek Gap, and took possession of the hills which overlook the place, which my division occupied on the 9th. On the morning of the 14th, I was ordered to move to Lay's Ferry, about 5 miles to our extreme right, throw a pontoon bridge across the river, and hold the place, if possible. I made my arrangements accordingly, and succeeding in effecting a lodgment the following morning.

"After the second regiment had crossed, I commenced laying down the pontoon bridge, when the enemy commenced massing his troops in front of me, with the intention of gobbling those on the other side, and preventing any more crossing.

"I knew Walker's Division of infantry was on the other side, and the passage of a river in the face of an enemy is always a hazardous undertaking. I also knew that as long as Johnston was able to hold the line of the Oostanaula he was safe; but if I succeeded in cutting it, his rear and communications were threatened, and he would be compelled to retreat.

"Though driven from Dalton, his new position behind the Oostanaula was much stronger, because his forces were more concentrated in the vicinity of Resaca, which was the objective point. I hurried my troops across, and placed batteries on this side to command the position, when Walker and his whole force swept down with the hope of driving me across the river.

"Our fellows met him with great firmness, the 7th Iowa was thrown on his flank, which completely broke and routed him.

This was their last attempt to dislodge me. I threw my bridge across to be prepared for any emergency, and fortified both sides of the river. In this affair I lost a number of men. But the enemy's loss must be serious, at least so the prisoners I took say. Walker was put in arrest for allowing me to cross. I made a reconnaissance to the front, and found the enemy retreating. . . .

The story of General Sweeny's division crossing the Oostanaula is a little busier than he let on to his friend Bodge. On May 14, as Federal infantry were testing Johnston's lines around Resaca, Sweeny's division was ordered to lay two pontoon bridges at Lay's Ferry, four miles downstream, effectively outflanking Johnston's position north of the river. Confederates on the south bank were there in force, however, so Sweeny proceeded farther downstream still, where Snake Creek empties into the Oostanaula, and managed to get a bridgehead across. Fearing a counterattack, though, Sweeny called it back.

Johnston learned of all this and ordered that on the night of the 14th-15th, Maj. Gen. William H. T. Walker's division march toward Sweeny's crossing point.

At 8:00 a.m. on May 15, Sweeny's infantry recrossed the river on a big flatboat and chased away a few Rebels. When Walker arrived, he ordered an attack on the Federal bridgehead but was repulsed. Walker reported to Johnston that the Federals, now on the south bank of the Oostanaula, threatened the Confederates' railroad supply line to Atlanta. Johnston consequently ordered a retreat from Resaca during the night of May 15-16.

Thomas Sweeny's claim that Confederate General Walker had been arrested for failing to prevent the river-crossing of his division is perhaps the most colorful statement in this article. It is also incorrect.

12

At the Octagon House—A Northerner's Remembrance

George E. Dolton, "Battle of Adairsville"

(June 18, 1891, p. 3)

Mark Esgar, "Adairsville, Ga."

(August 13, 1891, p. 3)

Sam Watkins, like many veterans of both sides, could write of his war experiences with emphasis and exaggeration. One example is his article, "Battle Near Adairsville" (Confederate Veteran, *April 1902), in which he characterizes the fight at the Octagon House, May 17, as "a scene of blood and courage and death almost without a parallel in the history of the war."*

After another Southerner claimed that a hundred Federal batteries had shelled the Octagon House, one Union artilleryman who had been there, George Dolton, wrote in to set the record straight. Dolton's Battery M, 1st Illinois Light Artillery, was attached to Brig. Gen. John Newton's Second Division, XX Corps; chief of artillery for the division was Capt. Charles C. Aleshire, the "Long-range" to whom he refers.

EDITOR NATIONAL TRIBUNE: I recently saw a Confederate account of a little engagement at the famous Octagon House, one mile north of Adairsville, Ga., which occurred on the Atlanta campaign.

It is written with all the spread-eagle common in Confederate war narratives. He tells how bravely the 1st and 27th Tenn., consolidated, held the Octagon House against the assaults of the infantry and the shelling of 100 batteries of artillery at close range.

I have a little account of that skirmish, which I wrote at the time. Besides, I have some very good reasons for remembering it. That day the rebels had been pretty near as hard to drive as a herd of swine. They were very unruly, and some of the time did not act as though they wished to be driven at all.

Early in the afternoon, when they were thus contrary, a lot of them having gotten in and around a log house about a mile north of the Octagon House, two guns of Battery M, 1st Ill. L. A., were planted on the skirmish-line, and fired at the house. One of the shells passed through it, and about two feet above a bed on which was lying a woman who had only a few minutes before given birth to a child. There were two other women in the house. The rebels soon fell back, leaving several dead around the house.

Their next stand was in the woods at a creek immediately north of the Octagon House. Our skirmish-line, followed by a thin line of battle, had advanced into the woods. The main column of the infantry was in the road running almost due north and south, and on a straight line with the Octagon House. My battery (M, 1st Ill.) was in a grass field, in column of sections, just east of the road, and I was sitting on a squared log in a yard in front of a house just west of the road, talking with our Chief of Artillery, "Long-range," when the rebels opened from a battery near the Octagon House, the first shell sailing along the road but a few feet above the heads of the infantry, and striking the ground in the rear well beyond the curve in the road. The shell had scarcely passed when Long-range sprang to his feet and saddle, and dashed to the rear as rapidly as his horse would take him, simply remarking "I must go!" We were soon ordered by the brigade commander to open fire on the men in the woods. We told him that those were our men. He insisted that they were not, and again ordered us to fire on them. This we positively declined to do, when he ordered another battery, which took position immediately on our right (we having gone into battery just south of the field immediately south of the house) to fire on them, which they did, and we learned beyond doubt immediately that they were our men.

Considerable was said that evening and next morning about the battery firing into our own men, and it was charged that it was Battery M that did it. But Battery M fired only at the Octagon House, and the rebels immediately around it. Early next morning I went over the field to see what damage, if any, the battery had done. There I found a portion of the remains of a soldier. One of the shells fired from a Union battery had struck him about the middle of the back, and exploded in him. His chest was thrown forward over a log, behind which he was lying, his musket-barrel being driven through him, and projecting at the back of his neck. His limbs and trunk were torn into very fine fragments and scattered for over a rod at either side. I found a piece of the shell by the log, and it was a spherical shell. This proved that it was not fired by Battery M, we having nothing but rifled guns.

Whether the other battery fired on the Octagon House or not I do not know. Battery M did fire it, and this leaves, according to the rebels' account, 99 other batteries to be heard from, and I wish every other battery that fired on that house would make the fact known. This Johnny says that the shell would make a hole large enough through the walls for hogsheads to be thrown through, and the cannonading made the earth tremble around the house as with an earthquake.

Certainly Adairsville should occupy a more conspicuous position in history than it has yet.—GEO. E. DOLTON, 18 North Main St., St. Louis, MO.

Dolton's article brought forth this response.

EDITOR NATIONAL TRIBUNE: In your issue of June 18 I read an article on the battle of Adairsville from the pen of George E. Dolton, Battery M, 1st Ill. L. A. It was interesting to me from the fact that I was a participant in that little affair, and brings before me scenes after a lapse of 27 years that are not altogether pleasant.

I can endure all he says in regard to the rebels being hard to drive that day. The firing of one of our batteries into our own ranks and of the soldier who was mangled by one of our shells I will not write. Neither will I attempt to state at this late day what particular troops were engaged, for I could not do it. Let every comrade write for his own command. But I know that the 88th Ill. was there, and had been on the skirmish-line since early morning. The rebels had been hard to drive all day, and along in the afternoon, when we occupied a little hill near the Octagon House, they absolutely refused to be driven any farther and proceeded to make it rather warm for us.

It soon became not warm, but hot, when the shells began to drop among us from one of our own batteries a short distance in the rear. For a few minutes the south side of the trees were the safest. I probably knew at the time what battery it was, but cannot recall it now.

We were relieved soon after dark, were marched a short distance to the rear, and camped near the battery that fired into us. We found the boys loud in their denunciation of the officer who had ordered them to fire; for, said they, "We knew we were firing at our own men."

The soldier whom Comrade Dolton saw mangled so fearfully by one of our shells was Thomas Drake, Co. F, 88th Ill. He was a good boy and deserved a better fate. We buried him next morning on the spot where he fell, and his gun was buried with him, for it was impossible to withdraw it from his body. Adairsville is mentioned as only a skirmish in history, but it is easily magnified into a severe battle by those engaged there May 17, 1864.—MARK ESGAR, Co. F, 88th Ill., Wauponsee, Ill.

13
Cassville

O. O. Howard, "Atlanta Campaign. Chapter V"

(November 22, 1894, p.1)

From October 25, 1894 to April 18, 1895, the National Tribune *printed 26 installments from General Howard's* Autobiography, *which was published as two volumes in 1907. This is part five.*

In the forward movement from Adairsville, May 18, 1864, the three armies, namely, that of the Tennessee, the Cumberland, and the Ohio, were a little mixed up by Gen. Sherman's orders. They were, substantially, however, from right to left as I have named them, their confident commanders aiming for the points designated taking divergent roads. McPherson started toward Rome, Thomas toward Kingston, with one corps (Hooker's) toward Cassville, and Schofield, above Echota or Newtown, gaining ground with infantry and cavalry to the eastward, had the village of Cassville for final destination.

One division under the enterprising Gen. Jeff C. Davis, with Garrard's Cavalry, was detached from Thomas and sent directly to Rome. This division on the 18th drove out the small garrison of Confederates there, capturing some 10 heavy guns, other war material, supplies of all kinds, including a trainload of salt, and a few prisoners-of-war. The Confederate detachment displaced from Rome, like those from Dalton, Resaca, Calhoun, Adairsville, and Kingston, joined Johnston's main army, now concentrated, as they have continuously fallen back before us, at Cassville.

After reading all the leading reports, Johnston's proclamation, and the controversies, which began at the time and continued as long as the great actors in them were living, some things are very plain.

First. That Gen. Johnston had fully determined to give Sherman battle at Cassville, or in its neighborhood. To this end, he had selected well-defined heights, which were most favorable, and covered them with the usual temporary intrenchments.

PLACES FOR ARTILLERY

were carefully chosen by good engineers and artillerists, and epaulements set up for proper cover. Strengthened by a small reinforcement, he located Hardee's Corps so as to meet all the Army of the Cumberland and of the Tennessee, which were likely to approach Cassville from the west—that is, from the Kingston route; Polk's command in the center would meet Hooker's Corps with sufficient force to hold him in check, and have strong enough reserve to strengthen Hood, who, on Johnston's extreme right, was directed to meet and withstand the Army of the Ohio.

Second. With regard to position at this time, Gen. Johnston had greatly the advantage of his adversary, for his troops were concentrated. He could move on the inner lines. Sherman was coming in upon Cassville, after having his four columns greatly separated the one from the other. The nature of the country was such that it was next to impossible, before actual junction, for Thomas to send help to Hooker, and worse still for McPherson or Thomas to reinforce Schofield—I mean in a reasonable time.

But Gen. Sherman was so anxious for battle on the more favorable ground north of the Etowah, rather than upon the ragged country south of it, that he declared to his commanders, as in his dispatch to Schofield: "If we can bring Johnston to battle this side of the Etowah, we must do it, even at the hazard of beginning battle with but part of our forces."

Third. It is very evident that Johnston hoped to be able to dispose of Hooker and Schofield, as he endeavored to do of Heintzelman and Keyes the first day of the Fair Oaks battle in Virginia; that is, to strike them with a superior force and crush them before help could come. Gen. Johnston's intention to make an "offensive-defensive" battle appears plain from his own language and the instructions that are on record. He says in effect that after consultation with his engineer officer, who was questioned over the map in the presence of Gens. Polk and Hood, who were informed of this object, he found the country on the direct road open and

FAVORABLE FOR AN ATTACK;

that the distance between the two Federal columns would be greatest when those following the railroad reach Kingston. Gen. Johnston's Chief of Artillery warned him that our artillery, planted on a hill a mile off, could enfilade his right. Johnston ordered traverses to be constructed, though he declared that such artillery firing, more than a half-mile away, could do little harm, seeing that there were many protecting ravines.

My corps, the Fourth, as we already know, followed the wagon-road nearest the railway, turning to the left of Kingston about 8 a.m., May 18, 1864. We had hardly passed through this much-scattered hamlet, when skirmishing opened southeast of the place. Pressing back the skirmishers, we delayed any positive action till about 11 a.m., waiting for other troops to come into position, when my command again took up the march.

Then, shelling the low ground, mostly covered with broad patches of thick underbrush and straggling trees, we moved slowly forward, forcing back the outer lines of what was reported to be Cheatham's and one other division of the enemy. These obstinate divisions retired perforce, skirmishing all the time, to within two miles of Cassville; we now, with thick timber all around, appeared to be in front of the Cassville Confederate works.

Hooker's troops had done the same thing as mine on the direct Adairsville and Cassville road, that is, had been moving forward and skirmishing up to within striking distance of Johnston's intrenchments.

Palmer's Corps, off to my right, had at least one division (Baird's) deployed.

About this time a deserter came into our lines and reported that Gen. Johnston had received reinforcements of about 6,000 men. Just at this juncture we reckoned his force to be fully 70,000 strong.

So far as the Fourth Corps, which I commanded, is concerned, the journal of Lieut.-Col. Jos. S. Fullerton, the Adjutant-General, gives quite an animated account of the series of combats which took place between Kingston and Cassville. He says:

"Three-fifty p. m., advance commenced. * * * [*asterisks in original*] The enemy was driven by us. We again took up the march in column, and

AGAIN MET THE ENEMY

one mile beyond his first position at 5:30 p. m.; halted and formed line-of-battle; 5:40 p. m., Gen. Sherman ordered Gen. Howard to put 30 or 40 pieces of artillery in position; formed two or three brigades in line-of-battle; then to shell the woods in our front vigorously, afterward feel the enemy."

This was done. The journal continues:

"Six-thirty p. m., firing ordered to cease and skirmishers ordered forward, followed by main lines."

Here we connected with Palmer's Corps on the right and Hooker's on the left. Then we find in the journal:

"Now the line advanced, trying to move to Cassville; skirmishing very heavy and progress slow."

At 7 o'clock, apparently within about one mile of Cassville, I halted my command in place, and all slept in line-of-battle that night. The day had been warm and clear, but the roads were very dusty.

In these exchanges of artillery shots 10 of our men had been killed and 35 wounded. Fullerton remarks in closing this day's journal:

"The whole of Johnston's force was before us in Cassville. * * * The enemy thought to strike him (Hooker) before we got up. * * * The enemy had strong rifle-pits and works, and Johnston had published an order to his troops, saying that he would make his fight there; this (was issued) the night before we arrived."

That Gen. Johnston did intend and expected to make a stand here will be seen from the tenor of this order, which was as follows:

"SOLDIERS OF THE ARMY OF TENNESSEE: You have displayed the highest quality of the soldier—firmness in combat, patience under toil. By your courage and skill you have repulsed every assault of the enemy. By marches by day and by marches by night you have defeated every attempt upon your communications. Your communications are secured. You will now turn and march to meet his advancing columns. Fully confiding in the conduct of the officers, the courage of the soldiers

I LEAD YOU TO BATTLE.

We may confidently trust that the Almighty Father will still reward the patriots' toils and bless the patriots' banners. Cheered by the success of our brothers in Virginia and beyond the Mississippi, our efforts will equal theirs. Strengthened by His support, those efforts will be crowned with the like glories."

Gen. McPherson, under Sherman's orders, had also turned to the left, and was close in support of Thomas' right.

All the movements of our armies are now before the reader, except that of Gen. Schofield, whose forces, according to the design of Gen Johnston, were in a more perilous situation than those of the other columns. Let us see how he approached the projected battlefield. Luckily for all concerned, Schofield had a long march to make. Leaving Resaca the night of the 15th, he took the Spring Place and Cassville road, and went via Field's Mill, Big Spring and Martseller's Mill around to the vicinity of Cassville. He was not, however, near enough for Hood's Corps, supported by Polk, to strike him a heavy blow during the 18th of May. As he came up the evening of the 18th, moving westward along the Canton road, the enemy's bold attack might possibly have been made, but it was certainly too late after 5 p.m. of that day; for by that time the armies all touched elbows,--were close around the works of Johnston,--and were never before or afterward more concentrated or better able to give battle. It was, however, Schofield's cavalry, under Stoneman, some horse-artillery being with it, that appeared off to the right and eastward of Hood's command during the 19th of May. It was decidedly to our advantage that the valiant and

INDOMITABLE HOOD

was thus deceived by a force which perhaps dismounted and acted as infantry. Gen. Stoneman, who has recently died at Buffalo, N.Y., deserved special recognition from Schofield and Sherman for his good work. Hood's mistake as to infantry upon his flank may have arisen from rumors.

A single instance is given by Capt. David B. Conyngham, who was present at Cassville as soon as we occupied that village. He speaks of three men of the Twenty-third Corps who entered a house and were betrayed to a detachment of Confederate cavalry by some of the inmates. They barricaded themselves in the house and resisted several attacks. Just as the Confederates were setting fire to the house "a squad of Stoneman's cavalry heard the firing and hastened to the spot. The Union cavalry attacked the besieging party in the rear, soon putting them to flight, and so released their friends." Of course, one bird does not make a Summer, but these three infantrymen may indicate the presence of more of the same sort near the cavalry of Stoneman.

With reference to the enfilading, Gen. Johnston spoke of the bare possibility of our enfilading him with artillery. The report of one of my commanders, Lieut. [Lyman A.] White, Bridges' Illinois Battery, says: "At 6 p.m., Gen. Howard brought this battery, with others, into position, from which we were able to fire with raking effect upon the flank of the rebel lines occupying Cassville, while their front was to the left meeting the attack of Gen. Hooker's command."

This operation took place, as we have before seen, the evening of the 19th of May, and will account for some of the serious impressions of Gen. Polk, if not of Gen. Hood, as were subsequently evinced at the council.

There are several accounts of this most important council, held informally, it is true, but far-reaching in its conclusion. Gen. Sherman speaks of it, in fact, describes it in his Memoirs in his own brilliant and graphic way. He also relates a subsequent interview at New Orleans, with Gen. Hood.

Probably Gen. Johnston's narrative is the most nearly accurate. This council doubtless indirectly caused Johnston's relief at Atlanta, and resulted in Hood's

SERIES OF DISASTERS

and his ultimate complete discomfiture by Thomas at Nashville. It probably rendered possible the great "March to the Sea," and the more troublesome ordeals of the Carolinas, which ended in Bentonville and bore no small weight upon the operations in Virginia—those operations which closed the war. Here is Gen. Johnston's account:

"On reaching my tent, soon after dark, I found in it an invitation to meet the Lieutenant-Generals at Gen. Polk's quarters. Gen. Hood was with him, but not Gen. Hardee. The two officers, Gen. Hood taking the lead, expressed the opinion very positively that neither of their corps would be able to hold its position next day, because, they said, a part of each was enfiladed by Federal artillery. The part of Gen. Polk's corps referred to was that of which I had conversed with Brig.-Gen. Shoup. On that account they urged me to abandon the ground immediately and cross the Etowah.

"A discussion of more than an hour followed, in which they very earnestly and decidedly expressed the opinion, or conviction rather, that when the Federal artillery opened upon them next day, it would render their positions untenable in an hour or two."

Hardee's note is of interest. He wrote:

"At Cassville, May 19, about 10 o'clock in the evening, in answer to a summons from you (Gen. Johnston), I found you at Gen. Polk's Headquarters, in company with Gens. Polk and Hood. You informed me that it was determined to retire across the Etowah. In reply to my exclamation of surprise, Gen. Hood, anticipating you, answered: 'Gen. Polk, if attacked, cannot hold his position three-quarters of an hour, and

I CANNOT HOLD MINE TWO HOURS.'"

The results of this remarkable council appear in Gen. Johnston's concise statement which follows: "Although the position was the best we had occupied, I yielded at last, in the belief that the confidence of the commanders of two of the three corps of the army of their inability to resist the enemy would inevitably be communicated to their troops, and produce that inability. "Lieut.-Gen. Hardee, who arrived after this decision, remonstrated against it strongly, and was confident that his corps could hold its ground although less favorably posted. The error was adhered to however, and the position abandoned before daybreak."

Gen. Sherman's subsequent account of the Hood and Johnston controversy will bear repetition:

"In the autumn of 1865, when in command of the Military Division of the Missouri, I went from St. Louis to Little Rock, Ark., and afterward to Memphis. Taking a steamer for Cairo, I found as fellow-passengers Gens. Johnston and Frank Blair. We were, of course, on the most friendly terms, and on our way up we talked over our battles again, played cards, and questioned each other as to particular parts of our mutual conduct in the game of war.

"I told Johnston that I had seen his order of preparation in the nature of an address to his army, announcing his purpose to retreat no more, but to accept battle at Cassville. He answered that such was his purpose; that he had left Hardee's Corps in the open fields to check Thomas and gain time for his formation on the ridge just behind Cassville, and it was this corps which Gen. Thomas had seen deployed, and whose movement in retreat he had reported in such complimentary terms.

"Johnston described how he had placed Hood's Corps on the right, Polk's Corps in the center, and Hardee's on the left. He said he had ridden over the ground, given each corps commander his position, and orders to

THROW UP PARAPETS

during the night; that he was with Hardee on the extreme left when night closed in and Hardee's troops fell back to the position assigned them for the intended battle of the next day [*May 20*], and that, after giving Hardee some general instruction, he and his staff rode back to Cassville [*sic: during the early afternoon of May 19, Confederates had passed through the town, allowing Federals to enter and occupy it after brief skirmishing with Johnston's rearguard*].

"As he entered the town, or village, he met Gens. Hood and Polk. Hood inquired of him if he had had anything to eat, and he said no; that he was both hungry and tired; when Hood invited him to go and share a supper which had been prepared for him at a house close by.

"At the supper they discussed the chances of the impending battle, when Hood spoke of the ground assigned him as being enfiladed by our (Union) artillery, which Johnston disputed, when Gen. Polk chimed in with the remark that Gen. Hood was right; that the cannon-shots fired by us at nightfall had enfiladed their general line-of-battle, and that for this reason he feared they could not hold their men.

"Gen. Johnston was surprised at this, for he understood Gen. Hood to be one of those who professed to criticise his strategy, contending that, instead of retreating, he should have risked a battle.

"Gen. Johnson said he was provoked, accused them of having been in conference, with being beaten before battle, and added that he was unwilling to engage in a critical battle with an army so superior to his own in numbers with two of his three corps commanders dissatisfied with the ground and positions assigned to them, He then and there made up his mind to retreat still farther south, to put the Etowah River and the Allatoona range between us, and he at once gave orders to resume the retrograde movement. * * *

Subsequently, in the Spring of 1870, when I was at New Orleans, en route for Texas, Gen. Hood called to see me at the St. Charles Hotel, explained that he had seen my speech reprinted in the newspapers, and gave me his version of the same event, describing the halt at Cassville, the General Orders for battle on that ground and the meeting at supper with Gens. Johnston and Polk, when the

CHANCES OF THE BATTLE

to be fought the next day were freely and fully discussed. He stated that he had argued against fighting the battle purely on the defensive but had asked Gen. Johnston to permit him with his own corps and part of Polk's to quit their lines, and to march rapidly and overwhelm Schofield, who was known to be separated by an interval of nearly five miles, claiming that he could have defeated Schofield and got back to his position in time to meet Gen. Thomas' attack in front.

"He also stated that he had contended with Johnston for the 'offensive-defensive' game, instead of the 'pure defensive' as proposed by Gen. Johnston; and he said that it was at this time that Gen, Johnston had taken offense, and that it was for this reason he had ordered the retreat that night.

"As subsequent events estranged these two officers, it is very natural that they should now differ on this point; but it was sufficient for us that the rebel army did retreat that night, leaving us masters of all the country above the Etowah River." * * *

The morning of the 20th of May the works so well prepared were vacant. The Confederates had crossed the Etowah. Then did we all unbend and rest for three happy days.

In the fearful skirmishes which took place on the 19th day of May, in the rough woodland between Kingston and Cassville, Kingston served as a field-hospital.

Small tents were erected for the wounded, and for the many others who fell sick from

OVERHEATING AND FATIGUE.

Rev. E. P. Smith, afterwards Commissioner of Indian Affairs, relates an [*line missing in the creased newspaper*] of similar character. He then represented the Christian Commission in our portion of the Western armies. In his sketch of army incidents he says:

"Late one afternoon I was summoned to see an officer who was supposed to be mortally wounded. It was Capt. James H. Burk, of the 37th Ind. It did not take long to discover that he was a devout Christian. He asked me to telegraph to his wife of his condition, praying me, however, to break the news to her gently—not to say that his wound was mortal. He spoke to me freely of his past life, and of the slight hope there was that he would survive his wound. I asked:

"'Captain, how does it seem to you to be thus stricken down here in Georgia, with all your prospects and hopes cut short? Isn't it hard for you to give up life and leave your family at your age?'

"'It has come suddenly upon me," was his answer: 'but I feel prepared for it. I have lived close to my Saviour in the army, and tried to keep my accounts square every night.'

"He did not die so soon as we at first expected, but lived to get as far home as Nashville, whither his wife came to nurse him. The few months during which he lingered confirmed my impressions at Kingston. He had indeed lived close to Christ, and kept his accounts square. As he grew weak, his mind sometimes wandered; he would call for his comrades, and seemed determined to go to them; but his wife could always calm him by saying: 'My dear, Jesus is here; that is all you want.' His sweet, assured reply was always: 'You are right, wife; that is all I want—all I want.'"

I am sorry to say that when we at last passed on from Kingston to establish field hospitals in other places, we were obliged to leave poor fellows there; they were too badly injured to be taken back to Chattanooga; many of them, mortally wounded, remained at Kingston to meet their death.

It is gratifying to think these comrades had double care from the faithful hospital attendants and from the Christian Commission. The delegate of the Commission would sit by the bedside of a young man, and act as amanuensis; so that many a last message too sacred for publication found its way to a sorrowing household beyond the scenes of war, but not beyond the sacrifices the dread war produced.

In this article, General Howard proves himself a thorough researcher. He refers to reports in the Official Records, *which for the Atlanta Campaign were already published; Lieutenant Colonel Fullerton's journal, quoted by Howard, appears in volume 38, part 1, published in 1891. He had also read Johnston's bellicose battle address to his troops and had waded through the dispute between Hood, who called off his attack on the morning of May 19 when Federal cavalry were reported on his flank, and Johnston, who believed they weren't there.*

Howard carefully describes events of May 18-19: how Johnston's three corps took position south of Two Run Creek, with Hardee's Corps southwest of Cassville, Polk's and Hood's north of town (see map in Castel, Decision in the West*). He mentions the Confederates' "usual temporary entrenchments," though military maps of the time do not show them. He also refers to how Sherman's three armies were considerably spread out: Thomas and McPherson marching on Kingston, five and a half miles west of Cassville; Hooker's XX Corps was advancing via the more direct Adairsville-Cassville road. The two divisions of Schofield's XXIII Corps were marching by another, more easterly road that led south from Martseller's Mill (as mentioned by Howard; again, see Castel's map). This gave Johnston opportunity to pounce on Schofield/ Hooker before the bulk of Sherman's forces could come to their aid.*

Howard is also correct as to Johnston's strength, around 70,000, due to the arrival of Polk's Army of Mississippi plus troops detached from garrisons at Charleston, Savannah, and Mobile.

Johnston's confidence in his position and plans is reflected in the battle order distributed to his troops on the morning of the 19th. "The successes of our brothers in Virginia and beyond the Mississippi" refer to Confederates' blocking Nathaniel Banks's Red River Campaign at Alexandria in the first week of May and Lee's repulse of Grant's assaults at Spotsylvania in the second.

While Howard speculates as to whether Hood could have attacked Schofield's corps late on May 18, it was actually not until early on the 19th that Johnston determined to attack that morning, sending Hood's Corps to strike the left flank of Schofield's advancing column. Getting into position, however, Hood was told that Union cavalry was riding in from the east so as to threaten his flank. With the situation now dramatically changed, Hood called off the attacking battle and withdrew back to his start-off point. When he so informed headquarters, an incredulous (and furious) Johnston believed Hood had succumbed to panic, refusing to believe there were any enemy cavalry out there.

Not so, writes the esteemed historian Albert Castel. Howard refers to Maj. Gen. George Stoneman's cavalry attached to Schofield's army, but Castel identifies the threatening Federal force as two divisions, Stoneman's and that of Brig. Gen. Edward McCook (with Stoneman in overall command). General Howard states that the movement of Schofield's cavalry that morning was "decidedly to our advantage." Dr. Castel is more extravagant, terming Stoneman's and McCook's actions on May 19 "the most valuable service that will be performed by Sherman's cavalry during the entire campaign."

Reluctantly, Johnston ordered his army to withdraw through Cassville and take position in an entrenched line south of the town.

General Howard also accurately relates the postwar dispute between Johnston and Hood over the commanding general's order later on the 19th for the army to retreat across the Etowah. Modern day historians have criticized Johnston for giving up the river, the second of the three main water obstacles in Sherman's path (Oostanaula and Chattahoochee being the others). The argument here, between Johnston and Hood, centers on who was responsible for the retreat decision. In his Narrative of Military Operations *(1874), quoted here, Johnston blames Hood and to a lesser extent Polk. The after-dinner conference was held at Polk's headquarters, the home of a Mr. Haise, according to the Bishop-General's recent biographer (Huston Horn,* Leonidas Polk: Warrior Bishop of the Confederacy *[Lawrence: University Press of Kansas, 2019], 402-403). There Hood and Polk declared that their lines had come under enemy enfilading artillery fire and that if the Federals attacked the next day, their lines could not be held. General Hardee, as Howard points out, was late to the meeting, but upon arrival disagreed with Hood's and Polk's recommendation of retreat.*

"Hardee's note" was Hardee's letter to Johnston of April 10, 1867, which Johnston quotes in his Narrative, *323.*

*In his article, Howard seems to side quietly with Hood, as he quotes the report of Captain Lyman White, stating that Bridges's Illinois battery was able to enfilade the Rebel right (*OR *38, pt. 1, 495).*

*Johnston's reference to Hood as "one of those who professed to criticize his strategy, contending that, instead of retreating, he should have risked a battle" brings up a criticism of Hood leveled by a staff officer, Lieutenant Thomas Mackall, in a valuable diary he kept during the campaign: "June 4. One lieutenant-general talks about attack and not giving ground, publicly, and quietly urges retreat" (*OR *38, pt. 3, 991).*

*Sherman's recollection from the spring of 1870 (*Memoirs, *vol. 2, 41) that Hood favored a flank attack with Polk on the Federal left, May 20, is supported by Hood including, in* Advance and Retreat, *a long postwar letter from Walter J. Morris, Polk's chief engineer, to Hood stating the same but that Johnston instead ordered the army to retreat.*

The Confederate army withdrew to Allatoona Mountain and dug in. Satisfied with having gained the Etowah, Sherman allowed his troops several days' rest, May 20-22.

Since Howard was known as "the Christian general," it is appropriate for Howard to end his article with encomiums for the Christian Commission, the faith-based organization providing aid to Northern soldiers."

14

From New Hope Church to Pickett's Mill

John McElroy, "The Atlanta Campaign. Chapter VII"

(March 4, 1909, p. 2)

Allatoona.

Johnston was now clear out of the "Champagne Country," with his army upon the great ridges on the eastern side of the valley and running parallel to the western ridge, where he had made his first stand behind the palisades of Buzzard Roost. After crossing the Etowah River, which skirts along the base of the cluster of mountains, the railroad winds up thru these to gain the difficult pass of Allatoona, by which it descends into the creek of the same name and runs up the valley of this toward the second range of mountains, of which Kenesaw is the most notable elevation.

The farseeing Johnston had contemplated the possibility of his retreat to this place, and had already begun to strengthen the natural impregnability of the country by fortifications. These were rapidly extended and completed by the labor of 70,000 men working industriously to cover themselves. Both sides had learned the value of fortifications, and there was no limit to the energy with which they constructed these nor to the ingenuity and skill displayed in making them formidable to the last degree.

Without having fought a decisive battle or crippled his antagonist, Sherman now found himself with a constantly diminishing army 50 miles from his base at Chattanooga, and his only line of communications a single-track railroad of poor construction winding thru the mountains and subject at any hour to being broken either by the acts of his indefatigable enemies or the wrecking by storms and accidents such as were painfully frequent in the early days of railroad construction. He therefore halted to give his men rest, to put the railroad in as good shape as possible and to bring forward supplies. The question of supplies was all the time of the utmost urgency.

Nothing could be gotten from the surrounding country, of limited resources at best, and which had been thoughly skinned by Johnston's foraging parties. Everything which Sherman's men or animals ate had to be brought from the Ohio River. The difficulties of this operation had been foreseen from the first. Every preparation that could be foreseen had been made for contingencies. We have before described the system of block houses by which every culvert, bridge and tunnel between Nashville and Chattanooga were guarded by fortifications strong enough to repel a raiding party armed with only field guns. The industrious engineers of the army extended this system rapidly in the rear of the army as it advanced from Chattanooga, and in all built 22 block houses between Chattanooga and Atlanta. These were subsequently to do splendid service. The railway construction brigade of 2,000 men, under the command of Col. W. W. Wright, to whom Gen. Sherman took frequent occasions to give warm praise, was as active and efficient as its laborers were all-important.

The location, length and other features of every bridge had been ascertained beforehand, and timbers stored at Nashville for its reconstruction if destroyed. With these timbers and such material as could be obtained by the ready axmen from the neighboring forests were sufficient to immediately replace any destroyed crossing, and Col. Wright had his forces always at hand when and where they were most needed. When Johnston destroyed the bridge across the Oostanaula at Resaca he had calculated that Sherman would be retarded two weeks at least before the bridge could be rebuilt so as to bring his supplies forward. As a matter of fact, Col. Wright rebuilt the bridge in three days, and cars loaded with supplies reached Kingston as early as May 24.

Sherman's army was suffering daily diminution from the necessity of guarding every mile of country as he advanced thru it. The same process was strengthening Johnson's army, since the farther he fell back the stronger he became from the withdrawal of his outlying parties and concentrating them with the main army.

On the Allatoona Lines.

Sherman had no more idea of making an attack upon Johnston in his prepared position at Allatoona Pass than he had of attacking him squarely in front at Buzzard Roost. Sherman did not propose to fight a battle at any time where he could only attack with a small portion of his forces and be held in check by a still smaller portion of Johnston's army. He clung to his determination to maneuver Johnston out of his strongholds, and try to catch him in the open ground or in the embarrassment of crossing a river. Sherman now projected a wide, sweeping flank movement far more expansive than any he had before attempted. He would move the main part of his army directly against Johnston and gain a position so close to him that Johnston could not retreat unseen. While engaging Johnston's attention in front with the possibilities of a heavy assault columns were to march by a large circuit to the westward and strike at Marietta. Here the railroad, after crossing the mountains, begins to descend into the valley of the Chattahoochee.

This maneuver was one of the highest military skill and delicacy, inasmuch as it sent a considerable portion of the army far away from the reach of support and without any further line of supplies. The moving column would have to rely upon the supplies it carried with it. Therefore, Sherman had to accumulate about 20 days' supplies to fit forth this column and provide his army against any interruption "of the cracker line." The planning and execution of this great movement was on the highest planes of the art of war, and nothing is more lustrous than Sherman's genius. The country was but little known, even to the Southerners, and the maps secured were terribly imperfect and frequently misleading. Many important places could not be found on any map, and the locations given for others could not be relied upon. For example, no map had shown such a place as Snake Creek Gap, thru which Gen. McPherson had passed to turn Johnston's position at Dalton.

Maps of the country had to be made as the army advanced, and in this particular, as in every other, was evinced the wonderful ingenuity and fertility of resources of the American soldier. The map-making branch of the Engineers' Department was under the charge of Serg't Finnigan, 4th Ohio Cav., who displayed almost genius in the work. The State map of Georgia was used as a basis for the operations of the campaign, and this was enlarged to the scale of one inch to the mile. As the army advanced this map was filled in and corrected by assiduous cross-questioning of refugees, spies, scouts, peddlers, prisoners and inhabitants of the country. Every man connected with the headquarters was alert to learn interesting topographical features and communicate them to the map-makers. When a sheet was completed it was traced on thin paper. This was laid over a sheet coated with nitrate of silver and exposed to the rays of the sun. The result was a blackened sheet, with rivers, roads, town, etc., in white. This sheet was sent around for criticism and inspection, and sometimes several editions of the map were made in one day. Copies of the maps were furnished to corps, division and brigade headquarters and to commanders of independent expeditions, and many officers had copies printed on handkerchiefs. All maps being copies of the ones at Headquarters, the possibilities of mistakes were greatly reduced. An officer might find the roads in his front not in accordance with the maps sent him, yet he knew the objective point which he was directed to reach, and could carry out the general plan without serious mistake. Sherman's wonderful topographical insight came in good play, since he seemed to know instinctively the country in front of him and rarely made a mistake in the general direction he gave to his columns.

Beyond the Etowah.

South of the Etowah the country rapidly rises toward the mountain ranges, with the streams flowing down thru deep canyons to the Etowah. The country is far more rugged and difficult than that north of the Etowah, and the marches over the canyons were tortuous and tedious. As they were far out of sight of the commanding General, with little facility for communication, he had to rely upon the character of the commanders and their reputation for arriving at designated places at the specified time.

Sherman's orders contemplated moving troops by divisions and corps over a great chessboard 50 miles square, broken by mountains, streams and dense primeval forests. The object was to pass around the end of the range far to Johnston's left to reach the railroad upon which he depended for supplies. Sherman's orders were to begin the march on May 23. Schofield, with Stoneman's Cavalry, was holding the ground at Cassville Depot, Cartersville and Etowah Bridge. Thomas, with the Army of the Cumberland, was at Cassville, and McPherson, with the Army of the Tennessee, was near Kingston. The Army of the Cumberland was ordered to march upon Dallas on Johnston's extreme left flank.

On May 23 Gen. Sherman ordered Gen. Blair, with two divisions of the Seventeenth Corps, to move on Rome and Kingston from Huntsville, Ala. Col. Eli Long's Brigade of cavalry accompanied the infantry. The Army of the Tennessee, moving from Kingston, crossed the Etowah at the mouth of Conasere Creek, and advanced toward Dallas by the way of Van Wert. Dallas is a small village lying about 25 miles south of Kingston and 20 miles to the westward of Marietta. The road from Kingston to Dallas and Marietta followed generally the watershed of the region separating the streams flowing north into the Etowah from those flowing south into the Chattahoochee.

Gen. Thomas crossed the Army of the Cumberland about four miles south of Kingston, and moved thru Euharley Creek and Stilesboro. Gen. Schofield, with the Army of the Ohio, crossed near the Etowah Cliffs to the left of the Army of the Cumberland. McCook's Division of cavalry preceded the Army of the Cumberland, and reached Stilesboro on the afternoon of May 23, finding the enemy present with cavalry and infantry. After the nightfall the Fourth, Fourteenth and Twentieth Corps encamped south of Euharley Creek. Kilpatrick's Cavalry, under the command of Col. W. W. Lowe, was left to guard the line of the Etowah against a threatened incursion by Wheeler's Cavalry. Each division was followed by its trains carrying 20 days' rations.

The country traversed was formerly the gold mining region of Georgia, and was cut up by misleading paths and trails. During the day a courier was captured at Burnt Hickory, and on him was found an order from Gen. Johnston, dated at Allatoona, and which revealed the fact that Johnston had detected Sherman's turning movement, and was preparing for it.

It was altogether unlikely that he should not discover it, since he had lookouts on the high mountains which dominated the lower hills and rolling country, and the movements of Sherman's columns could be distinctly traced by the smoke of their campfires.

This information made Sherman cautious lest Johnston take advantage of the wide separation of his columns to draw then into ambuscade or overwhelm them. This was what Hood had been proposing to do in the advance upon Cassville, and it was the policy which he had been urging upon Johnston and upon Jefferson Davis, but which he had signally failed to carry out when given an opportunity. Sherman thinks the failure to do this was due to the fact that the Confederates were as ignorant of the roads and the country as the Yankees were. Therefore, Sherman hoped that his possession of Dallas would compel Johnston to yield Allatoona Pass, and allow our trains to come down some miles nearer the front. Dallas is on the eastern side of the Allatoona Ridge, but on Pumpkin-vine Creek, which flows northward into the Etowah. Dallas was on the point of concentration of a great many roads, and therefore admitted of Sherman marching upon it with converging columns.

The Battle of New Hope Church

On May 25 all the columns were moving steadily on Dallas, with Gen. Sherman riding, as usual, with the Army of the Cumberland, along the main road in the center of the line. The Army of the Tennessee and Davis's Division were near Van Wert, with the Army of the Ohio on the left and somewhat in the rear. Hooker had his three divisions on separate roads, all leading toward Dallas, and as he approached a bridge across Pumpkin Vine Creek he found it held by a cavalry force, which was driven back, tho not until it had set fire to the bridge. Geary's Division followed the Confederate cavalry on a road leading eastward toward Marietta, and about four miles from the bridge struck a heavy infantry force which Johnston had sent down from Allatoona. The 5th Ohio was leading the van, and deployed as skirmishers, when the enemy was encountered, and Candy's whole brigade was rushed up to assist that regiment. The brigade at first drove back the enemy, but the attack was renewed, and Gen. Geary brought up Ireland's and Buschbeck's Brigades in support. Some prisoners were taken, from whom it was ascertained that the whole of Hood's Corps was in front, with Hardee not far off in the direction of Dallas.

This made a highly critical situation, as the enemy had a far stronger force present than we had. Gen. Sherman came up, and found that we were near an important crossroad called New Hope, from a Methodist meeting house, and he ordered Gen. Hooker to secure it if possible before dark. Hooker put his central division on a hill, and directed it to open a hot fire upon the enemy while barricades were being constructed. He sent urgent orders to Williams and Butterfield to come up immediately, but they were several miles distant, and could not get up for some hours. As soon as they could be formed in line they were sent forward, with Geary's Division in reserve, to drive the enemy beyond New Hope Church and secure the meeting point of the Marietta, Dallas and Ackworth roads. Williams's and Butterfield's Divisions attacked with great impetuosity, and drove the Confederates back thru the woods and thick underbrush for one and a half miles to New Hope Church, where they ran up against a heavy line of works well manned. Tho they attacked this line with great energy, supported by Geary, they did not succeed in effecting a lodgment upon the strong log barricades, which were well supplied with artillery. Again and again Hooker's men assaulted, only to be beaten back. Gen. Geary says that the shell and canister were the heaviest of any battle in the campaign.

A Gloomy Night Settles Down.

The last part of the fighting was in the midst of a singularly heavy thunderstorm, with a cold, pelting rain, bringing on a night of intense darkness. In spite of this, the troops moved forward thru these difficulties, and established a line in close touch with the enemy, which they proceeded to barricade. Gen. Thomas sent the Fourth Corps to the assistance of Gen. Hooker, and it reached him by nightfall and formed on his left.

During the night all of the troops came up and went into position, the Army of the Tennessee moving toward Dallas, with Garrard's Cavalry on its right flank.

Gen. Schofield was so badly injured by being knocked from his horse in the darkness of the night in the forest that he was unable to exercise the command for several days, and Gen. J. D. Cox took his place.

The night was one of indescribable turmoil, confusion and fatigue. The rain poured down in torrents, the darkness was like Egypt, and no one could have any secure idea of where the line was nor where his regiment, brigade or division should form. The troops could only press forward in a general direction until they became aware by the musket shots, the sound of chopping or of the enemy's voices that they were near the Confederate line. As best they could the Union lines were formed confronting this, and the men went to work, tired as they were, to construct defenses. Brigades and divisions became inextricably mixed up, and any attempt to rectify the formation frequently resulted in confusion worse confounded. Gen. Sherman realized that Johnston had fathomed his designs, and, having the shorter line, was massing his men in front of him. There was a painful anxiety as to what the daylight would develop, and all felt certain that a bloody conflict would immediately open as soon as the light enabled a movement to be made.

Worn out at last by his anxieties and physical fatigue, Sherman threw himself down beside a log under the pouring rain and slept till daybreak. Every other officer and man had about the same lodgings.

May 26.

When daylight dawned on May 26 the Union army saw a heavy line of breastworks stretching along its entire front. The Confederates, having better knowledge of the ground, had disposed of their troops to advantage and covered them well. Sherman realized that Johnston had his whole army in front of him, and that the movement on Marietta would have to take a different character. The thing to do now was to force him back still farther, so as to compel his abandonment of Allatoona Pass and the railroad leading thru it. The morning was actively employed in rearranging the position of the troops and in getting the brigades and divisions together.

The much-feared attack upon some portion of the line did not come. Johnston was having as much trouble in concentrating his troops as Sherman was. As soon as the latter was relieved from the fear of one of the usual Confederate attacks in mass he began to threaten Johnston's left flank, and Gen. McPherson, whose force had been increased by Davis's division, advanced to Dallas, with Sherman and Thomas going over in that direction to see what success he would have.

The Army of the Ohio was advanced on the left to find and turn Johnston's right flank, with Stoneman's Cavalry extending to the left. Both Howard and Schofield pushed up so close to Johnston's main line that there was a constant interchange of musketry during most of the day. Gen. Thomas resumed command of Davis's Division, and sent it to fill the gap between the Army of the Cumberland, and McPherson reconnoitered toward Dallas. Davis advanced on the Burnt Hickory road, drove the enemy back, and connected with the Army of the Tennessee. Col. E. M. McCook, with the First Cavalry Division, was sent out far to the left, where at 4:30 in the afternoon he came across Wheeler's whole cavalry force, which he attacked, breaking thru Wheeler's lines, taking 52 prisoners and driving the enemy back toward Ackworth. McCook kept up the pursuit until he encountered infantry. He lost Lieut.-Col. Stewart, commanding the Second Brigade, and about

25 men and officers. He estimated that he killed and wounded about 80 of the enemy. In the afternoon the lines were everywhere confronting each other, within easy musket shot, with the artillery in position, and it looked very positively as if an engagement of the most sanguinary character was about to ensue.

Pickett's Mills.

Gen. Sherman now determined upon a heavy assault on Johnston's right to reach the railroad in his rear. Accompanied by Gens. Howard and Thomas, he went over to the left to superintend this, and Gen. Howard was directed to form the assaulting column. A point was selected for the attack, but before the order was given Gens. Thomas and Howard made a careful reconnaissance, and discovered that the enemy had a cross-fire upon the ground in front and that they were yet some distance from Johnston's right flank.

Howard was therefore ordered to move far to the left beyond all the troops then in line, and endeavor to reach the extremity of Johnston's flank. Gen. Howard sent Wood's Division on this errand, supported by R. W. Johnson's, which in turn was near the Army of the Ohio. At a place called Pickett's Mills Howard felt sure that he had reached Johnston's flank, and at 6 p.m., May 27, ordered Wood to assault. Wood formed his division six lines deep, with Hazen's Brigade leading. They drove back the enemy's skirmishers, and assaulted the main line with great energy. The resistance was so decided that Wood rushed up his supporting lines, and Scribner's Brigade was hurried forward on Hazen's left. Before Scribner could reach Hazen he was struck in flank from the opposite side of the creek to his left, which brought him to a halt to change direction and repel his assailants. Gen. Wood reports as to the conduct of his men during this engagement:

"At 4:30 p.m., precisely the order was given to attack, and the column, with its front well covered, moved forward. And never have troops marched to a deadly assault, under the most adverse circumstances, with more firmness and more truly soldierly bearing and with more distinguished gallantry. On, on, thru the thickest jungle, over exceedingly rough and broken ground, and exposed to the sharpest direct and crossfire of musketry and artillery on both flanks, the leading brigade, the Second, moved (followed in close supporting distance by the other brigades), right up to the enemy's main line of works. Under the unwavering steadiness of the advance the fire from the enemy's line of works began to slacken, and the troops behind those works first began perceptibly to waver and then to give way, and I have no hesitation in saying that so far as any opposition directly in front was concerned, tho that was terrible enough, the enemy's strongly fortified position would have been forced. But the fire, particularly on the left of the column, which was at first only en echarpe, became, as the column advanced, enfilading, and finally took the first line of the column partially in reverse. It was from this fire that the supporting and covering division should have protected the assaulting column, but it failed to do so. Under such a fire no troops could maintain the vantage ground which had been gained, and the leading brigade, which had driven everything in its front, was compelled to fall back a short distance to secure its flanks, which were crumbling away under the severe fire by the irregularities of the ground. (It is proper here to observe here that the brigade of the Twenty-third Corps which was ordered to take post so as to cover the right flank of the assailing column by some mistake failed to get into a position to accomplish this purpose.)

Hazen's Brigade.

"From the position taken by Hazen's Brigade when it retired a short distance from the enemy's works it kept up a deadly fire, which was evidently very galling to the foe. The brigade was engaged about 50 minutes. It had expended the 60 rounds of ammunition taken into action on the men's persons; it had suffered terribly in killed and wounded, and the men were much exhausted by the furiousness of the assault. Consequently I ordered this brigade to be relieved by the First Brigade, Col. William H. Gibson, 49th Ohio, commanding. So soon as the First Brigade had relieved the Second Brigade I ordered Col. Gibson to renew the assault. I hoped that with the shorter distance the brigade would have to move after beginning the assault to reach the enemy's works, and with the assistance of the knowledge of the ground which had been gained a second effort might be more successful than the first had been. I also trusted some cover had been provided to protect the left flank of the column. This had been partially, but by no means effectually, done.

"At the signal to advance the First Brigade dashed handsomely and gallantly forward up to the enemy's works. Men were shot down at the very base of the parapet. But again the terrible fire on the flanks, and especially the enfilading fire from the left, was fatal to success. In addition, the enemy had brought up fresh troops, and greatly strengthened the force behind his intrenchments."

Gen. Howard saw that the assault had failed, and ordered a withdrawal. This was done with such deliberation as to bring off all the wounded. The losses cost Gen. Wood 1,400 men in killed, wounded and missing. The Confederates reported a loss of 450 killed and wounded. Only two advantages had been gained at this terrible price—an important position was secured, and it was developed that Johnston's army was well concentrated in shorter lines than those occupied by Sherman. Wood and Johnson intrenched their positions, and held them for future movements.

While this was going on Johnston made a return thrust in front of Newton's Division, but was handsomely repulsed by Wagner's and Kimball's Brigades. Col. Dan McCook's Brigade seized a valuable pass in front of the Confederate center, and held it against a night attack by Polk. Therefore, the day closed with the losses and repulses on both sides somewhat equal.

McElroy's article touches on a number of points, including Sherman's logistical system (a common topic in the campaign literature) and his mapmaking operation (which isn't). It offers a sound survey of events, May 23-25, including Sherman's decision to bypass Allatoona Mountain and move his troops southwest, away from the railroad and toward Dallas.

McElroy sides with Hood as to his claim that he had lobbied Johnston for an "offensive-defensive" at Cassville. He is off the mark, though, in writing about "the much-feared [Confederate] attack" and "the usual Confederate attacks in mass." As a rule, throughout the campaign Johnston adhered strictly to defensive positions. Only at Resaca had Southern infantry charged; although, as we have seen, Johnston had ordered an attacking battle at Cassville (that never came to fruition).

Like other chroniclers writing well after the war, McElroy had access to the Official Records. *Brigadier General Thomas J. Wood's report, which McElroy quotes at length, is to be found in vol. 38, pt. 1, 377-378.*

*Our author's narrative of the battle of New Hope Church is brief but to the point: Federals charged Hood's prepared position and were easily repulsed. When he relates Geary's statement about the Rebel artillery at New Hope Church, he is supported by Hooker's campaign report (*OR *38, pt. 1, 123): "The discharges of canister and shell from the enemy were heavier than in any other battle of the campaign in which my command was engaged." A surgeon in Williams's division later wrote, "our men suffered severely, especially from his grape and canister, at short range" (Stephen Davis, "No Hope of Success,"* Civil War Times, *[April 2018], 40).*

As McElroy relates, General Schofield indeed fell from his horse on the night of May 25 and gave up his command for two days. He returned on the 28th, though only partly recovered (Jack D. Welch, Medical Histories of Union Generals *[Kent OH: Kent State University Press, 1996], 291).*

His summary of the battle of Pickett's Mill, so named for Benjamin and Martha Pickett's creekside gristmill, is also concise and correct. Sherman sought to get Howard's troops around by the left and attack the Rebel right on May 27. Late in the afternoon, they found that Cleburne's division had been extending its right; buglers sounding orders alerted the Confederates to the Federals' movement across Cleburne's front. Without the possibility of a flank attack, Sherman ordered an assault anyway. As we shall see, Brig. Gen. William B. Hazen's brigade suffered severe loss.

15

Hooker Attacks, May 25

Thomas Gilmore, "New Hope Church"

(September 1, 1887, p. 3)

Contributors to the National Tribune *used the name of "New Hope" to refer to the actual battle of New Hope Church, May 25, 1864, but also to the engagements fought at Pickett's Mill on May 27, as well as Dallas on the 28th. Johnston's defensive line ran from Pickett's Mill, on the right, a half-dozen miles westward toward Dallas.*

As Thomas Gilmore states, the fight on May 25 involved Hooker's XX Corps infantry attacking Maj. Gen. Peter Stewart's division of Hood's Corps. The Confederates had constructed slight works just before the Federal assault, though certainly not "long before he was called upon to occupy them," as Gilmore states. They were enough, however, to help Stewart's men repulse Hooker's attack, and at that rather easily. Union casualties totaled 1,664. The Southerners counted about 475 men lost in their smart, little, defensive victory (Stephen Davis, "No Hope of Success," Civil War Times, *[April 2018], 39).*

EDITOR NATIONAL TRIBUNE: There is still much controversy and misunderstanding in regard to the time and the troops engaged at the battle of New Hope Church, Ga., which some call Pickett's Mills, others Dallas, others Pumpkin Vine Creek. I think the whole trouble is that comrades get different battles fought on different dates mixed together, simply because they were fought within a few miles of each other. Some of the comrades seem to think that the battle of the 25th of May, 1864, was a small affair, and the only battle of New Hope Church was fought on the 27th of May, while others claim that the battle of New Hope Church, or Dallas, was fought on the 28th of May.

I claim that there were three distinct and separate battles fought in that vicinity—viz., the battle of New Hope Church on May 25, Pickett's Mills on May 27, and Dallas on May 28. The battle of New Hope Church proper was fought by Hooker's (Twentieth) Corps, and mainly by Williams's Division (First) of that corps. The battle was begun by Geary's (Second) Division driving in the rebel pickets at Pumpkin Vine Creek, near Owen's Mills, on the afternoon of May 25. Geary pushed the enemy across the creek, but on reaching the other side found that the rebels greatly outnumbered him. He bravely held his position until the remainder of the corps was brought to his relief.

The First Division, under Gen. Williams, was at that time well advanced on its march toward Dallas, but was halted on the road, about-faced, ordered to "load at will," and marched back, "left in front," to the support of Geary. We crossed the creek at Owen's Mills and formed on Geary's right about 4 o'clock p.m. Butterfield's (Third) Division also arrived about the same time. The First Division formed in column of brigades and advanced to the attack at double-quick, and as desperate fighting as was ever done in any war was done there that May afternoon. The enemy's position was simply impregnable. His lines were formed on a ridge in a dense wood, with strong earthworks thrown up and the whole front protected by a row of stakes driven in the ground, with the upper end sharpened and pointed outward, like a line of bayonets. His artillery was masked by shrubbery, and opened on our men with canister when our line was so close that the embrasures of their batteries were in plain sight and only a few rods off.

It seems that Gen. Johnston had the works at this place laid out and built long before he was called upon to occupy them. I think Gen. Hooker had no idea of the strength of the works, or he would not have persisted in his efforts to break their line. We charged up close to the works, and although unable to penetrate, we held our position, pouring volley after volley into the rebel works until our ammunition was exhausted and darkness closed over the field. A heavy thunderstorm came up about this time, and the rain fell in torrents. As soon as it began to get dark the firing gradually ceased.

Our losses in this battle were very heavy. The brigade to which my regiment belonged was composed of the following regiments: 3d Wis., 2d Mass., 13th N. J., 27th Ind. and 107th N. Y. There were regiments in that brigade who fought with McClellan at Malvern Hill, with Pope at Cedar Mountain, with Banks at Winchester, with Hooker at Chancellorsville, and with Meade at Gettysburg, whose records will show that they lost more men at New Hope Church, for the time engaged, than in any other battle. So it was not such a small affair after all. My own regiment (107th N. Y.), out of a little more than 300 men, lost 43 killed and 132 wounded; and I understood that the other regiments of the brigade suffered in about the same proportion.

The Fourth Corps, under Howard, was sent to the relief of Hooker, and formed its line of battle in the rear of the Twentieth Corps a little before dark. At that time the writer of this was lying on the ground, wounded, and was an eye-witness to the beautiful manner in which the troops of the Fourth Corps came into position. Although in the rear of Hooker's Corps, they were under a heavy fire from the enemy's artillery, but formed their lines with as much coolness as if on dress parade, although men were falling fast in their ranks. About the time they were ready for action it was getting dark, and the battle of New Hope Church was ended.

They were moved farther to the left that night, and I understand that they were the troops (Fourth Corps) that fought the battle of Pickett's Mills on the 27th of May, this being four or five miles from the New Hope Church battleground. I always understood that Logan's Fifteenth Corps fought the battle of Dallas on May 28, which is quite a distance from either the Pickett's Mills or New Hope Church battlefields. Now, I don't know what troops fought the battle of Pickett's Mills, but always understood that it was fought by the Fourth and part of the Fourteenth Corps, and that Logan fought the battle of Dallas; but I do know that Joe Hooker's Twentieth Corps fought the battle of New Hope Church, and that there was some "tall fighting" done there.

—THOS. GILMORE, Co. I, 107th N. Y., Harrison, Ill.

16

Pickett's Mill, May 27

Arnold Brandley, "Fighting Them Over. What Our Veterans Have to Say About Their Old Campaigns. Only a Few Left. Lively Times for Co. C, 23d Ky., at New Hope Church"

(December 17, 1896, p. 3)

EDITOR NATIONAL TRIBUNE: How few soldier readers have ever heard about Dallas, or New Hope Church, Ga. For the number of men engaged, and the short time the fight lasted, it was one of the most hotly contested battles of the war. Co. H, 23d Ky., lost more men there in 30 minutes than it did in two days' fighting at Stone's River, two days at Chickamauga, Mission Ridge, or the 100 days under fire from Chattanooga to Atlanta. The balance of the regiment's loss was nearly as great; and, for all I know, the 6th Ind., who joined on our right, may have lost equally as heavily.

Gen. Howard has given the engagement considerable notice. I am sorry to say, Sherman speaks of it as a very slight affair; while Gen. Joe Johnston (Confederate) says he never saw more bravery displayed anywhere than by the enemy during that fight; that we fought desperately, with great losses.

I am satisfied none of these gallant commanders saw the matter as I did in the ranks, on the charge, in the front line. As well as I can recollect, the 1st Ohio, 41st Ohio, 5th and 6th Ky., 6th Ind., and 23d Ky. constituted Hazen's Brigade, of Gen. Wood's Division, Howard's (Fourth) Corps, Sherman's army.

On May 26, 1864, we charged the enemy near a mill, with a loss of two men in my company. We gained possession of a ridge opposite, from which could be seen the enemy's works. Part of a battery was brought forward to this ridge, after which Gen. Howard dismounted, went to one of these cannon, and aimed the piece himself before the shot was fired.

I can see him yet in my mind, as he stood there, with one empty sleeve, to watch the effect of his aim. The shot was a good one.

While at this place we lost our First Sergeant, Wm. Jackson. On the morning of the 27th we proceeded onward in a left-oblique movement through the forest. The commands were imparted by the Headquarters bugler of Willich's or Beatty's Brigade. That organization drilled chiefly by bugle calls; consequently each regimental and company bugler repeated the order from Headquarters, making it a perfect din of sounds.

It was over brush and logs until about 4 o'clock in the evening, when, crossing a small creek, we halted. A few scattering shots came from the front. No doubt the Johnnies had moved in the same direction, as they were informed by our bugles the direction we had taken. I felt as if before many minutes our command would find the enemy in force.

While the line rested I stepped to the rear a few yards to procure water. All soldiers looked out for that necessary article before going into battle. While filling my canteen several officers rode up near me and dismounted. Among them I recognized Gens. Howard and Hazen. Being so close I did my best to hear what passed between them, as I felt interested in in what lay before us.

"General," said Howard to Hazen, "you will have to charge and turn the enemy's flank, if you sacrifice your brigade."

This was enough for me. I skipped for my company, where I imparted the news to some of my fellow-Sergeants.

The order soon followed:

"Fix bayonets! Charge bayonets! Forward—Double-quick—March!"

Away we went—through the timber, up a hill, over a fence to an open field, down to a ravine, up another hill to another fence.

Many brave comrades fell before reaching the second fence. What a shower of bullets met us! We fought each other through that fence. One Confederate Colonel was pulled over the rails and made to surrender by Corp'l Cooper, of Co. I. He started for the rear with his prize, but the Colonel was killed by his own men's bullets before he took many steps. I loaded and fired so fast my gun-barrel grew dangerously hot. A ball struck a rock, glanced, then hit me on the foot near the instep. It made me dance; then maddened me. I forgot the heated gun-barrel. I fired away, not more than 100 feet from the Johnnies. While loading, a ball hit my gun just above the lower band, smashing it flat. It saved my life. I picked up a dead comrade's gun.

Our line was considerable thinned by this time. Casting my eyes to the left I saw, to my dismay, we were on the extreme left of this line-of-battle, with our flank exposed. True, a considerable body of our troops were to our left, but so far in our rear that they were no protection.

Serg't Mahaffey, of Co. I, was our extreme left flanker. He motioned me to him. I observed he was facing to the left, not paying any attention to the front. As I reached close enough to be heard, he said: "Look down this fence and see what will happen." He loaded and laid his gun on the top rail. Soon a tall Confederate raised his head above, looked across to the rear line in his front. Then he took aim. Serg't Mahaffey's bullet closed his earthly career before the Johnny could fire.

We now both watched this part of the line, and followed out the example set by our illustrious commander, Gen. Howard, the day before. "Take good aim, and be sure you do good execution," he had said. The rebels we had been firing at were located behind a pair of bars a few yards to our left; they had stuck rocks and chunks between the bars as a protection to themselves. From some cause, they failed to notice us on their flank, as they always looked across the field to where, I am informed, the 57th Ind. held a position.

We finally crowded our enemy behind the bars; none showing their head any longer, we made up a squad and charged the bars. I saw enough there to make my blood run cold; plenty of dead men, with a very lively line behind them. We hastily fired into them and hastily retreated; not before they shot the most of our squad. They now located us. Some of them got over the fence and were making their way under the brow of the hill we occupied, so as to gain our rear.

I notified Capt. Tift of our danger, he being occupied in encouraging what few men were left. He went with me to the left, and very coolly focused a pair of fieldglasses to his eyes, with which he overlooked the crawling rebels.

"Lower your glasses, Captain; don't you see them, not 25 feet from you?" I said.

Before he got the range with the glasses they fired at us. One of the balls penetrated the Captain's knee. It made him spin around on one leg, but failed to down him. The wounded man showed an unusual amount of nerve and grit. He replaced the glasses.

"Can I help you?" I asked.

"No; go tell Lieut. Whiting to take charge of the company." That day ended the Captain's military campaigns. He crawled away from the enemy and made his escape. We never met again until 31 years after, when I had the pleasure of shaking his hand at Capt. Wm. Mundy's office, Louisville, Ky. I was so overcome with feeling that I was unable to speak to him for minutes. He was blind. Kind relatives had assisted him all the way from Sanborn, Iowa, to the State he once so nobly defended and represented in the struggle.

To return to my narrative of New Hope Church. I found the Lieutenant lying on the ground near the fence. The facts were soon made known. Our ammunition was about exhausted. We had already emptied our own and the dead comrades' cartridge-boxes. A stranger ran past us toward the right, calling out "retreat!" The command was repeated by those having authority. Most of our regimental survivors rallied around our colors in the hands of Serg't Henry. He leisurely rolled up the flag around the pole, after which we started. I found lying on his back Wm. Johnson, the Second Sergeant of my company. "Brandley, don't let the rebels get me," he implored. I had once hated this man for his overbearing disposition while in line of duty. I looked behind me; the rebs had already gotten over the fence, and were firing on our retreating troops. Before me was life, liberty, and my comrades. To stay meant possible death or worse—a rebel prison. But he wore the blue, was a defender of our cause, and never was known to flinch in battle.

"Where are you wounded?" I asked.

Said he: "Cross your fingers, put your hands under my head, and lift me up stiff-legged." I did as directed. He threw one arm around my neck. We started toward the left-rear, as he could not bear to go straight down-grade.

By this time the rebs were up with us. It is a mystery to me why they did not capture or shoot us. They certainly showed us mercy not granted others on that day. We were the last to leave the battlefield. Our movements were slow and exceedingly painful to Johnson, for he groaned at every step.

We reached the ravine in safety. "I can go no further," said Johnson. "Lay me down." I did so as gently as possible. I examined his wounds and found all the fingers of one hand shot off, except the first one and thumb, a flesh wound through the thigh, another through his side, from left to right, above the hips. How he had managed to walk so far, even with my assistance, is more than I can explain.

Unable to save him alone, I gazed around for help. Seeing a comrade fortified behind a log I called for him to come to me. It was Ed Bruehl, of my company. We took the Sergeant and lay him on a blanket. We heaved on the blanket; this doubled up our comrade so he screamed with pain. "I can never be moved that way," he said.

"Ed, remain with him while I go to the rear for more help," said I. I ran the gantlet to the first fence. The balls made the dirt fly as I ascended the opposite hill in plain view of the enemy. However, I got over in the woods, where I was sheltered by the trees.

In a very few minutes I met coming toward me a fine, robust looking comrade of powerful frame, carrying a pair of stretchers.

"You are the very man I want; come with me to a wounded comrade, who must be saved."

"Where do you belong?" he asked. Then he declined to help me, saying: "I belong to the 49th Ohio, and am now on my way to carry a wounded officer of my regiment from the field."

"My friend is also an officer." I insisted on his help. I promised that if he would go with me I would, in payment thereof, help him with the officer. Together we returned over the fence to be shot at. We reached my two comrades, and placed Johnson on the stretcher. We found where our wounded had been deposited—near the stream where I had filled my canteen. I now offered my services to the owner of the stretcher to help secure his friend. He declined my services. Nevertheless, I still thank him for his kindness through these columns, and hope he lives to remember the incident. I hardly think he secured his officer, as I am under the impression the enemy held most of that part of the battlefield.

Our troubles had not yet ended for that day. The enemy commenced shelling our wounded. Several shells exploded right among them. I got permission from my Colonel to stay with Johnson until I could send him away to the rear. The battle for us was over for the present; there were hardly enough able-bodied men left in the regiment to look after the wounded. Again procuring assistance, we removed Johnson to the right, behind a higher hill, more protected from the artillery. The balance of the wounded were also carried to this place.

Darkness soon after spread her black wings over the mournful sight of wounded and dying soldiers. One rebel officer, with his arm shattered, had come with us; he was a member of the 8th Ark. He was as well cared for as our boys.

As I sat by Johnson, between 10 and 11 o'clock a horseman approached carefully among the wounded. He came so near stepping on Johnson, however, that I yelled out: "You wagon boss, what in thunder are you doing among our wounded, tramping on them as if they were stones; you wouldn't be up so near the front if it was daylight!"

At this he shied off a little to the left, near the fire. He turned his head. It was Gen. W. B. Hazen. I dropped to the ground to keep from being recognized, but he passed in deep reflection, not saying a word in response to my impudence. A few days later I heard that on that day Gen. Hazen shed tears over the loss of his brigade.

At 3 o'clock in the morning of the 28th I succeeded in getting Johnson in an ambulance. He was taken to the field hospital, where death ended his suffering. At break of day I was with my command. Co. H mustered five men for duty, with Lieut. Whitney in charge of two companies (H and E). He turned over the command of Co. H to me, as I was the only non-commissioned officer left. —ARNOLD BRANDLEY, First Lieutenant, Co. C, 23d Ky., Elkins, W. Va.

The recent authority on the battle of Pickett's Mill, Brad Butkovich, quotes Lieutenant Brandley several times in his The Battle of Pickett's Mill: Along the Dead-Line *(Charleston: The History Press, 2013), but he makes no mention of a Confederate colonel captured in the fighting by the 23d Kentucky in the cornfield on the far left of Hazen's assault.*

After the war, more than one Northern soldier complained about all the bugle-blowing—Lieutenant Brandley's "perfect din of sounds"—from Brig. Gen. August

Willich's brigade, which they believed had alerted Maj. Gen. Patrick Cleburne's Confederate division to the impending Federal attack at Pickett's Mill (Stephen Davis, "Simply Criminal," America's Civil War, *vol. 32, no. 2 [May 2019], 31; Stephen Davis, "The Bugle Was to Blame,"* Civil War News, *vol. 45, no. 1 [January 2019], 23).*

17

Pickett's Mill: A Grieving General Hazen

Silas Crowell, "The General Wept. Pathetic Incident of the Battle of New Hope Church"

(December 31, 1896, p. 3)

Lieutenant Brandley's remark that "Gen. Hazen shed tears over the loss of his brigade" is borne out by this recollection.

EDITOR NATIONAL TRIBUNE: I indorse all Comrade Brandley, 23d Ky., says about there being so little heard about Dallas, or New Hope Church, Ga. We were with you, but perhaps we were so few in numbers that you overlooked us; less than 300. The 93d Ohio was in Hazen's Brigade from the time of the reorganization of the two corps that merged into the Fourth. Well, we remember the 23d Ky. I do not think any of the commanders saw the fight as the rank and file did.

In looking through "Sherman's Memoirs" for notes on this same fight I was very much disappointed at the slight he gives it.

In memoranda taken from a comrade's diary I find the following:

"On May 27 we were ordered to the front, but our movements were slow. We moved to the left toward Laurel Hill to press the rebel right, and marched about two and one-half miles before we found any heavy forces. This was about 3 p.m. We were ordered to charge a hill, our brigade in the lead.

"We got about two-thirds way up when we were met with a galling fire that checked us. We could not see any distance before us, on account of the underbrush. The 93d was on the right of the brigade and advanced almost to their works, and were caught in V-shaped works. We maintained the fight until our ammunition was exhausted. Finally, we were relieved by Gibson's Brigade, but they did not go up as far as our brigade did, by a long ways. The loss in the division to-day was 1,500. We worked all night on earthworks. Our regiment lost eight killed and 42 wounded."

The above was noted while the 23d Ky. were on the left. We were on the right. I can yet see in my mind's eye Gens. Howard and Hazen sitting on their horses in the woods after we had come out of the fight. A fragment of the several regiments had rallied around a set of colors, I do not remember of what regiment. A Lieutenant took charge of us. We passed to the right on a blind road, and came near the officers, when the Lieutenant halted us, stepped forward and saluted:

"General, where is our brigade?" he said; "we wish to report to our regiments."

The General looked at him a moment. The tears began to roll down his cheeks, and he said:

"Brigade, h—l. I have none. But what is left is over in the woods."

He addressed us kindly, and told us to get all the rest we could. I was an eye-witness to this, and know he did shed tears about his brigade on that day.

Now, as to the bugle. It was Willich's, and it was that bugle which caught us. The 32d Ind. was on the skirmish-line for his brigade that day, and they drilled by the bugle. From some prisoners taken that day we learned that they were sent double-quick from their left to intercept us, and they did, too. There was only a thin line, but the bugle gave our movements away, and the line was reformed so strong that we did not get there.

One of the boys of our company, Christian J. Sensenbaugh, was killed near their works, and after the rebels had left, three of us went up to find him if we could. This comrade had been slightly wounded at Chickamauga, pretty severely wounded at Mission Ridge by a piece of shell striking him on the top of the head, and he would often say that if hit the third time it would kill him.

We went to the trees that we took shelter behind during the fight, locating the tree he stood behind when shot, and found near it a grave. We did not know then, of course, that it was his body. One of the boys who had the spade dug down until he came to his head, and then we could not tell whether it was he or not. One of my companions asked if we remembered the scar on his head. We did, and his head was raised high enough, and we could see the scar of the second wound, and in that way identified him.

We left a cracker-box board as his headboard, with his name cut on it. His remains were afterward taken up and placed in the cemetery at Chattanooga.

Our brigade was made up of the 1st, 6th, 41st, 93d, and 124th Ohio, 5th, 6th, and 23d Ky., and 6th Ind.; at least, that is what I find in my memoranda. If I remember right, it was said at the time that the nine regiments would only make three full regiments.

Come again, comrade; tell us of some of the other parts we took in that campaign.—SILAS CROWELL, Co. I, 93d Ohio, Springfield, O.

Historian Albert Castel confirms Crowell's observation about Pickett's Mill in Sherman's autobiography (1875): "the Memoirs *contain not a single word. It is as if it never occurred, despite its being the second bloodiest defeat experienced by the Union forces during the Atlanta Campaign" (Castel,* Winning and Losing in the Civil War: Essays and Stories *[Columbia: University of South Carolina Press, 1996], 97).*

Crowell's recollection is published in Larry M. Strayer and Richard A. Baumgartner, eds., Echoes of Battle: The Atlanta Campaign *(Huntington WV: Blue Acorn Press, 1991), 115-116.*

18

A Yankee Trick

J. W. Clemson, "Surprised the Johnnies. Yankee Trick Played at New Hope Church, From Which the Rebs Suffered"

(September 30, 1897, p. 2)

EDITOR NATIONAL TRIBUNE: While at New Hope Church, Ga., our lines were advanced until the Second Brigade of the First Division, Fifteenth Corps, had advanced and intrenched, by actual count afterwards, to within 120 steps of the rebel works. The only guard duty we did was to make a detail of three men from each company as camp-guard at night, with instructions to watch very carefully, lest the rebels should surprise us while it was dark.

We could plainly see the Confederate works during the day, and no man dare raise his head above the works lest it became a target for watchful sharpshooters. Col. Walcutt, of the 46th Ohio, on June 4 or 5, 1864, thought to give the rebs a surprise. He arranged with the other regimental officers for their regiments to give the accustomed "Yankee yell" as the bugles sounded the charge. The Johnnies would think we were charging their works, and fall in line, exposing themselves above the works. This would give the 46th Ohio a fair chance at them.

Our boys were armed with Spencer rifles—seven shooters. They were ordered to load and every man be ready to fire at the sound of the bugle and the yelling of the remainder of the brigade.

All was ready; the bugle sounded the charge. The 46th Ohio rose behind their works, gave the Johnnies seven volleys, and fell down again, without the loss of a man.

The Johnnies did not see the point until the Ohioans had killed and wounded many of them. The rebels evacuated this part of their line that evening, and the writer of this went over inside of their works and saw many old hats with bullet-holes through them, and many other marks of death.

The rebels, when they saw the trick that the 46th had played on them, heaped all kinds of slurs on the men of the 46th Ohio. I will give a few of their remarks: we could plainly talk across the line to line.

"You green-eyed Yankees, that's another of your Yankee nutmeg tricks," shouted the Johnny.

One of the boys of the 46th called over:

"Say, Johnny, how many of you are there over there?"

A tall, lank reb yelled back:

"Well, I guess there's enough for another killin'."

"Say, Yank, what kind of guns have you-all got over there?" asked another.

"Wind 'em up on Saturday night and they run all week."

"What are you-all down here fighting we'uns? We-all ain't mad at you-all," was a call that brought a laugh.

The 46th Ohio fought all along this line. The regiment, on account of their superior arms, held the key at Dallas Hill in single line of May 28, when the Johnnies charged, three lines deep defending their own regimental front, and only by the galling crossfire saved the front of the 97th and 100th Ind. when the lines came very nearly being broken.

The 46th Ohio was in every battle fought in which Gen. Sherman commanded, beginning at Shiloh. Why don't you wake up, boys, and let us hear from you? —J. W. CLEMSON, Co. I, 46th Ohio, Crawfordsville, Ind.

Corporal Clemson's anecdote about the Federals' "trick" to get the "Johnnies"—a common term in the National Tribune*—to pop their heads over the parapets as targets is quoted in Russell W. Blount, Jr.'s* The Battles of New Hope Church *(Gretna LA: Pelican Publishing Company, 2010), 150. On the other hand, writers on the Atlanta Campaign usually place the "about enough for another killing" incident after Ezra Church in late July, beginning with Union general Jacob D. Cox's* Atlanta *(New York, 1882), 186. Larry J. Daniel quotes another Northern soldier writing about the "two more killings" incident on July 23, the day after the battle fought east of Atlanta (*Days of Glory: The Army of the Cumberland, 1861-1865 *[Baton Rouge: Louisiana State University Press, 2004], 414).*

Clemson is correct: the 46th Ohio was armed with seven-shot Spencers (Earl J. Hess, The Battle of Ezra Church and the Struggle for Atlanta *[Chapel Hill: University of North Carolina Press, 2015], 89).*

This piece is reprinted in Larry M. Strayer and Richard A. Baumgartner, eds., Echoes of Battle: The Atlanta Campaign *(Huntington WV: Blue Acorn Press, 1991), 126.*

19

"Charlie, I am going to get killed to-day"

Charles F. Kimmel, "The Fight at Dallas"

(October 30, 1884, p. 3)

As Thomas Gilmore states in his previously quoted piece on New Hope Church, there was a sharp fight near Dallas on May 28. After observing the eastward march of Howard's corps, General Johnston guessed that all of Sherman's forces were heading in that direction. To test his assumption, he ordered Maj. Gen. William B. Bate, on the Confederate left, to feel forward and ascertain the enemy's strength in his front. Johnston was wrong. Major General John A. Logan's XV corps held the Dallas sector in strength and had no trouble repulsing Bate's assault. Confederate casualties ran 600-800; Logan counted 379.

An accounting of this battle of Dallas, May 28, is not to be seen in the National Tribune*—a lesson that despite its voluminous text, the newspaper sometimes missed even important events. Instead is this piece, featuring a soldier's dramatic foreboding, and briefly mentioning fighting during the night of the 29th and 30th.*

TO THE EDITOR: Seeing a call from a comrade in THE TRIBUNE for an account of the skirmish at Dallas, Ga., May 31, 1864, I beg leave to offer the following, made up from my diary. In your issue of September 25, 1884, Mr. S. H. Henderson, of Co. B, 4th independent battalion of Ohio Cav., would like to see an account of the skirmish at Dallas, Ga., Tuesday, May 31, 1864, especially Co. G, 66th Ill. W. S. S. Here is the full account of the part taken by the company at Dallas, Ga., from my daily journal.

Tuesday, May 31, 1864.—Weather warm and pleasant. Skirmishing commenced at daylight. The Western Sharpshooters (66th Ill.) were ordered out on the skirmish-line in front of the Second Brigade, Second Division, Sixteenth Corps, by Gen. Thos. W. Sweeny, commanding. At 8 o'clock a.m. I was writing a letter home, and Corporal John Henderson was also doing the same, while the stray shots were passing over our heads and the skirmishing on our right and left quite lively. Just as I was about finishing my letter, Henderson said to me, "Gunboats (my nickname), this is my last letter home." I said, "John, take that fool notion out of your head." He then said, "No, Charlie, I am going to get killed to-day," and handed me some things he wished to have sent to his mother in Dayton. Just then Gen. Sweeny rode by us and said, "Boys, put up your traps; we will have hell here in a few minutes!" And, if I mistake not, Old Bulldog Sweeny was correct, for I had hardly put away my traps when orderlies and staff officers came riding up, and Lieut. Perry P. Ellis called out, "Fall in, Co. G, fall in!" Our regiment had been lying in reserve since the all-night's Sunday battle, May 29. Maj. A. K. Campbell and Adj't W. Wilson formed the regiment in the rear of the 52d Ill. and 66th Ind.; Col. August Mersey (9th Ill.) gave the order, "Forward, Second Brigade!" and away we went over the works under the fire of the rebel batteries on the hills in front of Dallas, Ga. As soon as we passed over our works the rebel skirmishers opened on us a brisk fire, which we returned. I was then slightly wounded in the right knee and fell back in the works held by the 52d Ill. The 66th Ill. W. S.S. charged across Dallas Run and drove the Johnnies out of their rifle pits, but the regiment having no support, we were forced back by the rebels, and here we lost Corporal John Henderson and Private Joseph Smith killed, and Privates Geo. P. Peters, Chas. F. Kimmel and James Farley of Co. G., 66th Ill., wounded. In the evening we fell back form Dallas, Ga., to New Hope Church. The sortie in front of the Second Division, Sixteenth Corps, was to draw the attention of the rebels from Gen. John A. Logan's Fifteenth Corps, who were then occupying the extreme right of Gen. Wm. T. Sherman's army, so that the Fifteenth Corps could withdraw from Dallas and form a new position near New Hope Church. The 81st Ohio and 12th and 66th Ill. were on the skirmish-line in front of Dallas, while the First and Third Brigades were holding our line of works. In this skirmish at Dallas Lieut. Van Lew, of Co. E, was killed and Lieut. Henry Sanders, of Co. F, wounded. At 10 o'clock in the night the Second Division, Sixteenth Corps, fell back on the Burnt Hickory road five miles to Lone Mountain, Ga., where we lay in line of battle all night. I was walking with a musket for a crutch.—CHAS. F. KIMMEL, Serg't, Co. G, 66th Ill.

20

"Just to see the splinters fly": A Veteran Recalls May 25-June 1

C. M. Castle, "Dallas Woods"

(June 23, 1887, p. 3)

Here again a veteran jumbles the battle of New Hope Church, fought May 25, with another (Dallas, the 28th). It is instructive to us who know the whole story of the war—or at least have access to it—that Union veterans a few decades later were trying to assemble a narrative of their war experiences. (Notice that concerning Hooker's attack of May 25, the author makes no mention of the Federals' bloody repulse.)

But Castle's point is salient: "those who were there and took a hand in the engagements of the dates mentioned" would remember them, regardless of names.

EDITOR NATIONAL TRIBUNE: Comrade De Land, Co. D., 1st Ohio, thinks there is some confusion of names in regard to the battles at and near New Hope Church, Ga. We belonged to the Third Division, Twentieth Corps. The battles referred to were fought in the tract of country known as Dallas Wilderness, or Dallas Woods, as it is more commonly called. I have always understood that Pickett's Mill was on Pumpkin Vine Creek. I remember that on the morning of May 25, 1864, our division commander, Gen. Butterfield, issued an order and gave the name of the encampment as "Burnt Hickory Grove," in which he cautioned the men of the command to guard against sunstroke by putting green leaves in their caps. Gen. Geary was in the lead with his White Star Division, and we were close behind. About 3 o'clock p.m. of that day we found the enemy. A battle at once began, and continued until darkness and rain put an end to it.

Our brigade—the First, of the Third Division—was deployed and advanced close upon the enemy, but was ordered to halt before we became actively engaged. On our left the battle was as hard as any we were ever in for the time it lasted. We occupied a ravine all that night, while the rain poured down in torrents, and the heavy forest, with the smoke of battle around, made the night one of inky blackness.

At a little before dawn we moved forward to our most advanced position of the night before and began fortifying. The boys who were there will remember how wet and foggy the morning was and how hot it was on the skirmish-line, as the enemy's works were in plain sight, only 75 yards in front of our works. Capt. Dan Sedwick, with Co. E of our regiment, had driven the rebels into their works that morning, losing a number of men wounded in doing so. Our works were the next morning pierced with embrasures, and artillery was placed in position. For several hours they threw shot and shell into the rebel lines with scarcely a moment's interruption. There was a rebel battery in front of us, which with our Spencer rifles we kept from being fired or removed.

I remember of being on the skirmish-line in the afternoon of the 26th with a Spencer rifle, with orders to keep up an annoying fire on the guns in our front. Just after I had got in a good position a team of six horses made a rush to draw off one of the guns, but horses and riders went down in less time than it takes to write this sentence; and when I could see no rebels to shoot at I would shoot at the cannon-wheels that I could see through the embrasures, just to see the splinters fly.

We were relieved from the front line on the 27th, but remained in the vicinity until June 1, when Gen. John A. Logan and the Fifteenth Corps relieved us and we moved several miles to the left. During all the time from May 25 until June 1 it was a continuous battle. We always called our part of it New Hope Church, but I have heard men of other corps call it by the different names that Comrade De Land suggests. Those who were there and took a hand in the engagements of the dates mentioned will recognize the place if we call it "Dallas Woods."—C. M. CASTLE, Co. D, 102d Ill. Yorktown, Iowa.

In his article, "New Hope Church," carried by the National Tribune *on April 21, 1887, W. P. De Land refers to the battle of May 27 not only as "Pickett's Mills," but also as New Hope Church, Dallas, and Burnt Hickory.*

21

Thick of the Fight

A. S. Fitch, "Some Tragic Scenes at the Battle of Dallas, Georgia"

(November 15, 1883, p. 3)

This article was less a narrative of the battle of Dallas, May 28, 1864, than a veteran's recollection of memories about comrades shot in battle. As such, it offers a novel element to our newspaper's coverage of the war.

Moreover, the National Tribune *noted that this article was reproduced "from a paper by Lt. A. S. Fitch, 107th N.Y.V."—evidence of a polished style, rather exceptional in the newspaper.*

Of the many incidents of that dreadful day, the first that always comes to my mind is the death of Louis Vreeland, of my company. The advance of our line had been stopped by the terrible fire of the enemy close in our front. Our men had closed up and begun a return fire. I was acting as lieutenant, and took my position in rear of the company. Vreeland had just prepared himself to begin firing, when, without a word or exclamation, he sank down to a sitting posture directly in front of where I stood. I spoke to him some word of inquiry as to whether he was hurt. I did not realize that anything serious was the matter. He did not reply. Some comrade called to me to unloose his belt and straps. I undid the buckles of his knapsack, unclasped his waist-belt, and as the straps parted he sank back upon his knapsack, his face became of a peculiar ghastly pallor, his jaws relaxed, his eyes became glassy and set, and to my horror some one spoke, "Why, he is dead!" A closer inspection disclosed a sickening wound in the breast, through which the bright red blood was gushing rapidly. He had been shot dead within arm's reach of where I stood. I shall never forget the sensations of that moment, when I fully realized the truth. A few moments later my attention was directed toward the left of the company, and I saw Comrade Hay Greve, of the finest soldiers in the company, throw up his arms and fall backward to the ground. He had been struck in the head by a rifle ball and instantly killed. In a very short time the ranks had become so thinned by the dropping out of the wounded that directions were given to the men to take advantage of such protection as the scattered timber afforded. I had seated myself on the ground and was watching the men as they loaded and fired. An Irishman named Martin McGuire, one of the oldest men in the company, and a steady, resolute man, stood immediately in front of me, busy with his gun; he suddenly dropped, turned, and with an indescribable look of terror and entreaty upon his face, crawled upon his hand and knees to me, and as I bent my ear to his lips he gasped, in words almost unintelligible: "I am hit; where can I go to get out of this?" "Poor fellow! I was helpless to aid him to escape from the death trap that held us all. I told him to try to crawl to the rear of the line and lie down until some relief could be had to remove him. He gave me a mute look of despair and crept painfully back a few feet and died—he was shot through the body and beyond human power to save. Brave old Martin, one of the many sons of Erin who gave their lives for their adopted land.

A MATTER OF NERVES.

These incidents filled me with a nervous dread. I sat down by Captain George Swain, and I shall never forget the questioning look that passed between us, as if asking whose turn next. It seemed impossible to escape. The air was noisy with the flying missiles. They flew all about us; they scattered the loose sticks and leaves at our feet and crashed through the trees over our heads. There was nothing to do but to await the blow that should prostrate us beside the rest of the fallen ones. The strain became unendurable and I picked up a gun, and possessing myself with a handful of cartridges, I began to load and fire, aiming at the flashes of the enemy's guns as the most effective point discernible in the gloom that began to gather about us. This occupation gave instant relief to my half paralyzed nerves, and I had no further return of that feeling. About this time Captain Swain was hit just above the ankle. He started with a hasty stride toward the rear, turned, came back, sat down by my side and pulled up his trousers, removed his stocking and disclosed the spot where he had been hit. He examined it carefully, took out his pocketknife, opened it and coolly picked out from the punctured leg a buckshot that had lodged beneath the skin. He placed it in his vest pocket with the remark that "that would do to keep," and binding his pocket handkerchief about the wounded limb, resumed his duty. Such coolness and pluck had an inspiring effect upon the few who witnessed the little incident. It seemed as though every man there was possessed with a determination to stay and fight as long as he remained capacitated so to do.

UNCLE DAN KEENER.

There was Daniel KEENER, "Old Uncle Dan," the boys called him, for he was old—having a grown-up son in the company with him. Uncle Dan was a little, nervous old man, very excitable at times. During the conflict he came running to me, fairly dancing with excitement, exclaiming in half-breathless tones that his boy Charlie was wounded, and that he wanted to go back with him in search of help. He pointed to his own breast, and said: "They have hit me too, but I'll come back when I have got Charlie safe." I said "go," little expecting to see the old man again that day. What was my surprise, a few minutes later, to see Uncle Dan again on the scene, shaking his head and calling to me, as he resumed his loading and firing: "I told you I'd come back; here I am." He escaped any serious hurt, and was living near Big Flats a few years ago. His son Charlie died a few days after the battle from the effects of the wound there received. Where can one find finer specimens of devotion to duty than in this action of brave old Dan Keener?

We had in the company a bight little Irishman, Thomas Maher by name. He was one of the youngest of us—not out of his teens, and full of genuine Irish vivacity and humor. During the action my attention was attracted by a series of emphatic exclamations to the rear of where I stood. The "brogue" at once told me whence they proceeded, and nearer inspection disclosed "Tommy," standing behind a tree, the rammer of his gun stuck half way down the barrel, and he endeavoring to force it and the cartridge home by punching it against the tree, accompanying each stroke with his inimitable Irish oaths, cursing the "dirty gun," the "rebels," and "the luck" generally. His gun had become so fouled by the rapid firing, it was his only method of ramming home the cartridge. It was ludicrous in the extreme.

A TREACHEROUS COVER.

Another instance of like nature occurs to me. Sergeant Charles Solotski had found shelter behind a huge tree. He called to me to come and partake of the same safe cover. I shook my head "no." I was well enough off. He reiterated the advantages of his retreat, when crash came a shell into the tree above his head, bringing down a perfect avalanche of limbs and splinters upon his head. The tree was a dead one, a fact he had failed to notice, and he speedily picked himself out from the mass of debris that covered him and sought more reliable shelter. As we were falling back at the close of the battle, I began to rally him about this "safe retreat" behind the rotten tree, when, as I was speaking, a grape shot came skipping along the ground, bounded up, and struck my wrist a stinging blow, glanced off, and caromed against my leg and went on. I became very suddenly quiet. I laughed no more. The sergeant was very hilarious over my discomfiture. I had scarcely gained my equanimity when, as we emerged from the timber into the open road that ran toward the rear, I met Major Lathrop Baldwin coming toward me. He seized hold of me in his impulsive way and began shaking me, exclaiming, "Oh! Arthur, thank God you are safe." Just then a missile, probably a grape-shot, came skimming down the road, struck the inside of my left foot and went ricochetting on. I suppose I made the most extraordinary leap of my life. The major's congratulations ceased, and as I went limping on to the rear, I realized the force of the old proverb, "Don't halloo until you get out of the woods."

A MIRACULOUS ESCAPE.

One of the most miraculous escapes of that day was that of Sergeant Lauren T. Reeder, of my company. While in the act of loading his gun it was struck near the hammer by a grape or canister shot, and the entire stock was torn from the barrel, leaving it literally a piece "without lock, stock or barrel." He threw down the disabled arm, picked up another that had been dropped by a disabled comrade, and, as he was ramming home a cartridge, a bullet struck the rammer, between the hand which held it and the muzzle of the piece, and bent it half-way double. Disheartened, he threw down the gun and lay down flat with his face to the ground, growling like an enraged bear. A moment later a shot of some kind passed obliquely downward through the rim of his slouched hat, filling his face, mouth and eyes with the loose dirt. A madder man I never saw. He leaped up, seized another gun and began loading and firing with infuriated energy. He escaped farther accident, but that night when we were taking inventory of our damages, Reeder found that in addition to his rent hat brim that no less than seven balls had struck different parts of his person and equipments. One shoulder-strap of his knapsack was cut clean through, the buckle which fastened his haversack was shot off, his canteen was perforated by a ball, and another ball had passed across his left leg near the ankle, cutting clean through his trousers leg and drawers, without breaking the skin; and an iron fry-pan that was strapped on the outside of his knapsack was riddled and rendered unserviceable. He escaped unhurt, however, and did gallant service to the end of the war.

Another comrade went to a brook that ran near by our bivouac to get a drink of water. As he dipped his cup into the stream he found to his dismay that two large holes had been made by the flying shot and the utensil was no longer serviceable.

These incidents show how deadly severe was the fire we had been exposed to. Scores of like incidents might be related. I will give but one more: A comrade of company, next to my company, found after the battle that a grape-shot had struck the brass U. S. plate on his cartridge-box, penetrated to the interior of the box and was lodged within the little tin canister that holds the cartridges. A fact that he was unconscious of until after the fighting was over.

It is improbable that all of the incidents Arthur Fitch relates in this article occurred in the comparatively small battle of Dallas. Given the confusion among National Tribune *readers as to the names of the three battles fought May 25-28 (New Hope Church, Pickett's Mill, and Dallas itself, as we have seen), it is likely that Fitch is referring to New Hope Church, May 25, at the end of which, as he writes, "we were falling back." Confirming evidence is that Fitch's regiment, the 107th New York, was part of Hooker's XX Corps, which did the attacking at New Hope.*

What is nonetheless striking is that two decades after the war, this veteran could relate in singular detail a dozen "close calls."

22

That Fateful Cannon Shot, June 14

P. M. Mitchell, "Gen. Polk"

(September 8, 1887, p. 3)

D. H. Chandler, "Death of Bishop Polk"

(July 9, 1885, p. 3)

Throughout the pages of the National Tribune *one may count more than 40 articles or letters related to the death of Confederate Lt. Gen. Leonidas Polk, Episcopal bishop of Louisiana and commander of the Army of Mississippi, which eventually became the third infantry corps in the Army of Tennessee. Polk was killed by a Northern artillery shell on Pine Mountain, Georgia (north of Kennesaw) on June 14, 1864. While observing Federal positions from the top of the mountain with Generals Johnston and Hardee, Polk was struck by a shell that passed across his chest, breaking both arms and mangling his torso, before exploding on a nearby tree.*

A number of Tribune *correspondents claimed to be able to name the battery that fired the deadly round. The contestants include:*

- *Battery I, 2d Illinois (National Tribune, February 5, 1885)*
- *15th Ohio Battery (April 23, 1885)*
- *5th Indiana Battery (July 9, 1885)*
- *Knap's Pennsylvania Battery/Battery E, Pennsylvania Light Artillery (September 8, 1887)*
- *Bundy's Battery/13th New York Independent Battery (August 30, 1888)*
- *Landgraeber's Battery (February 10, 1898)*
- *1st Missouri Light Artillery (August 1, 1901)*
- *Battery M, 1st Illinois Light Artillery (June 4, 1903)*
- *Battery I, 1st Michigan Light Artillery (October 15, 1903)*

One Ohio veteran claimed to have heard Brig. Gen. John Geary, commanding the Second Division, XX Corps, call for 1st Lt. Joseph M. Knap's Battery to fire at the Rebels on Pine Mountain, and that Geary even sighted one of the guns; "I heard him say, 'That struck right among them'" (P. M. Mitchell, Co. D, 6th Ohio, Collinwood O., "Gen.

Polk. Why a 66th Ohio Comrade Thinks Knapp's Battery Killed Him," [September 8, 1887], p. 3).

On the other hand, the 5th Indiana Battery, Capt. Peter Simonson, enjoyed the strongest support for its contention that its guns had fired the salvo that killed Polk, as one sees in various letters sent to the National Tribune. *Historians today have sided with the 5th Indiana, which Sherman himself credited with the fateful round (Stephen Davis, "The Death of Bishop Polk,"* Blue & Gray, *[June 1989], 13).*

TO THE EDITOR: Maj. [*sic: Lt.*]-Gen. Bishop Leonidas Polk was killed June 14, 1864, by a shell from a steel gun in the middle section of the 5th Ind. battery, Capt. Peter Simonson. Corp. B. F. McCollum sighted the piece and Charles M. Miller pulled the lanyard. The battery was in line directly opposite Pine Mountain, on the point of which was a rebel redoubt mounting two guns. We were shelling the rebel lines. Gens. Sherman and Stanley, with their staff officers and escort, rode near, and dismounting, came up to the battery to reconnoiter. While doing so Gen. Sherman called the Captain's attention to a group of rebels and said: "Try 'em." Three shells were thrown and one of the men was seen to fall, the shell exploding in their midst. Two hours after an orderly brought Capt. Simonson a message from Gen. Sherman saying that Polk was killed by that shot. Simonson was himself instantly killed two days after while gallantly fighting his battery on almost the same ground.—D. H. CHANDLER, 5th Ind. battery, Xenia, O.

As for the "three shells," years later a veteran wrote the National Tribune, *stating that his infantry company "was directly in the rear of the gun that fired the shots," adding, "there were but three shots fired in all. . . . They were all fired by one gun," a Rodman rifle; "there was no volley fired" (Lewis C. Killian, First Sergeant, Co. A, 25th Mich., First Brigade, Second Division, Twenty-third Corps, Tacoma, Wash., "Death of Gen. Polk. Shot First by an Indiana Battery of Rodmans" [October 2, 1902], 3).*

The Fifth Indiana, like most Northern artillery batteries, possessed six guns (as opposed to Confederate batteries' four). In June 1864 they were 2 three-inch Rodman rifled steel guns and 4 Napoleon 12-pounder smoothbores (S. J. Arnold, Co. B, 40th Ohio, "How Gen. Polk Was Killed" [April 28, 1898], 7).

23

Extract from a Diary

G. H. Blakeslee, "Pine Mountain and the Death of Gen. Polk"

(May 21, 1903, p. 3)

EDITOR NATIONAL TRIBUNE: There being some controversy still existing as to what battery fired the shot at Pine Mountain, Ga., that caused the death of Gen. Leonidas Polk, of the Confederate army, and believing that credit should be accorded to the proper parties, I take pleasure in adding my mite regarding the matter. I herewith append notes from my diary of June 14, 1864:

"We are facing Pine Mountain, our lines being, I think, about 800 yards distant from the crest of the mountain, along which runs the Confederate line of works. Have been exchanging compliments with the rebel skirmishers all morning. The batteries are now and then firing a shot to let the Johnnies know we are here. The nearest battery is 'Simonson's 5th Ind.,' just to the left of our regiment, which has just come up and taken position. Along the crest of Pine Mountain, on the rebel line rides a squad of cavalry, apparently Confederate officers and their staffs. Some of them, dismounting, advance close up to their works and are intently watching our movements. Gen. Sherman, who has just ridden by, seeing them, ordered the battery men to 'touch them up; teach those fellows to keep cover,' meaning the group of Confederates. Three shots were fired, and one of the men was seen to fall. Just before night, Capt. Reed tells me an orderly brought Capt. Simonson a message, saying that Maj.-Gen. Leonidas Polk was killed by those shots, and that Simonson remarked upon hearing what the shots from his battery had done: 'I am satisfied; I have avenged my brother.' The battery boys tell me that it was Corp'l Frank McCollum who sighted the gun and Charley Miller who pulled the lanyard."

Thinking that notes made at the time are more likely to be, in the main, correct, than the memories of the old comrades after a lapse of near 40 years, I am writing this. I would like to hear from some member of the 5th Ind. Battery, to know if I have the names of the boys who took part in that day's work right. Are there any of them still living? It may be new to some to learn that Capt. Simonson himself was killed a few days later.—G. H. BLAKESLEE, Eddyville, Nebr.

24

Kolb's Farm, June 22

Frank Elliot, "A June Evening Before Atlanta. Cothran's Battery and Knipe's Brigade Repulses Stevenson's Division"

(October 26, 1905, p. 3)

The author of this piece is Sgt. Frank Elliot of Battery M, 1st New York Light Artillery—six 12-pounder Napoleon smoothbores, Capt. John D. Woodbury, commanding—which was attached to Brig. Gen. Alpheus S. Williams's First Division in Maj. Gen. Joseph Hooker's XX Corps. Here he describes his part in the battle of Kolb's Farm, fought near Kennesaw Mountain on June 22. In the days preceding, Sherman had been maneuvering around Johnston's lines, hoping Schofield's XXIII Corps could outflank his left. To counter this movement on June 21, Johnston ordered Hood to march from his position on the right of the Confederate line through Marietta and to extend the Confederate left. With Schofield and Hooker's XX Corps coming up, on the afternoon of the 22d, Hood either saw an opportunity to launch a flank attack of his own, or sought to block the enemy's further advance with a strong assault at Kolb's Farm, some five miles south of Kennesaw. He accordingly ordered Carter L. Stevenson's and Thomas C. Hindman's divisions to attack the Federals who, as Elliot relates, had taken position there and were waiting for them.

Editor National Tribune: In January, 1862, Cothran's Battery, of which I was a member, was a part of the First Division of the Second Corps, and later the First Division of the Twelfth Corps, then the Twentieth Corps. The same men marched together and fought together to the close of the war.

About June 20, 1864, the Twentieth Corps was in motion going south, around the west end of Kenesaw, which was yet in possession of Johnston.

We were halted to let some regiments pass us. A sergeant with a small bag on his shoulder stopped and said to me:

"I have carried this bag to-day about as far as I care to. It is a bag of musket balls. Will you put it into one of your guns for my benefit?"

I went to the rear chest of my caisson, raised the lid, and he dropped the bag in. We moved on a few miles and halted on a long ridge, which we at once began to fortify, facing the works to the east toward Marietta. This ridge ran parallel with the Chattanooga & Atlanta Railroad, and about two miles from it.

By midnight we had everything in good shape for defense. We moved south two miles on June 21. The Fourth Corps occupied the works as we moved out. After our removal we seemed to be on the same ridge. By midnight we had as good a line of works as those we had vacated. The right of First Division was in heavy timber, awhile a beautiful valley was east of us reaching north of Kenesaw.

This part of the valley was Culp's [*Kolb's*] farm. I saw no house; only well-fenced fields and an old cotton-gin with a large press to the right of it. This stood well to the other side of the open ground.

On the morning of June 22 Gen. Knipe [*Brig. Gen, Joseph F. Knipe, brigade commander in Williams' division, XX Corps*] sent a line of skirmishers (the 125th New York) into the timber half a mile away on the other side of the farm. The battery section I belonged to followed after. We came to a ridge. When about half-way Gen. Knipe said we had better take position there, which we did, and he went over into the timber with his men to ascertain if any of the enemy were lurking in that vicinity.

He certainly found some, for the firing soon became brisk. He came back and sent 200 men to reinforce his skirmishers. He told us to use one of our guns to put a shot through a designated tree-top, and to continue, at intervals of about five minutes, firing about three feet lower each time until he gave us a signal, when we were to use both guns. He disappeared for a short time in the woods, and after our third shot he reappeared and waved a white handkerchief.

We delivered about 10 rounds from each gun. Our men did some lively shooting and some lusty cheering and advanced into the woods. A rebel battery in our front opened up and gave us a few shots. Knipe soon came running back to us and said:

"We have driven them back. They are trying to build breastworks. They left one poor devil over there with his leg shot off. I am going to fortify this ridge for an outpost."

His brigade came, and after lining up behind the caissons, stacked arms and went to the front to get all the rails in the vicinity. The four remaining guns of our battery came down and stopped beyond the stacked rifles. Rails at a "right-shoulder shift" were coming by thousands from the front, left and right, and were being laid in line. The skirmishing became animated for a time. Then followed a lull.

Since the campaign opened Hood's corps had been at the right of the rebel lines, but it was reported that Hood was ambitious to try a tilt with "Hooker's soft-bread Potomac boys." Afterward it was said he had requested and secured from Johnston permission to cross his corps over and try a round with Hooker.

About the time we began to fortify that little ridge Hood's three divisions were massing back of the timber. The ridge we occupied sloped down gently for about 12 rods, then dropped rather abruptly for another 10 yards, then a space of level ground, and beyond an upslope to the woods. The cotton gin stood at the foot of the upgrade.

We had begun using our picks and shovels, when I noticed that for about two miles toward Kenesaw our main line of works was covered with Yankees, who seemed to be looking at us. They could see the enemy getting in readiness to pounce upon us, as we could not. The skirmish lasted only for a short time. Then came the "zip, zip, zip" of missiles from the muskets of the men in gray, and a new act was on. Some of our men dropped their rails, others put them in place, and within five minutes the men of the brigade had recovered their arms and lined up with us behind the rails.

Our skirmishers now came swarming out of the woods at thrice-quick time, not even looking back. They had no occasion to, for not more than 15 rods behind them came a long line of battle, four ranks deep, at double-quick. The other four guns took position on our right and left and we poured into the advancing rebel ranks a rapid and destructive fire; but a second, then a third line came at 30 paces interval, and all merged at the foot of the hill and opened fire on us.

For 30 minutes the scrap was animating and everybody kept busy. I did not see a Yankee who was not doing his very best. The rebel line was much longer than ours; they overlapped our left, but the batteries in the main line opened on them and they were forced back to our left front, and soon a similar movement was tried on our right, with the same result.

Their whole force then moved forward under cover of the hill and the firing slackened. We distinctly heard the order, "Fix bayonets," and we were expecting them to try a rush upon us. From the beginning of our service we had never been budged from any place we tried to hold, and we had no thoughts of being driven then. The 46th Pa. occupied the space between the sections. The old cotton-gin was about 40 rods to the front and somewhat to the right, a two-story building about 25 to 40 feet in size. The left half of the first story was open and occupied by a large horse-power engine. We had a fair view of the west end of the building; a stovepipe hole was visible a few feet below the peak.

I was at the right of my gun when a ball crashed through the top of the head of the man standing at arm's length from me. He was a young fellow about 17. He fell on his back, and every muscle seemed strained to its utmost tension. His Captain, standing near, assisted by another comrade, raised him to his feet, when he opened his eyes, seized the Captain's coat collar with both hands and exclaimed:

"Captain, am I killed?"

The Captain laughed and replied:

"You certainly don't act much like a dead man."

But he was dead, and did not hear the Captain's reply.

I saw a gun stuck out of the stovepipe hole mentioned, and another rifle ball shattered the stock of a soldier's musket near me. I stepped to the side of my gunner, and requested him to blow a shell through that stovepipe hole. He sighted the piece and fired, but the shot went too high by several feet. Out came the rifle again, and down went Charles Hatch, my No. 5, who was coming up with a round in his leather bag. The shot penetrated his right temple and passed out at the base of the brain. He fell about 15 feet back of the trail. I stepped up to him and tried to arouse him, calling him by name. His eyes were wide open. but they were sightless. I then noticed the wound. Evidently he never knew what hit him. I then said to the gunner:

"You shot too high. You must shoot lower and hit that fellow or he will kill the whole of us."

Two comrades with a stretcher were about to carry Hatch's body away. I told them he was as safe there as anywhere, but to leave the stretcher as we might have use for it. John Dryer, my No. 1, then said to me:

"We are out of water and this sponge is dry and sticky, and I am about out of wind. I wish someone would load a few times for me."

I reached for the sponge staff, when a ball struck him in the right breast, passing out at a point between the shoulder blade and the spine.

"Frank, I am shot," said he, as I caught him under the arms.

"I know it," I replied.

The stretcher was quickly brought, and as I laid him back on it—the blood gushing out between his fingers as he held his hand over the wound, he said:

"Frank, I don't care a ---- for the wound if we only lick them."

I swabbed the gun and sent the charge home. As I stepped back a musket ball passed close enough to my left ear to be suggestive. My gunner had lost his head and missed again, and I said to him:

"You get around here and load this gun; I can hit him," and we exchanged places.

In my two years' previous service as gunner I had fired or aimed a 10-pounder Parrott for more than 1,500 rounds, and with the old gun could have hit a man's face every time at that short range. This gun was a brass 12-pounder Napoleon, and I had not studied the ranges; consequently my first shot was three feet too high and passed through the roof. My second shot was as much too low. It hit the main part of the horse power, knocking it down and the big drive wheel with it. My next aim was correct, and as I gave the finishing turn to the [elevating] screw the fellow shot again and knocked the muzzle sight off the piece. I gave the order to fire. The shot seemed to burst against the building, three feet below the pipe hole. For an instant the atmosphere in that vicinity was filled with smoke, splinters, clapboards and building materials. There was a hole in the end of the old gin that a mule and cart could have gone through. Some 20 long-legged rebels who were inside concluded that was a good place to make tracks from, and they started for the woods with much cheering from our side, emphasized by a few shots from the infantry boys.

Sergeant Hood, of the right gun, placed his hand on my shoulder and said:

"Can you see those fellows in my front? They have fixed bayonets and are going to charge on us."

"Yes," I replied, "I can see them, but the gun sits too low to be brought to bear on them," and he went to his gun.

We loaded with two charges of canister, 12 pounds each. I then thought of the bag of musket balls—over 20 pounds—and they were added to the charge in the gun, which we ran by hand a rod or so to the front and right. A slight depression in the hill led down to Hood's front lines. We forced the gun up on a small pile of rails and thence had a fine view of about 200 of the enemy. I depressed the muzzle, aiming by guess, as the muzzle sight was off, and fired. The gun backed off that rail pile, and the way the grass and gravel and jumping bullets went down that hill was a caution.

The shot mowed a swath 20 feet wide through that line and over 400, with guns in hand, believing there was more to follow, walked up into our lines and were received with great rejoicing as our prisoners.

At this time the enemy appeared to abandon the project of capturing the hill, and large numbers of men in squads from 10 to 100 would break cover and make for the timber from whence they had come. The rebel line, however, remained under cover of the hill until night let down her sable curtain, when they withdrew, taking their dead and wounded with them.

Our losses for the day were reported as killed and wounded, 175. We will let the other fellow tell his side of the story. Here it is from Rebellion Records, page 841:

Headquarters Carter L. Stevenson's
Division, August 19, 1864.

Major: I have the honor to submit the following report of the part taken by my division in the engagement of the 22d of June last, on the Powder Springs road. My division had for one or two days previous to the 22d been lying in reserve on the extreme left of the infantry of the army, about three miles from Marietta on the Powder Springs road. About 12 m. I moved the command further from Marietta, and halted it at Mount Zion Church. The enemy, as I moved forward, were driving in the cavalry. About 2.30 p.m. I was directed to take position on the left of Gen. Hindman's Division, about half a mile in advance of the church. I at once advanced my skirmishers, and, driving those of the enemy, established my line under fire of his artillery. Brown's and Cummings's Brigades formed the first line Reynolds's and Pettus's the second. The men hastily constructed breastworks of logs and rails. Soon afterward I received order to advance from my position and drive the enemy on the road toward Manning's Mill. The division of Gen. Hindman was also directed to advance on my right. I placed Gen. Cummings in charge of the first line, Brown's and Cummings's Brigades, commanded by Cols. Ed. C. Cook, 33d Tenn., and E. P. Watkins, 56th Ga., respectively, and Gen. Pettus in charge of the second line, Reynolds's and Pettus's Brigades, commanded by Col. R. C. Trigg, 54th Va., and C. M. Shelly, 30th Ala., respectively. A good deal of time was occupied in getting and giving instructions and making the necessary preparations. About 5 p.m. we advanced and soon struck the enemy, driving him quickly before us from his advanced works, which consisted of one line of logs and rail works complete, and one partially constructed. The fire under which this was done was exceedingly heavy, and the artillery of the enemy, which was massed in large force and admirably posted, was served with a rapidity and fatal precision which could not be surpassed. The nature of the ground over which we passed was most unfavorable to such a movement. The two right brigades moved for much of the way over open fields; the two left through dense undergrowth. The line thus became more irregular and broken every moment; and when the two right brigades had driven the enemy into his main works the line was so much broken and mixed up that, although the men were in good spirits and perfectly willing to make the attempt, it was not deemed practicable to carry the works by assault. The commands were halted and the best possible line, under the circumstances, formed. Brown's, Triggs's and Reynolds's Brigades lay in a swampy ravine within pistol-shot of the enemy's works. The other two brigades held the road on their right. The dead and wounded were all removed to the rear, and after holding our position for several hours, in compliance with the orders of General Hood, the division returned to its old position. With perhaps some few exceptions the conduct of the troops was highly creditable. My loss was heavy—870 killed and wounded. Among the killed were Col. Ed. C. Cook, 32d Tenn., and C. H. Walker, 3d Tenn. Losses in the division, May 7 to 12, 138; Resaca, 575; June 22, 870; July 20, 689; total, 2,272.—C. L. Stephenson, Major-General.—Frank Elliot, Eagle Harbor, N.Y.

Elliot is correct in stating that "Hood's corps had been at the right of the rebel lines" throughout the campaign; Johnston had repeatedly placed Hood's troops on his right flank at Dalton, Resaca, Cassville, and here at Kennesaw. Not corroborated, however, is the author's statement that Hood knew Hooker's XX Corps infantry, including a lot of New Yorkers formerly of the Army of the Potomac, was in front of him, and he wanted to get at "Hooker's soft-bread Potomac boys."

At the same time Elliot's article is notable for detailing the Rebels' deadly sharpshooting in the front of his artillery section and for its mention of Confederates surrendering rather than taking more Union artillery fire. According to a member of the 19th Ohio Battery, Federal officers yelled, "Don't shoot those men coming over" (Eldon B. Richardson, Kolb's Farm: Rehearsal for Atlanta's Doom *[privately printed, 1979], 14). Finally, to provide context for his recollection, Elliot transcribes Confederate Gen. Carter Stevenson's report on Kolb's Farm (*OR *38, pt. 3, 814-815). More importantly, at one point Elliot even corrects General Stevenson. In his report, he had written that "the other two brigades (Cumming's and Pettus's) held the road on their left," but Elliot changed it to "their right." The artillery sergeant was correct, as will be shown by Earl J. Hess's map in his* Kennesaw Mountain *(Chapel Hill, 2013), 30.*

Finally, the Tribune *thought so much of this article that it authorized an illustration to complement Elliot's text. Titled "I Changed Places with the Gunner and Aimed at the Stovepipe Hole," it shows a soldier, presumably Sergeant Elliot, sighting the Napoleon's barrel toward the cotton gin structure out in the field, with a dead comrade lying to his left, near a water bucket and sponge staff.*

This article (minus Stevenson's report) is included in Larry M. Strayer and Richard A. Baumgartner, eds., Echoes of Battle: The Atlanta Campaign *(Huntington, WV, 1991), 154-158.*

25
Kennesaw Mountain, June 27

"A Memory of the War. The Amputation of Gen. Rice's Limb—How the Gallant Soldier Endured the Operation"

(June 1879, p. 8)

Mr. C. D. Reese, an old resident of Columbus, Ohio, was present when the leg of the gallant General Rice was amputated, upon the dark and bloody field of Kenesaw Mountain, and thus relates the occurrences of the time: "There had been" said he, "a fortnight's fierce onslaughts upon the heights of Kenesaw Mountain. It was in June of 1864, and Sherman was pushing on his triumphal march to the sea. But before Atlanta was reached the rebels had concentrated their forces near Dallas, and about Lost Mountain and the heights of Kenesaw, endeavoring to their utmost to shut off the communication of Sherman's troops with their base of supplies. To thwart this, it was determined that the enemy's position must be taken. All during the day from June 18th to the 27th there were repetitions of the fierce sallies and the terrible mowing down of our troops by the enfilading fire from Big Kenesaw, which was lined with rifle-pits, while from Little Kenesaw the musketry added to the frightful slaughter.

"During one of these repeated charges and repulses, Gen. A. V. Rice, whose name now honors the second place upon the Democratic Gubernatorial ticket, was shot, the ball striking the leg, below the knee.

"It would not have been so serious a wound had the limb been sound, but at Vicksburg, shortly before, another ball from an enemy's musket had sped through the air and lodged in that fated limb. The wounds were very near each other. The Vicksburg wound had been received when the general, with that intrepidity almost akin to rashness, had refused to enter a rifle-pit, but sat crouching upon the ground. The ball struck the knee in front, penetrating both portions of the limb, bowed as it was, and lodged in the groin.

"Thus it was that Dr. Messenger, of Cleveland, when the brave general was brought at midnight from the battle-field of Kenesaw to his field hospital, decided that naught but amputation would suffice to save life. Dr. J. B. Potter, of Canal Winchester, Surgeon-in-Chief of the Second Division, Fifteenth Corps, was called in consultation, and agreed that the mutilated member must be severed. None but a brother-in-law of the general objected.

"There, in that hospital tent, which the blackness of midnight surrounded, amid the moans of the wounded and the shrieks of the dying, upon the rude, improvised couch the heroic Rice lay, not a murmur of pain escaping his lips. Ever since the wound received at Vicksburg he had limped about, resting upon a sword or cane, and now the pain must have been intensified beyond conception.

"When the decision of the surgeons was announced, without the moving of a muscle, or the slightest remonstrance, the general signified his acquiescence and his immediate readiness for the terrible ordeal.

"'Who will do it?' was asked, and Dr. Messenger agreed to perform the operation.

"I held tallow dips, the only available lights, while the unnerving work progressed. Louis Parker, quartermaster of the general's regiment, the 57th Ohio, also stood near and held lights.

"The incision was quickly made, and then the severance cut with the steadiness and rapidity of the trained surgeon. The ligatures were fastened, and everything bid fair for a perfectly successful operation. But Hospital Steward Luhrens, of the 116th Illinois, had first administered the anaesthetic, and kept the sponge and funnel close to the mouth until the critical moment of the effective use of the knife. Then, absorbed in watching the operation, he relaxed his care, the result being that just as the ligatures were bound the unconscious general revived, and suddenly clapped his hand down upon the limb, breaking the ligatures. Fears of loss of blood and death from exhaustion inspired a dreadful anxiety, but the robust constitution overcame all draughts upon its vital forces.

"Thus it was that Gen. Rice was made a 'stumper.'

"This sad incident of those days spent beneath the frowning peaks of Kenesaw may serve to recall to the many heroes who scaled the heights and saw their comrades swept away before the enfilade of the enemy, all the scenes of heroism and suffering enacted.

"The general has a cork leg now that does its utmost to supply the functions of the flesh-and-blood one."

Americus Vespucius Rice was colonel of the 57th Ohio in June 1864. Earl J. Hess uses Reese's National Tribune *article as a basis for his recounting of the colonel's wound (Earl J. Hess,* Kennesaw Mountain: Sherman, Johnston, and the Atlanta Campaign *[Chapel Hill: University of North Carolina Press, 2013], 158, 290, n.56.). As for the medical details, Jack D. Welsh, M.D., writes, "At Kennesaw Mountain on June 27, 1864, Rice received three gunshot wounds almost simultaneously. The right femur was fractured, and the knee joint penetrated. The skin of the forehead was lacerated but there was no fracture of the skull. The remaining bullet carried away pieces of bone from near the left ankle. Because of the fracture, he underwent a primary circular amputation in the lower third of the femur 12 hours after receiving his injury (Welsh,* Medical Histories of Union Generals *[Kent: Kent State University Press, 1996], 276). Rice was appointed brigadier general in May 1865.*

This was the first article relating to the Atlanta Campaign published in the National Tribune, *which became a weekly newspaper on August 20, 1881.*

26

McCook's Brigade Charges Cheatham Hill

H. McKinsay, "The Charge at Kennesaw"

(December 25, 1884, p. 5)

After giving up Pine Mountain, Johnston had his army take up a new line that stretched from Lost Mountain on the left to Brush Mountain, eight miles to the east. This was abandoned on the night of June 18-19, when the Confederates took up their new position anchored with its right flank on Kennesaw Mountain.

Schofield's Army of the Ohio had been Sherman's maneuvering force, but after Schofield reported that he could not safely march farther past the Rebel left, Sherman determined on an assault against Johnston's entrenched position. The attack, scheduled for June 27, would have two prongs: against Little Kennesaw Mountain and Pigeon Hill on the Southerners' center-right, and against a salient farther to the south held by Maj. Gen. Frank Cheatham's division (and which has since been given the name "Cheatham Hill").

Sherman's attacking battle involved eight infantry brigades, totaling 15,000 troops. Two brigades, those of Col. Dan McCook and Col. John Mitchell, both from Brig. Gen. Jefferson C. Davis's division (XIV Corps) advanced against Cheatham's salient around 8:00 a.m. on the 27th.

As McKinsay states, the 125th Illinois was the lead regiment in McCook's assault column. Colonel McCook, shot in the chest, was carried to the rear; he would die three weeks later at home in Ohio. Colonel Harmon died almost instantly when he was shot five minutes after McCook fell.

TO THE EDITOR: As I have not seen anything of the charge at Kenesaw, I thought I would see if I could get some of my comrades to reply to me. It would be consoling to me to hear from you something about the narrow escapes we underwent during that charge, in which I was a member of Co. G., 125th Ill., Third Brigade, Second Division, Fourteenth Corps, Col. Dan McCook commanding Third Brigade. When the orders were issued, as my Colonel was the ranking Colonel of the brigade, we took the front line, supported by the 22d Ind., 86th Ill., 85th Ill. and 52d Ohio. We marched in line of battle to the foot of the hill or ridge. We were ordered to raise the yell and charge up the hill through a rye field. After reaching the works we found them so strong we could not take them and fell back, when Gen. McCook seized the colors, mounted the rebel works, and yelled, "Come on, boys, the day is ours!" He at that moment was shot, falling outside of the works, still holding the colors. Turning to Col. Harmon, of the 125th Ill., he said: "Colonel, take command." At that instance the Colonel was killed, when the brigade fell back some 20 paces and threw up works, and held them till the rebs evacuated.—H. McKINSAY, Havensville, Kan.

By the end of 1884–the National Tribune*'s eighth year—the newspaper had published fewer than a half-dozen pieces about Kennesaw Mountain (modern spelling includes two n's). None of them pertained to the charge against Cheatham Hill, so McKinsay's request for comrades to write in about it is logical. It also demonstrates the role that the* National Tribune, *just a few decades after the war, was serving for Union veterans eager to read about the drama in which they had played a role.*

27

General Harker Is Killed

R. Grove, "Picket Shots. Gen. Harker's Death"

(November 24, 1898, p. 3)

About the time that McCook's and Mitchell's brigades advanced against Cheatham at 8:00 a.m., Brig. Gen. John Newton's Second Division (IV Corps) sent its three brigades forward. One of them was led by Brig. Gen. Charles G. Harker, who had predicted, "I shall not come out of this charge today alive."

He was right.

R. Grove, Co. F, 79th Ill., Chehalis, Wash., writes: "I saw in the issue of October 20 last a note from Comrade J. A. Therman, Co. C, 64th Ohio. The comrade is correct in stating that Brig.-Gen. Harker gave up his life on the Atlanta campaign, in the charge at Kenesaw Mountain. I was less than 100 feet from the General when he fell from his horse. Adjutant Lamb, 79th Ill, was on Harker's staff at the time, and took the body home."

General Harker was shot from his horse by a rifle ball that broke his right arm and lodged in his chest. He was carried to a field hospital, where he died a few hours later (Welch, Medical Histories of Union Generals, *152).*

28

If Only We Had Formed Outside Our Works

John K. Shellenberger, "Kennesaw Mountain. The Causes that Led to the Repulse of Harker' s Charge"

(December 11, 1890, p. 4)

Often, one veteran's article in the National Tribune *would spark another, as shown here.*

EDITOR NATIONAL TRIBUNE: In his article describing the assault on Kennesaw Mountain, published in THE NATIONAL TRIBUNE of Nov. 6, Comrade A. M. Potter, of the 74th Ill., has given such a full and accurate account of that bloody and disastrous affair, that little remains to be said to complete the picture. I write to point out the prime cause of the failure of Harker's Brigade to break through the rebel line. I have never seen it given in any history of the war, and I hold it to be of the highest importance that all of the causes of our failures be fully disclosed in order that our coming soldiers may profit by the study thereof.

The conditions in front of Harker's Brigade were especially favorable to a successful assault. The opposing lines were here not to exceed 500 yards apart, and the intervening space was covered with a heavy growth of timber which afforded an effectual screen against the observation of the enemy, and there was not sufficient undergrowth to seriously impede our advance. The ground descended in front of our works with an easy declivity to a stream about mid-way between the lines, so small that it could be jumped over. Beyond the stream the ground rose at first with a gradual ascent, and then more abruptly. About 15 or 20 yards beyond the crest of this abrupt ascent was the rebel line, the ground rising but very little across the intervening space. Our column would therefore not come under the effective fire of their line until its head would appear above the crest of this abrupt ascent, and so close to their works that they would have only time to fire a single volley before we would be upon them while in the act of reloading. There was no artillery in our front to mow down our men with double charges of canister, nor was there any abatis or other obstruction to delay us while we might be picked off by their infantry. The chevaux-de-frise which covered this part of their line, when some of us went out under a flag of truce to bury our dead the morning of the 29th, had been placed there after our assault was repulsed. There was no ditch on the outside of their works, all the dirt having been thrown from the ditch inside, the depth of which formed a good part of their works.

On our side, therefore, their line was covered by a low embankment, over which we might have charged without any serious delay.

Three regiments of the brigade were left to hold the intrenched line we had been occupying for several days—the 3d Ky., the 42d and 79th Ill. The remaining five regiments reached the ground selected for our assault a little before 9 o'clock a.m. We had no previous intimation of the work cut out for us. When we halted, Gen. Harker called together the regimental commanders and gave them his orders. They returned to their respective regiments, and calling up the company commanders, gave their instructions, which were then communicated to the men. We were informed that our task would be to break through the rebel line in front, and having accomplished this much we would be relieved at once by the other troops, who would then take up the fight. The 125th Ohio was selected to carry the rebel picket line, which was well intrenched and strongly held, the pits being large enough to hold about a dozen men each.

The main column was composed of the 51st and 27th Ill. and the 65th and 64th Ohio, in the order named. The 64th counted off into eight equal companies, and I presume the other regiments did the same. We then formed column, doubled on the center and closed in mass. This formation gave us a front of only two companies and a depth 16 battle-lines—a human battering-ram. The preliminary arrangements occupied but a few minutes, when the order was given to advance.

Right here the great mistake was made. Our formation was made inside our own line of breastworks, with no proper provision for getting outside. Each man climbed over as best he could. When our advanced divisions got over, instead of moving out a short distance and there halting until the entire column got over and was properly formed outside, they charged headlong on the rebel works. They were probably carried forward prematurely by the movement of McCook's Brigade, assaulting a short distance to our right, or by Wagner's on our left. I cannot state how many of our brigade were engaged in this premature advance, but I know from what I saw and heard that the head of our column was being repulsed on the rebel breastworks while the main body was still struggling with the difficulties encountered in climbing over our own breastworks. My own experience will best illustrate this part of the affair. I was commanding the third division of the 64th Ohio. When the second division had got out of the way my men began to climb over. I carried a sword, haversack and canteen only, and yet I had about all I could do to get over. It was not until I had slipped back two or three times that I found a crevice large enough into which securely to stick my toes, and then succeeded in getting on top of the works. The men of Stanley's Division, holding this part of line, gave all the assistance they could, "boosting" many of our men over bodily. When I got over, the last of the second division was disappearing in the woods in front where the roar of battle was swelling in its awful majesty. I had gathered about me only five or six men of my division, among them my First Sergeant, Harry Lawrence, a cool, intrepid soldier, in whose judgment I had much confidence. When I inquired of him, "Harry, shall we go forward with the men we have, or wait till they all get over?" he replied, "Better go forward with those we have. It sounds like our boys are having a mighty hot time out there. They are probably on the rebel works, and may be in desperate need of the help of every man as quick as they can get it."

Without waiting longer we then ran forward. When we approached the top of the hill on the opposite slope we found all of the brigades which had preceded us lying massed in a slight depression behind the cover of the crest of the steep ascent already described. We joined them there, as did also the remainder of our regiment as it came straggling forward. Those of our men along the top of the crest were keeping up a hot fire in reply to the fire which was coming from the rebel works. Occasionally some gallant soldier would rise up with a stand of colors in his hands and would start for the breastworks. The movement would begin to spread, when a volley would come from the works, cutting down the leaders, and the movement would then subside. It needed a leader who could carry the men forward in mass, and such a one now appeared on the scene. Gen. Harker came riding up the slope from our rear. His cheeks were pale but his eyes were burning and his lips were compressed with a grim determination. He passed around the right of the brigade and riding to the center along the crest, not more than 15 yards from the muzzles of the muskets behind the breastworks, he lifted his hat and called out: "Forward, men, and take these works."

The brigade arose as one man to follow his lead; his horse was just turning his nose toward the breastworks when the gallant Harker reeled in his saddle, stricken with a mortal wound. A bullet from the breastworks broke his right arm and penetrated his breast, and he did that night.

Just as Gen. Harker fell from his horse orders came from the rear to fall back, a movement which we immediately executed on the principle of "the devil take the hindmost."

The 51st Ill., leading the assault, had planted its colors on the rebel breastworks, and had effected a lodgment there, but there were too few of them left to jump over and engage in a hand-to-hand contest with the enemy. They lay down on the outer slope waiting for their supports to come up, but these did not arrive in sufficient numbers in time to enable them to hold the position. The rebels vigorously assailed the men of the 51st. Some were shot, some were bayoneted and some were dragged over the works by the hair of the head and made prisoners.

The remnant, finding their position was a hopeless one, fell back behind the cover of the crest of the hill, where they were eventually joined by the remainder of the brigade coming forward in the straggling manner already described.

I believed then, and I believe now, that if our column had been formed outside our own breastworks, it would have gone straight over the rebel line; McCook to our right and Wagner to our left would have immediately widened the breach, and the day would have closed with very disastrous results to the rebel army.—JOHN K. SHELLENBERGER, Humboldt, Iowa.

29

Approaching the Chattahoochee

Oliver O. Howard, "Atlanta Campaign. Masterly Monographs From a Trenchant Pen. By O. O. Howard, Major-General. XV—Crossing the Chattahoochee"

(January 31, 1895, pp. 1-2)

General Johnston held his Kennesaw Mountain position until July 2, when Sherman's flanking maneuvers compelled him once more to retreat. In the next week, the Confederates took up two more defensive lines between Kennesaw and the Chattahoochee, near Smyrna and along the north riverbank. Here, Sherman directed possibly his most adroit flanking maneuver. Having throughout the campaign turned Johnston on his left, Sherman now feinted toward the Rebel left, sending McPherson and cavalry downstream. Johnston took the bait and sent considerable mounted troops in that direction. But on July 8-9, Union infantry and cavalry succeeded in finding several points upstream from the railroad bridge where they crossed against weak Rebel resistance. During the night of July 9-10, Johnston could only respond by ordering his army to retire south of the Chattahoochee.

The National Tribune *did not relate these events, save in the narrative of John McElroy and in the autobiography of Union general Howard. Here is how the latter did so, in number 15 of his chronicle.*

THE CROSSING of a broad river in face of an able and active enemy is one of the hard problems of war. By the last Monograph it will be noticed that we had pressed hard against Johnston's bridgehead below Vining's Station, and caused Wheeler to cross the Chattahoochee at Paice's Ferry, near by.

* * *

In the minds of the readers of a story of a military campaign wonderment often arises why there are so many delays. Our people at home and our authorities at Washington, at the time of which we write, were always impatient at such delays, and could not account for the waste of so many precious days behind the Chattahoochee. "Hadn't Joe Johnston cooped himself up there at the railroad crossing? WHY NOT NOW BE BOLD and strike below him for Atlanta, already in plain sight, and for Johnston's lines of supply?"

A few answers in answer to my memory. 1. As we, who belonged to Thomas, pushed up a few miles against those "inner lines" [*Johnston's "river line" near the Chattahoochee, occupied by his troops, July 5-9*], the Confederate cavalry had crossed the river and taken on the other high bank fine positions for their cannon—cannon to be well-supported by mounted and dismounted men. Every crossing within reach was to be diligently watched by our foes, and every possible effort put forth to prevent or delay our attempted passage of the river; Confederate Jackson [*Brig. Gen. William H. Jackson, commanding a division in Wheeler's cavalry*] and his active cavalry were working below the Confederate army, and Gen. Wheeler above the Marietta & Atlanta Railway crossing of the Chattahoochee, to and beyond the Roswell Factories [*along the river, some fifteen miles northeast of the railroad bridge*].

* * *

Sherman quickly moved his Headquarters belongings up to Vining's Station, on the Marietta and Atlanta Railroad. . . . While his mind was quite settled as to his manner of crossing the river, yet there were still many things to be considered. Thomas had found it impracticable to cross over in face of the fortified points on his front or left [*the area of the railroad*]. The water, which had risen from the recent rains, was now too high for fording.

Sherman saw, however, that the water was slowly falling and that in a short time all the fords would be practicable; so that by-and-by something more than artillery and cavalry would be required by the Confederate General over there to keep him back.

* * *

Sherman…had also sent Garrard's Cavalry Division to the Roswell Factories. As soon as Garrard could charge into the place he drove out the detachment of Wheeler's cavalry, and destroyed the factories. The Confederate guard rushed over the Chattahoochee Bridge, there located, and SUCCEEDED IN DESTROYING IT.

Sherman by the 8th of July had determined to make his first crossing near these Roswell Factories; McPherson, with Dodge, then Logan, and finally Blair, were to go up there, back up the cavalry of Garrard and Col. McCook, which must ford or swim the river, and clear the way for a bridgehead. Who could build a trestle bridge like Dodge, who was not only a superb commander of men in battle, but was already an imminent practical engineer?

Sherman decided that Garrard should attempt a crossing the morning of the 9th at dawn. Gen. Howard must send a division to support Garrard's effort. So Newton's Division, starting before light, marched up the 12 or 14 miles from his camp. Garrard crossed at 6 a.m. with little loss, and Newton followed him during the morning; the ford there by this time had become practicable. The men were not long in putting up a strong work for a bridgehead, and so the upper crossing was secured. [*On the morning of July 9 a brigade of Brigadier General Kenner Garrard's cavalry division waded across the river at a two- to three-feet-deep ford near the burned Roswell bridge. Firing their seven-shot Spencers, they quickly drive off the small Confederate force on the south bank. Brig. Gen. John Newton's infantry division (IV Corps, Thomas' army) arrived to reinforce their bridgehead.*]

But meanwhile something else even more important had been done. As soon as Schofield had been crowded out by Johnston contracting his lines from the "outer" to the "inner" protection of his railroad over the Chattahoochee . . . [*On July 5, Johnston withdrew his army to a shorter line on the north bank of the Chattahoochee. Pursuing Federal infantry adopted an accordingly shorter line themselves, causing Maj. Gen. John M. Schofield's XXIII Corps to be "crowded out."*] . . . Sherman brought his (Schofield's) corps back near to Thomas' left [*upriver, to the east*] . . . Sherman set him reconnoitering for a convenient river-crossing somewhere above Thomas.

He discovered a practicable ford just above the mouth of Soap Creek. There was but a small picket of the enemy's cavalry opposite, and a single section of artillery. The whole work of preparation and approach was done so well that the enemy suspected no movement there till Schofield's men of Cox's Division about 3 p.m. July 8 were making their way across by ford and by detached pontoon-boats. . . . [*Here, Sergeant Leeds' article, following, picks up General Howard's narrative.*]

30

Federal Pontoon Crossing at Soap Creek, July 8

L. C. Leeds, "He Volunteered. Then Crossed the Chattahoochee in a Pontoon"

(March 14, 1895, p.1)

EDITOR NATIONAL TRIBUNE: In a recent issue, in one of O. O. Howard's accounts of movements during the Atlanta campaign, I noticed where and how Schofield crossed the Chattahoochee, and I remembered that I belonged to Schofield's command, and participated in that crossing; in fact, was an early crosser, and all owing to my fool habit of volunteering, which always got me into places that I wished I wasn't in.

On the morning of July 9, 1864, we had been advancing slowly until about 10 a.m., when we halted in the woods, alongside an old road, and remained standing in line-of-battle, not knowing what might be ahead of us in the woods. Our Lieutenant-Colonel (Benjamin F. Orcutt) rode on ahead. He was commanding the regiment, and presently came riding slowly back, and did not stop until he got up to the center of the line. Then he looked up and down the line for a few minutes. Finally, he said:

"Boys, I want some volunteers who can row boats."

Now, that just suited me, for I had been raised near Lake Michigan and upon the St. Joe River, and had an idea that I could row a boat with any of the boys. I stepped to the front, and was immediately accompanied by another Sergeant, named Ben --- (I have forgotten his name), from Co. G, and in a minute or two enough had volunteered, and Lieut. B. F. Travis, of Co. E, was placed in command of the squad.

The first order was to leave everything except our clothes on us. Ben and I were at the head of the column. In a few minutes we reached a creek named Soap Creek, and along the bank, standing in a row on the edges, were a number of canvas pontoons, and immediately in their rear was the 16th Ky., commanded by Lieut.-Col. Hobson, I think. Soon as we got there we were told-off in twos, and every two were to man a boat. Ben and myself got the first boat, and someone said, "Launch the boats," and they went into the water. As soon as our boat got straight into the water as many as could stand up in it of the 16th Ky. piled in with the Lieutenant-

Colonel, when Ben and I commenced pulling on the oars. Everything went along smoothly for a few minutes, when I looked back of me to see where and how we were going. I saw a river, and upon the bank next us above and below the mouth of the creek was a line-of-battle stretched, all standing and looking over the water toward the far bank. I then and there told Ben that we were in for it.

So soon as the nose of our pontoon commenced passing in to the river the entire line-of-battle along our bank opened up, firing toward the other side, and the other side opened with a small battery, shooting toward the mouth of that creek. I saw grapeshot skipping and jumping around on the water hunting someone to hit. We were pulling for the shore opposite hard as we could and the Lieutenant-Colonel in the pontoon was ordering us to pull harder and just dancing around and hallooing. When we got almost over we saw that we could wade. Ben jumped in first and then I. The water was about waist deep. We could get foothold and push better than to row.

When our pontoon was within two or three yards of the bank I saw that the next boat was getting away from the boys rowing and was starting down the river, and as our boat was out of the current I started back to help them. Then I did get a blessing from the Lieutenant-Colonel for leaving his boat, so I came back to his craft, and about that time the pontoon hit the bank and the troops were getting out and starting up the hill.

They went right up and captured the battery and the few men manning it, and we had made a crossing of the Chattahoochee River and was firmly planted on the bank nest to Atlanta. We continued to carry over troops for a short time. Then the pontoon men took charge and commenced building a pontoon-bridge.

Our regiment crossed the river the next morning. I did not get back to my regiment until after dark that night, tired, hungry and wet; found nothing to eat, and lay down to sleep at once.

Of the men mentioned Lieut.-Col. Orcutt stayed, and went home with the regiment the latter part of June, 1865; was elected Sheriff of Kalamazoo County; was shot and killed one night by some criminals who were escaping. Lieut. B. F. Travis is yet alive, living at Climax, Mich., and is writing a history of the regiment. My partner Ben I have never heard of nor seen since we mustered out at Jackson, Mich., and disbanded early in June 1865.—L. C. LEEDS, Sergeant, Co. C, 25th Mich., Dallas, Tex.

Late on July 7, Schofield informed Sherman that he had found two possible points where his infantry could cross the river downstream from Roswell. First, a submerged fish-dam, over which men could walk, was apparently undefended. Then, a half-mile below (to the southwest) was Isham's Ford at the mouth of Sope Creek. There, because of recent rains, the Chattahoochee was 300 yards wide, with a swift current and too deep to be waded. Yet, Schofield judged it a good point to build a pontoon bridge, especially as on the south bank some 400 yards from the river there could be seen a commanding ridge—an excellent place for troops to establish a defensive bridgehead. Even better, he thought it was guarded by "only a squad of cavalry and one or two pieces of artillery." Sherman liked the plan for the twin-crossing the next day and ordered two dozen canvas pontoon boats brought to Schofield's troops at Sope Creek.

It is here that Sergeant Leeds picks up the story. The appeal of his article derives from the importance of his topic—Schofield's crossing of the Chattahoochee on July 8 led Johnston to retreat across the river during the night of July 9-10—and his first-person remembrance as one of the lead pontoniers in the river crossing.

As usual, the National Tribune *contributor trips up on some details—it was July 8, not 9—and it was the 12th Kentucky—not the 16th, that got across the river on pontoons (Albert Castel,* Decision in the West: The Atlanta Campaign of 1864 *[Lawrence: University Press of Kansas, 1992], 336, 339).*

But the conclusion of the story is undisputed. On the afternoon of July 8, a Union regiment walked across the fish-dam undetected. At Isham's/Sope Creek, Federals fired across the river at the small group of Rebels on the south bank, while others were rowed across on their canvas pontoons. The Southerners resisted meekly, firing a few rounds with their small, six-pounder cannon. Schofield's troops landed and drove them away, capturing the Confederates' "pop gun." By nightfall, the two bridgeheads had linked, and a pontoon bridge had been built, allowing Brig. Gen. Jacob Cox's infantry division to cross and establish an entrenched defensive line on the commanding ridge. The next day, Schofield's other division (Brigadier Milo Hascall's) also got across (Gould Hagler, "Crossing the Hooch without a Hitch," Civil War News, *vol. 45, no. 9 [September 2019], 26-27).*

Benjamin Travis's The Story of the Twenty-fifth Michigan *was published in 1897 (Allan Nevins, James I. Robertson, Jr., and Bell I. Wiley,* Civil War Books: A Critical Bibliography, *2 vols. (Baton Rouge: Louisiana State University Press, 1967, 1969), 1:170)].*

31

Crossing at the Fish-Dam

George Redway, "A Bloodless Victory. Securing a Crossing of the Chattahoochee and Turning Joe Johnston's Impregnable Line of Defense"

(September 18, 1902, p. 6)

Almost of necessity war stories are apt to portray pictures of carnage and death. Their interest is often absorbing in proportion as the details are harrowing. A tale of war without fire and sword, killing and mangling, is like the play of Hamlet with Hamlet omitted.

Therefore he must be a bold soldier indeed who should attempt to describe a military victory in which there was no bloodshed. It is this kind of bravery only that I propose to exemplify on this occasion; for my narrative relates only to a bloodless victory. It is the story of the way in which Gen. Sherman's grand army effected the crossing of the Chattahoochee River, Ga., on July 8, 1864.

The two greatest campaigns of the war for the Union are supposed to have been those of Gen. Grant toward Richmond in 1864-'5 and of Gen. Sherman toward Atlanta in 1864.

The 130 miles from Chattanooga to the Chattahoochee River, 10 miles this side of Atlanta, was through a rough and mountainous country, peculiarly well adapted to defensive military operations.

Every one of those 130 miles was won by hard fighting, through dense forests, or over rugged mountains, or through or over rushing streams, or by narrow gaps and gorges—all defended by veteran Confederates. They were commanded by Gen. Joe Johnston, whom Gen. J. D. Cox, in his history of the campaign, described as "by common consent of military men of both sides reckoned second only to Gen. Lee; if, indeed, he was second" to any Confederate General.

The last great natural barrier to Sherman's advance upon Atlanta was the Chattahoochee River, with practically only one bridge, and that defended by some 60,000 veteran rebel soldiers, in impregnable earthworks, with ditches and abatis, reaching six miles up and down the river, and over 200 pieces of artillery ready to belch forth their iron hail upon our approach. For miles to the right and left of this six miles of continuous works were long lines of cavalry and picket posts, with occasional forts and artillery.

Sherman's advance reached and confronted this river-line on the 5th day of July, 1864. More than a month previous he had telegraphed to Washington that if Johnston should select this line of defense he (Sherman) "must stop and study the case a little." The next day, after reaching it, he again telegraphed to Washington, as follows:

"I propose to study the crossings of the Chattahoochee, and, when all is ready, to move quickly. * * * [*asterisks in original*] At present the waters are turbid and swollen from recent rains. * * * We have pontoons enough for four bridges; but, as our crossing will be resisted, we must maneuver some. All the regular crossing places (fords and ferries) are covered by forts; but we shall cross in due time."

The last clause has the same ring as Gen. Grant's famous dispatch—"I shall fight it out on this line if it takes all Summer."

He therefore sent one strong column a few miles down the river, and another (Gen. Schofield's Army of the Ohio, to which my regiment belonged) a few miles up the river, to look for a place where it might be considered easiest to force a crossing. At the same time he put on a bold front in the center near the bridge, as if intending an assault there in overwhelming force; though that was probably about the last alternative in his mind.

In my company morning report book I find this entry: "July 7, 1864—Moved two miles northeastward up the Chattahoochee." We were not, however, within sight of the river, being in a deep ravine separated from the river by a parallel ridge some 200 to 300 feet high. Through this ravine ran a considerable stream called Soap Creek, which emptied into the river a mile or less below. Gen. J. D. Cox's Division of the Twenty-third Corps occupied the ravine, with the rest of Gen. John M. Schofield's command close in the rear, and all were kept out of sight of the enemy, who at this point were all on the south bank of the river.

Gen. Cox (afterward Governor of Ohio, and still later Gen. Grant's Postmaster-General and Secretary of the Interior) in his history of the campaign says:

> "Early in the morning of the 8th the corps, with Colonel Buell's pontoon-train, moved, by roads back from the river, to the mill near the mouth of Soap Creek. The leading division (Cox's) was ordered to take position as close to the river as was consistent with remaining unseen by the enemy—to permit no campfires, and no exposure of men to view. The river was to be picketed, but the videts to conceal themselves from the opposite shore. A fish-dam was learned of half a mile above the mouth of the creek, which had been made by piling rough stones across the current. * * * In the condition of the river that day this was a difficult and dangerous ford, but it was determined to use it."

In Special Field Order No. 46, issued by Gen. Schofield the day before the crossing, he directed as follows:

> * * * "The brigade commander will deploy a strong line of skirmishers, with large reserves, behind the ridge near the river, and prepare a party of about 50 good men to lead the crossing and effect a lodgment on the opposite side. The men should be tall and strong, on account of the possible difficulty in fording. It is not necessary to select men from the Twenty-third Corps for their bravery. * * *

Volunteers from all the regiments of my brigade, to the number of about 60 men, were selected as a sort of forlorn hope to try this ford in advance, to see whether it was possible for the brigade to wade it, and to develop the strength and take the first fire of the enemy. I had the honor of commanding this advance of 60 men.

But first the pontoniers set up and launched their canvas boats in the creek, and one entire brigade was loaded into them ready to push out into the river and row for the other shore as soon as my advance guard had secured a safe footing there. Other pontoons were made ready for throwing a bridge across the river.

Let me quote again from Gen. Cox: "Col. Cameron (commanding my brigade) was ordered to conceal his men near the fish-dam, push an advance guard (my 60 men) over it, if possible, at the time appointed, and if the ford proved practicable, follow it with his brigade," at the same time the brigade in the pontoon boats should try to row from the mouth of the creek.

I did not in person quite meet Gen. Schofield's requirement of "tall and strong," inasmuch as my army measurements was only 5 feet 5 1-2, and I had been recently ill and was hardly yet convalescent. So that, when I reported with the advance guard to my Colonel (J. S. Casement), who superintended the fording, he said, apparently surprised: "Capt. Redway, what are you doing here?" "I am here for duty, Colonel," was my reply, "under orders, in command of the advance guard." He protested that I was not yet strong enough for such work, but I assured him I was all right, and with some apparent misgiving he acquiesced and led the way to the fish-dam ford. This was the only occasion I ever saw his face blanched, and I knew it was not so then from fear, at least on his account.

The place was wooded down to the water's edge, so that it was easy for us to remain concealed until we entered the river. The opposite bank was perhaps eight feet high from the water, and beyond lay an open, level bottom, say 50 yards wide, and beyond that a rather steep hill some 200 feet high, crowned at the top with heavy timber. We could see all this from among the trees while awaiting the signal to advance. At the top of the hill opposite, all along the edge of the woods, there appeared what looked like a line of earthworks, which, of course, ought to be full of Confederates. No Union troops except my 60 men were then within our sight.

Knowing well what was the mission of this advance guard that day, very few of us expected ever to reach the south shore, or any other shore save that of eternity. I think most of us saw in imagination our wounded or lifeless bodies floating down the rushing current of the swollen Chattahoochee. But when the signal was given, at about 4 p.m., we marched into the river by twos, right in front, I on the right and a First Lieutenant of the 65th Ill., whose name I have forgotten, taking charge of the rear. My Colonel remained on the north shore until the regiment crossed, a half hour or so later. The rocky way under our feet was rough and slippery, the current was swift, and the water much of the way up to my mouth. We had to hold our guns, ammunition and accouterments over our heads. A few slipped and went under, but got up again with help and pushed on, till all clambered safely up the bank on the rebel side, and not a shot had been fired.

My orders were to deploy in skirmish line as fast as my men were across, and push obliquely up the hill and toward a piece of timber which hid a bend in the river just opposite the mouth of Soap Creek. I was to commence firing as soon as I heard firing, whether the enemy was in sight or not. We had not reached this piece of timber when, "boom!" went a rebel cannon in front of us beyond the timber. Immediately we commenced firing into the woods that concealed the rebels, and at the same time a perfect thunder of artillery opened from our own guns in ambush on the north bank of the river.

The Johnnies had not seen us. Their first intimation of the proximity of a Union force was, evidently, when our armed pontoons shot from the creek, across the river from their little fort. When whistling minie-balls and shrieking shell came raining on them so suddenly from front and rear flank, they hurriedly abandoned their cannon and fled as fast as legs and horses could carry them. Meantime, Col. Casement was leading our 103d Ohio across the ford, and soon a pontoon bridge was laid, and before morning the entire Third Division had crossed upon it and intrenched along the hills south of the river. The next morning the remainder of the corps crossed.

Thereupon the rebel General made haste to abandon his impregnable line north of the river and to cross his entire army at the bridge a few miles down stream, and fall back to his outer line of defenses around Atlanta.

Thus was overcome the most serious natural defense of the Confederates against Sherman's advance upon Atlanta, and a great victory won without the loss of a man.

Immediately thereafter Gen. Joe Johnston was superseded in command of the rebel army by Gen. Hood, greatly to the advantage of the Union cause.

Gen. Sherman, in his Memoirs, speaks of this crossing as one of the greatest military achievements in the annals of modern warfare. In this estimate he has reference, of course, to all of the elements that contributed to its success; as, for example, the selection of a place for the crossing where the river might be forded, and where the pontoons might be set up and manned unobserved by the enemy, and to the secrecy and celerity with which all the operations were conducted, resulting in a complete surprise to the enemy. Credit was, of course, due chiefly to the officers who planned and directed the movement; namely, Gens. Sherman, Schofield, Cox and Casement—the latter then Colonel of the 103d Ohio.

The only entry I find in my company morning report book for July 8, 1864, is this "Marched up the river and forded it below Phillip's Ferry."

I am glad to have enjoyed the good fortune of being the first officer of Sherman's grand army to cross the Chattahoochee, and to have commanded what was supposed to be the forlorn hope of that important advance. I am also very glad that the forlornness was eliminated from the hope.

Two strong-limbed fellows reached the south bank a step or two before me—Corp'l Tom Branigan, of my own company, and a stalwart Sergeant of the 24th Ky., whose name I am unable to recall.

The inconvenience of dripping clothes after our wade through the river that afternoon must have seemed slight; for I have no recollection of how the wet garments felt, although I well remember the boys picking blackberries just after they scrambled up out of the river, and while deploying as skirmishers.

That night my detachment held the extreme left flank of our skirmish line. The next morning, as soon as I could see (not far from 3 o'clock), I began to examine our situation. I found our skirmish line lay just in front of a tolerably well-defined road through open timber, running along a little south of the top of the river hills. Going along this road, I discovered only a few rods to the left of our outermost picket post in that direction, another road running at right angles with the river road. Both sides of the latter road, looking southward, were flanked by dense woods, except for one or two acres about a deserted log house in our front. I went along the river road some distance and then came back to my outpost, and was just directing the tall Sergeant of the 24th Ky. to extend the picket line across the north-and-south road, when I heard a thundering noise up that road. I knew it must be rebel cavalry, and hurriedly cautioned the men to hold their fire until the command. Just then we noticed a lot of bluecoats from our main line in the rear, with canteens and unarmed, getting water from a spring to our left and front. They were on and near the road down which the rebel cavalry were galloping. Some of them were in plain view of the rebs, who rushed on, at the same time treating the canteen-boys to a lively fusillade from their carbines. At this my men could no longer wait for the command to fire, but blazed away and emptied every gun-barrel in a jiffy. Before this my skirmish line had not been seen by the rebs, as we were somewhat sheltered from their view by open timber. My idea was to let this rebel company get somewhat into our rear and then to throw my men across the road and capture at least some of them. We had plenty of support within easy reach. But when I ran toward the road and called to my men to follow, they waited to reload their muskets. So I found myself near the road alone, and slipped behind a big oak tree.

By that time the whole of our division in my rear was in line of battle, expecting a rebel charge. When the foremost of the Johnnies got sight of this line through the timber they turned tail, and came scurrying back. All this had happened in less time than it takes to tell it, and my own men had not yet reloaded their guns and followed me to the road. Just then I heard a reb call out to his commander, "Captain, I've got one of the - - Yanks." Looking that way, I saw him driving a bluecoat before him with a carbine close to his head. At this I gave him every charge but one in my revolver, as rapidly as I could fire, and he put spurs to his horse and was soon out of sight—probably unhurt, though at first not over two rods away.

The released Union prisoner went slowly back to camp, breathing very hard, and swearing to himself at his late captor. From the lettering on his cap I noticed that he was a member of the 65th Ill., with which my regiment was brigaded; but I did not offer congratulations at his escape from Andersonville, nor stop to receive his thanks, and I never chanced to recognize him afterward.

Captain Redway's article informs us that, in addition to the Official Records *pertaining to the Atlanta Campaign (vol. 38, parts 1-5, 1891), writers at the turn of the century also consulted Union general Jacob D. Cox's* Atlanta *(1882), part of Scribner's "Campaigns of the Civil War" series (13 volumes, 1882).*

Redway rather overstates the strength of Johnston's position as Sherman's forces approached the Chattahoochee in the first week of July. During the night of July 4-5, the Confederate army occupied a five-mile fortified line on the north bank of the Chattahoochee, centered on the railroad and wagon bridges eight miles northwest of downtown Atlanta. Johnston's main problem was not to hold this "river line" but to guard the many fords and ferries upstream and downstream, where Sherman would surely attempt a troop crossing. For instance, there were 6 ferries in the 14 miles downstream from the W. & A. bridge. At one of them, Aderhold's (10 miles downriver from the Confederate line), on July 3, 100 state troops drove off some snooping Union cavalrymen. Altogether, Johnston's troops had to guard possible crossing points along fully 35 miles of riverbank (Stephen Davis, Texas Brigadier to the Fall of Atlanta: John Bell Hood *[Macon: Mercer University Press, 2019], 204-208).*

Sherman's statement that at the Chattahoochee he would have to "study the case a little" is disingenuous. On April 10, 1864, three weeks before the campaign even started, Sherman confided to Grant that while he planned to outflank Johnston's line by his right (and the Rebels' left) throughout his advance in north Georgia, once he reached the Chattahoochee he would feint right but cross his troops from his left flank, upriver from Johnston's presumed position (Davis, Hood, *206).*

It is noteworthy that for this article, Captain Redway (like other writers for the National Tribune*) was able to consult wartime documents kept long afterward, in this case his company report book. It reminds us that with such factual underpinning, Civil War veterans' recollections, written a generation after the war, can still be considered reliable.*

In quoting from Cox's Atlanta *(138-139) and Schofield's Special Field Order No. 46 (*OR *38, pt. 5, 85), Redway makes only slight divergences from the texts.*

Together with Sergeant Leeds's article, Captain Redway's gives us as close to first-person accounts of the crossings of Schofield's troops on July 8 (the Soap Creek pontoons and the fish-dam) as we are to see in the literature. This article is reprinted in Larry M. Strayer and Richard Baumgartner's Echoes of Battle.

32
Sherman's Construction Corps
E. J. Holman, "Bridging the Chattahoochee"
(July 28, 1910, p. 3)

*In Chapter 2 of his Atlanta Campaign narrative (*National Tribune, *January 28, 1909), John McElroy had lauded the ability of Sherman's engineers to build or repair the bridges, railroad track, and roads needed to supply an army of 100,000 men and 50,000 animals.*

Johnston's army, in its retreat of July 9-10, burned the railroad and wagon bridges across the Chattahoochee. During the week of Sherman's troop crossings (July 10-16), Captain Orlando Poe, the army group's Chief Engineer, oversaw construction of various pontoon and wooden trestle bridges to get the troops over the river and keep them supplied while his workers rebuilt the Western & Atlantic bridge. This they completed by August 5 atop the tall stone pillars still standing in the river (Poe report, OR *38, pt. 1, 130-134).*

How they did it is explained in the following letter sent into the newspaper by one of the head engineers.

E. J. Holman, Leavenworth, Kan., writes:

"In a late issue of The National Tribune a correspondent expresses his astonishment at the entrance of a railroad train into Atlanta soon after its occupation, knowing that the bridge over the Chattahoochee was destroyed. The Construction Corps, whose duty it was to repair and build railroads and bridges as fast as Sherman advanced, was as perfect an organization as any other part of Sherman's army. It consisted of about 75 trackmen and mechanics.

"The length of this bridge was 769 feet, and it was 80 feet high. We felled timber on both sides, and, commencing at both ends, erected sections of bents. On this section another was placed, and as fast as it was in position a rodman stood on the cap and gave me the reading (I stood behind the instrument on the west bank), from which I gave the builders the length of the top section, they sawing the four lengths or legs of the bent accordingly and placing it. The stringers were then stretched, ties placed and rails laid. On the third day at noon the top section met in the center, a piece of timber was thrown across and the writer was the first to cross, just two and one-half days from commencement.

"When Sherman left Atlanta we went to Baltimore, where we loaded on the steamship Baltic, and went down the coast, [*dis*]embarked at Morehead City, N.C., where we built additional wharfing and terminal facilities and put in order the road between Goldsboro and Raleigh, when the circuit was completed and we were again with Sherman, ready to build his bread line wherever he went."

The Baltic, *incidentally, was the steamer that carried Maj. Robert Anderson and the Fort Sumter garrison to New York after their surrender in April 1861 (E. Milby Burton,* The Siege of Charleston 1861-1865 *[Columbia: University of South Carolina Press, 1970], 58).*

33

Events of July 17-19

John McElroy, "The Atlanta Campaign. Chapter XVII"

(May 13, 1909, p. 2)

After Federals crossed the Chattahoochee and the Confederates retreated south of it, General Johnston aligned his army south of Peachtree Creek, which flowed from the east into the Chattahoochee some five miles north of Atlanta. He gave Sherman a full week, July 10-16, to rest his troops and prepare for his next move.

Sherman did not intend to attack the Rebels in the city's fortifications, which ringed it in a perimeter of rifle pits and two dozen artillery forts. Instead, he planned to starve the enemy out by cutting the railroads leading into the city that supplied both Johnston's men and the thousands of civilians still in it.

Besides the Western & Atlantic to Chattanooga, three railroads ran into Atlanta: the Georgia Railroad (east to Augusta), the Macon & Western from the south, and the Atlanta & West Point, leading southwest toward Montgomery. A Union cavalry raid had cut the latter in east central Alabama in mid-July. To get at the Georgia line, Sherman directed his forces to start moving on July 17. McPherson's Army of the Tennessee would swing wide to the southeast, aimed at striking the railroad between Decatur and Stone Mountain, well east of Atlanta, then marching toward it. Thomas's Army of the Cumberland would march south directly toward the city; Schofield's Army of the Ohio would keep position in the gap between Thomas and McPherson.

Here is where the National Tribune *editor's article begins.*

Johnston Removed.

While the army was making this grand wheel, with the Army of the Tennessee far to the left tearing up the railroad near Decatur, news came which Sherman and his officers welcomed as equivalent to a victory. This news reached Sherman by a man who appeared to be a citizen, but who was really one of our spies in Atlanta. He arrived at Gen. Sherman's headquarters with a newspaper containing Gen. Joe Johnston's order relinquishing the command of the Confederate forces in and around Atlanta, and the order of Gen. J. B. Hood assuming command in his stead.

This change was not wholly unexpected by any one. Johnston had been put in command of Bragg's badly defeated army much against the wishes of Jefferson Davis and Braxton Bragg. Davis hated Johnston with all his vindictiveness, which was notorious, and only assigned him to command because of the strongest pressure was put upon him and it was necessary to do something to vindicate himself to the army for his persistence in keeping Gen. Bragg in command after his repeated failures.

Bragg was as vindictive as Davis, hated Johnston for his intellectual and professional superiority and was only too willing that Johnston should fail where he himself had not succeeded. Therefore, from the first he and Davis kept nagging Johnston to make an advance and destroy Sherman's army, and held out to the country that he was in a position to do this. Far able soldier than either of them, Johnston saw the folly of an offensive movement against an army of at least as good men as he could muster, and 50 per cent more of them.

Johnston had really done wonders, especially when compared with Bragg's administration of the same army. Bragg had left the army dispirited by defeat, with much of its artillery and transportation captured from it, and little hope for the future in any man's breast. Johnston had increased it in numbers, reorganized it, systematized its means of supply, provided it with clothing, rations and ammunition, and in every way brought it to a far higher standard of contentment with itself and hope for the future.

Every backward step that Johnston made brought down the censure and cavilings of Davis and Bragg. They kept insisting should fight and at least cripple Sherman, and they gave him no credit for the battles which he did win nor for his successful withdrawals in front of superior forces. Johnston was following the policy of defense, fighting whenever he could do so with advantage and skilfully retreating, so as to embarrass his opponent, diminish his force, and render any blow which he might receive much more damaging.

Pollard says in his "Third Year of the War" that Johnston had lost about 10,000 in killed and wounded and 1,700 from "all other causes." That is, he had lost about one-fourth of his command in two months, which certainly indicates that there had been some hard fighting done by him in that time, particularly as his campaign was purely defensive.

In spite of these losses, however, he turned over to Hood an effective total of 41,000 infantry artillery and 10,000 cavalry, in all 51,000 men, or nearly as many as he had when he confronted Sherman at Dalton in the beginning of the campaign. This shows that he had rare talents as an organizer and disciplinarian, and held his men well in hand, gathering in recruits constantly and keeping them. That he had not been able to delay Sherman longer or strike him a crushing blow was due to

Sherman's exceptional skill and ability and the energy with which he pushed his campaign. After all, Johnston had struck as hard a blow at Sherman as Lee struck at Gaines's Mill, White Oak Swamp or Chancellorsville. That Johnston's blows had not been so effective as Lee's at those places was simply because the commanding General was of a very different mold from those whom Lee had encountered.

Orders From Richmond.

Altho Gen. Johnston's correspondence with Richmond had been so tart as to be near the limits of military insubordination, he hardly expected his supersedure to come when it did. Bragg had visited him personally a few days before, coming directly from Richmond, saying that he was going to Lieut.-Gen. S. D. Lee's headquarters to confer with him and communicate with Lieut.-Gen. E. Kirby Smith, across the Mississippi, in hopes of obtaining reinforcements for Johnston. He had said that his visit was wholly unofficial. All the same, he had sent telegrams to Davis very prejudicial to Johnston, of which the following is a sample:

"Atlanta, July 15, 1864.
"His Excellency Jefferson Davis, Richmond:

"I have made Gen. Johnston two visits and been received courteously and kindly. He has not sought my advice, and it was not volunteered. I cannot learn that he has any more plan for the future than he has had in the past. It is expected that he will await the enemy on a line some three miles from here, and the impression prevails that he is now more inclined to fight. The enemy is very cautious, and intrenches immediately on taking a new position. His force, like our own, is greatly reduced by the hard campaign. His infantry now very little over 60,000. The morale of our army is reported good.

"Braxton Bragg."

J. B. Hood, who was anxious to supersede Johnston, was striking at his chief behind his back, as will be indicated by this dispatch to Gen. Bragg:

"Near Atlanta, Ga., July 14, 1864.
"Gen. Braxton Bragg, Commanding Armies Confederate States, Richmond, Va.:

"General: During the campaign from Dalton to the Chattahoochee River it is natural to suppose that we have had several chances to strike the enemy a decisive blow. We have failed to take advantage of such opportunities, and find our army south of the Chattahoochee, very much decreased in strength. Our loss cannot be less than 20,000, without having fought a decisive battle. I deem it of the greatest importance that Gen. Kirby Smith should be ordered at once, with at least half, if not a larger portion, of his army, on this side of the Mississippi River. Our success west of the Mississippi River has proven a disadvantage to us, since the enemy has re-enforced his army on this side, and we have failed to do so. The strength of the Army of Tennessee is such at this time as to render it necessary to have aid from Gen. Kirby Smith—allowing that we should gain a victory over Sherman—to follow up our success and regain our lost territory. Our present position is a very difficult one, and we should not, under any circumstances, allow the enemy to gain possession of Atlanta, and deem it excessively important, should we find the enemy intends establishing the Chattahoochee as their line, relying upon interrupting our communications and again virtually dividing our country, that we should attack him, even if we should have to recross the river to do so. I have, General, so often urged that we should force the enemy to give us battle as to almost be regarded reckless by the other officers high in rank in this army, since their views have been so directly opposite. I regard it as a great misfortune to our country that we failed to give battle to the enemy many miles north of our present position. Please say to the President that I shall continue to do my duty cheerfully and faithfully, and strive to do what I think is best for our country, as my constant prayer is for our success.

"Respectfully,

"J. B. Hood, Lieutenant-General."

Transferring the Command.

At 10 p.m., July 17, while Johnston was in his tent with this Chief Engineer planning for fortifications, the following dispatch was handed him:

"Lieut.-Gen. J. B. Hood has been commissioned to the temporary rank of general under the late law of Congress. I am directed by the Secretary of War to inform you that as you have failed to arrest the advance of the enemy to the vicinity of Atlanta, far in the interior of Georgia, and express no confidence that you can defeat or repel him, you are hereby relieved from the command of the Army and Department of Tennessee, which you will immediately turn over to General Hood."

Gen. Johnston wrote an order relinquishing the command, and the next morning replied to Richmond thus:

"Your dispatch of yesterday received and obeyed. Command of the Army and Department of Tennessee has been transferred to Gen. Hood. As to the alleged cause of my removal, I assert that Sherman's army is much stronger compared with that of Tennessee than Grant's compared with that of Northern Virginia. Yet the enemy has been compelled to advance much more slowly to the vicinity of Atlanta than to that of Richmond and Petersburg, and has penetrated much deeper into Virginia than into Georgia. Confident language by a military commander is not usually regarded as evidence of competence."

Gen. Hood went to Johnston's headquarters, and remained with him during the day, while Johnston says:

"In transferring the command to Gen. Hood I explained my plans to him. First, I expected an opportunity to engage the enemy on terms of advantage while they were divided in crossing Peach Tree Creek, trusting to Gen. Wheeler's vigilance for the necessary information. If successful, the great divergence of the Federal line of retreat from the direct route available to us would enable us to secure decisive results; if unsuccessful, we had a safe place of refuge in our intrenched lines close at hand. Holding it, we could certainly keep back the enemy, as at New Hope Church and in front of Marietta, until the State troops promised by Gov. Brown were assembled. Then, I intended to man the works of Atlanta on the side toward Peach Tree Creek with those troops, and leisurely fall back with the Confederate troops into the town, and, when the Federal army approached, march out with the three corps against one of its flanks. If we were successful, the enemy would be driven against the Chattahoochee where there are no fords, or to the east, away from their communications, as the attack might fall on their right or left. If unsuccessful, the Confederate army had a near and secure place of refuge in Atlanta, which it could hold forever, and so win the campaign, of which that place was the object. The passage of Peach Tree Creek may not have given an opportunity to attack; but there is no reason to think that the second and far most promising plan might not have been executed."

Did Not Disobey Davis.

Gen. Johnston denies Gen. Bragg's charges that he had "persistently: disregarded" the President's instructions, and says:

"The President did not give me the benefit of his instructions in the manner of conducting this campaign, further than a brief telegram received early in July, in which he warned me against receiving battle with the Chattahoochee behind the army and near it. But as Lieut.-Gen. Pemberton's retreat from the Tallahatchie to the Yallobusha, in December, 1862, before an army which he thought not quite double his own; and General Bragg's, first from Murfreesboro' to Tullahoma, then from Tullahoma beyond the Tennessee River, and afterward the rout on Missionary Ridge and flight to Dalton, apparently had not lowered the President's estimate of the military merit of these officers, I supposed that my course would not be disapproved by him; especially as General Lee, by keeping on the defensive, and falling back toward Grant's objective point, under circumstances like mine, was increasing his fame. I believed then, as firmly as I do now, that the system pursued was the only one at my command that promised success, and that, if adhered to, it would have given us success."

Satisfaction in the Union Army.

Gen. Cox says of the way in which this news was received in Sherman's army:

"It is certain that the change of Confederate commanders was learned with satisfaction by every officer and man in the National Army. The patient skill and watchful intelligence and courage with which Johnston had always confronted them with impregnable fortifications, had been exasperating. They had found no weak joints in the harness, and no wish was so common or so often expressed as that he would only try our works as we were trying his. It was now known that this was likely to come, not only because Hood's character as a soldier implied it, but because the reasons for the change were known to be based upon a determination to pursue a more aggressive policy. It was understood that hard blows were to be received; but Sherman's whole army was supremely confident in its ability to take such prompt advantage of natural and artificial means of defence, as to punish aggression on the part of the enemy severely enough to reduce his strength with great rapidity. It is not over-praise of the National Army to say that its veterans were panic-proof; and its well-tried courage was so intelligent and quick-witted that the smallest detachments could be relied upon to do a wise and bold thing in almost any juncture.

If aggression was to be tried, it would be hard to find any commander better fitted than Hood to test it. He had gained renown as a division commander under Longstreet in Virginia, and at Gaines's Mills, Second Manassas, Antietam, and Gettysburg he had shown the kind of courage and dash which made him to be looked upon as a soldier of the Jackson school. It was a fatal error to suppose that the Army in Georgia could afford to take the kind of initiative now intended; but it was the error of the Richmond government, and Hood, though he had been freely critical of Johnston's cautious strategy, seems to have been sincerely reluctant to take the command under the implied conditions.

A Bold Push on Atlanta.

July 18 Gen. Sherman wrote to Gens. Thomas, McPherson and Schofield that he wanted "a bold push for Atlanta" the next day, and he expected to be soon in the city or very close to it. He found it hard to realize that Johnston would give up Atlanta without a fight, but it might be that he would. He wanted the army to find out. The next day he issued the following important special field order.

"Headquarters Military Division of the Mississippi,
in the field, near Decatur, July 19, 1864.

"The whole army will move on Atlanta by the most direct roads to-morrow, July 20, beginning at 5 a. m., as follows:

"I. Maj.-Gen. Thomas from the direction of Buck Head, his left to connect with General Schofield's right about two miles northeast of Atlanta, about lot 15, near the houses marked Howard and Col. Hooker.

"II. Maj.-Gen. Schofield by the road leading from Dr. Powell's to Atlanta.

"III. Maj.-Gen. McPherson will follow one or more roads direct from Decatur to Atlanta.

"Each army commander will accept battle on anything like fair terms, but if the army reach within cannon-range of the city without receiving artillery or musketry file he will halt, form a strong line, with batteries in position, and await orders. If fired on from the forts or buildings of Atlanta no consideration must be paid to the fact that they are occupied by families, but the place must be cannonaded without the formality of a demand.

"The General-in-Chief will be with the center of the army, viz, with or near Gen. Schofield.

"By order of Maj.-Gen. W. T. Sherman.

"L. M. Dayton,
Aid-de-Camp."

Crossing the Creek.

The night of July 17 the Army of the Cumberland was on Nancy's Creek, having pushed back the enemy's skirmishers from the Chattahoochee. On the 18th the army advanced until Palmer's right rested in the junction of Nancy's and Peach Tree Creeks, and Howard's Corps was at Buckhead. Gen. Schofield was in the neighborhood of Decatur, while Gen. McPherson was on the Augusta Railroad, a few miles east of Decatur. The line was a very long one, thin in places and with intervals which were dangerous. Gen. Sherman's field order was intended to consolidate the line and throw his whole force against Johnston. Early in the morning of July 19 Wood's Division, leading the Fourth Corps, reached Peach Tree Creek, on the Buckhead and Atlanta road. The bridge was burned, and the enemy was in a heavy work on the high ground beyond. Wood was ordered to force a passage of the creek, and secure a lodgment on the other side. He communicated his orders to Col. Knefler, of the Third Brigade, who immediately proceeded to its execution. The average width of the creek was about 30 feet and the depth about five. Col. Knefler detailed 50 picked men from the 79th Ind. and a like number from the 9th Ky., who were to rush across the creek, deploy as skirmishers and drive the enemy back. The brigade moved down the stream to a ravine, where they were hidden from the view of the enemy. The pioneers were each given a pole about 30 feet long to make a sleeper for the proposed bridge, and each of the 100 picked men took a rail. When all was ready the men moved rapidly but quietly down the ravine, threw down the sleepers, crossed the creek, each man rushed up with his rail and laid it for a bridge, and the whole 100 men were soon over, actively engaging the enemy's skirmishers. The enemy was taken by surprise and as he fell back the brigade rushed over the bridge, deployed, moved to the left, struck the flank of the enemy's intrenchments and drove him out, capturing some prisoners. This uncovered the stream for a considerable distance, when the First Brigade threw a bridge over and quickly joined Knefler's Brigade. A line was formed and hastily intrenched under a fire of artillery and musketry, which our artillery on the other bank kept down as much as possible. Wood's casualties were very small, which was remarkable considering the risks he took and the possibility that he would have to encounter the half of the Confederate army. Gen. Hazen's Brigade came up in the rear, and at once began the construction of a permanent bridge, which was completed early in the evening. Gen. Wood very naturally took much credit to his men for the brilliant passage of the stream, which, he asserts, was as handsome and artistic a piece of military work as was performed on the campaign. Gen. Stanley crossed the north fork of the creek some distance to the left, meeting strong opposition. His men rebuilt the bridges which had been burned, and he encamped on a line facing Atlanta.

Gen. Davis' Crossing.

July 18 Gen. Jeff C. Davis went into camp on Peach Tree Creek, a short distance from Howell's Mill, and the next day sent out Dilworth's Brigade in search of a crossing in the neighborhood of Greenbone Creek. At the best crossing it was found that the enemy was in considerable force, and they offered a strong resistance, but Dilworth forced them back and crossed the creek, but it had hardly formed on the other bank when a brigade of the enemy sallied out of their works and attacked him. The two forces were about equal, and a sharp action ensued, with heavy loss on both sides. The enemy was at last repulsed, Mitchell's Brigade coming in at the close of the fight to assist in winning the victory. Baird's Division crossed, and took position on Davis' left for the night. Geary's Division had a similar experience, but managed to cover the construction of its bridge with a heavy artillery fire, and then crossed to take up a strong line and repulse the enemy in his efforts to recover it.

Each of the commands at once intrenched itself strongly for the night. These operations contracted the line a great deal, but there was still a gap of about two miles between Gen. Thomas's left and Gen. Schofield's right. Gen. Thomas sent two divisions of the Fourth Corps to fill this gap, leaving only Newton's Division, which was on the south side of the creek, from the other two, which were on the north side. Gen. Newton had advanced and secured a good position in open ground at the distance of a division's interval from Geary's left. Everything indicated the presence of the enemy in strong force, and the Union commanders made their dispositions accordingly. Gen. Johnston had expected to attack Sherman in the confusion and lack of support involved in crossing the deep gorge of Peach Tree Creek, and he had fully informed Hood of these plans. Hood now saw the opportunity that Johnston had mentioned, and it was more favorable than he had anticipated. The Army of the Cumberland was across Peach Tree Creek, but it was minus the two divisions sent to the north side and which were beyond helping in case it was assailed. Hood thought he had an admirable chance to roll up the Army of the Cumberland in the narrow ground between Peach Tree Creek and the Chattahoochee River, and deliver a crushing blow upon it. He decided to attempt it, and resorted to a ruse to throw the Army of the Cumberland off its guard. He called in his skirmishers as if he were about to withdraw, and sent trusted men into the Union lines, under the pretense of being captured, to tell the commanders that there were no heavy bodies of troops within two miles. In the meanwhile he was massing everything for his tremendous blow. He ordered Cheatham's Corps and the Georgia State troops to hold fast on his right in a salient, which interposed between the two wings of Sherman's army, while Stewart and Hardee were instructed to attack with their corps by a division in echelon, crushing Thomas' left flank and driving the Army of the Cumberland backward into the muddy and difficult bed of Peach Tree Creek.

McElroy gets right the story of how the Federals learned of the Confederate army's command change. On July 19, a spy (possibly Milton Glass or J. C. Moore) brought out the Atlanta Appeal *of July 18, and Sherman thus learned of the Confederate army's change of commanders (Wilbur G. Kurtz, "A Federal Spy in Atlanta,"* Atlanta Constitution Magazine, *June 8, 1930, pp. 5, 14).*

The National Tribune *editor, however, distorts Jefferson Davis's complex relationship with Joseph E. Johnston, which at the start of the war had been amicable. After Manassas, Davis had given Johnston command of the main Confederate army in Virginia. After the Peninsula and Vicksburg Campaigns, though, Davis had become disenchanted with Johnston, but after Bragg's disastrous failure at Missionary Ridge, he still gave him command of the Army of Tennessee—hardly the act of an executive who "hated Johnston with all his vindictiveness."*

On the other hand, McElroy is right in referring to the president's "persistence in keeping Gen. Bragg in command after his repeated failures": Perryville, Murfreesboro and the sluggish pursuit after Chickamauga.

Bragg's alleged hatred of Johnston for "his intellectual and professional superiority" is not commonly seen in the literature, and it is not sustained by the facts. Bragg graduated from West Point fifth in his class; Johnston ranked thirteenth in his. Both men went into the army. When Bragg resigned in 1856, he had risen to lieutenant colonel—the same rank Johnston held at the time.

McElroy is on firmer ground concerning the argument between Davis and Johnston about launching an offensive into Tennessee in the spring of '64. The general maintained that the enemy forces were more numerous and in a strong position at Chattanooga; the country was rough; and he had insufficient subsistence and transportation. Johnston argued it was better to stand and await the enemy's advance—which is what he did.

McElroy clearly takes Joe Johnston's side in referring to the Richmond authorities' increasing alarm at his retreats from Dalton, Resaca, Cassville, Allatoona, Dallas, and Kennesaw. It was logical for McElroy to quote The Third Year of the War *(1865), written by Edward A. Pollard, who as an editor of the* Richmond Examiner *had voiced persistent criticism of Davis and his administration.*

The editor is correct as to the strength of the Army of Tennessee when Johnston handed it over to Hood on July 18. He does not, however, mention that during May 1864, the administration sent Johnston about 24,000 reinforcements: Lt. Gen. Leonidas Polk's Army of Mississippi, garrisons from Savannah and Mobile, plus other commands (E. C. Dawes, "The Confederate Strength in the Atlanta Campaign" in Robert U. Johnson and Clarence C. Buel, eds., Battles and Leaders of the Civil War, *4 vols. [New York: Century Co., 1888], 4:281-283).*

McElroy appropriately criticizes Johnston's correspondence with Richmond. A year before the Atlanta Campaign had even begun, a War Department clerk in Richmond entered in his diary that Johnston, then a western theater commander, "has written another of his brief, unsatisfactory, almost captious letters" (March 22, 1863) and "has written another sharp captious letter" (April 12, 1863). (Edward Younger, ed., Inside the Confederate Government: The Diary of Robert Hill Garlick Kean *[New York: Oxford University Press, 1957], 46, 50). (N.B.: captious is defined as critical, fault-finding, quibbling and carping.)*

But our author is off the mark in stating that Johnston hardly expected to be relieved. As early as June 24, Senator Louis Wigfall of Texas—something of a foe of President Davis, hence something of a friend of Johnston—warned the general that officials in Richmond were so disillusioned by his retreating there was talk of relieving him.

Moreover, distressed by Johnston's "brief, unsatisfactory" telegrams (Kean's words), on July 9, Davis sent his military advisor, Bragg, from Richmond to Atlanta to confer with Johnston and report back on the situation. Bragg arrived on the 13th and immediately wired, "indications seem to favor an entire evacuation of this place" (OR *38, pt. 5, 878).*

Bragg stayed in Atlanta July 13-15, meeting with Johnston and his key officers. McElroy accurately quotes Bragg's wire to Davis of the 15th (OR *38, pt. 5, 881). Bragg spent considerable time with Lieutenant General Hood and probably coaxed him to write the letter correctly quoted above* (OR *38, pt. 5, 879-880), which Bragg sent by train back to the capital.*

Before it could reach there, however, an alarmed Jefferson Davis determined that Johnston had to go. On the 17th, he therefore had Secretary of War James A. Seddon send the telegram that McElroy again quotes correctly (OR *38, pt. 5, 885).*

As a Johnston loyalist, McElroy faithfully quotes the general's memoir, Narrative of Military Operations *(1874), in which Johnston claims to have had a plan to attack Sherman's forces just about the time he was relieved of command. Most historians today, though, don't believe this, and assume Johnston was fabricating a narrative to make him look better in history. McElroy does not point out that on July 16, two days after his cabinet had voted unanimously that Johnston must be fired, Davis gave him one more chance to save his job by asking for a statement of his plans and intentions. In his reply, Johnston did not mention a Peachtree Creek attacking battle but instead stated that he intended for the Georgia militia to hold Atlanta while he maneuvered his army "freer and wider"* (OR *38, pt. 5, 883). Davis could only infer this as a hint of evacuating Atlanta.*

On the basis of all this, historian Albert Castel concludes, "rarely if ever has a military commander striven harder to persuade the head of his government that he is incapable of defeating by his own efforts the army he opposes" (Castel, Decision in the West: The Atlanta Campaign of 1864 *[Lawrence: University Press of Kansas, 1992], 329).*

The quote by Union general Jacob D. Cox, who commanded a division during the Atlanta Campaign, is from his Atlanta *(Dayton OH: Morningside, 1987 [1882], 148-149).*

McElroy accurately describes events in the field. By nightfall of July 17, all seven infantry corps in Sherman's army group had gotten across the Chattahoochee. Major General John Palmer's XIV Corps advanced on the Federal right flank, nearest the Chattahoochee. Major General Joseph Hooker's XX Corps held Thomas's center. Major General O. O Howard's IV Corps formed the left. Major General James B. McPherson's Army of the Tennessee (XV, XVI, and XVII Corps) approached Atlanta from the east, tearing up the Georgia Railroad as it went. Schofield's Army of the Ohio/XXIII Corps was northeast of the city, between Thomas and McPherson.

Confederate cavalry burned the three bridges over Peachtree Creek, which, as McElroy states, was not very deep but whose steep embankments made crossing difficult for the Federal infantry. The creek was only two or three miles north of the strong Confederate fortifications encircling Atlanta.

McElroy's account of how the Northern troops bridged the stream is a valuable element of his article. He focuses on Brig. Gen. Thomas J. Wood's division of the IV Corps (including Brig. Gen. William B. Hazen's 2nd Brigade and Col. Frederick Knefler's 3rd), but during July 19 Brig. Gen. John W. Geary's 2nd Division of the XX Corps, as well as Brig. Gen. Jefferson C. Davis's 2nd Division of the XIV Corps and Brig. Gen. Absalom Baird's 3rd Division of the XIV also crossed Peachtree Creek.

Robert D. Jenkins covers the "sharp action" at Greenbone Creek—called the battle of Moore's Mill, fought between Col. Caleb Dilworth's and Brig. Gen. Daniel Reynolds's Arkansas Brigade on the afternoon of July 19—in To the Gates of Atlanta: From Kennesaw Mountain to Peach Tree Creek, 1-19 July 1864 *(Macon: Mercer University Press, 2015), 208-248.*

As we shall see, it was the two-mile gap between Thomas's left and Schofield's right, northeast of the city—and the Confederate cavalry's discovery of it—that gave General Hood his idea for an attacking battle against Thomas's infantry, just after it had gotten south of Peachtree Creek.

Today, historians are divided on whether to accept Johnston's claim that he planned to attack at Peachtree Creek and that he imparted this idea to Hood before he left Atlanta on the evening of July 19 (Stephen Davis, Texas Brigadier to the Fall of Atlanta: John Bell Hood *[Macon: Mercer University Press, 2019], 274-276). Generally, Johnston's biographers side with him, while Hood's do not. Recent historians (e.g., Castel, Woodworth) dismiss Johnston's claim, although as far back as 1953 Stanley Horn reasoned, "There is strong suspicion that the plans of which he [Johnston] wrote so confidently in 1874 were the product of reflection after the event" (Horn,* The Army of Tennessee: A Military History *[Norman: University of Oklahoma Press, 1953), 348).*

Hood's attacking battle at Peachtree Creek was set for July 20. His plan called for Hardee to lead off the assault from the right, committing his divisions one after another in echelon, as McElroy states. This was the same battle plan Lee had followed on the second day of Gettysburg.

*The author's claim that Hood employed "a ruse" on July 20 is sustained by the campaign report of Brig. Gen. John W. Geary, dated September 15, 1864. After Geary ordered the 33rd New Jersey forward as skirmishers, he wrote, "I went forward to the hill to reconnoiter . . . . On my way I met 3 prisoners, sent in from the skirmish line. They were quite communicative, saying that there were no large bodies of their troops within two miles" (*OR *38, pt. 2, 138). It is clear that John McElroy had done his homework in writing this piece; volume 38, part 2 of the* OR *was published in 1891.*

34

Union General Johnson Surveys Events, July 20-September 2

Richard W. Johnson, "How Atlanta Fell. Gen. R. W. Johnson's Reminiscences of a Ceaseless Struggle"

(May 13, 1897, p. 3)

Brigadier General Richard W. Johnson commanded the 1st Division, XIV Corps during the Atlanta Campaign.

EDITOR NATIONAL TRIBUNE: The march from Chattanooga to Atlanta was one continuous battle. It might almost be said that during those long months of combat which culminated in the capture of Atlanta and northern Georgia, like the Israelites of old, we followed a cloud by day and a pillow of flame by night.

For in that time Dalton, Resaca, Kenesaw, New Hope Church, Pickett's Mills, Peach Tree Creek, Jonesboro, Altoona [*Allatoona, post-Atlanta, fought October 5, 1864*], and all those other crimson names of battle, had been traced bloodily into the history of our devoted army. Every day had the smoke-cloud of battle kissed the heavens, and each night had flamed and flashed with the lament light of our blazing guns, and we had followed that smoke-cloud and those blazing guns over a hundred fields of strife, until the old flag floated in exultation over the great "Gate City" of the South.

I will begin my reminiscence on July 20, 1864, when our army was in position on Peach Tree Creek. The morning was a beautiful one, the sun rising in a cloudless sky. While riding along my lines I met Col. Mackay, of Gen. Sherman's staff. I had known him in Texas, years before, and he was well acquainted with Hood. He said to me:

"We are going to have a hard battle to-day."

I asked him why he thought so, and he replied:

"I have just seen an Atlanta paper which contains an order placing Hood in command; and" said Mackay, "a man who will bet a thousand dollars without having a pair in his hand will fight when he has the troops with which to do it."

Sure enough, about 3 o'clock that same afternoon Hood moved his army out, as if forming on parade, and when all was in readiness let loose his "dogs of war."

The main portion of his army was thrown against our left, his extreme right being opposite to my left brigade, commanded by that brave and gallant soldier,

Col. A. G. McCook, of the 2d Ohio. My other brigades and the two other divisions of the Fourteenth Corps—Davis's and Baird's—were not engaged.

The assault was a desperate one, and the casualties great on both sides. Hooker's Corps, immediately on my left, suffered most heavily. Hood was finally repulsed and fell back on his intrenchments. When the smoke of battle had lifted, I went over to see Hooker, and he said:

"They put me in a place where they supposed I would have no fighting, but Joe Hooker cannot be kept out when fighting is going on."

His loss was about fifteen hundred. In this battle my loss was light, but my Adjutant-General, Capt. E. T. Wells, was dangerously wounded. I had attached to my division an Illinois battery, commanded by Capt. Dilger, an officer of the Prussian army. It was said that he, in company with another young Prussian officer, came to this country to witness war, and that they might see both sides they cast lots for choice. Dilger chose the Federal side and his friend joined the Confederates.

Through certain influence he secured the command of Battery C of Illinois artillery. Dilger dressed in buckskin, and was known throughout the army as "Leather Breeches." He was a gallant fellow, and when an engagement took place generally rushed his battery out to the skirmish-line. I was in constant fear that through his rashness the battery might be captured, so I had him instructed not to go in front of the main line unless ordered.

In the battle of the 20th, regardless of my orders, he moved forward to the front line, and had several of his cannoneers killed by the enemy's sharpshooters. After the battle I sent for him, and said:

Capt. Dilger, you violated my orders in going too far to the front and in doing so you have lost some of your men." To this he replied: "No, no, General, I did not lose any men."

I told him it had been reported to me that several of his men had been picked off by the enemy's sharpshooters.

"Oh, yes," said he; "mit dem leetle balls."

Belonging to the artillery, he did not count a man killed unless by a cannon-ball or shell. He did not again return to his own country, but remained in the United States. While Gen. Palmer was Governor of Illinois "Leather Breeches" was his Adjutant-General.

On July 22 Hood made another sortie, this time striking our extreme left. Again the losses were heavy. It was on this occasion that McPherson fell. As soon as his death was known Gen. John A. Logan took command, and by his good judgment showed himself to be a splendid soldier and an able commander. A few days after this battle Gen. O. O. Howard was assigned to the command of McPherson's Army.

Sherman decided on the movement of his army to the right [*meaning, marching Howard's Army of the Tennessee from its position east of the city, behind Thomas' to the north of it, then south, heading past the western reaches of Atlanta, aiming to break Hood's last supply line, the Macon & Western Railroad.*] It seems that his movement was not known to Hood. [*General Johnson is incorrect: Howard's march began before dawn of July 27; Hood knew of it within hours and planned a counterstroke.*] On July 28 he moved out on the Lick Skillet road to attack our right. Here he encountered the same troops he had fought on the 22d, and with about the same result.

This was Howard's first battle with his new command, and so well did he manage it that his army was convinced that the brave McPherson had a worthy successor. Hood and his army were driven back into Atlanta, and he sent a telegram to Richmond, in which he said:

"I have fought a bloody battle on the Lick Skillet road, but I still hold the road." [*Hood's exact phrasing in his telegram to Richmond, the evening of July 28 was, "About 1:30 o'clock a sharp engagement ensued with no decided advantage to either side. We still occupy the Lick Skillet road"* (OR *38, pt. 5, 917). Actually, the Confederate attack in this battle of Ezra Church was easily repulsed by Howard's troops, who after the battle still held the key Lick Skillet Road crossroads near the Methodist chapel.*]

True, he held the road, but it was the end of it which was lost in the streets of Atlanta [*meaning, the road running east from the chapel into the city suburbs*]. This was a bloody engagement. I passed over the field before the dead were buried, and could easily trace the line-of-battle of the Louisiana Tigers by the dead of that organization who fell in the line. The losses did not seem near so great at any other points of the battlefield. It was here that it was said a Federal officer called out:

"Johnny, how many more men have you?"

The answer came back:

"Enough for one more killin'."

To pass over a field of battle and then visit the hospitals will convince anyone that, refine war as much as possible, still it is cruel, bloody work. After a few more unimportant engagements Hood evacuated Atlanta, and our victorious army entered the city....Gen. R. W. JOHNSON, U.S.A.

General Johnson relates his conversation with Colonel Mackay ("without having a pair in his hand") in his memoir, A Soldier's Reminiscences in Peace and War *(1886). A variant appears in Lloyd Lewis's biography of Sherman (1932): "Through the Federal ranks went the story that a Kentucky colonel had come up to tell Sherman how in a poker game, 'I seed Hood bet $2,500 with nary a pair in his hand'" (383).*

35

Hood Plans His Attack at Peachtree Creek

John B. Hood, "Advance and Retreat. XII"

(May 3, 1906, p. 8)

After his disastrous Tennessee Campaign, November-December 1864, John B. Hood was demoted by the C.S. Senate from full general to lieutenant general. He signs himself with that rank for this article, one of 26 installments printed by the Tribune, *February 15-June 21, 1906, from his memoir,* Advance and Retreat. *The book was published a year after Hood's death from yellow fever in New Orleans, August 1879.*

On the night of the 18th and morning of the 19th, I formed line of battle facing Peach Tree Creek; the left rested near Pace's Ferry road, and the right covered Atlanta. I was informed on the 19th that Thomas was building bridges across Peach Tree Creek; that McPherson and Schofield were well over toward, and even on, the Georgia Railroad, near Decatur. I perceived at once that the Federal commander had committed a serious bunder in separating his corps or armies by such distance as to allow me to concentrate the main body of our army upon his right wing, whilst his left was so far removed as to be incapable of rendering timely assistance. General Sherman's violation of the established maxim that an army should always be held well within hand, or its detachments within easy supporting distance, afforded one of the most favorable occasions for complete victory which could have been offered; especially as it presented an opportunity, after crushing his right wing, to throw our entire force upon his left. In fact, such a blunder affords a small army the best, if not the sole, chance of success when contesting with a vastly superior force.

Line of battle having been formed, Stewart's Corps was in position on the left, Hardee's in the center, and Cheatham's on the right. Orders were given to Generals Hardee and Stewart to observe closely and report promptly the progress of Thomas in the construction of bridges across Peach Tree Creek and the passage of troops. General Cheatham was directed to reconnoiter in front of his left; to erect, upon that part of his line, batteries so disposed as to command the entire space between his left and Peach Tree Creek, in order to completely isolate McPherson and Schofield's forces from those of Thomas; and, finally, to thoroughly intrench his line. This object accomplished, and Thomas having partially crossed the creek and made a lodgment on the east side within the pocket formed by Peach Tree Creek and the Chattahoochee River, I determined to attack him with two corps—Hardee's and Stewart's, which constituted the main body of the Confederate Army—and thus, if possible, crush Sherman's right wing, as we drove it into the narrow space between the creek and the river.

Maj.-Gen. G. W. Smith's Georgia State troops were posted on the right of Cheatham, and it was impossible for Schofield or McPherson to assist Thomas without recrossing Peach Tree Creek in the vicinity of Decatur, and making on the west side a detour which necessitated a march of not less than 10 or 12 miles, in order to reach Thomas' bridges across this creek. I immediately assembled the three corps commanders, Hardee, Stewart, and Cheatham, together with Maj.-Gen. G. W Smith, commanding Georgia State troops, for the purpose of giving orders for battle on the following day, the 20th of July.

Hood's Plans.

I here quote from my official report written soon after these events:

"On the morning of the 19th the dispositions of the enemy were substantially as follows:

'The Army of the Cumberland, under Thomas, was in the act of crossing Peach Tree Creek. This creek, forming a considerable obstacle to the passage of an army, runs in a northeasterly [sic: westerly] direction, emptying into the Chattahoochee River near the railroad crossing. The Army of the Ohio, under Schofield, was also about to cross east of the Buckhead road. The Army of the Tennessee, under McPherson, was moving on the Georgia Railroad at Decatur. Finding it impossible to hold Atlanta without giving battle, I determined to strike the enemy while attempting to cross this stream. My troops were disposed as follows: Stewart's Corps on the left, Hardee's in the center, and Cheatham's on the right intrenched. My object was to crush Thomas' Army before he could fortify himself, and then turn upon Schofield and McPherson. To do this, Cheatham was ordered to hold his left on the creek, in order to separate Thomas's army from the forces on his (Thomas's) left. Thus I should be able to throw two corps, Stewart's and Hardee's, against Thomas. Specific orders were carefully given these Generals, in the presence of each other, as follows: The attack was to begin at 1 p. m..; the movement was to be by division, en echelon from the right, at a distance of about 150 yards; the effort to be to drive the enemy back to the creek, and then toward the river, within a narrow space formed by the river and creek; everything on our side of the creek to be taken at all hazards, and to follow up as our success might permit. Each of these Generals was to hold a division in reserve.

Instructing the Corps Commanders.

The three corps commanders, together with General G. W. Smith, were assembled not only for the purpose of issuing to them orders for the battle, but with the special design to deliver most explicit instructions in regard to their respective duties. I sought to "make assurance double sure" by direct interrogatory; each was asked whether or not he understood his orders. All replied in the affirmative. I was very careful in this respect, inasmuch as I had learned from long experience that no measure is more important, upon the eve of battle, than to make certain, in the presence of the commanders, that each thoroughly comprehends his orders. The usual discretion allowed these officers in no manner diminishes the importance of this precaution.

I also deemed it of equal moment that each should fully appreciate the imperativeness of the orders then issued, by reason of the certainty that our troops would encounter hastily constructed works thrown up by the Federal troops, which had been foremost to cross Peach Tree Creek. Although a portion of the enemy would undoubtedly be found under cover of temporary breastworks, it was equally certain a larger portion would be caught in the act of throwing up such works, and just in that state of confusion to enable our forces to rout them by a bold and persistent attack. With these considerations I timed the assault at 1 p. m., so as to surprise the enemy in their unsettled condition.

Early on July 20, McPherson's Union troops marching from east of Atlanta had gotten so close to Hood's defensive lines that he had to order his entire line to shift a mile and a half to the right, so that Cheatham's infantry and Wheeler's cavalry could better contain the Federals' advance. This movement consumed several hours; Hood's hoped-for attack on Thomas's army, set for 1:00 p.m., did not begin until Hardee's infantry attacked around 3:45, maybe 4 o'clock.

36

"A chaos of riderless horses"

John McElroy, "The Battle of Peachtree Creek"

(May 20, 1909, p. 2)

The National Tribune *could only print what the veterans sent in. Of the dozens of pieces it published about Peachtree Creek, almost none touches on how the battle began with the attack against Thomas's left by Hardee's corps—the divisions of Major Generals William B. Bate, William H. T. Walker, and George E. Maney. (Hardee, for some reason, held Cleburne's division, his best, in reserve.)*

To give us the big picture, as usual, we turn to John McElroy's long narrative on the Atlanta Campaign. The editor was thorough, if not encyclopedic (and accordingly, at times, a little dull). As the author states, about a mile south of Peachtree Creek, Johnston's engineers had overseen slaves' digging of an outer defense line running roughly seven miles west-east, and another two to the south, ending near the Georgia Railroad. McElroy mentions Peavine Creek, which flows into Peachtree Creek from the southeast, near the salient created by the southward shift of the defense line.

From the confluence of Peachtree Creek and the Chattahoochee River to Decatur is ten miles as the crow flies—a distance lengthened by the salient in the Confederate outer defense line that McElroy mentions. McPherson was marching in from Decatur (Sherman's left) and Thomas, holding the right, was at Peachtree Creek near the river. Schofield was in between. Thomas tried to bridge the gap between his army and Schofield's by sending two divisions of the IV Corps in the latter's direction. Still, there existed a two-mile gap that left Thomas's left flank open to attack—the "serious blunder" Hood writes of, above.

By mid-afternoon on July 19, the seven infantry divisions of Thomas's Army of the Cumberland were south of Peachtree Creek in an approximately four-mile line stretching from its right (Maj. Gen. John Palmer's XIV Corps) to its left—Brig. Gen. John Newton's division of the IV Corps, astride today's Peachtree Road. A half-mile westward is Collier's Mill (on Tanyard Branch, which flows north into the creek). Nearby Collier Road runs west from Peachtree Road. Confederates marching north out of their works would have to cross the road to get at the Federals posted north of it.

John McElroy was not afraid to editorialize, as he does in the start of this article stating his opinion about Davis's decision to replace General Johnston with Hood.

A FALSE POLICY.

The supersession of Johnston by Hood is impossible to reconcile with Mr. Jefferson Davis's claims to high military ability. Hood was represented to be another Stonewall Jackson, but the time for Stonewall Jackson-like achievements was passed. Union Generals and Union soldiers were not nearly so badly shaken by flank attacks as they had been in their earlier and greener years. It must be said that the Union soldiers themselves were never as profoundly disturbed by these attacks as their commanders. McClellan, Pope and Hooker lost their nerve entirely under a sudden assault from an unexpected quarter, but the Union soldiers would receive these attacks, and usually beat them off, as at Gaines' Mill, White Oak Swamp, Bristoe Station and Gettysburg. Their worst effect was to shake the confidence of the Union Generals themselves. McClellan and Hooker could then think of nothing but retreat. Grant, Sherman, Sheridan, Meade and Thomas were of different metal.

Gen. John B. Hood had early distinguished himself when a Lieutenant serving against the Apaches, by his disposition to come into close quarters with the enemy and maintain a stubborn fight with him. He was a man of great determination, of high courage, but of moderate abilities. In spite of the vehemence and pertinacity of his flank attacks, he had very few substantial successes to boast of. It is true that he had demoralized [*Union Brig. Gen. William B.*] Franklin at the White House Landing by a sudden sharp attack; but, then, everybody demoralized Franklin. At Gettysburg Hood made what he hoped would win him lasting renown, but was beaten back by an inferior force in the decisive struggle for the possession of Little Round Top. He had succeeded no better at Chickamauga, while his assaults during the Atlanta campaign had never succeeded even when chance favored him. Still, Mr. Davis and his military adviser, Gen. Braxton Bragg, thought it best to put him in command in place of Johnston, and dash out against the Union force the army which that able commander had carefully conserved behind strong defenses. As said before, the Union soldiers wanted nothing better than that their enemy should come out in the open and fight them. Hood was now about to oblige them.

The Battle of Peachtree Creek.

Circumstances were singularly favorable for Hood to signalize the advent of command by a crushing victory. The outer line of works which Johnston had prepared began at the railroad about two miles from the river, and ran along about six miles to the northeast. They were on a ridge forming the boundary of the valley of Peachtree Creek, and near the junction of Pea Vine Creek with that stream, the intrenchments turned sharply toward the southeast to follow Pea Vine Creek until they crossed the [*Georgia*] Railroad, entering Atlanta from the east. This sudden change in the direction of the fortifications made a sharp salient, which separated the Union line and left the two flanks out of reach of mutual support. In other words, the Armies of the Tennessee and Ohio, with two divisions of the Army of the Cumberland, were to the eastward, pressing down toward Atlanta and the railroad. They were the more anxious to destroy the railroad, because of Grant's fears that the Confederates who had been operating in the Shenandoah Valley had been sent to reinforce Johnston with 20,000 men. McPherson destroyed the railroad for seven or eight miles east of Atlanta.

On the southwest side of this salient was the Army of the Cumberland minus two strong divisions. The army had crossed Peachtree Creek by various fords and bridges, and had not yet formed a complete connecting line. Hood not only had a thoro acquaintance with the country, but he had his men well in hand, so that he could hope to move out of his works and strike and crush the isolated divisions of the Army of the Cumberland, roll them up one after another without their being able to help each other until he had finally forced them, a confused, broken mass, into the miry bottom at the junction of the Peachtree Creek with the Chattahoochee.

The organization of the Confederate army had been somewhat changed. Gen. A. P. Stewart had succeeded to the command of the corps made vacant by the death of Bishop Leonidas Polk, and Gen. [*Benjamin F. "Frank"*] Cheatham had succeeded to the command of the corps formerly commanded by Hood. Besides this, there was a large body of Georgia militia under the command of Gustavus W. Smith, an officer who had aroused the highest expectations in the minds of the Confederates in the beginning of the war, but who soon fell under the displeasure of Mr. Davis, and had been retired to the rear since the Peninsular campaign, during which he had held a highly important command.

Hood's plan was for Cheatham and Smith to hold the east side of these defenses that stretched along Pea Vine Creek, and check the advance of McPherson and Schofield, while Hardee and Stewart, issuing from their works, should fall upon the divisions of the Army of the Cumberland. This was to begin by an attack on Newton's Division of the Fourth Corps, isolated from the rest at Collier's Bridge.

On the morning of July 20 Stewart, with his corps, was holding the extreme left of Hood's line, with Hardee in the center and Cheatham and Smith on the extreme right. Thomas was pushing the heads of his columns cautiously and steadily forward, keeping them as much as possible within touch of one another. Each of the divisions was moving in the formation of two brigades at the front and one in reserve. Besides these divisions, 10 brigades had been sent across Peachtree Creek to facilitate manuvers, but necessarily had to go from one part of the Union line to another, involving recrossing the bridge and making a wide circuit, whereas the enemy in front had a far easier and shorter line of communication between the various parts.

The Attack on Newton.

Gen. Newton, with one division of the Fourth Corps, after crossing at Collier's Mill, had pushed forward toward the crossroad, with his left flank reaching toward Clear Creek. Newton, an engineer officer, was ever cautious, and had, by a temporary halt, covered his front with barricades of various kinds. He had one battery on the road in his center and another in reserve. The next division to him was Ward's of the Twentieth Corps, but at that time Ward had not come up into position, and had not been able to get his artillery across. Newton's line had assumed a singular shape, that of the capital letter T [*upside-down T, as two of Newton's brigades faced south and Brig. Gen. Luther P. Bradley's, in reserve, formed the T-stem*]. Bradley's Brigade was along the main Atlanta road [*today's Peachtree, which runs from downtown north to Buckhead*], forming the upright of the letter and facing to the left [*east, as Newton's was Thomas' left-flank division*]. Wagner's Brigade commanded by Col. [*John W.*] Blake, 40th Ind., was the left half of the horizontal top line, while [*Brig. Gen. Nathan*] Kimball's Brigade was the right half [*aligned from Blake's right to the west, just north of Collier Road*].

While Kimball's and Blake's Brigades were building a rail barricade the skirmishing in front of them began, rising with that sharpness of sound which at once arrested attention. Then came the wild, piercing, ominous rebel yell from the throats of thousands rushing out from the cover of the woods. It was a portentous wave of men, which did not seem to march out of the woods, but simply burst out, as a wave dashes upon the seashore. The skirmishers, skilful soldiers as they were, saw the futility of attempting to stem this tide, and ran back to their regiments. The enemy was Walker's splendid division, charging straight for Newton's front, while Bate's Division passed to the flank to strike at the rear and gain the bridge.

By a lucky chance Capt. [*Wilbur F.*] Goodspeed, Newton's Chief of Artillery, had been laboring to get 10 guns across the bridge from the north to the south side of the creek, and was succeeding. It was at once seen how urgently the guns were needed, and Goodspeed rushed them forward to the point to where they could open at 70 yards with canister. Never was artillery more welcome to infantrymen, and the rhythmic thunder of those guns was sweetest music to the ears of the startled men of Newton's command. It was a joy to look up, while loading their muskets, and see, as the powder smoke drifted away, the great ragged holes torn in the enemy's line by the hurtling, slaying canister. Four guns of Smith's 1st Mich.

Battery [*Capt. Luther R. Smith's Battery I, 1st Michigan*] secured a fine position on the right, where they could rake the advance, and presently thru the drifting smoke the formidable wave was seen to be a chaos of riderless horses, disorganized regiments and shattered brigades. What 20 minutes before had seemed a miracle of human power was now largely a mass of dead or wounded men. The men, infantry and artillery, whom Sheridan had drilled and commanded had shown splendidly the excellence of their schooling.

During this critical time Thomas was present, as he had a habit of being, at the nerve center of the battle, and gave personal direction to the artillery, complimenting Capt. Goodspeed upon his work, and when the repulse was assured said a few words of praise to the infantry which they prized above rubies.

Ward's Advance.

While all this was occurring Ward's Division was lying in the hollow below and further to the right and rear. For a moment it seemed to him as if Newton's Division was yielding to the heavy attack, and without waiting for orders the brigade commanders rushed forward to attack the assailants in flank and relieve Newton. The skirmishers in front of the division were commanded by Lieut.-Col. [*Edward*] Bloodgood, 22d Wis., but the solid ranks were soon on the heels of the advance. There was a sharp, bitter fight for 15 minutes, but the enemy had to yield, and when they did so Ward's Division had seven battle flags wrested from their stubborn foes. Coburn's and Wood's Brigades had carried the left of the line, while Harrison's did the same on the right, and all three saw the back of the last of their enemies disappear into the woods. With the battle flags came 154 prisoners.

The Attack on Geary

The tied of battle now rolled over to the left across Shoal Creek [*now Tanyard Branch*] and upon Geary's Division. Geary's left was on open ground, covered by a ravine leading down to Shoal Creek. There he put [*Col. Charles*] Candy's Brigade and the artillery of the division. [*Col. Patrick H.*] Jones's Brigade was on Candy's right, with a heavily-wooded country before it, and [*Col. David*] Ireland's Brigade was in the rear of Jones. Geary's men had time to put up a slight barricade. The enemy tried to interpose between Ward's right and Geary's left, but there they came into contact with Geary's batteries, as well as the still more destructive infantry fire both in front and in flank.

Tho the fight lasted only a short time, the slaughter was unusually heavy even for that later and harder fighting period of the war. A portion of the battle reached the extreme right [sic: *left*] of Palmer's Corps, with the brigade of Anson McCook being sharply engaged and losing quite severely. The rest of the Fourteenth Corps did not suffer any loss.

Gen. Ward's Report.

Gen. W. T. Ward says:

"The first line of the rebels was shattered in a few minutes; my advance was hardly checked a minute; the enemy had evidently believed themselves in a gap between Geary and the Fourth Army Corps. Meeting my line of battle seemed to completely addle their brains. Their first line broke, mixing up with the second line; they were now in the wildest confusion, firing in all directions, some endeavoring to get away, some undecided what to do, others rushing into our lines. I still advanced my men, keeping up a steady fire, crossed a deep ravine to gain the next hill to make good my connections with Gen. Newton on my left and Gen. Geary on my right, and also to gain a position which commanded the open country for 600 yards in advance. Once they had made a feeble effort to rally, but they were too badly broken. They succeeded in making a slight attack, but it was not a concerted movement; it commenced on the left, running at intervals toward the right. It only resulted in giving us more prisoners, two more battle-flags, and swelling the already frightful number of rebel dead and wounded. They then fled to the woods, leaving dead, wounded and arms in our possession. I took up the chosen position, and commenced to fortify it. The enemy was rallying his men in the woods, keeping up a constant fire on our lines, and made several attempts to charge. We returned the fire vigorously; repulsed the charges before they got far out of the woods. This was kept up briskly until 6 p,m., when the fire began to abate, but a brisk skirmishing fire was kept up until dark. The Ambulance Corps worked faithfully all night, carrying off the wounded of both armies."

Gen. Geary's Report.

Gen. J. W. Geary says:

"I have never seen more heroic fighting. For three hours the fury of the Battle along our entire line could not have been surpassed. Then the tempest of sounds and missiles began gradually to decrease, and by dark nothing but heavy skirmishing remained. Gen. Hood had massed the greater part of his entire army in this furious assault upon a single corps (and that one the smallest in our army), and was whipped back to the ground he had left in the morning. It is with a feeling of unusual admiration for the troops under my command that I record the history of their part in the battle of Peachtree Creek. Attacked by overwhelming numbers from front, right flank and rear, five regiments with the artillery held the key position while fighting terribly all the time. The rest of my command changed its front, formed a connected line, and threw themselves into the combat with such determination and valor that they overcame five times their number. This result was largely due to the fact that by changing my front in the manner described our troops delivered an effective and persistent cross-fire upon the enemy at the moment when they were flushed with the anticipation of victory, and supposing themselves entrapped, they retreated, broken and dismayed. This battle was a very remarkable one as a test of discipline and valor of our troops, and as the first defeat of the newly-appointed commander of the rebel army it was glorious in its results. The field everywhere bore the marks of the extreme severity of the contest, and recalled to my mind, in appearance, the scene of the conflict where the same division fought at Gettysburg. Not a tree or bush within our entire range, but bore the scars of battle. The appearance of the enemy as they charged upon our front across the cleared field was magnificent. Rarely has such a sight been presented in battle. Pouring out from the woods, they advanced in immense brown and gray masses (not lines), with flags and banners, many of them new and beautiful, while their general and staff officers were in plain view, with drawn sabers flashing in the light, galloping here and there as they urged their troops on to the charge. The rebel troops also seemed to rush forward with more than customary nerve and heartiness in the attack. This grand charge was Hood's inaugural, and his army came upon us that day full of high hope, confident that the small force in their front could not withstand them, but their ardor and confidence were soon shaken. My artillery, served with the utmost rapidity, even while receiving volley from the rear, poured out steady discharges of canister and shell, and we could see the great gaps in that compact mass of human beings as each shot tore thru their ranks. Those masses of the enemy that charged upon my right and rear reached at one time within a few yards of Bundy's Battery, but by the cool bravery of my officers and men were driven back. I cannot refrain from specially mentioning Maj. [*John A.*] Reynolds, Chief of Artillery of the corps, who, with Capt. [*Charles C.*] Aleshire, my own chief, was present on my line and rendered distinguished service throughout the severest portion of the battle."

THE LOSSES.

There are no means of knowing precisely what the losses were in these hotly contested little battles, into which both sides entered with the utmost determination and elan. The Confederates were animated by the expectation of inflicting a crippling blow on the Army of the Cumberland, and the Union soldiers at last saw their enemies come out from behind their intrenchments for a fight in the open. This was something that the Union soldiers had been earnestly praying for, and they went into the struggle with unusual spirit.

The official reports give the losses of the Army of the Cumberland, outside of Palmer's Corps, as 1,707 killed, wounded and missing. Strangely enough, Newton's Division only lost 100 of these, although it received the first brunt of the attack. It had had warning of the blow, and the defense with which it hastily covered itself seems to have been unusually efficient. Probably, also, its small loss was due to the terrific artillery fire directed by Thomas himself, which broke the force of the assault. Thomas was even seen to strike the battery horses with the flat of his sword to hurry them forward.

Ward's Division lost 550 killed, wounded and missing; Geary, 406, and Williams 580. These divisions fought in the open, and were attacked as they came into position. Of the total loss there were very few missing, of whom 165 were from Geary's Division alone, the result of the momentary confusion on the right, which was in the air at the opening of the engagement.

Nothing satisfactory can be learned of the Confederate losses, and the strongest factor in the statement is that Hood does not criticize Hooker's estimate of 4,400 killed and wounded in front of the Twentieth Corps alone. Geary reports having buried 409 Confederates in front of his division, tho it may be that this number included some killed in front of Ward's, since Ward makes no report. Williams merely reports that there was severe fighting in his front, but gives no numbers as to those whom he buried. If his division did as well there as it did at Gettysburg, the dead in his front must have been at least equal to those in Geary's front. Some 1200 of the enemy are reported as buried in front of Newton's Division, the impression being that this was far from all. Therefore, it would seem fair to assume that the Confederate dead was in the neighborhood of 1,000 with the wounded and prisoners carrying the total up to 6,000 or 7,000, which was the current report at the time.

Hood's Initial Failure.

Hood's absolute failure in this his first engagement after assuming command, and from which he had every reason to hope so much, must have been exceedingly depressing. Neither he nor his subordinates conceal the fact that this engagement was intended to be a decisive one, and the orders which went out and were transmitted down to the Colonels of regiments were to attack desperately, whatever might be in their front, and to push whatever success they made home to make the engagement the final one of the campaign. Savage as the fighting was at times, and headlong as were the attacks, they did not shake the Army of the Cumberland as a whole. The brunt of the fighting fell on four divisions only, with the strongest corps in the army—the Fourteenth Corps—hardly being touched. Yet these four divisions had each one held its ground without unusual difficulty, and there was at no time any possibility of a rolling up of the left flank, upon which Hood had confidently counted, from the weight and spirit of the assault which he launched against it. He had expected, and there were grounds for the expectation, that by throwing the weight of his army upon one division after another, he could break in succession the outstretched portions of the Army of the Cumberland and finally huddle it into a disastrous position in the swamps at the junction of the Peachtree Creek with the Chattahoochee. But he had not even forced back a single rod the extreme left of the army. This should have been, indeed, disheartening to him. Hood seeks to palliate his ill-success by saying that at a critical time in the fight he learned that the advance of the Armies of the Ohio and Tennessee were much more rapid than he had supposed. He thought it necessary to move Cheatham and the Georgia militia further to the east to arrest the flank movement and direct advance of Schofield and McPherson. To cover the Decatur Railroad Cheatham had to string out his men in a single line, so that one division covered a front of two miles.

Hood also blames Hardee for not attacking with sufficient determination, but the number of dead in front of Newton and Ward and the closeness with which they lay to the Union lines was sufficient answer to this. There was a feud between Hood and Hardee, and Hood was a bitter hater.

The men of Newton's, Ward's, Williams's and Geary's Divisions naturally took much pride in the success with which they had arrested Hood's impetuous advance. They had had nothing like the cover behind which the enemy had been sheltering themselves, and yet they withstood the attack with the greatest firmness, and inflicted a heavier loss upon their opponents than they themselves had suffered when attacking such strongly-built works as those at Kenesaw. It was mainly a man-to-man, open-field fight, a role which gave the Union soldiers the utmost confidence in themselves, and could not fail to be dispiriting to the Confederates.

McElroy's description of the battle is efficient, if a little spotty. Lt. Gen. William J. Hardee's corps held the Confederate right, and led off the attacking battle around 4:00 p.m.—a delay of three hours from Hood's desired starting time. Hardee's right-most division, Maj. Gen. William B. Bate's, advanced into the two-mile gap separating Newton's division from the other two IV Corps divisions off to the east. They were so far off Newton's flank that they never really became engaged. That left Hardee's next division, Maj. Gen. William H. T. Walker's, to launch the main attack against Newton, near the Peachtree Road. The Federals' high ground (today it's known as Cardiac Hill, from the Peachtree Road Race), their slight barricades, plus artillery support drove back Walker's troops in less than an hour. Maj. Gen. George E. Maney's division, advancing in echelon, achieved even less success.

Next came the turn for Lieutenant General A. Peter Stewart's corps (formerly Polk's), led off by Maj. Gen. William W. Loring's division. Brigadier General Winfield S. Featherston's brigade locked horns with Brigadier General William T. Ward's division west of Peachtree Road. After some initial gains and losing half their strength, Featherston's troops also fell back.

Though McElroy's article of 1909 came out nearly two decades after publication of the Official Records *volumes treating the Atlanta Campaign, his quoting of the reports of Generals Ward and Geary (vol. 38, pt. 2, 137-141, 327-329) would have been seen as an educational service for the veterans reading the* National Tribune.

Brigadier General Geary's remark that the Rebels attacking his line were "flushed with the anticipation of victory" reflects their initial success. Part of Brigadier General Thomas Scott's brigade attacked and took three Napoleon guns as they drove back the Federals. But a Union counterattack in turn forced a Confederate retreat. Geary's Gettysburg allusion reflects his earlier service as commander of a division in the Army of the Potomac's XII Corps. Later that year the XI and XII Corps were consolidated into the XX Corps and transferred west to the Army of the Cumberland.

Our author is definitely on the mark as to Union casualties. In Thomas's army on July 20, Newton's division, Hooker's XX Corps, and Palmer's XIV Corps (only slightly engaged), casualties totaled 1,733 (William D. Whipple, "Circular," July 28, 1864, OR *38, pt. 1, 174). McElroy is way off, though, in his assumption of 6,000-7,000 Confederate casualties at Peachtree Creek. Modern historians, such as Albert Castel, place Hood's losses at around 2,500 (Castel,* Decision in the West: The Atlanta Campaign of 1864 *[Lawrence: University Press of Kansas, 1992], 381). More recently, Robert D. Jenkins counts a slightly lower figure, 2,316 (Jenkins,* The Battle of Peach Tree Creek: Hood's First Sortie, 20 July 1864 *[Macon: Mercer University Press, 2013], 397).*

*Moreover, Geary exaggerates the "overwhelming numbers" attacking him. According to Hess, the two Confederate brigades (Scott's and Edward O'Neal's) carried 2,370 men into the fight; Geary had 3,000 engaged (*The Battle of Peach Tree Creek, *248, 253).*

McElroy's statement that General Thomas thwacked the backs of artillery horses with the flat of his sword is sustained by the literature (Francis F. McKinney, Education in Violence: The Life of George H. Thomas and the History of the Army of the Cumberland *[Chicago: Americana House, 1991 (1961)], 349).*

Our author correctly refers to Hood's having to shift Cheatham's Corps farther to the right to face McPherson's army marching in toward Atlanta from Decatur. The division-length shift affected Hood's entire line and led to his attack, originally set for 1:00 p.m. on July 20, to actually start around 3:30 or 4:00.

*McElroy's statement that Hood blamed Hardee for his failure at Peachtree Creek comes from Hood's campaign report (1865), in which he wrote, "Hardee failed to push the attack, as ordered (*OR *38, pt. 3, 630-631), and also from his memoir (1880), in which he alleged "the troops of Hardee—as their losses on that day indicate—did nothing more than skirmish with the enemy" (*Advance and Retreat, *171). Historians have generally not addressed the question of why Hardee held in reserve Cleburne's Division, arguably the best in the army, while sending forth into the fight Bate's, Walker's, and Maney's Divisions.*

John Bell Hood may have been, as McElroy claims, "a bitter hater," but it was William J. Hardee who asked President Davis to be transferred from Hood's army. Davis declined to do so during the campaign, but after the fall of Atlanta, agreed in mid-September to send Hardee to Savannah.

37

A Confederate's Account

J. P. Cannon, "Inside of Rebeldom"

(November 18; continued November 25, 1897, p. 7)

Southerners' capture of the 33rd New Jersey's flag during the battle of Peachtree Creek is a highlight in the following remembrance by Dr. J. P. Cannon, a private in the 27th Alabama, part of Scott's Brigade. Altogether, the National Tribune *published Cannon's memoir in 40 installments, October 7, 1897-April 13, 1899. The* National Tribune *Co. published the assembled series as a book in 1900.*

Brigadier General Geary had his three brigades stacked one behind another, with Col. Charles Candy's in front. Right to left were five infantry regiments and two batteries in this order: 147 PA, Sloan's By E PA Arty, 5 OH, Bundy's 13 NY By, 29 OH, 28 PA, and 66 OH. Some 300 yards in front, as Dr. Cannon writes, was the 33rd New Jersey.

Peach Tree Creek, Ga., July 20, 1864.—

The enemy has crossed the Chattahoochee and fortified in our front, while a column is moving around our right flank. Skirmishing was heavy all the morning, and everything indicated that a battle would be fought during the day. We all know that Gen. Hood was placed in command of this army for the express purpose of making a desperate effort to hold Atlanta, and while we have not the same confidence in his generalship that we had in Gen. Johnston, we have resolved that if there is a failure it shall not be our fault.

It is a fearful thing to charge an enemy in his works, especially when outnumbered two or three to one, but feeling that it had to be done we nerved ourselves up the point to do our whole duty. So when orders came to form in front of the breastworks we were ready. [*When General Hood succeeded Johnston on July 18, his army occupied an outer line of entrenchments a mile and a half north of Atlanta's main defensive perimeter, and an equal distance south of Peachtree Creek.*] The line being formed, we had to move half a mile or more to the right to fill a gap between us and Hardee's Corps.

This delayed us till 4 o'clock p.m., when we halted and Gen. Stewart made a little speech in which he informed us that we "were going to assault the enemy in his works, and we must carry everything, allowing no obstacle to stop us; that the fate of Atlanta probably depended on the result of this battle."

The order was to charge en echelon, by divisions, at intervals of 200 yards, so when the division on our right had gained the proper distance the command was given "By the right of companies to the front, march," and it was well that such was the order, for we could never have gone through that tangled mass of timber and brush in line-of-battle. It was a heavy timbered section and the trees had been felled, lapped and crossed until they presented an almost impassable barrier, but we finally made our way through the worst of it and were then halted and wheeled by the left flank into line-of-battle, being then under fire of the pickets.

The order to "fix bayonets, forward, double quick, march," was given. We raised the old rebel yell, and rushed on the works, but the yell was soon drowned by the roar of musketry and thunder of cannon, grape and canister, and minie-balls mowed great gaps in our ranks, but on we went until it seemed a hand-to-hand conflict was inevitable, when our boys began to waver and soon the line fell back under cover of a little hill, where we reformed our shattered columns and forward again with the same result.

The three gun battery was immediately in our front, and the enemy were massed in the ditch, and indeed it seemed like a forlorn hope to attempt to dislodge them, but having rested a short time we made the third charge and drove them from the works, capturing the three cannon and the flag of the 33d N.J., and planting our colors on the breastworks.

We thought the battle was won, and were rejoicing over what we supposed would result in a glorious victory, but, alas! Hardee's Corps was repulsed on our right, and in short time the Yankees were pouring a galling fire into us from front and flank, which, with an enfilading fire of artillery from our right, proved so destructive that we were ordered to retire, leaving our captured guns, but holding to the New Jersey flag, which we carried out as a trophy.

Sorrowfully the survivors retired to our breastworks, mourning the loss of many of our friends, but thankful that we had escaped. Thus Gen. Hood's first battle was a failure, with a loss of probably 4,000 or 5,000 men [*Hood's actual losses were 2,300 to 2,500*], but it was no fault of the troops on our part of the line, for Stewart's Corps literally obeyed his orders, carrying everything, and with proper support on the right could have driven the enemy across Peach Tree Creek.

One of Cannon's comrades in the 27th Alabama, John Abernathy, is credited with capturing the Jerseymen's colors (John G. Zinn, The Mutinous Regiment: The Thirty-Third New Jersey in the Civil War *[Jefferson NC: McFarland, 2005], 130).*

Earl J. Hess quoted Dr. Cannon's "it is a fearful thing" remark in The Battle of Peach Tree Creek: Hood's First Effort to Save Atlanta *(Chapel Hill: University of North Carolina Press, 2017),133.*

Dr. Cannon weaved his memoir into a history of his regiment that is repeatedly quoted by Robert D. Jenkins in The Battle of Peach Tree Creek: Hood's First Sortie, 20 July 1864 *(Macon: Mercer University Press, 2013).*

38

A Female Rebel at Peachtree Creek

J. F. Pettit, "Wounding of a Young Lady"

(April 7, 1910, p. 3)

W. W. Ewing, "Wounding a Young Lady"

(July 1, 1910)

J. F. Pettit, 335 West Broad Street, Hazleton, Pa., says that he enlisted for the first three months' service in the 6th Pa., and re-enlisted as Second Sergeant of Co. F, 147th Pa., in which he took part in Chancellorsville and Gettysburg, and then was sent West under Gen. Hooker to open up communications for Gen. Rosecrans at Chattanooga. Their (Gary's) [sic: *Geary's*] Division fought at Lookout Mountain, Mission Ridge and other battles under Gen. Sherman. He thinks his regiment should have the credit for saving the battle of Peach Tree Creek, and he remembers the young lady who was wounded in the fight. She was in the Confederate ranks, and was wounded in the charge that Hood made on the First Brigade, Second Division, Twentieth Corps. This division was the first in Atlanta and also first in Savannah. He would like to know what battery covered the Plank road leading to Fredericksburg on the night of May 2, 1863. That battery should be given the credit for Stonewall Jackson's wounds. Jackson's Orderly was wounded and left behind. Our men carried him to the Chancellorsville House.

Pettit's recollection of a Southern woman fighting at the battle of Peachtree Creek did not go unchallenged. W. W. Ewing wrote, "that young lady was a fine-featured young man."

However, Pettit's claim of female Rebels at Peachtree Creek has been accepted by historians. Lee Kennett quotes Union soldier Judson Austin's letter to his wife, written the day after the battle, on how he had found "a female dressed in men's clothes & a cartridge box on her side"; she had been shot in the chest but was "still alive & as gritty as any reb I ever saw" (Kennett, Marching Through Georgia: The Story of Soldiers and Civilians During Sherman's Campaign *[New York: HarperCollins, 1995], 45-46). DeAnne Blanton and Lauren M. Cook quote Austin, as well as Federal soldier James L. Dunn, who wrote his wife on July 22, "among the reble wounded we found several women in mens clothes also among the killed." The authors count at least four women among Hood's casualties at Peachtree Creek (Blanton and Cook,* They Fought Like Demons: Women Soldiers in the American Civil War *[Baton Rouge: Louisiana State University Press, 2002], 19-20).*

David P. Conyngham, the New York Herald *correspondent who accompanied Sherman's forces and who wrote* Sherman's March through the South *(1865), went further. He relates a conversation with a Northern soldier who had been captured at Peachtree Creek, including the story of a Confederate "she-major . . . strangely dressed; she wore a cap decked with feathers and gold lace, flowing pants, with a full kind of velvet coat coming just below her hips, and fastened with a rich crimson sash, and partly open at the bosom" (Conyngham,* Sherman's March through the South *[New York: Sheldon & Co. 1865], 194-96). Blanton and Cook correctly term Conyngham's anecdote as "clearly a tall tale," but cite it as a "northern veteran's picture of southern female militarism" (*They Fought Like Demons, *159). Robert D. Jenkins quotes the passage about the female major in* The Battle of Peach Tree Creek: Hood's First Sortie, 20 July 1864 *(Macon: Mercer University Press, 2013), 389, and adds the recollection of Pvt. Frederick N. Kollack (Co. B, 29th Pennsylvania) that among the Rebel prisoners taken at Peachtree Creek were "two females in uniform."*

39

Sherman's Blunder Gives Hood an Opportunity

J. R. Donaldson, "Sweeny's Fighters"

(May 19, 1898, p. 3)

Arguably General Sherman's biggest blunder in the Atlanta Campaign was sending Brig. Gen. Kenner Garrard's cavalry division off to wreck railroads on July 21.

On the 18th, Garrard's horsemen and some of McPherson's infantry had struck the Georgia Railroad east of Decatur. As they marched westward, they tore up more of the railroad—so thoroughly that the line to Augusta remained out of operation for the rest of the war.

That was not enough for Cump, however. On the 21st, he ordered Garrard to ride off to Covington, 35 miles east of Atlanta, burning railway bridges and destroying depots.

The problem, though, was that Garrard's division was guarding the left (southern) flank of McPherson's Army of the Tennessee. With his flank "in the air," Mac worried that the Rebels would launch a surprise attack. He consequently protested the order to Sherman, but to no avail. The commanding general wanted more track ripped, even if it endangered one of his armies.

Sure enough, after Garrard rode off in the early afternoon of July 21, Wheeler picked up on it and notified HQ, allowing General Hood—barely 24 hours after his repulse at Peachtree Creek—to plan just the kind of flank attack that McPherson feared.

At the time, the Army of Tennessee occupied an outer line of entrenchments north of Atlanta's main defensive perimeter, a mile south of Peachtree Creek. Hood's plan was for his troops to withdraw during the night of the 21st-22nd back into the main works. Hardee's Corps would keep marching southward, through the city and out of it, then turn northeast. Guided by Wheeler's cavalry, the troops would take position in McPherson's flank and rear before launching their assault.

Hood had multiple problems. An all-night march in late July heat would exhaust the troops, especially Cleburne's men, who had been fighting that morning at Leggett's Hill. Second, Hood unrealistically called for a dawn assault after (third) the infantry had trudged along a route that would eventually measure 13 miles. After Sherman refused to rescind his orders for Garrard's ride, McPherson began warning his corps commanders against a surprise attack from the south and deploying parts of the XVI and XVII Corps to receive it. In particular, he placed the division of Brig. Gen. Thomas W. Sweeny (XVI Corps) at the end of his line, facing south.

Hardee's four divisions deployed right to left: Bate, Walker, Cleburne, and Maney. Sweeny's division of the XVI was the first to be engaged, when Bate's Confederates attacked around noon on July 22.

It is here that our author's narrative begins.

EDITOR NATIONAL TRIBUNE: A recent article reminded me of experiences July 22, 1864, east of Atlanta, the day Gen. McPherson was killed.

Our division, Gen. Sweeny's, was on the reserve two miles in the rear of the heavy fighting that was going on [*at Leggett's Hill, but Bate's assault on Sweeny, around noon, actually preceded Cleburne's advance, which began about 1:15 p.m., according to Gary Ecelbarger,* The Day Dixie Died: The Battle of Atlanta *(New York: Thomas Dunne Books, 2010), 79, 112*]. Gen. Sweeny ordered the 2d Iowa and the 66th Ind to fall in immediately. We fell in and marched right-oblique toward the rear in quick time.

We supposed that Sweeny was marching us to a position out of danger. It was reported that Gen. Sweeny said the 2d Iowa and the 7th Iowa were the two best regiments in the service. We know that he said Battery H, 1st Mo., was the best battery he ever saw.

We looked back and saw Battery H following the infantry. We marched about two miles. We could hear an occasional shot. It sounded as if our cavalry had been deployed in the timber and had discovered some stumps in front and imagined they were Confederate infantry.

Finally we came to a halt. We found a lot of cavalry behind breastworks of rails. The breast works were in an open field about 200 yards from the timber.

There was a hollow about 80 yards in front of us, running parallel with our works, so deep that we could not depress our guns enough to hit a man in the center of the hollow.

The 2d Iowa lay down behind the rails on the left, the 66th Ind. on the right and battery H, 1st Mo., was placed to the left of the 2d Iowa. The 14th Ohio battery came up to the right of the 66th Ind.

The cavalry skirmishers had just reached the works as we arrived, and reported that the woods were full of rebel infantry. Gen. Sweeny ordered one company of skirmishers from the 2d and one from the 66th to deploy immediately and march to the timber in front, double-quick. They started on a slow trot. When the skirmishers got near the timber they turned and ran toward the works.

Gen. Sweeny was a little, ordinary man with a weak voice. He kept a big, burly Orderly with him, who had a voice like a big gray timber wolf. Before the skirmishers got to the hollow the 5th Ky. [*Confederate*] emerged from the woods in fine style. They made as fine an appearance as any yellow butternuts I ever saw.

Comrade Donaldson describes the opening of Bate's attack led by the charge of Brigadier General Joseph H. Lewis's Orphan Brigade—so called because its five Kentucky regiments had lost their home after Federal occupation of the state. Facing them were Donaldson's regiment, the 2nd Iowa, and the three others of Brigadier General Elliott W. Rice's brigade. As our author states, the infantrymen were aided considerably by Battery H, 1st Missouri Light Artillery (Ecelbarger, The Day Dixie Died, *78).*

When the skirmishers got near the hollow Gen. Sweeny's Brigade-Orderly bellowed out for the skirmishers to break in the center; 2d Iowa to file to the right of the hollow, and 66th to file to the left down the hollow, out of range of the guns.

After the 5th Ky. emerged from the woods the 2d Ky. appeared; then the 9th Ky. came out of the timber. As soon as the skirmishers were out of sight we opened on the enemy.

The first shots were by Battery H, six at once. The shells struck the ground about four rods in front the of the enemy and knocked dirt in their eyes. The shells bounced over the rebs and burst near the timber.

At the second volley from the infantry the Confederates turned and made for the timber much faster then they had come toward us. The Color-Sergeant of the 5th Ky. (McDowell) was shot, and another man took the colors. He, too, fell. The third man fell; then they left their colors.

After the firing cease J. A. Cease, of Co. C, 2d Iowa, jumped over the works, ran out to the colors of the 5th Ky., and brought them in. The inscription on the flag was: "5th Ky. Ivy Mountain; Chickamauga; Princeton; Mill Creek."

While the battle was in progress we learned that the 3d Mich. battery lay upon a hill 400 yards to our rear. They opened on the Confederates, and did their part as well as the other batteries mentioned.—J. R. DONALDSON, Co. C, 2d Iowa, Goff, Kan.

*Citing Donaldson, Gary Ecelbarger tells the story of Cease bringing in the banner of the 5th Kentucky (*The Day Dixie Died, *81).*

40

Taking and Holding Leggett's Hill

M. B. Loop, "Veteran Campaigns of the 68th Ohio"

(May 23, 1901, p. 7)

In November 1861, Myron B. Loop (1838-1922) enlisted as a private and served in Company I of the 68th Ohio. His memoir, The Long Road Home: Ten Thousand Miles Through the Confederacy with the 68th Ohio, *was the basis for two series in the* National Tribune*: "Campaigning with the Buckeyes" and "Rounding-up the Confederacy," 26 articles in all, appearing September 1900-July 1901. "Rounding-up" was subtitled "Veteran Campaigns of the Gallant 68th Under Uncle Billy Sherman" (10 parts). Its first (May 9, 1901) has the regiment joining Sherman's army June 8, 1864, near Acworth; it became part of the 2nd Brigade (Col. Robert K. Scott, commander), 3rd Division (Brig. Gen. Mortimer D. Leggett), XVII Corps. The series chronicles the 68th's service in the Atlanta Campaign and the Carolinas, all the way to mustering out (*National Tribune, *July 11, 1901).*

In this article, third in the series, Loop refers to his unit's march to Decatur and turning west toward Atlanta, wrecking the Georgia Railroad as it went. The heart of the piece involves the fighting around the "bald hill," held first by Wheeler's cavalry. As our author states, during the night of July 20-21, Cleburne's Division reinforced the horsemen. Then, the next morning, Leggett's division attacked and drove the Rebels from the hill.

*Private Loop is also accurate in stating that, once the hill had been won, Federal artillery began shelling Atlanta. Two days earlier, on July 19, Sherman had issued an order that when any of his cannon should get within range of Atlanta—for rifled artillery, that was 2 ½ miles—they should begin bombarding the city. General Leggett reported that his guns were able to open up before 9:00 a.m. on July 21 (*OR *38, pt. 3, 564).*

The "Col. Welles" Loop writes about was Lt. Col. George E. Welles, commander of the 68th Ohio. As he states here, the 32nd Ohio was transferred to the 1st Brigade, 4th Division, XVII Corps, on July 10; Col. Benjamin F. Potts took command of the brigade on July 18 (William R. Scaife, The Campaign for Atlanta *[Saline MI: McNaughton and Gunn, 1993], 164-165). An Ohioan may be forgiven for ignorance as to Georgia geography: "Rossville" was the town of Roswell.*

While we lay in camp on the Chattahoochee several of our comrades established a medium of exchange with the rebs on the opposite side of the river. We would meet each other in the middle of the river and trade coffee for tobacco. The latter was a very scarce commodity with us, and as coffee was highly prized by the rebels, they would gladly make the exchange, which would take place after the shadows of night had fallen.

It was amusing to see a comrade stick to his choice morsel, as long as there was any taste to it, after which he would dry it and smoke it in his pipe, and as he finally knocked out the ashes would draw a long sigh.

About July 12 the 32d Ohio, with which we had been associated since November 1863, was transferred to the Fourth Division, Seventeenth Corps, to give Col. Potts a chance to command a brigade. About the same time the noble 17th Wis. was assigned to our brigade, which military composition--20th, 68th, 78th Ohio, and 17th Wis.—we maintained to our muster-out.

The three Ohio regiments had been associated at Bolivar, Tenn., in the Summer of 1862; and it is a very remarkable fact that they served their first enlistments, veteranized, returned from veteran furlough, and were again brigaded together, so to remain to the close of the war, thus forming and cementing a comradeship that will last forever.

Early July 16 we started in the direction of Rossville, on the Chattahoochee River. The object was to cross the river and if possible plant ourselves on the east side of Atlanta. After a march of about 20 miles under a hot July sun we camped one mile from Marietta.

The following day we marched to Rossville, 10 miles east of Marietta, and the same evening crossed the Chattahoochee on a pontoon bridge, and went into camp for the night. From Rossville our line of march was about 20 miles in a southerly direction to Decatur, a little village on the Augusta Railroad, eight miles from Atlanta, where we arrived on the evening of July 19.

PEACH TREE CREEK.

The next morning an incessant crash and roar of artillery and musketry on our right told us that a battle was being fought at a place which afterwards was known as "Peach Tree Creek."

We devoted a portion of our time while near Decatur to tearing up and thoroughly destroying the railroad and bridges. We also picked blackberries, which grew in profusion around us.

Early in the afternoon our division moved forward along the railroad in the direction of the defenses of Atlanta. After marching about three miles, the enemy was discovered to be posted about half a mile in our front in a strip of heavy timber.

The Fourth Division now came up and immediately deployed into position on our right, after which they advanced upon the enemy, driving them pell-mell about one mile to a high range of hills. In the meantime our division was rapidly moving forward and swinging as a pivot on the left of the Fourth Division. We moved forward across an open plain to the timber beyond, and just as the sun was sinking we came to a halt on the banks of a creek, from the opposite side of which came rebel shot and shell whizzing all around us. Night now coming on, we lay down in line of battle.

The next morning [*July 21*] just as the great orb of day commenced to lighten up the eastern horizon a general advance was ordered against the enemy, who were in position on what afterwards became known as "Leggett's Hill."

Our lines were quickly formed, our flags unfurled in the early morning breeze, and our comrades as they saw the colors sparkle in the morning sun realized in them everything we held dear in Government, and again resolved to follow the grand old flag on to victory.

We moved across the creek and up the slope toward the enemy, who had been reinforced during the night, and were prepared to dispute every inch of ground. Our division, however, with the First Brigade in front, moved forward on the double-quick, driving the enemy from the hill and taking about 100 prisoners.

The enemy again being reinforced made an attempt to retake the hill, but at this opportune moment the muskets of the Fourth Division, which were rapidly moving on our right, gave tongue, causing the enemy to retreat in disorder.

Before 10 o'clock Gen. Leggett had a battery in position on the hill and was throwing shells into Atlanta, one and a-half miles distant. The position thus secured was one of great importance, as the occupation of the hill forced the enemy to give up his line of works in our front and fall back toward Atlanta. The balance of the day was spent in extending our lines and strengthening our position against an assault by the enemy.

Early July 22 we discovered that the enemy had withdrawn from our front, and while engaged in preparing our breakfast we were aroused by the well-known voice of Col. Welles, shouting "Fall in men, fall in!" That earnest voice called us to our feet in an instant, and grabbing muskets we formed in line and were soon marching rapidly to the rear to repel, as we supposed, an attack by rebel cavalry, upon our corps hospital and Seventeenth Corps headquarters.

IN A TRAP.

Upon reaching our position imagine our surprise to find in our front, instead of cavalry, a long line of rebel infantry, while at the same time another line of rebel troops were forming across the road in our rear. Our regiment was thus being sandwiched between two lines of the enemy, who appeared to have been wholly unaware of the position of our little Buckeye band.

From our position, being partly concealed in a dense copse, the commands of rebel officers could be distinctly heard, and prisoners were taken who unknowingly ran into our line. Still the enemy moved on; something must be done, and done quickly, in order to get out of a trap which was about to spring upon us.

Those were anxious moments, which to waste meant a visit to some Southern prison-pen.

Col. Welles hastily surveyed the ground on our left, and a moment later whispered down the line, "Be cool, men; be cool! Forward by the left flank—march." We sprang to our feet and moved to the left on the double-quick, and dropping behind a rail fence which lay in our path, poured a volley into the enemy, who were forming in line in an open field on our right. The alarm thus given by the muskets of our regiment was immediately responded to by a battery of artillery, and the battle of July 22 opened in earnest.

The Third Division engaged the enemy so promptly that our regiment was enabled, by making a rapid move to the left and a wide detour of about two miles, to pass around the enemy's right, and again join our brigade and division on Leggett's Hill.

Gen. R. K. Scott, commanding our brigade, and Capt. A. C. Urquhart, picket officer on Scott's staff, accompanied our regiment in the early morning, but upon our return they took a shorter route than that followed by the regiment, and were taken prisoners. The next day, the next week, the next month, we anxiously discussed the matter of the capture, whether living or dead, but could hear nothing until about September 28, when they joined us in camp near Atlanta, having been exchanged.

Upon reaching our division we found our comrades hotly engaged with the enemy, who were advancing in solid columns to storm Leggett's Hill. My pen utterly fails me in an attempt to describe in detail the events of that fearful struggle.

ASSAULTS UPON LEGGETT'S HILL.

Nearer and nearer came that line of rebel gray, indicating that they felt able to brush us away, but as they ran against the muskets of Leggett's Division they were sent reeling backward, suffering great loss, our loss being slight, as we lay behind a hastily-constructed line of rails and dirt.

The next attack came from the direction of Atlanta: a skirmish line followed by a heavy force was observed moving upon us from that direction. We now hastily changed front—as the first attack had been from the east—and again repulsed the enemy in handsome style.

The enemy now fell back, reformed their lines, and again returned to the attack, but were again repulsed and driven back, leaving their killed and wounded on the ground.

During the afternoon the enemy again advanced upon us from the direction of Atlanta, at the same time furiously attacking us on our flank, using their heavy artillery. If ever we were in a position to fight like demons it was then. "Get into the works," shouted Col Welles. "Which side, Colonel?" was asked. "I don't care which side," yelled our Colonel, "but get into the works!" And get into the works we did, but it was a puzzle to us to know which side of the works would be the safest, as the attack came from front and flank, which compelled us to fight first on one side of a barricade of rails and dirt and then on the other.

At one time a portion of our division was on one side of our works firing in one direction, while a little farther along the line the rest of our division was on the opposite side of the works, where a few rails were hastily thrown together, and behind these we hugged the ground. Still on came the enemy, rolling and surging up against our lines in another determined effort to take Leggett's Hill. But Leggett's noble men were just as determined that they should not have it. We saw them coming to take the hill, with officers in front, lines well dressed, and following each other in quick succession.

Such a scene one does not often behold, even in the wild tumult of war, as here it was the tidal wave of war beat with its wildest fury against us. Volley after volley of musketry, accompanied by the bellowing of heavy guns, seemed to have no more effect than so much chaff would have done in the ranks of those advancing hosts.

A HAND-TO-HAND STRUGGLE.

On the enemy came until they became engaged in a hand-to-hand struggle with a portion of Leggett's Division. Wild yells rent the air, and bayonets clashed together as the men gave the glistening steel. Men with uplifted blades sought each others' lives, but the swift, unerring ball reached them before the blows were delivered, and they fell side by side.

The crash of cannon and roar of musketry were deafening, and the enemy were hurled back only to spring forward with greater fury in a vain effort to burst Sherman's coils that were tightening around them.

As we glanced to the right or left we found it the same—a struggling, fighting mass of men, now party hidden by clouds of powdersmoke and then again in plain view. Thus the battle raged till night dropped her mantle over the scene. Little by little the enemy were driven back, and when darkness fell they gave up the fight and quietly quit the field.

Wearied with the confusion and excitement of battle we threw ourselves down to rest, but not to sleep. The voice of a comrade is heard calling; we hurry here and there—now holding our canteen to the lips of a dying comrade, now endeavoring to smooth the couch of a wounded brother, and now hastily answering the voice of a friend, "Oh, give me water."

The morning of July 23 a muffled shout, that was taken up by brigade after brigade and division after division, rolled gloriously along the lines. There was no enemy in our front, and the victory was ours; but, oh, what a fearful loss of life there had been. The ground over which the enemy made their successive charges was thickly strewn with dead.

In front of Leggett's Division the rebel dead lay so close together that one could have walked for some distance, stepping from one body to another. During the day the enemy sent a truce, and there was delivered to them to be buried about 1,000 of their dead.

These were collected from the ground in front of Leggett's Division, which went to show how well Leggett's noble lads had responded to Logan's battle cry, "McPherson and revenge!"

July 23 was a sad day to us. There was no excitement to keep up our strength as with mute lips we gathered together those of our own regiment who had fallen on July 22, and with many an aching heart laid them tenderly away.

Our total loss in killed and wounded was about 70. Yet it does not appear in Ohio's records that our regiment suffered any loss in wounded. This discrepancy, however, may to some extent be accounted for from the fact that during the last year and a half of our service a very small per cent of our wounded were reported. Only those who were wholly disabled were sent to the hospital, while those who sustained less severe wounds remained with the regiment, and in many cases were doing duty before their wounds healed.

DEATH OF GEN, M'PHERSON.

The most severe loss we sustained on July 22 was our beloved commander, Maj.-Gen. James B. McPherson. He had just left Gen. Sherman, where he had been in consultation, and was hastily riding forward accompanied by one Orderly, his other Aids having been sent on different missions, when, while passing through a belt of timber, which but a few moments previous had been in our possession, he encountered a body of the enemy's skirmishers, and was shot dead.

The first time we heard of McPherson was at Corinth, Miss., he then being a Colonel on Halleck's staff.

In October following McPherson was made a Major-General, and upon organization of the Seventeenth Corps, Army of the Tennessee, he was made its commander. He remained in command of the Seventeenth Corps, leading it in all its marches and campaigns until March 1864, when he took command of the Army of the Tennessee.

Gen. McPherson's death was soon known throughout his entire army, awakening, first, bitter grief, and then the honest thirst for vengeance. That afternoon "McPherson and revenge!" rang from right to left along the line. Ten thousand of the enemy went down before it, and at night the dripping earth bore mute testimony of the terrible vengeance his devoted army had visited upon his slayers.

A braver man never drew a sword. In the fight where the pressure was the heaviest he was sure to be found, encouraging his men by his presence. He never used profane language; he needed no oaths to emphasize his orders; yet in the heat of battle his words rang out like a bugle-call. There he was in his element, and his clear eye blazed like a meteor as he rode at the head of his columns, a hero admired and loved by his men.

Full of honor and noble generosity, he finished his short, bright career. Noble in all his impulses, pure in all his actions, true to the integrity of his country, and great as a military chieftain, his fall was a sad calamity to our cause and our country.

Soon after McPherson's death his body was recovered and taken to Gen. Sherman's headquarters. Sherman ordered McPherson's personal staff to escort the body to the home of his boyhood, in Clyde, Sandusky County, Ohio, where his remains now rest under a beautiful equestrian monument erected by the Army of the Tennessee.

Private Loop is vivid but also accurate in describing how Leggett's men were compelled to jump over their parapets back and forth to meet the rebels attacking them from the southeast (Pat Cleburne's division) and from the southwest (George Maney's). He also relates well the hand-to-hand combat on Leggett's Hill. Around mid-afternoon, Cleburne's troops got so close to Leggett's line that the two sides engaged in what historian Gary Ecelbarger calls "a rudimentary gang fight."

*As for casualties in the fight for Leggett's Hill, Ecelbarger figures that Frank Blair's XVII Corps (the divisions of Leggett and Giles Smith) lost 1,800 officers and men killed, wounded, and captured (*The Day Dixie Died*, 210). Cleburne's division, which repeatedly attacked the hill, lost 1,388 out of 3,500 officers and men (40%—Ecelbarger, 212).*

Loop's memoir, The Long Road Home, *has been reprinted by Blue Acorn Press (Huntington, WV, 2006). An excerpt from "Sounding the Alarm: The 68th Ohio's Trying Time at the Battle of Atlanta" (*National Tribune, *December 1, 1898) is reprinted in Larry A. Strayer and Richard Baumgartner, eds.,* Echoes of Battle: The Atlanta Campaign *(Huntington, WV: Blue Acorn Press, 1991), 240-241. The editors have added, pp. 243-244, an excerpt from Loop's "Rounding-up The Confederacy,"* National Tribune, *May 23, 1901.*

41

General Leggett Writes on Defending His Hill

Maj. Gen. M. D. Leggett, "Battle of Atlanta. The Fierce and Bloody Struggle of July 22, 1864. Crowding the Foe. Within his Lines Around the Doomed city. Seizing the Bald Hill. This Important Position Wrested from the Enemy"

(May 6, 1886, p. 1)

Maj. Gen. M. D. Leggett, "Battle of Atlanta. II"

(May 13, 1886)

Mortimer Leggett writing about the July 22, 1864, fight to control the hill that came to bear his name is arguably one of the most important officers' remembrances about that dramatic engagement. Yet, in the prominent secondary literature on the battle of Atlanta, this long article is not mentioned—either by Albert Castel in Decision in the West *(which does not cite any* National Tribune *article) or by Gary Ecelbarger in his account of the engagement,* The Day Dixie Died *(which cites only a speech Leggett made in 1883).*

*This piece, and its continuation in the issue of May 13, are much more detailed than Leggett's after-action report of July 25 (*OR *38, pt. 3, 564-566). Here he recounts the Federals' capture of the "bald hill" east of Atlanta on July 21, the counterattack of Maj. Gen. Patrick Cleburne's infantry division, and the opening of the battle around noon on the 22nd. General Leggett's apprehensions of a surprise Rebel attack that day, and his precautions against it, are telling, and are not seen elsewhere in the battle literature. Notably, he refrains from criticizing General Sherman for sending Garrard's cavalry division off toward Covington on a railroad raid in the early afternoon of July 21, leaving the left flank of McPherson's army "in the air." This fact, quickly discovered by Wheeler's cavalry, led to Hood's decision for a night march and morning surprise attack by Hardee's corps—the "battle of Atlanta" that so arduously tested Leggett's division and Blair's XVII Corps on the 22nd.*

To our knowledge, this narrative by General Leggett has not been previously reprinted from the National Tribune.

The battle of Atlanta, fought on July 22, 1864, was undoubtedly one of the most intense battles of the war. Other battles have had more troops engaged and lasted longer, but none, probably, exhibited more heat of passion, more violent ardor, mor impetuous vigor in both attack and defense, than did this great battle in which the noble McPherson fell. From 11:30 a.m. till nearly 9 p.m. the battlefield was literally red-hot. Although other troops were engaged some part of the time, yet the battle was fought principally by the Army of the Tennessee, consisting of the Fifteenth, Sixteenth and Seventeenth Corps. I commanded the Third Division of the Seventeenth Corps, and it is this part taken by this division in the battle that I am invited to describe, but, of course, must mention other troops to some extent, in order to make known the part taken by this division.

THE BATTLE OF PEACH TREE CREEK

was fought on the 20th of July, and on the evening of that day we crowded closely up to the enemy's outer works about Atlanta, with my division on our extreme left. [*Maj. Gen. James B. McPherson, commanding the Army of the Tennessee, was leading his 25,000 infantry toward Atlanta from the east, along the line of the Georgia Railroad that connected Atlanta with Augusta. Opposing them was Confederate cavalry leader Major General Joseph Wheeler and 3,500 mounted troops.*] It was noticed that the enemy occupied a bald hill in an open field in front of the left of my division, the hill being so high as to give them a very commanding position. [*The hill, often called Leggett's Hill in the campaign literature, was located two miles east of downtown Atlanta.*] The enemy's ground at their right of this hill was vailed from our view by a dense strip of woods at our left. Col. G. D. Munson, of my staff, pressed our skirmish-line through this strip of forest and discerned that the hill was the extreme right of the Confederate line. On our immediate right the Fourth Division of our corps, under Gen. W. Q. Gresham, had just carried, after a brisk but short engagement, a hill of less elevation, in doing which the gallant Gresham fell severely wounded and was carried from the field. [*Brigadier Walter Q. Gresham was shot in the lower left leg, breaking the bone. No amputation was performed, but Gresham was out for the war.*] In camp and on the march, Gresham was always a quiet, kind, affable, unassuming gentleman, but rigorous in discipline; while in battle he was brave, intrepid and enthusiastic, always inspiring his men to deeds of bravery. His loss to the whole corps was severely felt. His division fell to the command, for the time being, of Col. William Hall, of the 13th Iowa, who was the ranking officer in the division under Gresham.

Bald Hill, in front of my extreme left, was considerably in advance of our main line, yet it seemed necessary that we should occupy it, in order to render our position tenable. When we discovered that this hill was the enemy's right, I determined that we would at once occupy it. But just at this time Gens McPherson and Blair, (Blair commanded our corps), rode up. Gen. McPherson at first approved of an immediate assault on the hill, but on further consultation he concluded that we had better defer it until the morning. He thought it would

PROBABLY BRING ON A BATTLE

involving at least the whole of our corps, and it then being nearly sunset, and the Fourth Division having just changed commanders, we all cheerfully accepted his decision. [*It was now 4:00 or 4:30 in the afternoon on July 20, with perhaps two hours of daylight left; McPherson judged this was not enough time to launch a successful assault. The delay gave Confederate General Hood time to send Maj. Gen. Patrick Cleburne's division, which had not participated in the battle of Peachtree Creek, on a nighttime march through the city to reinforce Wheeler. Cleburne's infantry began arriving early on the morning of the 21st. The right of the division—Brigadier James Smith's Texas brigade—occupied Bald Hill, where the troops began strengthening the cavalrymen's rifle pits.*]

During the night of the 20th I adjusted my division in the strip of woodland mentioned. My First Brigade, under Gen. M. [*Brig. Gen. Manning*] F. Force, was on my right and immediately facing Bald Hill; my Second Brigade, under Gen. R. [*Col. Robert*] K. Scott, was on the left of Force. The Third Brigade, under Col. Maloy [*Adam G. Malloy*], of the 17th Wis., occupied a refused line on the left of the Second Brigade to protect our left flank.

It was understood that the duty of leading the assault would devolve upon Gen. Force. His brigade consisted of the 20th, 30th, 31st and 45th Ill., and the 12th and 16th Wis. These regiments, except the 12th Wis., had fought together on many sharply contested fields, and each had implicit confidence in the other. The 12th Wis. was a full regiment, splendidly officered; but it had joined us only a few days before, and had not been thoroughly tried in our division. In putting the troops in position this regiment was accidentally put in the front line and in the most exposed position. When this was discovered both Gen. Force and myself expressed regret, but its Colonel (George E. Bryant) and other officers of the regiment besought us to make no change, and assured us we should have no cause to regret having put them in the position they occupied.

Early in the next morning (the 21st) Gen. Giles A. Smith was placed in command of the Fourth Division, with orders to press the enemy in his front at the time of our assault to prevent those in our front from begin reinforced. [*Smith's division (formerly Gresham's) was positioned to the north of Leggett's line, which ran north-south, facing the Bald Hill to its west.*] He reported his line ready soon after sunrise, when my First and Second Brigades were ordered forward. During the night the enemy had considerably strengthened his position on the hill. Our formation was in double line, with a strong skirmish line, under Col. Munson. When the command to advance was given the skirmishers were pushed forward

TO DRAW THE ENEMY'S FIRE,

which they did the instant they emerged from the woods. The skirmishers were closely followed by Force's lines. Gen. Force's coolness and self-possession and utter forgetfulness of danger when under fire was well known throughout the corps; but here he seemed to excel himself. To lessen the exposure of his officers, he had directed his field officers to leave their horses behind, only himself and a portion of his personal staff being mounted [*which meant Force, his adjutant general, Capt. J. Bryant Walker, and two aides*]. He had directed his men to hold their fire until in the enemy's works, and his personal presence, conspicuously mounted, enabled him to enforce this order and prevent a halt for a single moment. The resistance to his assault was determined and sanguinary. His men fell thick and fast around him, but forward they went, stubbornly holding their fire until they mounted and entered the enemy's works, capturing a considerable number of prisoners. [*Force's assault quickly sent Wheeler's cavalrymen fleeing, then tangled with Smith's Texans. Bitter hand-to-hand fighting ensued before the Confederates were driven off the hill.*] Some of the prisoners said, with both pride and chagrin, that it was "the first time Pat Cleburne's Division was ever routed." [*General Smith counted nineteen men captured, as well as at least one member of the 1st Georgia Cavalry.*]

Gen. Force was now in possession of Bald Hill. He made the charge through an open field, up the side of the hill, against a confident enemy strongly entrenched on its summit. Few charges were ever so successful under such unfavorable circumstances. I have not been able to find Gen. Cleburne's report of the affair of the 21st, but Gen. Hardee, in his report of the military operations around Atlanta, says that Gen. Cleburne described this fight for the hill on the 21st of July as "the bitterest of his life." [*Leggett is correct; Hardee quoted Cleburne's "bitterest of his life" remark in his campaign report (*OR *38, pt. 3, 699).*]

As before stated, this hill was considerably in advance of our main line. The Fourth Division, under Gen. Giles A. Smith, advanced at the same time as we did, with an effort to keep the left of Smith's Division closed on the right of mine, but, finding the enemy

TOO STRONGLY INTRENCHED

and too well supported with artillery, was compelled to fall back into the temporary works thrown up the night before. This left Gen. Force very greatly exposed, for he was occupying the right of the enemy's line while the enemy was still in possession of the same line to our right.

We immediately began to turn the works we had captured, but the enemy rallied in large force in a piece of woods to our right front and made several desperate efforts to dislodge us, but without avail. [*Several Confederate counterattacks failed to recover the hilltop; the fight was over by 11:00 a.m.*] Gen. Force was there to stay. He never had yielded an advantageous position to the enemy, and he was not ready to extend such courtesy to Pat Cleburne at that time, although we had all learned long before to have a most thorough respect for the fighting qualities of Gen. Cleburne and his troops.

In the midst of these conflicts we continued the work of changing the captured intrenchments so as to face them toward Atlanta. As soon as this had extended far enough to afford partial protection, we placed Elliott's Michigan battery of Rodman guns in position, and very soon shelled the enemy out of the woods and out of their line in our immediate vicinity, and threw shot into Atlanta. [*Captain Marcus Elliott's Battery H, 1st Michigan Light Artillery, with its three-inch ordnance rifles, was brought atop the hill and severely harassed Cleburne's troops some 150 yards away.*] We found that this Bald Hill not only overlooked our line, but overlooked Atlanta as well. As soon as the enemy were driven from our immediate vicinity, and our works had been sufficiently strengthened, we replaced the Rodman guns with Williams' 3d Ohio battery of 20-pound [rifled] Parrotts, when our shots were sent into Atlanta, and drew a response from the heavy guns of their inner line.

I had three batteries attached to my division—Capt. W. [*William*] S. Williams' 3d Ohio [*Light Battery*], 20-pound Parrotts; Capt. M. D. Elliott's 8th Mich. [error: *Battery H, 1st Michigan*], Rodman guns; and Capt. E. [*Edgar*] H. Cooper's 1st Ill. [*Battery D, 1st Illinois Light*], 24-pound howitzers—all under the direction of Capt. W. S. Williams, my Chief of Artillery, who was constantly on the alert to do all that was in the power of artillery to do.

The weather was extremely warm, and the hill being in the open field, with no protection from the direct rays of the sun [*hence its characterization as "bald"*], many of our officers and men

SUFFERED WITH SUN-STROKE.

Among these were some members of Gen. Force's staff, whose constant activity and exposure had greatly exhausted them, and the General himself suffered greatly from the same cause. [*The temperature that afternoon, reaching well into the 90s, debilitated Northerners and Southerners alike. One of Force's aides had to be taken off the field due to sunstroke.*]

This hill has since been known as "Leggett's Hill," but I have always thought it should have been christened "Force's Hill," for he captured and held it on the 21st by a rare display of soldierly qualities, and because, in defending it the next day, he there fell so terribly wounded. [*Leggett's modest deference to General Force about the naming of the hill is commendable, but ineffectual. In the 1950s, a Georgia Historical Commission highway marker was placed at the hill site. It is titled "Leggett's Hill," with a text that does not mention Manning Force.*]

In the charge and capture of the hill the 12th Wis. covered itself with glory. Not an officer or man faltered. They maintained the front to the end, and suffered nearly one half of the entire loss in the killed and wounded. Their veteran steadiness was lauded by all who witnessed the charge. Gens. Sherman, McPherson, Blair, Logan and others of his rank were in position to witness the whole movement. [*In his two lines of battle, Force put the 12th and 16th Wisconsin in the front, and three Illinois regiments behind them. In their charge the Wisconsans suffered accordingly: 150 officers and men in the 12th; over 130 casualties in the 16th, many in 15 minutes of the advance.*]

Among the badly wounded was the gallant and witty Col. Tom Reynolds, of the 16th Wis. [*Maj. Thomas Reynolds, later Brevet Colonel*]. He fell with his thigh terribly crushed. The Surgeons at once pronounced his wound fatal. The weather was so extremely warm and the Colonel so exhausted by want of sleep the night before, and the violent and long-continued struggle of the day, that no hope was entertained for his recovery. When the Surgeons were examining his wound in the evening, to determine whether his leg should be amputated, the Colonel rallied and said: "Please spare that leg, gentlemen; I think a great deal of it; it is an imported article." The Colonel was of Irish birth, and brought the leg over with him when he came to America. The Surgeons thought he would die anyhow, and concluded to let him keep his imported leg; and through God and the Colonel's indomitable pluck he has both his life and his leg yet. After our march to the sea and up through the Carolinas, much to our surprise Col. Reynolds met us at Raleigh, N.C. After congratulating him on his resurrection, I said to him, that his wound had considerable shortened his leg. He answered, "Well, I don't know, General; lying so long in bed my leg got crooked at the knee-joint, and the doctors put me under the influence of chloroform to straighten it, and I believe the d—d fools

STRETCHED THE LONG LEG."

Late in the afternoon of the 21st, Gen. Force called my attention to a continuous column of troops moving out of Atlanta in direction of our left. With our field-glasses we carefully scanned this column, and finding it composed of only infantry and artillery, with ammunition wagons and ambulance, we both concluded that it meant no good to us. I sent back frequent notes of this movement to our corps commander—Gen. Frank P. Blair—by Capt. G. W. Porter, Capt. A. W. Stewart, and others of my staff, and urged that my left should be strengthened with additional troops. The destiny of these troops moving in our front is a mystery, in the light of Hood's, Hardee's and other Confederate reports, as they all agree in saying that the movement to our left commenced after dark--a little after 8 o'clock.

[*General Leggett here alludes to Hood's plan to launch an attack on the left flank of McPherson's army, after Sherman on the afternoon of July 21 sent Brig. Gen. Kenner Garrard's cavalry division, which had been guarding McPherson's left, off to the east to tear up track of the railroad to Augusta. Hood ordered Lt. Gen. William J. Hardee's corps during the night to march south through the city, swing to the northeast, get into position and attack McPherson's flank and rear on the 22nd. Leggett is correct in stating that Hardee's infantrymen were only to start marching after sunset for their surprise attack. Here he assumes that the Rebel troops movements he observed in the afternoon of July 21 were the beginnings of Hardee's flank-march. They were not; after the loss of the Bald Hill, and under pressure from McPherson's forces, General Cleburne asked that reinforcements be sent his way. Hood sent Maj. Gen. George Maney's infantry division. It was deploying in Leggett's front during the afternoon of July 21—the "continuous column of troops" that Leggett mentions.*]

The movement of which I have spoken was witnessed not only by Gen. Force and myself, but by all officers and men on duty on the hill, and on the picket-line in front of and to the left of the hill, and was much talked of at the time, because many thought they were evacuating Atlanta,. Whatever the movement was, it caused our left to be greatly strengthened, by sending there our Fourth Division (Gen. Smith's), and Gen. John W. Fuller's Division of the Sixteenth Corps. [*During the afternoon Blair shifted Giles Smith's division from Leggett's right to his left, south of the Bald Hill.*] The Fourth Division was relieved from my right by the Fifteenth Corps, and formed a refused line on my left, while Gen. Fuller bivouacked his Division directly in my rear, and in the rear of the woods in which my lines formed the night before.

As soon as the Confederate movement referred to was discovered in the afternoon, I immediately gave orders to strengthen our works as much as possible, and to throw out traverses to the rear, facing south at the left of each company.

[*A traverse is an earthen bank built at an angle to the infantrymen's main parapet, designed to protect the men from flanking fire.*] There was enough apprehension of danger among the men to

MAKE THEM WORK VIGOROUSLY.

The most of my First Brigade and the whole of the Second were in the line of the hill, and extending to the left of it, along what was known as the McDonough road, having woods immediately in the rear and open fields in front between us and Atlanta. Between these two brigades we stationed Capt. Elliott's 8th Mich. battery of Rodman guns. My Third Brigade, after being relieved by Gen. Smith's Division, was placed in a refused line from the right of Gen. Force's Brigade (the First) toward the left of the Fifteenth Corps. To fill this space I also called on Gen. Fuller for one regiment, and here I also placed Capt. Cooper's battery of 24-pound howitzers. Such was the position of our troops at night of the 21st.

In the evening I consulted freely with Gen. G. A. Smith, and we both regarded with considerable anxiety the movements of the enemy toward our left, noticed in the afternoon. Quite late in the evening I visited Gen. Blair also in relation to the same matter, but found him not apprehensive of danger, as he seemed quite convinced that Atlanta was being evacuated. He, however, supposed that a considerable force of our cavalry was at our left, which proved a mistake, as our cavalry had been sent to the rear of the enemy to cut their lines of communication.

From Gen. Blair's headquarters I went along my line to encourage the men in strengthening the works. Just before midnight an order came from Gen. McPherson to strengthen our works and be on a vigilant watch for an attack at daybreak the next morning. I met Col. George E. Welles, of the 68th Ohio, who reported considerable noise in front of our picket-line.

[*At 5:30 p.m. on July 21, McPherson was worried about the absence of cavalry on his flank, so he urged Blair to fortify and watch for an enemy attack. McPherson also passed on Leggett's observation of Confederates marching southward to Sherman, who mistakenly assumed early on the 22nd that Hood was abandoning Atlanta. McPherson knew better. He ordered John Morrill's brigade (John Fuller's division, Dodge's XVI Corps) to take position at the end of Blair's line, perpendicular to it ("refused"), facing south—the direction from which he feared the Rebels would be heading. (Fuller's other brigade was sent to guard the army's wagon trains at Decatur, a few miles east.) On the morning of July 22, a Federal signal officer in a treetop observed and reported the distant dust of marching infantry. This caused McPherson to send Brig. Gen. Thomas Sweeny's division (XVI Corps) to reinforce Morrill's refused line. In other words, even if*

Sherman was taking no precautions against a surprise enemy attack, McPherson was. So was Mortimer Leggett.]

WE CALLED FOR VOLUNTEERS,

and selected two reliable men to go out in front of our pickets far enough to discover the cause of commotion. They returned and reported Confederate troops moving to our left. I reported this to Gen. Blair as late as 1:30 the morning of the 22d.

It will be noticed that my line was not in a desirable shape. My First and Second Brigades and two of my batteries occupied a line considerably in advance of our main line; in fact, my line was a prolongation of the enemy's line. My right was refused so as to connect with our Fifteenth Corps, and Gen. Smith's Division was refused on my left; but the possession of Bald Hill was regarded of sufficient importance to warrant the risk of our awkwardly-formed line.

At break of day the troops were on the alert, but no attack was made. The silence in our front was phenomenal and profound. Both Gen. Smith's Division and my own had an admirable line—with numerous traverses—at least one to each company—facing to the left. It was soon discovered that the enemy had abandoned his outer works to the right of Gen. Force. [*During the night Cleburne's and Maney's divisions had withdrawn from the Confederates' outer line east of Atlanta to join in Hardee's march around the Federal flank. The rest of Hood's army also withdrew into the fortified perimeter surrounding Atlanta.*] I immediately swung my Third Brigade (Col. Maloy) forward into the vacated work on Force's right, and the Fifteenth Corps did the same to the right of my division. These troops immediately changed the works to face toward Atlanta, with traverses as in the Seventeenth Corps, for there was a general distrust of the strength and protection of our left flank.

Soon after sunrise Gens. McPherson and Blair visited our line and rode well out in front without drawing the enemy's fire. Both seemed to believe that the enemy had evacuated Atlanta, in which belief none of the officers and but few of the men of my command concurred. We succeeded in detaining Gens. McPherson and Blair until Gen. Smith and myself advanced our skirmish-line and drew the enemy's fire with sufficient vigor to cause the theory of evacuation to be abandoned. We were then told to advance our defensive works and

ESTABLISH OUR LINES

as near as possible to the enemy's inner line of works, and made details and commenced such works.

It must be remembered that my line was on the McDonough road, running nearly north and south, and facing almost due west toward Atlanta. Gen. Giles A. Smith's Division was on my left, having his right on the McDonough road, and his line refused from mine at an angle of nearly 45 degrees, with his extreme left still farther refused; his whole command being in a dense forest, except as the forest had been disturbed in building his defensive works. Smith's line was therefore established in a northwesterly and southeasterly direction facing to the southwest. Gen. Smith's left was "in the air," with no protection except such defensive works as they had thrown up. Both Gen. Smith and myself had urged upon Gen. McPherson that morning the exposed condition of our left flank in case of an attack in that direction, which we both feared.

One division of the Sixteenth Corps, under Gen. John W. Fuller, was bivouacked a short distance to the rear of my division, just in rear of the strip of wood in which we formed our line for assault the night of the 20th. We were assured that, if possible, he would further extend the refused line of Smith's extreme left. This he was doing by sending the Sixteenth Corps, under Gen. George [sic: Grenville] M. Dodge, who was in transit when the battle of the 22d opened at about 11:30 a.m. The Seventeenth Corps hospital was located nearly a mile in our rear, and as some Confederate cavalry had been discovered near it [*Wheeler's cavalry, riding ahead of Hardee's infantry and toward Decatur to attack McPherson's wagon train*], Gen. Blair directed me to send a regiment back to protect it. I sent the 68th Ohio, under Col. George E. Wells, which started about 11 a.m.

As soon as I had started this regiment on its mission I went down toward the left of our line to confer with Gen. Smith, for the

PRESENCE OF CONFEDERATE CAVALRY

near our hospital, a mile to our rear, was ominous; but I had not found him when, hearing skirmish firing, I hurried back to the hill occupied by Gen. Force, from the summit of which the hospital was in sight. When I reached the hill I received a dispatch from Capt. Peter Hitchcock informing me that the enemy had just captured a man from a picket-post closely in rear of Gen. Smith's left. From the hill I could see the 68th Ohio deployed and firing at an enemy not visible at my standpoint. Gen. Fuller, who was a brave and vigilant officer, quickly took in the position, faced his division to the rear, and double-quicked back on to the ridge under which he had been lying. The 68th was slowly moving toward us, but kept up a constant firing toward its left.

[*These were the first signs that the Rebel movement to the south of McPherson's left flank—which Leggett had feared all morning—was underway. During the night,*

Hardee's four divisions (Maj. Gen. William B. Bate's, W. H. T. Walker's, Cleburne's, and Maney's) marched south out of Atlanta, swung northeast and by late morning were getting into position to attack McPherson's flank.]

At this time Gen. Sweeny's Division of the Sixteenth Corps could be seen moving by the right flank toward Gen. Fuller, but had not yet joined him. At this point Col. A. J. Alexander, Chief of Gen. Frank P. Blair's staff, joined Col. Wells and urged him to press the enemy hard and hold him back until Gen. Dodge could close up Sweeny's Division on Gen. Fuller's. Just as Gen. Dodge's two divisions had united, the enemy, in double line, emerged from the dense forest in their front. Gen. Fuller, by good luck, had parked his artillery in exactly the right place, and it was very efficient.

These two divisions of the Sixteenth Corps [*Sweeny, Fuller*] immediately became hotly engaged [*under attack by Bate's and Walker's divisions*]. The enemy were evidently greatly surprised at finding such a force in that position and were easily repulsed, and fell back into the woods in a southeasterly direction. Just at this I espied Gen. McPherson in the immediate rear of Gen. Fuller, and I sent Capt. John B. Raymond, of my staff, to him to inquire if he had any orders for us, and at the same time I sent Capt. Geo. W. Porter, one of my Aids, to ascertain whether or not the left of Gen. Smith and the right of Gen. Fuller were sufficiently near together to antagonize any force seeking entrance there. [*They were not; at the time of the Confederate attack in the early afternoon, a half-mile gap existed between Smith's left and Fuller's right southeast of the Bald Hill.*]

The enemy in front of the Sixteenth rallied in the woods, and then, knowing what he had to meet, renewed his attack with increased vigor and bitterness; but the Sixteenth Corps had also had time to dress and readjust its lines and prepare for the second attack which it expected, and

MET THE ASSAULT MAGNIFICENTLY.

The conflict continued for some time, with no appearance on either side of any disposition to yield the ground, when finally the enemy gave way and fell back in confusion, closely followed to the woods by the Sixteenth Corps. The attack was not again renewed at that point. This flanking force consisted of the four divisions of Hardee's Corps, commanded by Gens. Bate, Walker, Cleburne and Maney. Bate and Walker were on the right of Hardee's infantry and Cleburne and Maney on the left, while Wheeler's cavalry was on his extreme right. It was this cavalry that had been annoying the hospital. The first attack upon the Sixteenth Corps was by Bate's and a part of Walker's Divisions, while the second was by the whole of these two divisions. These conflicts between Dodge's and Hardee's Corps were among the very few engagements in the war of the rebellion where the opposing forces met and struggled in the open field, with no works to protect or shield them on either side.

[*To be continued.*]

* * *

[*A week later, General Leggett resumed his narrative. This came after Confederate general Hardee's first assaults from Walker's and Bate's divisions against Sweeny's division (XVI Corps) were repulsed around 1:00 p.m. on July 22. Then Hardee's other two divisions, Cleburne's and Maney's, continued that attack, this time against Major General Frank Blair's XVII Corps. Blair's line ran generally north-south, with Brigadier General Giles A. Smith's division on the left (south) and Leggett's on the right (north), anchored on Bald Hill.*]

In Hardee's movement upon our left and rear, it was design[*ed*] to have his right reach to the right of our Fifteenth Corps and assault it, while his left should strike the left of our Seventeenth Corps; hence he swung his right much more rapidly than his left, and Bate and Walker struck the Sixteenth Corps before the [*Confederate*] left did the Seventeenth. The second assault was simultaneous with the attack upon the left of Gen. Smith's Division, which was the left of the Seventeenth Corps.

It will be remembered that Smith's line ran in a southeasterly direction, facing to the southwest. Hardee was evidently seeking to strike us in the rear and not in the flank. He intended to "take us in," rather than drive us away; but as they moved upon us from the southeast, they found Smith's line perpendicular to theirs, and consequently struck Smith directly on the flank, enveloped his left regiment and captured it before Smith could so change front as to resist his attack [*Lt. Col. Addison H. Sanders surrendered the 16th Iowa, at least 240 men*]. In changing front under a destructive fire and impetuous charge, Smith was compelled to uncover a portion of one of his batteries and lost two guns [*Lt. Walter Powell, thirty artillerists and two Napoleons*]. He succeeded, however, in repulsing the enemy's assault after a most desperate encounter of considerable duration.

In repulsing the divisions of Gen. Bate and Gen. Walker, the Sixteenth Corps had so advanced in following up the enemy as to materially widen the gap between the left of Smith's and the right of Fuller's Division [*Brig. Gen. John W. Fuller's division, XVI Corps*], so that Gen. Cleburne's command passed with little molestation between them and quickly appeared directly in rear of my division, which was occupying the works it took from Gen. Cleburne the day before [*on Bald Hill*], and Cleburne was now assaulting us from the same direction and over the same ground we assaulted him. From the assertion the prisoners made which we captured from him that it was "the first time Pat Cleburne's Division was ever routed," and Cleburne's report to Hardee that his fight with us on the 21st was the "bitterest of his life," we may easily imagine the spirit that inspired him and his men when they came upon us with their demoniac yells, so characteristic of Pat Cleburne's Texans. [*Brig. Gen. James A. Smith's Texas Brigade of Cleburne's Division advanced through the gap between Smith's and Fuller's divisions. Around 2:00 p.m., the Confederates managed to push back Smith's troops but were eventually halted and forced to withdraw.*] The soldiers of the Third Division immediately leaped their works, putting

THEIR BACKS TOWARD ATLANTA,

and for vindictive desperation this encounter was probably never exceeded. After a prolonged struggle, in which the bayonet and clubbed muskets and officers' side swords were freely used in a hand-to-hand encounter, the attack was repulsed. Cleburne's troops were driven only into the strip of woods at the foot of the hill, when we were obliged to return to our works to meet an assault from toward Atlanta by Gen. Cheatham's Corps, covering the front of my division and also that of Gen. Smith; and other Confederate troops at the same time struck the Fifteenth Corps to our right.

As soon as the attack was first made on the Sixteenth Corps we anticipated a co-operating attack from Atlanta; so I sent Col. G. D. Munson, of my staff, to take charge of a strong skirmish-line and retard as much as possible any assault from that direction. Col. Munson had no superior, probably, in ability to handle a skirmish-line. A skirmish-line under his control was equal or superior to a line of battle in the hands of some officers. He had a quick eye and excellent judgment, and that kind of fearlessness that give him staying qualities, and a personal magnetism that inspired his men to stay with him. On this occasion he made the skirmishers fight so desperately as to prevent effectually the intended simultaneous attack by Cheatham and Cleburne. Cheatham finally struck us savagely, and found our men again on the right side of our works facing Atlanta, and a sanguinary struggle ensued.

[*About 3:30 p.m., Hood ordered Major General Cheatham's three divisions, in the Confederate fortifications east of the city, to advance in an attack to support Cleburne's fight to take the Bald Hill. Leggett's division, and Morgan Smith's of the XV Corps to its right (north), faced the Rebel assault, which Leggett's troops repulsed. As Leggett states, his men literally had to jump over their parapets to face this new threat. A sector of Smith's line near the Georgia Railroad, however, was overrun, driving back four brigades. But a Federal counterattack, organized by General Logan and launched*

4:30-5:00 p.m., restored the XV Corps line and drove Cheatham's infantry back to its start-off positions.]

After a time the enemy began to waver, when our men leaped their works and forced them rapidly back at the point of the bayonet, leaving many prisoners in our hands. Capt. Williams, my chief of Artillery, had placed Capt. Elliott's battery of Rodman guns at a point between my First and Second Brigades, and Capt. Cooper's battery of 24-pound howitzers in our works on the hill, where both of these batteries did very effective service in repelling this assault. Twenty-four pound howitzers are

HARD CUSTOMERS TO CHARGE AGAINST.

A bucketful of missiles can be poured down their throats, and when vomited forth will cover nearly a whole regimental front. Capt. Elliott's Rodman guns were always very skillfully handled and very rapidly. The rapidity of their firing made the Rodmans nearly equal to the howitzers in this battle.

Capt. Williams early in the conflict moved the 3d Ohio battery of 20-pound Parrotts to a ridge near the right of the Third Division, where it did effective work, as we shall see further along.

Cheatham's Corps was but fairly repulsed when Cleburne, who had fallen back into the strip of woods to readjust his lines, renewed his assault upon our rear with more anger, if possible, than before; but he was more easily repulsed, for Gen. C. C. Walcutt, then Colonel, commanding the left brigade in the Fifteenth Corps, was on my immediate right [*following Cheatham's initial success, Col. Charles Walcutt's brigade was the only one of the XV Corps still in position north of Bald Hill, supporting Leggett*] and so changed front as to get an enfilading fire on Cleburne's attacking troops, which quickly caused them to seek shelter in the woods behind them, where they were not again able to rally and readjust; for Gen. Walcutt commanded these woods from his position, and so did Capt. Williams's 3d Ohio Parrott guns. And Gen. Fuller, becoming satisfied that the attack would not again be renewed upon his command, had faced to the rear and come to our assistance by attacking Cleburne in his rear, which compelled Cleburne to withdraw by his left flank.

Immediately Cheatham was upon us again from toward Atlanta with other Confederate troops, at the same time assaulting the Fifteenth Corps to our right. This assault was pressed with great vigor and determination, and succeeded in driving the whole Fifteenth Corps, except Walcutt's Brigade, from its position. Discovering this, I immediately rode to the right of my division and found Walcutt still holding his position, but while with him an order came from his commander directing him to fall back on a line with the rest of the corps. I said to him that the order was a mistake; that my orders were to

HOLD THE HILL AT ALL HAZARDS,

and that these orders were from Gen. Blair, Gen. Logan and Gen. Sherman; but to do so would be impossible if the enemy were to have, undisputed, my front and both my flanks. Gen. Walcutt responded very promptly that he could stay where he was as long as I could hold my position, and that he would take orders from me. I then told him to hold his position, and that we would finally win.

The position Walcutt held was one of great exposure. The enemy, flushed with a temporary victory on his right [*Cheatham's breakthrough to Walcutt's north*], was pushing him with renewed vigor and determination. To determine to stay there and hold his position, even discarding the orders of his division commander, was a test of personal courage and good judgment to which very few officers were subjected. Yet to this action of this gallant officer we were undoubtedly very likely indebted for our final and magnificent victory on that day. The right of his brigade was partially protected by a small swamp covered by dank undergrowth of brush, while his left occupied a high point of land overlooking my Third Brigade, the highest point occupied by Union troops north of the hill captured the day before. If the enemy had got possession of this elevation held by Gen. Walcutt, the position of my Third Brigade would have been utterly untenable. If I had been compelled to withdraw my Third Brigade, I should also have been compelled to abandon the hill, and to have abandoned the hill at that time would certainly have lost us the day, and the possible and probable consequences which would have followed the defeat of our army on the 22d of July, in front of Atlanta, are not pleasant to contemplate. [*At one point in the fighting, Leggett declared, regarding the Bald Hill, "the hill must be retained at all hazards and at whatever cost."*]

Thus far we had been extremely fortunate in being able to prevent the assaults in our front and rear from being simultaneous; in other words, the enemy had not succeeded in their plan of sandwiching us. We had been able to repel the enemy from one side, and then, leaping the works, repel him from the other. This leaping the works from one side to the other in fighting Hardee's troops, our soldiers, at the time, designated as "Hardee's Tactics."

[*In parrying the Southerners' repeated assaults from southeast and west, the Federals had indeed jumped from one side of their entrenchments to the other. In terming this "Hardee's Tactics," the general humorously refers to the infantry manual written by Major William J. Hardee for the U.S. Army in the 1850s.*]

Just about the time the Fifteenth Corps was driven from its position, Gen. Hardee having massed his divisions, with his artillery at short range, and so posted as to enfilade our whole line of works, made

AN IRRESISTIBLE CHARGE

directly upon the left flank of Gen. Smith's Division and doubled it back upon mine. For a time the two divisions were thoroughly intermingled, and fought as if they belonged to the same regiments and brigades. The traverses thrown out the night before were a valuable protection to our troops and enabled them to greatly retard the enemy's progress. Capt. Williams turned our 20-pound Parrott battery and two of the Rodman guns so as to enfilade the Confederate line occupying the works from which they had just driven the Fifteenth Corps, which enabled the Fifteenth Corps to recover its works, but our own troops, being between my batteries and the Confederates attacking our left, I could not use our artillery to defend our own position.

It at once became apparent that we must change our front. At this moment the 68th Ohio, under Col. Geo. E. Welles, whose soldierly instincts seemed always to guide him to exactly the place where he was most needed, having made a detour to the right around the Sixteenth Corps, made his appearance upon the hill at this critical moment exactly at the time and place where he could do us most good. Col. Munson aided Col. Welles in placing the 68th in a new line nearly at right angles with our former line, its right resting against the works on the hill and facing south, the direction from which Hardee's column was then coming and driving all before them.

While my staff were busily engaged in moving back my Second Brigade to this new line and rallying portions of the Fourth Division upon the same line, to aid them in so doing and to check and retard the enemy until this new line should become established solid and firm, I swung my Third Brigade forward, wheeling to the left, thus elongating this new line toward Atlanta. This movement enabled our 24-pound howitzer battery, by moving a little forward and facing to the left, to

PLAY UPON THE ADVANCING ENEMY

with great effect. Gen. Smith rallied his division on this line to the left of my Second Brigade, and the Sixteenth Corps continued the same line still further to the left. As soon as this line was well established I swung the Third Brigade back into its works again, and avoid its direct attack.

I presumed but few of this brigade ever understood why they were thus taken from their works and again returned to them, as they were not actively engaged during the movements. Their position on the west of the hill, however, not only furnished the needed support of the howitzer battery, but was also such an exhibition of strength in defense of the hill (which I had so often during the day assured Gens. Blair, Logan and Sherman that I would hold to the end) as to cause Hardee's charging column to hesitate and avoid its direct attack.

Probably no occasion during the war displayed so strikingly the discipline and soldierly qualities of the Army of the Tennessee as did this change of front under the circumstances. Hardee's Corps compactly formed was charging and rapidly doubling our left flank, while his artillery was enfilading our whole line with a destructive fire of grape and a galling cross-fire was being poured into us from Shoupe's battery in Atlanta. [*Brigadier General Francis A. Shoup was Hood's Chief of Artillery; in his after-action report (*OR*, vol. 38, pt. 3, 631) he writes that Shoup's artillery "was massed on the extreme right," and, as Castel notes, during the battle pounded Leggett's Hill (*Decision in the West*, 410).*] The new line was but barely formed when Hardee was upon us with his advancing columns, and a hand-to-hand conflict ensued which for fierceness and ferocity and personal bravery, on both attack and defense, was probably never exceeded in any battle anywhere or at any time. The Confederates seemed to fully understand, as we did, that

THE FATE OF THE DAY

depended on whether we could hold this line or not; but our men held their position and repulsed the enemy, but not until the ground in our front for a considerable distance was literally carpeted with the dead. No time was lost by our troops, and defensive works sprang up as if by magic all along this new line. [*By 5:00 p.m., Hardee's attack had pushed Giles Smith's division back 3/4 miles, but it and Leggett's division still held the hill. At 6:00 p.m., Cleburne launched a final attack that led to desperate hand-to-hand fighting, but which ended with a Confederate retreat.*]

The day was now nearly spent, and we felt certain that Hood's assaulting army was badly worsted. My First Brigade still held the hill. The Fifteenth Corps had recovered its line, and was again in the same position as when the battle opened. My Third Brigade held its position throughout the struggle, and so did so much of my First Brigade as was on the hill and north of it, but immediately south of the crest of the hill our line broke abruptly to the rear facing south.

Our line was therefore so formed at this time as to present a right angle at the hill, the summit of the hill being within the angle. I felt that this was an awkward position, but one forced upon us against our will. This angle was tempting exposure to the enemy and they were not long in discovering it. They again formed, and just at evening twilight they opened a terrible cannonading from Atlanta directly upon the hill, and followed it with a bitter and persistent assault directly upon this angle, and came up against our works, leaving only the earth wall between the two maddened lines. This last and bloodiest assault lasted until long after dark.

The struggle to recover from us the hill was fierce and desperate beyond description. The carnage at this point was terrible and sickening. The Confederates in force occupied the ditch outside our works on the hill, and to prepare them for this desperate charge they had been supplied with liquor, and were reckless to the utter disregard of their own lines. We succeeded in pushing out an angle of our works in such manner as to command this ditch, and then begged of them to surrender and come inside, or

ALL WOULD BE DESTROYED;

but they met our solicitations with curses. I told them that we could not longer permit them to remain where they were, and that if they would not surrender they might retire, and that in doing so they should not be fired upon; but they spurned my offer. We therefore opened an enfilading fire upon them and all were killed. This ended the battle of the 22d of July, 1864, or the "Battle of Atlanta," as it has been called.

During the whole of the battle Gen. Hood, the commander-in-chief of the Confederate forces in and about Atlanta, occupied a position where the hill and most of the Seventeenth Corps line were plainly within his view, and he witnessed all the movements and personally directed the attacks from toward Atlanta. Shoupe's battery was close by his position, and he kept it playing upon us all the afternoon and much of the night. From the opening to the close of the engagement, from 11:30 a.m. to 8 or 9 p.m., the fighting was incessant, and the Third and Fourth Divisions of the Seventeenth Corps were constantly engaged, except during the assault upon the Sixteenth Corps at the inception of the battle.

Almost at the very opening of the battle, the gallant McPherson, the typical soldier, who, as our former Seventeenth Corps commander, and now as the commander of the Army of the Tennessee had led us so successfully through so many tiresome marches and hard-fought battles, was shot by the enemy and fell dead from his horse.

AS A COMMANDER,

Gen. McPherson was most thoroughly respected, and as a soldier and man he was loved by every officer and man in the old Seventeenth Corps, and probably by every one in the Army of the Tennessee. He was not only intrepid and brave, but he was gentle and kind always—always and everywhere a perfect gentleman. His gentility was not like a garment, to be put on or off for occasions, but it was inbred, and constituted the very warp and woof of his being. He would always treat a subordinate in the ranks as kindly and considerately as he would the commanding officer over him. While he was unflinchingly brave and fearless, yet he was cautious and careful, and never unnecessarily exposed his men. Capt. Raymond was sent to him for orders, as before stated. He rode up to him, obtained orders, and started to return to me by a road which entered the woods when Gen. McPherson rapidly followed him. Capt. Raymond had ridden but a short distance in the woods when he found himself closely in front of Gen. Cleburne's line of battle, parallel with the road and moving rapidly toward it. They cried out "Halt" to him and commenced firing, but being in full gallop he passed about a regimental front, when his horse was killed and he fell into the enemy's hands. Capt. Raymond said he had scarcely extricated himself from his horse, when again he heard the word "halt," followed by firing, and

GEN. McPHERSON FELL.

McPherson knew that Capt. Raymond had come to him on this road and was returning on it, and so had no reason to apprehend danger from following him. He was also familiar with the road before, for he was at my headquarters that morning and rode to the front with me on this same road. The death of McPherson was quickly known to all the troops, and also the fact that Gen. Logan had succeeded to the command of the Army of the Tennessee. In Gen. Logan all had confidence. He was the original commander of my division, and was idolized by it. He was personally well known by every officer and man in our army, and his presence in battle was always a power. He had a wonderful influence to awaken the enthusiasm of troops, and to get out of them all the fight that was in them. His simple presence seemed to be sufficient for exciting to deeds of valor every officer and man.

Gen. R. K. Scott, the commander of my Second Brigade, rode out to the 68th Ohio as soon as he discovered it was engaged, but hearing firing on the front line, he started to return to his brigade, and followed Gen. McPherson into the woods. He had gone but a few yards when his horse was shot, he slightly wounded and captured by the enemy.

The same force that killed Gen. James B. McPherson and captured Gen. R. K. Scott and Capt. John B. Raymond a few moments later presented itself at the foot of the hill held by Gen. M. F. Force and commenced the assault, in the very beginning of which Gen. Force and his Adjutant General (Capt. Walker) both fell severely wounded—Capt. Walker through his thigh, from which he subsequently died, and Gen. Force by a minie ball through his head, entering just below the outer corner of the left eye and coming out close by the right ear. That he recovered, and was able five months later to go with us on the march to the sea, now seems almost miraculous.

Thus the Army of the Tennessee was deprived of its loved and trusted commander and my division of its First and Second Brigade commanders by Gen. Cleburne's advanced line in his first assault. Gen. Scott was a discreet, but a brave, daring and dashing officer, just the man to have commanded in such a battle, and his services

WOULD HAVE BEEN INVALUABLE.

Gen. Force was a born soldier, and greatly admired, not only by his own brigade, but by the whole division. His loss was severely felt, and at first threatened to be disastrous. The next in rank in his brigade was Col. Geo. E. Bryant, of the 12th Wis., who had been but a few days with the division and was but little known to the officers and men. When I directed him to assume command of the brigade and to hold the hill at all hazards, Col. Bryant modestly preferred to remain with his regiment, but reluctantly obeyed the order. He very soon, however, won the confidence of the officers and men of his brigade by his brave, cool and self-possessed manner and his careful and skillful handling of his command. It was a trying ordeal for one who had not before held a command larger than a regiment, but Col. Bryant proved equal to the emergency. He knew he was filling the place of one who was second to no officer of his rank in all those qualities which go to make up the successful commander.

My Second Brigade was commanded during the battle by Col. G. F. Wiles, of the 78th Ohio, my old regiment. Col. Wiles (afterward Gen. Wiles) was well known to the brigade and throughout the Seventeenth Corps, and had the full confidence of his command from the beginning of the battle. He was regarded as the best drillmaster in the Western army, and was well known for his skill in handling his men. In action he was always cool, brave, and self-possessed, and in this battle, calling so often for a change of front, fighting both to the front and the rear, his skill as a tactician was called into full play. Gen. G. A. Smith had been in command of the Fourth Division only 24 hours when this battle opened, and could hardly have been expected to have his division well in hand when called upon to resist a fierce and vigorous assault by overwhelming numbers directly upon his flank.

This assault upon the left flank of the Fourth Division so mixed its companies and men of different companies and regiments together as to have made troops of less nerve and patriotism perfectly worthless and an easy prey for the enemy. The same was true later in the day of the Third Division, and in fact the men of the two divisions became thoroughly intermixed about the time of our change of front, yet all this did not seem to materially affect the

FIGHTING OR STAYING QUALITIES

of the men. Wherever they were their faces were to the enemy, and every man doing soldierly work.

The use of clubbed muskets and hand-to-hand conflicts were frequent all along the line. Gen. W. W. Belknap, a gallant and brave officer in our Fourth Division, personally seized the Colonel of the 45th Ala. by his coat collar and dragged him over the works and made him a prisoner. Some privates in the 17th Wis., of the Third Division, seized the horse of a Lieutenant of a Confederate battery by the bridle and dragged the horse and rider over the works and made prisoners of both. Many prisoners all along the line were captured in the same way.

Where there were so many man-to-man encounters, interesting incidents were numerous; but I will not prolong this article, already much too long, to mention but few. Capt. John Orr, of the 78th Ohio, discovered a Confederate just about to bayonet a wounded color-bearer of the 78th Ohio, and, springing upon him with this light side sword, cut the Confederate's head almost clear from his body by a single blow, for which act he was awarded a gold medal. Capt. Orr was a short, compactly-built man, utterly devoid of fear, so far as any observer could discover. I afterward asked him how he was ever able to strike such a blow with so light a sword. He replied, "O, I weighed two tons when I struck that blow!" and it does not seem that a less weight could account for the execution. The conflicts for flags were numerous all along the line.

The number of men engaged in this battle was over 60,000. On the 20th of July there were present for duty in the Fifteenth, Sixteenth and Seventeenth Corps, including the artillery and not the cavalry, 27,593; while on the 10th of July there were present for duty in Hardee's and Cheatham's Corps, including artillery, 37,455. On the 20th at Peach Tree Creek the enemy's loss had been more than ours, and on the 21st about the same. The assistance afforded the Confederates by men and artillery in Atlanta, and not belonging to Cheatham's Corps, more than compensated for their losses referred to; so they must have brought into battle on the 22d fully 37,000 men against our 27,000, making in all 64,000 engaged.

The artillery did grand service throughout the battle. The 3d Ohio's heavy rifled Parrott guns could not, of course, be used against charging troops with the same facility and effect as could lighter and shorter guns. It neglected no opportunity, however, to put in effective work where it could be used. It was often brought to bear in enfilading a Confederate line or column. Its officers were vigilant, with their eyes open, watching for opportunities for getting in their work. It did magnificent service in aiding the Fifteenth Corps to

RECOVER ITS LOST WORKS AND GUNS.

Battery H, of Michigan, (Rodman guns,) under Capt. M. D. Elliott, was very effective. The guns were light and capable of being easily handled and fired very rapidly. This battery had a reputation for promptness second to none in the army. Wherever infantry could go this battery would also go, and its officers and men were very skillful in handling it. In the battle of the 22d, as in many battles before and some afterward, it was so handled as to very materially aid in winning the laurels of the day.

The McCallister (Ill.) battery of 24-pound howitzers was in its glory in this battle. It was just such fighting as these guns were intended for, and Capt. Cooper handled it with great courage and skill. He was wonderfully quick and accurate in calculating distance with his eye. He would direct the cutting of the dial fuze so as to burst his shell just where he pleased. He took his position on a stump in the midst of his guns, where he had a commanding view of his battery and all the approaches to it, and no amount of shot and shell from the enemy, or more gentle persuasion of his own officers and men, could induce him to leave his exposed position. There he stood as composed as if on review, and he made it simply impossible for any charging column or line to reach our works at the point where he was situated.

I must not extend this description with further special notices. Where all did so well, it is invidious to make special mention.

If the old Third Division had ever been defeated before, it probably would have been on that day. It had been well schooled on the battlefield, and knew no result of a battle but victory, and would accept no other. It was with Grant at Fort Henry, Fort Donelson, Shiloh, Thompson's Hill, Raymond, Jackson (Miss.), Champion Hills, Big Black, and Vicksburg, besides very numerous smaller affairs. At Vicksburg the division approached nearest the Confederate works; and it was this division that blew up Fort Hill and had the terrible fight for the crater after the explosion, and held it. By reason of this Gen. Grant designated the Third Division to first enter the works and erect its flags upon the public buildings and other points where the Confederate flags had floated.

It can truthfully be said of this division that it was never driven from a position it attempted to hold; never failed to capture any point it assaulted, and never failed, from Fort Donelson to the close of the war, to respond instantly to any order for battle or march, with a due supply of rations and ammunition. It received its staying qualities and its implicit confidence in results from its great and first commander, Gen. U. S. Grant, and much of its fire and dash and enthusiasm and indomitable pluck from Gen. John A. Logan, who first organized and commanded it as a division. So it fell into my hands after the surrender of Vicksburg with a grand record to maintain, a record which, I may say, grew brighter and brighter up to the close of the war.

[*The end.*]

42

He Found McPherson's Body

"Gen. M'Pherson's Death. What Private Reynolds Says About It. Where and By Whom the Dead Hero's Body Was Found. Details of the Sad Event. General Order No. 8, and a Medal of Honor"

(Pvt. George Reynolds, October 1, 1881, p.1)

A recent publication of the account of the death of Gen. McPherson, as given by Sergt. Thompson, and published in the *Army and Navy Journal* of August 27, threw doubt on the hitherto-received account that George Reynolds, of the Iowa Volunteers, stumbled upon McPherson as he lay dying at the foot of a tree. Mr. H. Seymour Hall, a neighbor of Reynolds, has received from him, and sends to the *New York Times*, this account:

"I enlisted when a mere plow-boy on my father's farm, at Ottumwa, Iowa, in 1862; was a private in Company D, Fifteenth Iowa Volunteers. In March, 1864, re-enlisted as a veteran at Vicksburg, went home on my veteran furlough, and on my return from furlough was detained for duty at Headquarters Third brigade, Fourth division, Seventeenth Army Corps, remaining there till July 22—the day Gen. McPherson was killed. In obedience to orders, five others, with myself, starting the morning of the 22d to rejoin my command. Starting out in the direction my regiment was supposed to be,

I SAW A LINE OF BATTLE

in the distance advancing toward us, and supposing them to be our men, one of our number called out, "What in the ---- are you shooting this way for?" As we approached nearer we saw that they were rebels, one of whom, when about ten feet from me, fired on me, his bullet grazing the upper side of my right arm, my abdomen, and passing through the under side of my left arm. My gun was seized by a rebel soldier, who said, "Give me that, and you 'git' to the rear." As I moved away the rebel line continued to advance on the flank and rear of our line, which they had broken, and I was left to take care of myself. I was afterward told that all but two of my comrades were killed. After checking the bleeding of my wound the best I could, I started to make my way out of there. The thought of being a prisoner was terrible to me.

EVERYTHING WAS IN COMMOTION,

and scarcely knowing which way to go, I finally started in a northwesterly course. I struck a road leading into Atlanta, where the rebels had captured a piece of artillery, and seeing their cavalry still in possession of this road, I went back into the timber and come out on the road further out and crossed, and some little distance after crossing the road I saw a man in blue uniform lying on the ground some distance ahead, and on nearer approach recognized our beloved commander, the brave Gen. McPherson, without a living being then in sight of him save myself. He was still living, but in his death struggles, and when I offered him water he made no reply. He seemed unconscious, but showed signs of life for 15 or 20 minutes, his struggles during that time changing his head to the opposite point from what it was when I first saw him. His sword and shoulder straps were gone.

BALLS AND SHELLS WERE STILL FLYING

around us in all directions, and one shell burst so close to the General's body that it swept every leaf or loose thing from the ground. A few minutes after the General's death I saw one of our men passing some distance off, and called to him, "come here!" He asked, "Is there any danger?" I replied, "No." He then came, and while we were talking of what was best to do, three rebel soldiers, one of them carrying part of a stretcher, came up, and talked of carrying off the General's body, but fearing they would encounter some of our forces, decided not to do so. As they went away they ordered us to accompany them, but as they were unarmed like ourselves, we declined the invitation. I think the name of the Union soldier who was with me was George Farlin. He and I then started

AT A DOUBLE QUICK

to try and find our lines. In about a quarter of a mile we came upon a train of ambulances. I asked the driver of the first to go with me and get the General's body, but he refused. I went to the next one, and just as I spoke to the driver General William E. Strong, Assistant Inspector-General, Army of the Tennessee, of Gen. McPherson's staff, rode up, and I told him my story. He at once ordered the ambulance driver to follow me, when Farlin and myself led back to General McPherson at double quick, followed by General Strong, his orderly, and the ambulance driver. We five put his body in the ambulance. Farlin and I got in, and the driver, following the lead of Gen. Strong, drove rapidly to General Sherman's headquarters, where Gen. McPherson's body was taken out of the ambulance, which was then driven on with me to the Twenty-third Corps hospital.

On the 26th day of July, four days after the above events, an ambulance was sent up to the hospital, with orders to

TAKE ME TO MY REGIMENT.

Ignorant of the purpose of this, on my arrival, I found my regiment drawn up on parade. I was taken to the front and General W. W. Belknap, at that time Colonel of the Fifteenth Iowa, read to the command an order, which was then for the first time known to me. It read as follows:

"H'DQ'RS SEVENTEENTH ARMY CORPS.
DEPT. OF THE TENNESSEE,
BEFORE ATLANTA, GA., July 26, 1864.
G.O. No. 8.

"During the bloody battle of the 22d inst., in which the Corps was engaged, Private George J. Reynolds, Company D, Fifteenth Iowa Infantry Volunteers, was, while in the performance of his duty on the skirmish line, severely wounded in the arm. In attempting to evade capture he came to the spot where the late beloved and gallant Commander of this Army, Major-General McPherson, was lying mortally wounded. Forgetting all considerations of himself, Private Reynolds clung to this old commander, and

AMID THE ROAR OF BATTLE,

and a storm of bullets, administered to the wants of his gallant chief, quenching his dying thirst, and affording him such comfort as lay in his power.

"After General McPherson breathed his last, Private Reynolds was chiefly instrumental in recovering his body, going with two of his staff officers, pointing out the body, and assisting it to an ambulance under heavy fire from the enemy, while his wound was still uncared for. The noble and devoted conduct of this soldier cannot be too highly praised, and is commended to the consideration of the officers and men of this command. In consideration of this gallantry and noble and unselfish devotion the gold medal of honor will be conferred upon Private George J. Reynolds, Company D, Fifteenth Iowa Infantry Volunteers, in front of his command. This order will be read at the head of every regiment, battery, and detachment in this Corps. By command of

Major-General FRANK P. BLAIR.
A. J. ALEXANDER,
Assistant Adjutant-General.

"Colonel Belknap then fastened to my breast the gold medal of honor, which is still and will remain in my possession as long as I live. Who gave the information to General Blair upon which this order was issued I do not know."

Mr. Hall adds: "General Strong, General Belknap, and too many officers of General Sherman's staff knew of this matter at the time to leave his statement unsubstantiated. The order of General Blair, issued at the time, speaks for itself. The post-office address of George J. Reynolds is Carrolton, Carroll county, Mo. He is a prosperous farmer and respected citizen, whose word is not doubted by any one who knows him. I know him to be a man of honor and truth, whose statement, even if not so satisfactorily proved as it is, could be implicitly relied on."

Blair's General Orders No. 8, commending Private George J. Reynolds for having helped retrieve General McPherson's body, is in the Official Records, *vol. 38, pt. 3, 556. William E. Strong, referred to in this* Tribune *article, was the author of an article in 1887 about McPherson's death. In it, he adds that coming upon the prostrate general, Reynolds "raised the dying General's head, placing it upon a blanket, tried to give him a drink of water from his canteen, and asked him if he had any message to communicate; but the General could make no reply, and died soon after" (Sydney Kerksis, ed.,* The Atlanta Papers *[Dayton OH: Press of Morningside Bookshop, 1980], 527). Historian Gary Ecelbarger affirms, "Private Reynolds witnessed McPherson take his last breath" (*The Day Dixie Died: The Battle of Atlanta *[New York: Thomas Dunne Books, 2010], 117).*

43

Cheatham's Breakthrough, July 22

"DeGress's Battery. The Rebels Now Disputing Over the Honor of Its Capture"

(August 10, 1899, p. 5)

A dramatic aspect of the fierce battle of July 22 was the late-afternoon, Confederate breakthrough on the Union right, part of the attack of Maj. Gen. B. Franklin Cheatham's corps on the Federal XV Corps in the vicinity of the Georgia Railroad. Brigadier General Arthur M. Manigault's and Col. Jacob Sharp's brigades sent Brig. Joseph A. J. Lightburn's division running to the rear. In the process, the Southerners overran two batteries. One of them was Capt. Francis DeGress's Battery H, 1st Illinois Light Artillery, four, 20-pounder Parrott, rifled cannon.

The Confederates chased the fleeing Federals awhile, then were called back to occupy the enemy's entrenched line. They were reinforced by a second wave, Col. Abda Johnson's brigade (more commonly named for Brig. Gen. Marcellus A. Stovall, out sick). By 4:30 p.m., Cheatham's troops held half- to three-quarters of a mile of Union earthworks (Stephen Davis, Texas Brigadier to the Fall of Atlanta: John Bell Hood *[Macon: Mercer University Press, 2019], 326-327).*

Years later, the ex-Confederates were arguing over who had taken DeGress's guns. Here is how the National Tribune *reported it in a reprinting from the* Savannah *(GA)* News. *The article refers to Stovall's Brigade, composed of five Georgia regiments, including the 42nd Infantry.*

At the Reunion of the 42d Ga. regiment in Social Circle last week a full history of that gallant organization was read and the truth of their claim of the capture of the Degress Battery on July 22, 1864 was established. This regiment, under the command of Col. Abda Johnson, of Cartersville, Ga., one of the ablest and bravest men in the State, charged across the track of the Georgia Railroad between Atlanta and Decatur and captured this famous battery of guns. The Degress Battery was being admirably served by Northern gunners and was carrying havoc to the ranks of the Southern soldiers. The 42d Ga. regiment was a part of Gen. M. A. Stovall's Brigade and was an organization conspicuous for gallantry throughout the war. It fought at Chickamauga and in the battles between Dalton and Atlanta and on this occasion, being one of hardest fought battles around Atlanta, distinguished itself by this memorable victory. A sign-board, to-day, on the edge of the railroad, marks the spot where the charge was made.

The significant part of the speeches and essays of the 42d Ga., bearing upon the capture of the Degress Battery, is that Gen. Manigault's South Carolina Brigade laid claim to the same achievement, and in its interest a pamphlet disputing with Stovall's Brigade the honor of this capture was published. At the meeting of the 42d Ga., however, last week the reports of Gen. Sherman upon the silencing and loss of this famous battery and the testimony of Capt. E. P. Howell, himself a gallant artilleryman, who was on the ground, is proof positive that Stovall's and not Manigault's Brigade should be given this credit. Capt. Howell says that he saw the charge of Col. Abda Johnson's Georgia regiment, witnessed the seizure of the guns, saw the 42d turn the Yankee battery upon the fleeing enemy, and described the effort to carry the horses of the Confederate artillery up to the guns to remove them into the lines of the Southern army. The heavy firing, however, frightened the horses so that they could not be harnessed to the captured cannon. No reflection was made upon the South Carolina troops who fought in the battle, but the fact remains that the credit of securing that artillery prize must be given to Stovall's Brigade. Palmam qui meruit ferat!

44

Taking Back Those Parrotts

An eyewitness, and one who was in the charge, "The Fate of that Ohio Battery"

(May 24, 1883, p. 7)

L. Smadley, "Who Recaptured the De Grasse Battery?"

(June 14, 1883, p. 7)

Charles D. Miller, "De Grasse's Battery"

(April 23, 1885, p. 3)

With the death of General McPherson, Maj. Gen. John A. Logan, XV Corps commander, took charge of the Army of the Tennessee on July 22. Hearing of the breach in the XV Corps line, he rode forth, rallying Lightburn's troops and ordering reinforcements to counterattack, retake DeGress's cannon, and restore the line. General Sherman, in his Memoirs, *credited two divisions of the XV Corps, Brig. Gen. Charles Woods's First Division and Brig. Gen. Morgan Smith's Second Division, as retaking the guns (vol. 2, 81).*

But there were other claimants. Among Logan's reinforcements was Col. August Mersy's Second Brigade of Brig. Gen. Thomas Sweeny's Second Division, XVI Corps; after the war, its members contended that in the afternoon counterattack they had "liberated" DeGress's guns.

So began the argument among Northern veterans as to who recaptured DeGress's battery. Over the years, at least a score of articles or letters discussed the issue. Here we excerpt a number of them, as an indication that long after the fighting had ended, Union soldiers were still playing it out in their memories.

- "De Grass' Ohio battery was . . . captured by Colonel Mercer's Second brigade, Second division, Sixteenth Army Corps, composed of the Sixty-sixth Illinois volunteer infantry, Twelfth Illinois volunteer infantry and Eighty-first Ohio volunteer infantry."

"Eye witness" misspelled Mersy's name as well as DeGress's name, misidentifying his Illinois battery, but he correctly named the three infantry regiments of Mersy's brigade. A month later, the National Tribune *printed a short note from "Drummer," who*

identified "Eye witness" as a member of Co. E, 66th Illinois; "Drummer" also resided in Oakland, Ill., and evidently knew him (Drummer, Co. D, 66th Ill., Oakland, Ill., "To the Editor National Tribune,*" [June 28, 1883], 7).*

* * *

- Smadley's regiment served in Col. Hugo Wangelin's Third Brigade, Brig. Gen. Charles R. Woods' First Division, XV Corps;
- he quotes Sherman's *Memoirs* (vol. 2, 81) in which the general states, "we saw Wood's troops advance and....at the same time, the division which had been driven back along the railroad [Brig. Gen. Morgan Smith's Second Division, XV Corps] was rallied by General Logan in person. . . . These combined forces drove the enemy into Atlanta, recovering the twenty-pound Parrott guns";
- Smadley thus affirms, "The Fifteenth Corps alone recovered the ground and the guns," adding, "no description of that engagement that I ever found mentions any brigade of the Sixteenth Corps."

* * *

The following supports the contention that Woods's division, XV Corps recaptured DeGress's Parrotts but that the feat had been performed by men of Col. Milo Smith's First Brigade, not Wangelin's Third.

- Miller served in color company C of the 76th Ohio, First Brigade, First Division, XV Corps;
- after the Confederate breakthrough and retreat of Morgan Smith's Second Division, Wood's division was ordered to counterattack; around 5 p.m. they drove the Johnnies off;
- "Capt. De Grasse soon came up and threw his arms around his pet guns and cried for joy. He thanked the 76th Ohio for saving his battery.

Miller's full article appears in Larry M. Strayer and Richard A. Baumgartner, eds., Echoes of Battle: The Atlanta Campaign *(Huntington, WV: Blue Acorn Press, 1991), pp. 250-251.*

45

Captain DeGress Sides with the Sixteenth Corps

A Veteran, "Fighting Them Over. Who Recaptured the De Gres Battery in the Battle Before Atlanta"

(June 28, 1883, p. 7)

In the back-and-forth between veterans of the XV and XVI Corps as to who recaptured DeGress's battery, an important piece of evidence surrounds the guns themselves, which had been spiked: the veterans who remembered and could write about the spiked breeches were obviously the men who reached the guns first.

- "Colonel Mersy formed the brigades, with the Twelfth Illinois on the left, Eighty-first Ohio in the center, and Sixty-sixth Illinois on the right";
- Mersy then ordered the charge, "recapturing Captain De Gres' four-gun battery of twenty-pound Parrott guns, the rebels not having time to take it away. They shot down the horses in a heap right in our sight as they fell back. . . .
- "The credit of recapturing the battery belongs to company G, Sixth-sixth Illinois (Lieut. P. P. Ellis, commanding,) and company K, (Lieut. Alvin S. Davis, commanding.) The rebels had only time to spike the guns with 10-penny nails. We pulled them out."

46

More on DeGress's Guns

J. B. Haldeman, "Other Versions"

(June 28, 1883, p. 7)

J. M. Naylor, "To the Editor of the National Tribune"

(June 28, 1883, p. 7)

Another recollection comes from this member of the 66th Illinois Western Sharpshooters, part of Mersy's brigade, Sweeny's division, XVI Corps.

We went up the hill with the usual Yankee yell, and when we got in sight of the Johnnies they very suddenly found out that they had urgent business in Atlanta, and did not stand on the order of going, but went at once.

When we reached the works we found a battery of 20-pound Parrotts, but spiked. Our boys, always in some devilment, got to monkeying around the pieces, and soon had the spikes out and the guns reloaded and gave the rebels our parting compliments. Up to this time there was no bursted gun in this battery; but with no rebs in sight some one suggested the idea of throwing a shot into Atlanta, and to do so it was deemed necessary to put in a double charge of powder, which was done, a ball was rammed home, the piece elevated as high as it would go, and all being now ready the word was given to fire—and she went off! Metal fairly rained around there awhile, and by the debris we concluded the gun had bursted! We anticipated a blessing when the battery boys came up, but instead they seemed thankful, as they informed us they had cracked that piece some time before and had been afraid of it; but, notwithstanding there was quite a crowd around the gun when it burst, not a man was hurt.

* * *

- In the Federal counterattack the 81st Ohio helped retake DeGress' battery;
- "Captain Dc Gres was himself with us. No other member of his battery being there just then, he formed some men of companies I and C, Eighty-

first Ohio volunteer infantry, into a squad to man his guns, of which squad I was a member."

- "We put the guns into use, but by awkwardness and the use of an imperfect shell, managed to burst the muzzle of the gun spoken of."

* * *

Captain DeGress wrote about the fight over his guns in an after-action report (E. Chris Evans, ed., "Report of the Battle of Atlanta by Capt. Francis DeGress Commanding Battery H, 1st Illinois Light Artillery," Blue & Gray, *vol. 11, no. 4 [April 1994], 28-30).*

The Enemy advanced in good order. Colors in the center and when I saw them the 2nd Company of my right gave away. I had the 2 left Guns spiked and fell back about 10 yards to my right section with which I fired on them until within 15 yards when I ordered the right Gun to be spiked, and waiting a short time I fired the left Gun myself, while Sergeant Peter S. Wyman poked it and fell back.

I had all my Prolongs fixed and made an attempt to pull the Guns off, but they were to heavy and my men were to much worn out. When I saw the left of the 30th Ohio fall back I ordered up my Limbers but it was to late, the enemy was between me and them. Going to the rear, I saw a brigade of the16th A. C. advancing and driving the Enemy from our Position and following them up I took possession of my Guns again.

In a very few minutes I had one Gun unspiked and with the assistance of Sergt. John McGeorge of my Battery and some Infantry men we fired at the retreating Rebels. By dark I had 3 Guns unspiked and was shelling the Woods, the Enemy's Batterys and the City.

I am sorry to report that one Gun Bursted after the third round, and the only cause I can give is that the wrought iron bands having been cracked for several weeks made the cast iron to weak. I first discovered the crack in the Reinforcement while firing at a very high elevation on Batterys on Kennesaw Mountain.

Not a man was hurt by the bursting of the Gun although they were standing thick around it and some of the pieces 50 to 100 pds heavy were thrown 100 yards. The carriage was much shattered.

47

Dodge Meets Sherman After the Battle

Grenville M. Dodge, "Battle of Atlanta"

(September 1, 1904, pp. 1, 6)

In May 1885, Maj. Gen. Grenville M. Dodge, commander of the Federal XVI Corps during the Atlanta Campaign, read a paper, "The Battle of Atlanta" before the New York Commandery of the Military Order of the Loyal Legion of the United States (MOLLUS). He later included it in his book, The Battle of Atlanta and Other Campaign Addresses, Etc. *(Council Bluffs IA: Monarch Printing Company, 1911). The* National Tribune *also printed the paper, which is a rather general account of the engagement of July 22. It contains, however, the following incident.*

At about 10 o'clock on the night of the 22d, the three corps commanders of the Army of the Tennessee (one of them in command of the army) [*Maj. Gen. John A. Logan, XV Corps commander, had taken over following McPherson's death*] met in the rear of the Fifteenth Corps, on the line of the Decatur road, under an oak tree, and there discussed the results of the day. Blair's men were at the time in the trenches; in some places the enemy held one side and they the other. The men of the Fifteenth Corps were still in their own line, but tired and hungry, and those of the Sixteenth were, after their hard day's fight, busy throwing up intrenchments on the field they had held and won. It was thought that the Army of the Cumberland and the Army of the Ohio, which had not been engaged that day, should send a force to relieve Blair, and Dodge [the author refers to himself in the third person], being the junior Corps commander, was dispatched by General Logan, at the requests of Generals Logan and Blair, to see General Sherman [to request reinforcements from Schofield or Thomas]. My impression is that I met him in a tent; I have heard it said that he had his headquarters in a house. [*General Sherman was quartered that day at the Augustus Hurt house, not far from the battlefield.*] When I met him he seemed rather surprised to see me, but greeted me cordially, and spoke of the loss of McPherson. I stated to him my errand. He turned upon me and said, "Dodge, you whipped them today, didn't you?" I said, "Yes, sir." Then he said: "Can't you do it again tomorrow?" I said, "Yes, sir"; bade him good night, and went back to my command, determined never to go upon another such errand. As he explained it afterward, he wanted it said that the little Army of the Tennessee had fought the great battle that day, needing no help, no aid, and that it could be said that all alone it had whipped the whole of Hood's Army. Therefore, he let us hold our position and our line, knowing that Hood would not dare attack us after the "thrashing" he had already received.

48

The McCook-Stoneman Cavalry Raid, July 27-August 12

"Cavalry Raids. The Ill-Fated Expeditions to the Rear of Atlanta"

(July 31, 1884, p. 3)

THE INQUIRY.

TO THE EDITOR: As a subscriber of the NATIONAL TRIBUNE I would like to hear through your columns something in regard to the McCook and Stoneman Raid in the rear of Atlanta, in the latter part of July, 1864. As to the intentions of the commanders or their orders given them to make the raid, the command to which I belonged (McCook's) lay nearly all day near Jonesboro waiting, as the soldiers supposed, for Stoneman's command, but it did not make its appearance. There has been a good deal of controversy between the soldiers of the two commands as to where the fault lay. Can you give us anything definite about it, and oblige many participants in said raid?—JASPER N. FINNEY, Co. E, 4th Ind. Cav., Valparaiso, Ind.

P.S.—That raid was the cause of my taking an excursion to Andersonville. The experience exceeded the pleasure of that trip by a big majority.

THE ANSWER.

An important feature in the Atlanta campaign was the series of raids made by the Union cavalry against the railroads leading southward and eastward from Atlanta. The first lines of communication selected to be broken was the railroad system connecting Atlanta with the southwest, comprising the Atlanta and West Point, and the West Point and Montgomery roads.

On July 10, Gen. Lovell H. Rousseau with 2,000 cavalry made an expedition from Decatur, Ala., to Opelika, a station on the latter road, where a road diverges east to Columbus, Ga., and thence to Macon. The column crossed the Coosa on the 13th near the Ten Islands, where in a sharp engagement the 5th and 8th Iowa Cav. routed a body of rebel cavalry passing through Talladega. He crossed the Tallapoosa, and on the 16th instant struck the West Point & Montgomery Road at Loachapoka, 10 miles east of Opelika, to which place the railroad was well broken up, the bridges and culverts destroyed, besides three miles of the branch toward Columbus and two toward West Point. Gen. Rousseau then turned northward and brought his command in safety to Marietta on the 22d, with a loss of less than 30 men.

The next raid was made against the Georgia Railroad, and the command of Gen. Kenner Garrard was designated for the expedition.

Gen. Garrard, in obedience to orders, marched to Covington, 41 miles east of Atlanta, and destroyed the railroad bridges over the Yellow and Ulcopauhatchie Rivers (branches of the Ocmulgee), the first bridge 550 feet and the latter 250 feet in length, destroyed three trains of cars, numerous depots, smaller bridges and culverts, and tore up the track for seven miles between the two rivers, besides burning 2,000 bales of cotton, a large hospital building at Covington, and a large quantity of hospital and commissary stores, bringing with him several hundred prisoners, horses and mules. He lost but two men in the expedition.

The success of these demonstrations upon the enemy's lines of communication emboldened Gen. Sherman to undertake the destruction of the Atlanta & West Point, and Macon & Western Railroads south and southwest from Atlanta. To aid in this enterprise, the Army of the Tennessee was ordered to take position with its right resting on East Point, where the above-mentioned railroads diverge from each other.

The two columns selected for this perilous enterprise, composed of the flower of the Union cavalry, were placed under command of Gen. Edward M. McCook, commanding the First Division of the Army of the Cumberland, and Gen. George B. Stoneman, commanding the cavalry of the Army of the Ohio. McCook's command comprised the following regiments: The First Brigade, consisting of the 1st Tenn., 2d Mich., 8th Iowa Cav., and the 4th Ky. M't'd Inf., under Gen. John T. Croxton; the Second Brigade, under Lieut.-Col. W. H Torry, was composed of the 1st Wis. and 2d and 4th Ind. Cav. The following picked regiments were added from other divisions: 2d Ky., 5th Iowa and 8th Ind. Cav. from the Third Division; 4th Tenn. Cav. from the Fourth Division, and the 9th Ind. Cav. from the Army of the Tennessee, forming a Third Brigade, under command of Col. T. J. Harrison.

Gen. Stoneman's division consisted of three brigades, under command of Cols. Horace Capron, James Biddle, and Silas G. Adams, comprising the 5th and 6th Ind., 14th and 16th Ill., 1st, 11th, and 12th Ky., 8th Mich., and McLaughlin's Squadron of Ohio Cav. Gen. Garrard's division, temporarily assigned to Stoneman's column, consisted of the three brigades commanded by Cols. Minty, Long, and Miller.

This force, when concentrated, was believed by Gen. Sherman to be amply strong enough to take care of Wheeler's cavalry and to effect the object of the expedition, which was to rendezvous at Lovejoy's Station, on the Macon Railroad, 30 miles south of Atlanta, on the night of July 28, and then make such a complete destruction of the road as would lead to the speedy abandonment of Atlanta. Stoneman's column moved southward on the east of Atlanta, making for McDonough, a town about 10 miles east of Lovejoy's, sending Garrard to Flat Rock, between Atlanta and his line of march, to cover his movement, while with his three brigades he marched towards the Georgia Central Railroad, following it as far as Covington, whence he struck due south and to the east of the Ocmulgee for Macon, distant 60 miles, in the neighborhood of which he arrived on the 30th. While moving southward a detachment of the 14th Ill. Cav., under Lieut. Davidson, was sent east to Gordon, on the Georgia Central Railroad, where 11 locomotives and several trains of quartermaster's stores were destroyed, together with several bridges between that place and Macon.

Meantime Gen. McCook marched down the right bank of the Chattahoochie, west of Atlanta, to the neighborhood of Riverton, where he crossed on pontoons and made for Palmetto Station on the Atlanta and West Point Railroad, 25 miles south of Atlanta, where he destroyed a section of the road. He thence moved eastward upon Fayetteville and burned 500 wagons belonging to the Confederate army, besides killing 800 mules and capturing several hundred quartermasters', commissaries' and train guards and exchanging their jaded horses for fresh ones.

Between Fairburn and Palmetto the1st Wis. Cav., in a severe action with Roddy's Confederate brigade, lost their gallant commander, Maj. Nathan Paine, killed at the head of his command. The regiment, forced back by superior numbers, was compelled to retreat across the Chattahoochie, thus ending its participation in the expedition.

Gen. McCook's column reached Lovejoy's, the point of rendezvous, on the morning of the 31st, nearly according to previous arrangement, but was unable to hear from Stoneman, owing to his disregard of the order to meet McCook at that point.

Thus far all had gone well, and if the contemplated junction had taken place the unified column would have been strong enough to force its way to Macon and possibly to Andersonville, where the expedition would have covered itself with glory by liberating the Union soldiers confined in that notorious prison-pen.

McCook destroyed a large quantity of cotton and a section of the Macon & Western Railroad, burning several trains of cars; but, finding his progress eastward barred by a constantly-accumulating force of the enemy, he turned off to the southwest, capturing a cavalry supply train, and beyond Newman [sic: Newnan], a station of the Atlanta & West Point Railroad, 15 miles south of Palmetto, encountered a force of the enemy's cavalry, under Gens. Roddy, Wheeler and Jackson. Roddy had taken position in his front, near the crossing of the Chattahoochie at Brown's Mills, Jackson and Wheeler came up in his rear, and the Union cavalry found itself surrounded by a largely-superior force. A sanguinary and disastrous engagement ensued, the command attacking and cutting its way through the enemy with the loss of many officers and men and all the prisoners and animals taken on the raid, crossing the Chattahoochie at Philpot's Ferry, near Franklin, on the 31st. A section of the 18th Ind. battery accompanying the expedition was destroyed, the guns being spiked and buried.

On this most unfortunate expedition the casualties among commanding officers was unusually severe. Col. J. T. Croxton, commanding the First Brigade, was captured, but, escaping from the enemy, he wandered for many days in the woods, fed and guided by negroes, and at last found his way, more dead than alive, to the Union lines. Col. Dorr, 8th Iowa Cav., who succeeded him, with Capt. Southerland, A.A.G. of the brigade, were also captured. Lieut.-Col. W. H. Torry,1st Wis., commanding Second Brigade, was killed while leading his command. A vigorous pursuit followed, in which the 4th Ky. M't'd Inf., under command of Col. R. M. Kelly, one of the finest regiments in the service, being left as rear-guard, held its ground until its ammunition was expended, when 300 of the regiment were captured. The command reached the Union lines, leaving a large number of its best officers and men in the hands of the enemy or hiding in the swamps of the Chattahoochie.

Stoneman's column was even more unfortunate. Before reaching Macon, Gen. Stoneman learned that the Union prisoners at that place had been sent away, and he decided to return at once by the way he had come. Nothing could have been more foolhardy. The whole country in his rear was aroused, and every road thronged with horsemen ready to carry intelligence of his movements to the nearest station. When Wheeler moved to the right, joining Jackson in pursuit of McCook, he left Gen. Iverson to attack Stoneman, whose force he encountered on the morning of the 31st near Hillsboro, Ga. After a brief engagement Gen. Stoneman decided to surrender, at the same time sending notice of his intention to his brigade commanders. Col. Adams, commanding the 1st, 11th and 12th Ky. Cav., immediately drew his men from the center of the line, mounted and rode away, reaching Marietta after a wide detour to the east, in safety. Col. Capron, being on the extreme right, did not receive the order so soon, and saw with surprise the sudden withdrawal of the Kentucky regiments. The enemy pushed thorough the gap in the center, captured Biddle's brigade and made a rush for the horses of Capron's regiments. In the race that ensued, the fleet-footed Confederates, unencumbered with heavy cavalry boots, outstripped the Union soldiers and a hand-to-hand fight ensued for the possession of the horses, in which many hard blows were given and received. Col. Capron, collecting about 200 of his men, set out in an eastward direction, hoping by a rapid march to elude his pursuers. He was overtaken, however, while in camp on the night of the 3d of August, after having marched 56 miles in the preceding 24 hours. His force had been considerably augmented by straggling parties who had joined him on the march, most of whom, however, were unarmed and dismounted. Maj. Davidson had joined him on the previous day, with his battalion of the 14th Ill. Cav., and Col. Biddle, with a small detachment of his brigade, who had escaped at Hillsboro.

The furious charge of the Confederate cavalry on the thoroughly-exhausted troops, scattered them in all directions. Many of them were drowned by the fall of a bridge, and by far the greater number were made prisoners. The heroic commander, with his son and one companion, mounted and escaped by the superior speed of their horses A large number, hiding in the densely-wooded swamps, finally found their way to the Union lines. Thus, in disaster, this expedition, planned in wisdom and blunderingly executed, came to an untimely end.

Gen. Garrard, while in position at Flat Rock, was attacked on the morning of the 28th by Hines's and Kelly's brigades of cavalry. The engagement lasted several hours, but resulted in holding these commands in check, while Stoneman pursued his course southward. A charge was ordered finally which drove and dispersed the enemy, when Garrard returned to his position on the left of the army, near Lithonia.

The following dispatches were received by Gen. Hood at Atlanta:

Wheeler says: "We have just completed the killing, capturing, and breaking up of the entire raiding party under Gen. McCook. Some 950 prisoners, two pieces of artillery, and 1,200 horses and equipments captured."

Iverson's dispatch of same date is as follows: "Gen. Stoneman, after having his force routed yesterday, surrendered with 500 men; the rest of his command are scattered and flying towards Eatonton. Many have been already killed or captured."

Hood says: "Gen. Shoupe, in recording these two telegrams in his diary, remarks that 'the first day of August deserves to be marked with a white stone.' He, doubtless, in common with every Southerner experienced deep concern in regard to the Federal prisoners at Andersonville, as it was reported that Sherman had arms in readiness for their use. Fearful, indeed, would have been the consequences, had they been turned loose upon the country in its unprotected condition."

This article is remarkable in several respects: first, obviously, for its broad perspective, relating four Union cavalry raids around Atlanta in July 1864; for its accuracy as narrative and attention to factual detail; and for its date, appearing in the National Tribune *years before publication of the* Official Records, *volume 38, which treated the Atlanta Campaign. Unsigned, it appears to have been the conscientious work of the* National Tribune *staff (possibly editor McElroy himself), responding to Corporal Finney's inquiry. Nonetheless, it has been overlooked by such scholars as David Evans in his* Sherman's Horsemen: Union Cavalry Operations in the Atlanta Campaign *(Bloomington: Indiana University Press, 1996).*

In Rousseau's raid, July 10-22, Union cavalry wrecked 26 miles of track in east central Alabama, cutting the railroad between Montgomery and Atlanta.

During July 21-24, Garrard's horsemen destroyed six miles of the Georgia Railroad linking Atlanta and Augusta. The author is correct as to the Federals' main achievement, burning the 555-foot trestle over Yellow River, some 30 miles east of Atlanta. They also destroyed the 250-foot bridge over the Alcovy (Ulcofauhachee) River. The article does not note, though, that the rail line to Augusta had already been knocked out of service; Federal infantry and cavalry on July 17-19 had torn up several miles of track near Stone Mountain, 15 miles east of Atlanta.

That left only the Macon & Western Railroad to bring in supplies for Confederate General John B. Hood's army defending Atlanta.

In the largest Federal cavalry operation of the Atlanta Campaign, Sherman planned to send some 5,150 troopers in two columns under Edward McCook and George Stoneman to break the railroad to Macon. By separate routes, both were to head for Lovejoy's Station on the Macon & Western, 20 miles south of Atlanta. After wrecking track and cutting the telegraph line, McCook and Stoneman were to ride back to the Union army north of Atlanta.

The two columns set out early on July 27, Stoneman around east of the city, McCook west. At Palmetto, 20 miles southwest of Atlanta, on the 28th, McCook's raiders fell upon a Confederate wagon train, burned 600 wagons, and sabered hundreds of mules before pushing on to Lovejoy's. There they tore up two miles of track (quickly repaired) and chopped down telegraph poles. Failing to see Stoneman's approach, McCook ordered his men to mount up for return to Atlanta.

Unknown to McCook, Stoneman had asked Sherman for permission to ride to Macon, free the thousand Union officers imprisoned there, and ride farther southwest to liberate the tens of thousands of Northern soldiers confined in the notorious Rebel prison camp at Andersonville. Sherman reluctantly consented but stressed that the railroad should be Stoneman's first objective.

Stoneman disobediently did not even head for Lovejoy's but rode straight for Macon. After being chased away there by local defense troops, Stoneman headed northeast. On July 31, at a place called Sunshine Church, Confederate brigadier Alfred Iverson attacked the Union force and so thoroughly thrashed it that Stoneman and 440 men surrendered; the rest made their way back to Atlanta as best they could.

The same happened to McCook's column on July 30 at Brown's Mill, near Newnan, when Gen. Joseph Wheeler attacked it, scattering the Federals in all directions.

McCook's and Stoneman's casualties for this failed raid totaled 2,559—49.7% out of 5,144 Federals who had set out (Evans, Sherman's Horsemen, *376).*

The author's most noticeable lapses involve Stoneman. He does not mention Stoneman's disobedience to Sherman's instruction and misleads as to why Stoneman withdrew from Macon without trying to liberate the officers confined there at Camp Oglethorpe.

Finally, it is also notable that the National Tribune, *the unofficial organ of Union soldiers' published recollections, depicted the McCook-Stoneman Raid as "blunderingly executed," ending in "disaster." It is also worth noting that the writer ended his article by quoting not McCook or Stoneman, but Wheeler, Iverson, and Hood, consulting no less than Hood's memoir,* Advance and Retreat *(1880).*

49

Hood's Third Attacking Battle, July 28

Albert G. Brackett, "Battle of Ezra Church"

(October 28, 1886, pp. 1-2)

In late July, Sherman's three armies were stretched from north of Atlanta (Thomas), to its east (Howard, succeeding McPherson) with Schofield in between. By this time, only the railroad running south to Macon kept Hood's army supplied. Rather than extend Howard's Army of the Tennessee farther to the left (southward), Sherman decided to swing it behind Schofield and Thomas, then beyond Atlanta's west side, marching south toward the Macon & Western. Howard's movement began early on July 27; within hours Hood knew of it and began to plan a counterstroke.

The battle of Ezra Church, which took place July 28, 1864, was brought on by one of the sorties made by the Confederates during the siege of Atlanta, and is frequently called the second battle of Atlanta. I was on the field and will endeavor to describe it, as I have nowhere seen a very full and satisfactory account of it.

In the first place it must be borne in mind that Atlanta, in July, 1864, was surrounded by dense woods, in which there were many roads, and it was as easy to take the wrong as the right one. Several were mere forest roads, while others led to pretentious farm-houses and plantations. There were a good many chestnut trees in the woods which made beautiful, straight rails, and fires that kept popping and cracking until completely burned up.

The houses in these woods during the siege continued to be occupied by their owners, as this was thought to be the surest means of keeping them from the flames or from harm in any other way. Whole families, principally made up of the female members, thus staid on their farms and plantations, and, except where the habitations obstructed military operations, remained unmolested to the end. The shade was dense and dark, and furnished fine places for our soldiers, though it often enabled the enemy to creep close up to our works and led to the death of Gen. McPherson on the 22d, near Decatur.

Gen. Sherman had determined to move the Army of the Tennessee from the left to the right of his line and boldly strike the railroad below Atlanta. This army consisted of the Fifteenth Corps, commanded by Gen. John A. Logan;

two divisions of the Sixteenth Corps, under Gen. Grenville M. Dodge; and the Seventeenth Corps, commanded by Gen. Frank P. Blair. Upon the death of Gen. McPherson there had been some difficulty in settling upon a man to lead the Army of the Tennessee, but after consultation Gen. Oliver O. Howard had been selected for this important position. He was

A BRAVE AND CAPABLE OFFICER;

had excellent judgment, and endeavored by all means in his power to secure the good will of those under his command. There was considerable jealousy at the time, and almost any one would have met with criticism who had been called upon to fill the place. Gen. Logan felt that he had a right to it, but was too good a soldier to make any trouble. Gens. Hooker and John M. Palmer had also considered themselves entitled to it, and not receiving it, had gone on leave of absence to the North.

[*Major General Joseph Hooker, commander of the XX Corps and former leader of the Army of the Potomac, had indeed wanted to replace McPherson. When he learned that Sherman had instead picked Howard (who had commanded a corps under Hooker in Virginia), the oversloughed general asked to be relieved of his corps command, complaining that "justice and self-respect alike require my removal from an army in which rank and service are ignored."*

Major General Palmer, commander of the XIV Corps, submitted his resignation on August 7, but it was unrelated to Sherman's choice for the Army of the Tennessee. During operations August 4-6, Sherman had directed Palmer to take orders from Major General Schofield, whom Palmer judged to be junior in both rank and service. Palmer therefore refused, and when he asked to be relieved, Sherman assented (Castel, Decision in the West, *454-456).*]

Things settled down rapidly in that period of stirring scenes, and soon the tide of events was running as smoothly as if Gen. Howard had been in command for months instead of days, and he was winning a warm place in the affections of his officers and soldiers.

All of the arrangements were made on the 27th, and that night and early on the morning of the 28th the movement was made. By some means Gen. Hood heard of it and sent out a strong force under Gens. Stephen D. Lee and Alexander P. Stewart to attack our men while on the march, or at least before they could get settled in their new position.

[*Hood's plan was a little more complex. Figuring that Howard's troops were marching toward a key crossroads on the Lick Skillet Road west of Atlanta, Hood ordered Lt. Gen. Stephen D. Lee (newly arrived to command Hood's old corps) early on July 28 to lead his forces out from town, seize the crossroads, and await Howard's approach. Then Lt. Gen. A. Peter Stewart would march his corps behind Lee, maneuver, and attack Howard's right (westmost) flank on the 29th.*

The problem was that Howard reached the crossroads near Ezra Church first and ordered his men to fortify against an expected Rebel attack. When Lee found the Federals ahead of him, he ordered a frontal assault that was predictably repulsed. As Stewart's infantry came up, Lee threw them into the fight as well.]

They were hurled upon the Fifteenth Corps, under Gen. Logan, with great fury about 11 o'clock in the forenoon, and were repulsed with severe loss. The Confederates reformed as soon as they could and were made ready for another attack. In the meantime our men had been

AS BUSY AS BEES

rolling up logs and rails and cutting down trees so as to make as good a breastwork as possible under the circumstances. Again the enemy came up in good style, and were met with determination by our soldiers, who threw them back again only to see them reform in full view. Ezra Church, a small edifice, was in front, and gave the name to the battle.

As soon as Gen. Sherman discovered that a general engagement was going on he went to Gen. Jeff C. Davis, who was on his way around to the right with his division of the Fourteenth Corps, belonging to the Army of the Cumberland, to hurry forward, but the men got lost in the woods and did not come up until the battle was over. Sherman himself was on the field when the fighting began.

The last time the Confederate officers endeavored to make a charge upon our lines the men refused to move forward, and so the battle ended. Among the Confederate officers wounded and disabled were Gens. Stewart, Loring, Brown and Johnson. [*General Stewart was struck in the forehead by a glancing bullet. Major General William W. Loring received a chest wound that knocked him out of action for more than a month. Major General John C. Brown suffered an injury so slight that he did not mention it in his after-action report. Brigadier General George D. Johnston took a shot in the leg that kept him on crutches for several months.*] The reserves of Gens. Blair and Dodge had been sent to support Logan and Howard massed his artillery to sweep the open field on his flank, but no rebels appeared, and about 4 o'clock p.m. they left the ground. At that time it is said that the Confederate officers coaxed and threatened their men to make them renew the attack, but without effect; they refused absolutely to move forward, having had enough rough treatment from the Federal soldiers.

Some of our soldiers chaffed the rebels while concealed in the thick woods, and told them to "bring on their 'graybacks' and they would make short work of them." The rebels replied that

THEY HAD HAD ENOUGH

to do with the "bummers" on that day, and would reserve what was left for a future occasion.

The wit of these times was not particularly polished, but was understood and appreciated as well as if couched in more polite terms. There was little argument in it, it is true, but coming from men intent upon taking each others' lives, or at least capturing them, it had a significance nothing else could produce. There was no anger involved, as, when prisoners were taken, it was "Come in, Johnny," or "Come in Yank," as the case might be.

The artillery was plied with great effect during the efforts of the Confederates to force our position, and the same may be said of that of the enemy, which was protected by a fresh earthwork. They seemed to fear that our men would make their way inside of their lines, and such indeed was the intention of our commander in case any opportunity occurred, as he was only too anxious to make a lodgment inside of their works. Our soldiers were especially fortunate on that day and picked off the enemy as they saw fit.

I noticed particularly a New York regiment moving through the woods, on account of the springiness of the steps of the men, who carried a musket on one shoulder and an ax or spade on the other. I never saw a body of men better equipped for action or who had apparently more confidence in themselves. They all seemed to be young, and acted more as if out on a pleasure excursion than anything else. They had been in several actions, and knew exactly how to turn everything to the best account. There was no noise or fuss about them. The went at their business

AS IF THEY UNDERSTOOD IT PERFECTLY,

and were in no way appalled by dangers or deterred by any obstacles which might be found in their way. Through the woods they passed in a stately way, there being no stragglers, and all keeping well in their places, like parts of a complete machine.

To Gen. John A. Logan must be accorded the praise for fighting this battle, for though Gen. Howard was in fact in command of the Army of the Tennessee he had not got sufficient hold of it to work it as well as Logan could, and therefore permitted Logan to conduct the affair as he thought best. True, there was little to do aside from repelling attacks, and Logan infused his men with an enthusiasm which swept all before them. Gen. Howard says that though Gen. Logan was ill and much worn, he was indefatigable, and the success of the day was as much attributable to him as to any one man.

Gens. Frank P. Blair and Grenville M. Dodge and their soldiers should also come in for their share of praise, as they did all in their power to strengthen Logan when he most needed assistance. The Generals pushed forward their soldiers as the enemy advanced, and shared in the glory of hurling them back within the limits of their own line of intrenchments. Some new intrenchments had been made near this particular locality, while others had been worked upon for many months before. Indeed, Atlanta was supposed to be so strongly fortified that it

COULD NOT BE CARRIED

by direct assault, and it is even now a question whether it could have been by the forces then commanded by Gen. Sherman. I heard Gen. Sherman say that Gen. Thomas was utterly opposed to the project of assaulting the place, as the loss of men would have been too great.

Although Gen. Hood pretends that he did not consider this a very important battle the reports of his subordinates show that it had been carefully planned and studied. Gen. Hardee was ordered to assume command, although neither of the corps engaged was his own, but he did not reach the field in time to participate in the fight.

[*By 5:00 p.m., Hood at his headquarters in southwest Atlanta had become aware that his battle plan for Ezra Church had gone awry. He summoned Hardee, his most experienced corps commander, to manage the situation, as Brackett states.*]

Gen. Sherman says his men were unusually encouraged by this day's work, for they realized that they could compel Hood to come out from behind his fortified lines to attack them at a disadvantage. In conversation with him the soldiers of the Fifteenth Corps, which he had formerly commanded, assured him that the affair of the 28th of July was the easiest thing in the world—that in fact it was a common slaughter of the enemy—and pointed out where the rebel lines had been and how they had deliberately shot down their antagonists, whose bodies still lay unburied and marked their lines of battle. The men were very proud to have

GEN. SHERMAN TALK WITH THEM,

and he appeared perfectly at home in their midst, they never presuming to trespass upon him or his time, but having the utmost confidence in him and a firm belief that no matter what emergency may arise, he would take care of them and see them through creditably. I cannot see how a General could bet a more firm hold upon the affections of his men than he had, or one who deserved them more.

All three divisions of the Fifteenth Corps were engaged, though the brunt of the fighting fell upon those of Gens. Wm. Harrow and Morgan L. Smith. Six successive charges were made on our men and as many times were they repulsed with great loss. Gen. Hood had determined in his own mind to annihilate the Federal forces on the right, but found himself unable to do so. His men fought with the utmost desperation and could not understand why they were unable to force our men from their position. The Confederates evinced the most undaunted courage, and formed as often as they fell back with promptitude and zeal. Their officers held them to their work well, and the Georgia militia proved to be of good material.

Some of these men who were captured were as cool and nonchalant as could be, and seemed to take their fate as a matter of course. They were fine-looking men, tall and large boned, without any superfluous flesh. They were animated by a desire to protect their homes and did all in their power to prevent the Federals from taking possession of Atlanta, which was a city of great consequence to the people of the South. When it fell I am convinced the men and women of Georgia and Alabama felt that

THEIR CAUSE WAS HOPELESS

and not worth striving for any longer. They had become very poor indeed, their property having been swept away and a condition of things bordering on famine existing in those States.

There were but two divisions in the Sixteenth Corps present in the Army of the Tennessee, namely those of Gens. Thos. W. Sweeny and J. C. Veatch. After the fall of Atlanta the Second Division was transferred to the Fifteenth Corps and the Fourth Division to the Seventeenth. The First and Third Divisions were left in the valley of the Mississippi by Gen. Sherman, and at the battle of Nashville rendered good service under Gen. Andrew J. Smith.

This was the last attempt made by Gen. Hood upon our lines. He had seen enough of it, and tried no more to turn the flanks of our army. His intentions were good in that direction, but his execution was poor, and he crippled his infantry terribly by his exertions. His Generals saw this and soon became convinced that he must resort to some other expedient, or his army would be used up so as to be of very little service to the Confederate States. He chafed like a madman under these reverses, and was soon discovered to be a man who had undertaken

MORE THAN HE COULD ACCOMPLISH,

or in homely soldier phrase he had "bit off more than he could chaw." The Southern men made excellent infantry soldiers, and were as a general thing good woodsmen, having been reared on farms and plantations, where they were taught to exercise their own wits and accustomed to ranging the woods in search of game, or for purposes connected with their house buildings and planting operations.

The battle of Ezra Church, or Ezra Chapel, had a good effect upon the Union troops and compensated in a great measure for the misfortunes of the 22d, when the commander of the Army of the Tennessee had been killed and a battery of artillery, with guns, horses, gunners and all complete, captured and marched into Atlanta without stopping. This was Murray's battery of Regular artillery. Our soldiers had not lost heart at all, but had grieved over the death of the brave young General whose prospects seemed so bright. The enemy had been driven back, it is true, but our loss had been considerable, and a feeling of sadness pervaded the army. Murray, who was captured, died shortly afterward at Macon, while a prisoner of war. He was a promising young officer.

The Union soldiers were only too glad to eat their suppers in peace after the events of the day, and he who has campaigned and knows the virtues of cold boiled pork, hard bread and coffee, knows how satisfying such a meal is. Fires could be readily kindled behind the earthworks, and many a good cup of coffee was made at these fires, where soldiers cracked their jokes and

BOUND UP THEIR WOUNDS

when not serious enough to take them to the hospital. It does not take very much to make men happy who are hungry and tired out, as the soldiers of the Army of the Tennessee were on this occasion.

Sleep in the open air is invigorating and somewhat exciting when you do not know what moment a body of the enemy may come storming over upon you, breaking in upon your slumbers and causing you to look well to your musket as your dearest and most cherished friend. Still men will sleep when greatly fatigued, and I believe our soldiers slept as soundly that night as they would have slept had they been in their own homes. The nights were warm, though it was intensely dark among the trees, and the glow of the campfires illuminated but a short distance around. There was some fear that the Confederates would make a night attack, and every precaution was taken to meet them and give them a warm reception should they attempt such a thing. Our men talked over the results of the battle in low tones, and prepared for the morrow as quietly as need be, for at that time the full gravity of the conflict was well understood by every one, and there was little or no

BRAVADO AND VAPORING

on either side. Some of our Generals seemed not to sleep at all, and it required a wonderful amount of endurance to undergo all that was required of them without completely breaking down. Others seemed to thrive on it, judging from their robust appearance.

Six hundred and forty-two Confederates were found dead on the field, and Gen. Hood admits that he lost 1,500 in killed, wounded and missing. Our loss amounted to 100 killed and wounded. [*Gary Ecelbarger puts Hood's loss on July 28 at "between 3,100 and 3,300 officers and men"; Gen Logan reported 562 casualties in his XV Corps, to which should be added maybe 60-80 more from the XVI and XVII Corps units engaged that day (Slaughter at the Chapel:* The Battle of Ezra Church 1864 *[Norman: University of Oklahoma Press, 2016], 184-185).*] The Confederate loss has been stated as much greater than the figures here given, but I am convinced they are nearly correct. The open space in front was well adapted for a charge, while the heavy woods on each side afforded a safe place to move into while withdrawing from the front. Our men by this time knew how to take advantage of every hill, hillock and copse, and could throw up a temporary breastwork as easily and skillfully as any men ever did. The old-fashioned impression that a soldier should stand up to be shot at had passed away, and he had learned to take what advantage he could of his enemy. In the early part of the war they did not understand things as well as they did later. There was a great deal of humbug and nonsense when the soldiers first took the field, and it required some time to eradicate this, but eventually it was done, and no better infantry ever stood in a field than that which belonged to Gen. Sherman's army, and served during the Atlanta campaign and on the march to the sea.

50

From a Northern Soldier's Diary

J. B. Ridenour, "Logan in Line. At Ezra Chapel July 28, 1864"

(December 8, 1887, p. 8)

EDITOR NATIONAL TRIBUNE: Looking over a diary that I kept during the war, I find the following, which I send you just as it was written at the time, as a tribute to the gallantry of Gen. John A. Logan:

"Ezra Chapel, (three and a half miles south of Atlanta,) Ga., July 28, 1864.—This morning our division (Second, Fifteenth Corps,) began to move slowly to the southwest, and took up a position on the extreme right, completing the formation of our lines about noon in an advantageous position, with brisk skirmishing in front. The 30th Ohio was on the extreme right; the 116th Ill. next on the left, on the north side of an open field, along a rail fence running nearly due east and west, facing south. Our regiment—the 55th Ill.—formed with our right resting on the left of the 116th at a right angle, facing west; from our left the line again running east and facing south.

"About 1 o'clock

OUR PICKETS CAME IN PELL-MELL.

Soon two rebel lines appeared, marching upon us in dress-parade order, file-closers with bayonets fixed, a color-bearer several yards in advance of the front line, leaning forward as he proudly leads the desperate rebel host, until he falls pierced by hundreds of balls. Bravely on and on came the unfaltering lines under a galling fire from the 116th Ill. and 30th Ohio, while ours is pouring in a left oblique and finally an enfilading fire. Still they pushed on; the crisis came; the line on our right is pressed hard. The boys look frightened and as if they would give way. The suspense is almost beyond endurance, for we expect a break on our fright. Pen fails a description here of those awful moments as they pass.

"To our right, at the angle of the 55th and 116th Ill., a rustling in the leaves and a firm step is heard. We anxiously look in that direction to see if our boys are running away. But no. A whisper goes up the line, 'It's Gen. Logan.' On foot and alone, passing quickly up the line, saying:

'STEADY, BOYS; HOLD THEM!'

Confidence is restored in a moment. The two rebel lines that have merged into one solid mass waver; confusion prevails; they are running—and gone, except the dead and dying. That determined charge is repeated five times, and repulsed as often with equal success.

"The question may be asked, Did the timely presence of Gen. Logan save the day and the turning of the flank of his army? I emphatically answer yes. The rebels confronted us two to one. Our boys were good for one, but it required the immediate presence of Gen. Logan to whip the two under equal advantages. The conflict lasted three and a half hours, our men averaging 100 rounds fired by each.

"Six hundred and sixty-two dead rebels were counted in front of the Fifteenth Corps, principally in front of the Second Division; 200 directly in front of the 55th and 116th Ill. and 30th Ohio. We captured near 300, 72 of which were wounded, and three of them females. The rebel loss was estimated at 6,000. [*Their papers subsequently admitted a loss of 7,000.*]

"The loss in the Fifteenth Corps was 61 killed, 439 wounded (mostly slightly), and 52 missing—total, 552. The 30th sustained the greatest loss of any one regiment, being the most exposed. We asked the prisoners how many they had left, and they said 'about another killing.' Hood's loss within ten days has been 22,000. They have fought with unparalleled courage and desperation. This may be called an open field fight, but we had a decided advantage in the position chosen by

THE SAGACIOUS LOGAN.

We had no protection except a fence, a few trees and logs, but most of the old veterans made every shot count."

In this, as in all other of our battles, Gen. Logan was a conspicuous figure, and yet I have never seen this fight mentioned in print. The histories say but little about it, but it is just like all of Gen. Logan's battles—gloriously victorious. I regret that I am not able to give a more animated picture of this great and beloved patriot. Who can? Who will do it?—J. B. RIDENOUR, Captain, Co. A., 55th Ill., Woodhull, Ill.

During the night of July 26-27, the Army of the Tennessee, now under command of Maj. Gen. Oliver O. Howard, quietly withdrew from its lines east of Atlanta, marched north and behind Thomas's army, and advanced west of the city in an extension of Sherman's right flank.

Hood picked up on the movement, and on the 27th ordered Lt. Gen. Stephen D. Lee to block the Federal advance, which Hood foresaw as heading for a key crossroads on the Lick Skillet Road. Lee marched his infantry corps out early on July 28, but by late morning learned that Logan's troops had already taken position on the road near Ezra Church, a Methodist chapel. Without seeking further maneuver, Lee ordered a frontal attack against Maj. Gen. John A. Logan's XV Corps.

The action described by Captain Ridenour occurred around 11:45 a.m. Another member of the 55th, quoted in The Story of the Fifty-fifth Regiment Illinois Volunteer Infantry in the Civil War *(1887), recalled that as the Rebels advanced, "General Logan passed along behind the line with words of cheer on his lips: 'Hold them! Steady, boys, we've got them now" (Gary Ecelbarger,* Slaughter at the Chapel: The Battle of Ezra Church, 1864 *[Norman: University of Oklahoma Press, 2016], 82-83).*

They did. As Ridenour explains, Howard's troops were in prepared defensive position; the general expected to be attacked that day. The Confederate assault was rather easily repulsed at a cost of 3,100-3,300 casualties (to Logan's 600-620).

After the battle, the Northerners talked about a woman in Confederate uniform who had been found dead near Ezra Chapel. An Illinois soldier wrote disapprovingly to his parents two days after the battle: "it is not a womans place in a fight" (Earl J. Hess, The Battle of Ezra Church and the Struggle for Atlanta *[Chapel Hill: University of North Carolina Press, 2015], 171).*

Ridenour's "about another killing" remark has appeared repeatedly in the literature of Ezra Church (Hess, 163). But as we have seen, John W. Clemson claims he heard a Rebel make the statement after the battle of Dallas, May 28.

As for the captain's statement, "I have never seen this fight mentioned in print," Ridenour seems to have missed at least two earlier articles in the National Tribune *about Ezra Church, including a long one by Col. Albert G. Brackett, 3d U.S. Cav. (October 28, 1886).*

Finally, as for the author's question--who will write Logan's biography?—it appears that the first appeared in 1884 when Logan was a Democratic candidate for the vice presidency. Another followed in 1887, a year after the general's death, and the year in which Ridenour's article asked its question (Allan Nevins, James I. Robertson, Jr., and Bell I. Wiley, eds., Civil War Books: A Critical Bibliography, *2 vols. [Baton Rouge: Louisiana State University Press, 1967, 1969], 2:36, 51).*

51

Utoy Creek, August 5-6

John McElroy, "The Battle of Utoy"

(June 24, 1909, p. 2)

After the battle of Ezra Church, it became clear to General Hood that Sherman would try to cut the Macon & Western Railroad by extending his right flank farther and farther south toward East Point. The Confederates consequently began digging entrenchments along the course of the railroad, which Atlanta historian Wilbur Kurtz has dubbed "the Railroad Defense Line."

On August 6, Sherman ordered General Schofield to test the strength of these new works with his two infantry divisions, Jacob Cox's and Milo Hascall's. The Federal assault was easily repulsed by Maj. Gen. William B. Bate's entrenched division. Bate lost a mere 15 or 20 men, but Union casualties numbered 76 killed, 199 wounded, and 31 captured, for a total of 306—all in the brigade of Col. James W. Reilly, Cox's division.

John McElroy's series of 28 articles on the Atlanta Campaign ran in the National Tribune *from January 21 to July 28, 1909. Number XXIII, "The Battle of Utoy," appeared in the June 24 issue. After completing his commentary on the failed McCook-Stoneman cavalry raids, McElroy turned to events in the first week of August, especially the sharp little fight near the Rebel railroad defense line.*

About a mile south of the battlefield on July 28, Utoy Creek flows westward into the Chattahoochee. It is here that McElroy resumes his narration, beginning with a lively tiff between two of Sherman's generals.

Trouble with Palmer.

There had been a growing trouble between Gen. John M. Palmer, commanding the Fourteenth Corps, and Gen. John M. Schofield, commanding the Twenty-third Corps. Palmer, who as a man of great natural ability and of the highest courage and patriotism, felt that undue preference and favoritism were extended to the Regular Army officers, and that the volunteers were not given their share. The passing over of Gen. Logan for a West Pointer [*after McPherson's death*] seemed a direct blow at Palmer. Palmer had resented on several occasions the claim of Schofield to exercise command over him. [*Palmer's XIV Corps was part of George Thomas' Army of the Cumberland, not of Schofield's Army of the Ohio.*] Palmer's commission as a Major-General was senior to that of Schofield, but Schofield claimed seniority in the previous grade [*Schofield had been promoted to brigadier general before Palmer had*] and also seniority as the commander of an army [*even if it was only one corps, the XXIII*]. Palmer felt, with much justice, that he was Schofield's superior. [*Both Palmer and Schofield had risen to the rank of major general with commissions bearing the same date, November 29, 1862. But Palmer's had actually been confirmed by the Senate that day, whereas Schofield's had been issued in early 1864 and granted retroactively. Palmer was also thirteen years older than Schofield and had seen more action.*] While Schofield had been a mere Lieutenant of Artillery, Palmer was one of the leading lawyers and politicians of Illinois, was one of the organizers of the Republican Party, had entered the army as the Colonel of a regiment, and by good soldiership had risen to the command of a brigade and a division. His handling of his division at Stone River and Chickamauga had greatly increased his reputation as a soldier, so that when Thomas was promoted to the command of the Army of the Cumberland the command of the Fourteenth Corps came naturally and deservedly to Palmer. He had so far commanded very successfully on the Atlanta campaign, but Sherman says of him that he lacked enterprise, "his three divisions were compact and strong, well commanded, admirable on the defensive, but slow to move or to act on the offensive. His corps, the Fourteenth, had sustained, up to that time, fewer hard knocks than any other corps in the whole army, and I was anxious to give it a chance."

Sherman expected one more hard fight before he reached the railroad and compelled Hood to evacuate Atlanta, and he now put Schofield in the advance with orders to the Fourteenth Corps to report to Schofield for a bold attack on the railroad somewhere about East Point. Schofield determined to force a crossing of the north fork of Utoy Creek, and detailed [*Brig. Gen. Milo*] Hascall's Division of the Twenty-third Corps and [*Brig. Gen. Absalom*] Baird's Division of the Fourteenth Corps to force the crossing. Hascall promptly made the crossing with little opposition, and went into position on a high ridge. Baird did not follow Hascall according to orders, since Palmer would not recognize Schofield's authority to command, and he did not move until Sherman himself came up late in the afternoon and ordered him to cross the creek. The next morning [*Brig. Gen. Jacob*] Cox's Division of the Twenty-third Corps crossed the creek and formed in rear of Baird, and Palmer was ordered to push Baird's Division against the enemy in front and support it with [*Brig. Gen. Jefferson C.*] Davis's and [*Brig. Gen. Richard*] Johnson's Divisions. Again Palmer balked on his orders, and the movement halted, but [*a brigade of*] Baird's Division pushed forward [*in a reconnaissance in force, August 4 at 4:00 p.m.*], capturing 25 prisoners, sustaining a loss of 26 killed and wounded. August 5 orders were issued [*by Schofield, directly to the XIV Corps division commanders*] for a general movement, but Gen. Baird notified Schofield that he did not recognize his authority, had received no orders from his corps commander [*Palmer*], and no notice that the Fourteenth Corps was under Schofield's command. By these halts and jangles two days were lost, and made what Sherman considered a most unpardonable delay.

Palmer Still Obdurate.

Gen. Sherman examined into the dispute as to the seniority, decided in favor of Gen. Schofield, and wrote the following letter to Gen. Palmer:

> "August 4, 10:45 p.m.
>
> "From the statements made by yourself and Gen. Schofield to-day my decision is that he ranks you as a Major-General, being of the same date of present commission, by reason of his previous superior rank as Brigadier-General [*Schofield had risen to this rank before Palmer*]. The movements of to-morrow are so important that the orders of the superior on that flank [*Schofield*] must be regarded as military orders, and not in the nature of co-operation. I did hope that there would be no necessity of making this decision, but it is better for all parties interested that no question of rank should occur in actual battle. The Sandtown road and the railroad, if possible, must be gained to-morrow if it costs half your command. I regard the loss of time this afternoon as equal to the loss of 2,000 men" [OR, *vol. 38, pt. 5, 356*].

In spite of this decision Palmer refused to obey Schofield on the next day [*August 5*] and again Sherman wrote to him, arguing the point with him as a friend, and advising him not to resign lest his motives be misconstrued and damage his career. At the same time he told him that the matter had been very unsatisfactory to him, Sherman. Still Palmer remained obdurate, and that night Schofield reported to Gen. Sherman:

"I am compelled to acknowledge that I have totally failed to make any aggressive movement with the Fourteenth Corps. I have ordered Gen. Johnson's Division to replace Hascall's this evening, and I propose to-morrow to take my own troops (Twenty-third Corps) to the right and try to recover what has been lost by two days' delay. The force may likely be too small."

Thereupon Sherman personally ordered Davis's and Baird's divisions to follow Schofield and Gen. Palmer to come to his headquarters. Gen. Palmer did so [*on the morning of August 6*], offered his resignation, and insisted upon it being accepted, and Gen. Sherman referred him to his immediate superior, Gen. Thomas. Gen.

Thomas accepted his resignation, and gave him the usual leave of absence to go to his home in Illinois, there to await further orders. Gen. Thomas recommended that the senior division commander of the corps be ordered back to Nashville to become Chief of Cavalry, and that Brig. Gen. Jeff C. Davis be promoted to Major-General and assigned to the command of the corps. These changes had to be referred to Washington, where the President promptly approved of them and Gen. Jeff C. Davis in the future operations was an entirely acceptable commander of the splendid old Fourteenth Corps.

[*McElroy's statement—that Thomas recommended the senior division commander in the XIV Corps be sent away so he could put Jefferson C. Davis in charge of the corps is not sustained in the* Official Records. *The senior division commander was Brig. Gen. Richard W. Johnson. He commanded the XIV Corps from August 7 to 22, when Davis took over. Moreover, Washington did not approve of promoting Brigadier General Davis, over whose head hung the allegation of murder after he shot and killed his ex-commanding officer, Brig. Gen. William Nelson, in September 1862. No charges were brought against Davis and he was returned to duty—just without further promotion.*]

Gen. Palmer was later assigned to command in Kentucky, and shortly after the war was elected Governor of Illinois. At the time of the fire in Chicago [*October 1871*] he got into a squabble with Gen. Philip H. Sheridan, who had long been associated with him as a division commander, and this and other things combined to take him into the Democratic Party. Later he was elected a senator from Illinois, and during the first Bryan campaign [*1896*] was the nominee for President of the Gold Democrats.

[*In the 1896 presidential campaign, the Democratic Party was divided. William Jennings Bryan, the Nebraska Populist, won the party's nomination on a platform calling for the government to abandon its policy of backing paper currency with gold alone and to adopt the minting of silver in order to deflate the currency (and help debt-ridden Southern and Western farmers). Conservative "Gold Democrats" favored retention of the gold standard. They organized a new "National Democratic" Party, with ex-Union general Palmer as presidential candidate and ex-Confederate general Simon Buckner as vice presidential nominee. Despite this pluralistic appeal, the Palmer-Buckner ticket won only 133,000 votes in the general election.*]

The Battle of Utoy Creek.

The delay of 48 hours consequent upon the dispute between Schofield and Palmer had encouraged Hood to hope for a defensive battle, where his men would have the advantages that the Union troops had enjoyed in the recent attacks. All during the night of August 5 the troops had heard the sound of busy axes, and they were not surprised when the morning dawned and showed the enemy behind a strong line of works well covered with abatis. Hood had the line of the Sandtown road, and filled the works with Hardee's Corps. Much dissatisfaction as Hood expressed with Hardee, yet, somehow, Hardee was always put to the front for heavy work. The line ran over the rough and high ground in front of Baird across a ridge dividing the branches of Utoy Creek and then down the east side of the branch of the main stream. The length of the work was about two miles.

Formidable as the intrenchments seemed, it would not do to lie idle before them, and Cox was ordered to send out a brigade to make a reconnaissance. [*Col. James W.*] Reilly's Brigade—112th Ill., 16th Ky., 101st and 104th Ohio and 8th Tenn. [*1,500, all told*]—was selected for this work, and supported by [*Col. John S.*] Casement's Brigade—65th Ill., 63d and 65th Ind., 24th Ky., 103d Ohio and 5th Tenn. [*which never got into action on August 6*]. Reilly formed his brigade on the open ground, sent forward his skirmishers in quick time across a brook and up a slope, with the brigade following closely. The skirmishers soon found themselves entangled in the limbs of the felled trees, but worked their way thru the abatis until some of them reached the foot of the works. By this time the fire from the enemy had become so heavy that the advance of the brigade was arrested about 100 yards from the works. A hasty survey of these showed that they extended far to the right and left and were well manned. Prisoners taken on the skirmish line gave the information that they belonged to Bate's Division [*Maj. Gen. William B., of Hardee's Corps*], which was there in force. Casement pushed his brigade forward to the east side of the valley, and attracted the attention of the enemy there so as to give Reilly an opportunity to retire, which he did with a loss of about 300 men out of his little brigade. He, however, left his skirmish line behind hastily constructed shelters close to the abatis, and the fire from this prevented the enemy from coming out in pursuit.

[*Reilly's brigade suffered 306 casualties at Utoy Creek on August 6: 76 killed, 199 wounded, and 31 missing. In its easy defensive victory, Bate's Division saw only fifteen or twenty casualties (Albert Castel, "Union Fizzle at Atlanta: The Battle of Utoy Creek,"* Civil War Times Illustrated, *[February 1978], 30.)*]

Hascall's Division [*beside Cox's, the other one in the XXIII Corps*] was in the meantime thrown across Utoy Creek, and had gained a hight which enfiladed Bate's line, and that night Bate's Tennesseans fell back to a still stronger line on the high hills near the north fork of Utoy Creek.

[*McElroy goes on to quote General Schofield's report on the battle, as well as Sherman's telegram to General Halleck in Washington, before turning to Confederate cavalry leader Joseph Wheeler's raid into north Georgia, which began on August 10.*]

52

In the Middle of the Campaign, General Sherman Reflects on the South's Blame for the War

"A Grand Letter From Gen. Sherman While in the Field Before Atlanta"

(October 1, 1885, p. 8)

A prewar friend of Sherman's, in January 1864, Daniel Martin was a farmer in southeast Tennessee who had written General Sherman asking for his help in reclaiming his runaway slaves. But he did not send the letter until July 24, which explains why Sherman had just—by August 10—received it (Brooks D. Simpson and Jean V. Berlin, eds., Sherman's War: Selected Correspondence of William T. Sherman, 1860-1865 *[Chapel Hill: University of North Carolina Press, 1999], 689).*

Sherman's reply to Martin was published in the New York Times, *September 7, 1865. It is not clear how editor McElroy and the* National Tribune *obtained it for publication.* Sherman's War *reprints Sherman's reply, 686-688.*

With "the dread missiles of war," Sherman is referring to the artillery bombardment of Atlanta, which he had ordered on July 19, and which began the next day when some of his artillerymen's rifled cannon had gotten within range (about two miles). Indeed, on August 9, the day before writing Martin, Sherman had ordered all rifled guns—his forces had about a hundred of them—to fire 50 rounds each into the city in indiscriminate bombardment. At the time, Atlanta had several thousand civilian inhabitants.

HEADQ'RS, MILITARY DIVISION
OF THE MISSISSIPPI,
IN THE FIELD, NEAR ATLANTA, GA.
August 10, 1864.

DANIEL M. MARTIN, Sand Mountain:

MY DEAR FRIEND: When in Larkinsville, last Winter, I inquired after you and could get no positive answer. I wish you had sent me your letter of Jan. 22—which I have just received—for I could have made you feel at ease at once. Indeed do I remember our old times about Bellefonte, and the ride we took to the corn mills, and the little farm where I admired the handsome colt and tried to buy it.

Time has worn on, and you are now an old man, in want, and suffering, and I also no longer young, but leading an hostile army on the very road I came when I left Bellefonte, and at this moment pouring into Atlanta the dread missiles of war, seeking the lives of its people. And yet I am the same William Tecumseh Sherman you knew in 1844, with as warm a heart as ever, and anxious that peace and plenty shall prevail in this land, and to prove it I defy Jeff Davis, Gen. Lee or Gen. Hood to make the sacrifice for peace that I will, personally and officially.

I will to-day lay down my power and my honor—already won—will strip myself naked, and my wife and child stark naked in the world as we came, and begin life anew, if the people of the South will but cease the war, elect their Members of Congress, and let them settle, by argument and reason, the question growing out of slavery, instead of trying to divide out country into two angry halves, to quarrel and fight to the end of time. Our country cannot be divided by an east and west line, and must be one, and, if we must fight, let us fight it out now, and not bequeath it to our children. I was never a politician, but resigned from the army and lived in California till 1857, when I came back with my wife and three children, who wanted to be near home—Mr. Ewing's, not Mr. Corwin's—but I had the old army so ground in my composition that civil pursuits were too tame, and I accepted an offer as President of the Louisiana Military Academy. Therefore, at the time of Lincoln's election, I was at Alexandria, on Red River.

I saw, and you must have seen, that the Southern politicians wanted to bring about secession—separation. They could have elected Mr. Douglas, but they so managed that Lincoln's election was made certain, and, after they had accomplished this, was it honest or fair for them to allege it as a cause of war? Did not Mr. Breckinridge, as Vice-President, in his seat declare Mr. Lincoln the lawfully-elected President of the United States? Was it ever pretended the President was our Government? Don't you know that Congress makes laws, the Supreme Court judges them, and the President only executes them? Don't you know that Mr. Lincoln, of himself, could take away your rights? Now, I was in Louisiana, and while the planters and mechanics and industrious people were happy and prosperous, the politicians and busy-bodies were scheming and plotting, and got the Legislature to pass an ordinance of secession, which was submitted to the people, who voted against it; yet the politicians voted the State out, proceeded to take possession of the United States Mint, the forts, the arsenal, and tore down our flag and insulted it. That, too, before Mr. Lincoln had got to Washington. I saw these things, and begged Bragg and Beauregard and Gov. Moore and a host of personal friends to beware. In that was high treason. But they answered: The North was made up of mean manufacturers, of traders, of farmers, who would not fight. The people of the North never dreamed of interfering with the slaves or property of the South. They simply voted as they had a right to do, and they could not understand why the people of the South should begin to take possession of the United States forts and arsenals till our Government had done something wrong—something oppressive. The South began the war. You know it. I, and millions of others living at the South know it; but the people of the North were as innocent of it as your little grandchild. Even after forts had been taken, public arms stolen from our arsenals and distributed among the angry militia, the brave and honest freemen of the great North could not realize the fact, and did not until Beauregard began to fire upon a garrison of United States troops, in a fort built by the common treasury of the whole country. Then, as by a mighty upheaval, the people rose and began to think of war, and not until then.

I resigned my post in Louisiana in March, 1861, because the public act on the part of the State in seizing the United States arsenal at Baton Rouge, and went to St. Louis, where I readily got lucrative employment, hoping that some change would yet avert war. But it came, and I, and all of military education, had to choose. I repeat, that then, as now, I had as much love for the honest people of the South, as any man living. Had they remained true to the country, I would have resisted, even with arms, any attack upon their rights—even their slave rights. But when, as a people, they tore down our old flag, and spit upon it, and called us cowards, and dared us to the contest, then I took up arms to maintain the integrity of our country, and punish the men who challenged us to the conflict. Is this not a true picture? Suppose the North had patiently submitted, what would have been the verdict of history and the world? Nothing else but that the North was craven and coward. Will you say the North is craven and coward now?

Cruel and inhuman as this war has been, and may still continue to be, it was forced upon us. We had no choice. And we have no choice yet. We must go on, even to the end of time; even if it result in sinking a million of lives, and desolating the whole land, leaving a desert behind. We must maintain the integrity of our country. And the day will come when the little grandchild you love so well will bless us who fought that the United States of America should not sink into infamy and worse than Mexican anarchy by the act of Southern politicians, who care no more for you, or such as you, than they care for Hottentots. I have never underrated the magnitude of this war, for I know the size of the South and the difficulty of operating in it. But, I also know the Northern races have, ever since the world began, had more patience and perseverance than the Southern races. And so it will be now; we will persevere until the end. All mankind shall recognize in us a brave and stubborn race, not to be deterred by the magnitude of the danger. Only three years have passed and that is but a minute in a nation's life, and see where we are. Where are the haughty planters of Louisiana, who compared our hard-working, intelligent whites of the North with their negroes?

The defeats we have sustained have hardly made a pause in our course, and the vaunted braves of Tennessee, Mississippi, Louisiana, Missouri, etc., instead of walking rough-shod over the freemen of the North, are engaged in stealing horses and robbing old people for a living, while our armies now tread in every Southern state, and your biggest armies in Virginia and Georgia lie behind forts, and dare not come out and fight us cowards of the North, who have come 500 miles into their country to accept the challenge.

But, my dear old friend, I have bored you too much. My handwriting is not plain, but you have time to study it out, and, as you can understand, I have a great deal of writing to do, and it must be done in a hurry. Think of what I have written. Talk it over with your neighbors, and ask yourselves if, in your trials and tribulations, you have suffered more from the Union soldiery than you would had you built your barn where the lightning was sure to burn or tear it down. Their course has provoked the punishment of an indignant God and Government. I care not a straw for niggers. The moment the master rebels the negro is free, of course, for he is a slave only by law, and, the law broken, he is free. I commanded in all Tennessee, Kentucky, Mississippi, Alabama and Georgia. The paper I endorse will be of service to you.

Love to Mrs. Martin.

W. T. SHERMAN,
Major-General.

By the way, there was no popular vote held in Louisiana on secession. The state convention that voted for disunion in January 1861 also rejected a motion for a plebiscite, so Louisianans never "voted against it" (John D. Winters, The Civil War In Louisiana *[Baton Rouge: Louisiana State University Press, 1963], 12-13).*

53

Sherman Sends Kilpatrick Off, August 18-22

Robert H. G. Minty, "Kilpatrick's Raid"

(July 10, 1809, p. 1)

Despite the disastrous failure of the McCook-Stoneman Raid in late July, General Sherman decided one more time to send cavalry to break the Macon & Western Railroad. After Utoy Creek, he gave up trying to extend his right farther toward East Point. Moreover, on August 10, General Hood sent Joe Wheeler and half the army's mounted troops on a raid into the Federal rear, so Cump figured the Rebel cavalry had to be weakened. Finally, Sherman had come to recognize Brig. Gen. Judson Kilpatrick, commander of one of his cavalry divisions, as a bold and energetic leader. Of Kenner Garrard, whose division he had sent off railroad-raiding on July 21, Sherman sniffed, "if he can see a horseman in the distance with a spyglass he will turn back" (James Hibbard and Albert Castel, "Kilpatrick's Jonesboro Raid, August 18-22, 1864," Atlanta Historical Journal, *vol. 29, no. 2 [Summer 1985], 33).*

On August 18, Kilpatrick set out with 4,700 troopers—his own three brigades plus two from Garrard's division, under Col. Robert H. G. Minty. His objective was Jonesboro, a train depot two dozen miles south of Atlanta, where, as Minty states, the men were to tear up as much track as possible before riding back to the army. Heading southwest from Atlanta, along the way they would cross the Atlanta & West Point Railroad, whose use to Hood and his army had been nullified by Lovell Rousseau's cavalry raid through east central Alabama in mid-July.

Having Robert Minty write about the Kilpatrick raid is another National Tribune *gem. He wrote a similar piece that appeared in the paper's issue of January 22, 1903. Our author focuses on the activity of his division, but this narrative is as authoritative a description of Kilpatrick's raid as we are to see in the pages of the* National Tribune.

Since my account of the battle of Shelbyville appeared in THE NATIONAL TRIBUNE of May 8, I have received numerous letters from old comrades who served under me indorsing all that I said, and urging me to describe other operations of the old "Saber Brigade."

[*In its "Fighting Them Over" section of May 8, 1890, Minty had written on the battle of Shelbyville, Tenn., June 27, 1863.*]

A hearty, soldier-like letter from Capt. [*George I.*] Robinson, the commander of that incomparable battery, the "Chicago Board of Trade," has so vividly brought to mind several incidents of the Kilpatrick raid around Atlanta, that I will endeavor to give an unvarnished account of the part taken by the First and Second Brigades of the Second Division of the Army of the Cumberland in that expedition.

About the 1st of August, 1864, Gen. Sherman, in carrying out one of those flank movements for which the Atlanta campaign was famous, ordered the Twenty-third (Schofield's) Corps from the extreme left to the right of the line, and two brigades (the First and Third) from our division (the Second) were dismounted and placed in the trenches vacated by the Twenty-third Corps. We occupied this position for about two weeks, performing all the duties of infantry during that time. On the 15th we returned to our horses and once more became cavalry, and took position near Decatur to cover the left of the army.

August 17, Gen. Washington L. Elliott, Chief of Cavalry of the Army of the Cumberland, received orders, which emanated from Gen. Sherman, to send two brigades from the Second Division to report to Gen. Kilpatrick, commanding the Third Division, on the extreme right; but not to send Gen. Garrard (the commander of the Second Division), as he outranked Kilpatrick.

I was ordered to take my own brigade (the First) and [*Col. Eli*] Long's (the Second) with two sections of the Chicago Board of Trade Battery and to report to Gen. Kilpatrick at Sandtown. At 1 o'clock a.m., August 18, I marched with the following force of all ranks: First Brigade [*Minty's, 4th Michigan, 7th Pennsylvania, 4th United States*], 925; Second Brigade [*Col. Eli Long's, 1st, 3rd and 4th Ohio*], 1,383; Chicago Board of Trade Battery, 90, and four guns [*10-pounder Parrott rifles*]—making a total of 2,398 men.

[*Sandtown was located on the south bank of the Chattahoochee a dozen miles west of Atlanta. Kilpatrick's Cavalry Division—three brigades under Lieutenant Colonels Robert Klein, Fielder Jones, and Robert King—numbered 2,618 on July 31, 1864 (*OR *38, pt. 1, 116), giving Kilpatrick close to 5,000 officers and men, plus two, four-gun batteries for his raid (Hibbard and Castel, "Kilpatrick's Jonesboro Raid," 34).*]

At 6 a.m. [*on August 22*] I halted on the banks of Utoy Creek, keeping the command under cover of the hills, rode over to Sandtown and reported to Gen. Kilpatrick, who immediately called his brigade commanders together, turned over the command of his division to Col. Eli Murray, of the 3d Ky, and assumed command of the corps. He then addressed us as follows:

"GENTLEMEN, WE WILL MARCH

at dusk so as not to be seen by the enemy. We should reach Red Oak, on the Atlanta &West Point Road [*a dozen miles southwest of Atlanta*], about 9 o'clock, and Jonesboro, on the Atlanta and Macon and Macon road, before daybreak [*on August 23*]. We will leave all ambulances and wagons here, and take no wheels but the artillery. Col. Murray, your division will take the advance. You will push as rapidly as possible for Jonesboro. The moment you strike the railroad at that point, you will commence the destruction of the road. When the length of your division is destroyed, you will move south and continue the destruction. Col. Minty, you will follow Col. Murray. Keep close to him until he arrives on the Atlanta and Macon road, when you will take position and form line of battle between him and Atlanta, facing Atlanta. The only force we are likely to meet will be that which may be send from there. What do you think, gentlemen? Give me your opinion, and speak freely."

He turned to me as he spoke. I said: "General, I like your program in every particular but one, and that is your order to leave ambulances in camp. I do not like the idea of leaving my wounded in the hands of the enemy. Men cannot fight cheerfully with the knowledge that if wounded they cannot be taken back with their comrades. Allow me to take my ambulances, and I pledge myself that they will not be an incumbrance to you."

[*In his* National Tribune *article of January 1903, Minty gives a slightly different statement to Kilpatrick. See David Evans,* Sherman's Horsemen: Union Cavalry Operations in the Atlanta Campaign *(Bloomington: Indiana University Press, 1996), 410.*]

Kilpatrick thought for a moment and then said: "Well, Col. Minty, you can take our ambulances, but if they impede our movement in the slightest degree you must burn them."

Here let me remark that in these ambulances I took back to camp 98 wounded officers and men of my division, besides a few of Kilpatrick's men.

At about dusk [*on August 18*] the Third Division marched and I followed. We did not reach the Atlanta & West Point Road [*fifteen miles southwest of Atlanta*] until daybreak, and then I was ordered to the front.

My rear brigade (the First) was sharply attacked when crossing the railroad, but Maj. [*William H.*] Jennings, commanding the 7th Pa., and Maj. [*Frank W.*] Mix, commanding the 4th Mich., promptly met the enemy, and with the assistance of one section of the battery repulsed and

DROVE THEM FROM THE FIELD.

[*In a nighttime brawl, Brigadier General Lawrence S. "Sul" Ross's Texas cavalry brigade attacked Kilpatrick's column. Though repulsed, Ross's riders dogged the head of the Federal column throughout the 19th as it headed for Jonesboro. Perhaps more important, Ross kept his division commander, Brigadier General William H. "Red" Jackson, apprised of the Federals' advance. Jackson in turn informed Hood in Atlanta. Alarmed by the Yankee raiders' obvious intent to strike the railroad, during the night of August 18-19 Hood ordered Brigadier General Samuel Ferguson's cavalry brigade out of the picket line west of Atlanta and at first light to ride to Rough and Ready (a depot thirteen track-miles south of Atlanta's central train station and ten miles north of Jonesboro). Ferguson, however, got lost and would not figure in repelling Kilpatrick's raiders. Hood also dispatched a small infantry brigade (Brig. Gen. Daniel Reynolds's) to reinforce the cavalry. Stationed at Jonesboro was Brigadier General Frank Armstrong's brigade of 1,500 horsemen. Six miles south of Jonesboro lay Lovejoy's Station, also a possible enemy target. Armstrong moved there; Reynolds soon joined him.*]

On gaining the head of the column Gen. Kilpatrick ordered me to push the enemy in our front, Ross' and Ferguson's Brigades [sic*: only Ross's Brigade*] to Jonesboro. The woods in our front were thick and impracticable for cavalry, and the road was obstructed by barricades. I ordered my advance regiment, the 3d Ohio, to dismount, and it moved forward as infantry, steadily driving the enemy before it until we arrived at Flint River [*two miles west of Jonesboro*], where I found the bridge partially destroyed and the Confederates in position on the opposite bank, where the rising ground was honey-combed with rifle-pits. [*After taking up the wooden planks of the Flint bridge—they had no time to burn it—Ross' Texans dug in on the east bank.*]

Lieut. [*Henry*] Bennett with his section soon silenced the artillery, and the two sections being placed in battery shelled the rifle-pits by volleys. Under cover of this fire my entire force, except the 7th Pa., which had been left at a crossroads to cover the flank of the Third Division [*Kilpatrick's, now under Colonel Murray*], dismounted and in line of battle charged across the open bottom to the bank of the river, and their [*Spencer*] carbines quickly drove the enemy from their pits. The 4th Mich. crossed on the stringers of the bridge, and were deployed as skirmishers. Fence-rails were thrown on the bridge as planking, and we crossed over, taking two of the guns, under Lieut. Robinson, commanding the battery, with us. The skirmish-line advanced steadily, driving the enemy, and was closely followed by the 1st Ohio and 4th Regulars in line, with the two guns, worked by hand, on the road between them, the 3d and 4th Ohio in column behind the guns, all dismounted, the 7th Pa. still covering the Third Division. [*Outnumbered and outgunned, Ross' brigade fell back on the morning of August 19; Kilpatrick's troopers crossed the Flint, heading toward Jonesboro.*]

Warming to our work, the guns were run forward to the skirmish-line, and Ross's and Ferguson's Brigades [*again, just Ross's; that morning Ferguson's brigade was on the march but would not join up with the Texans*] were driven back to the town of Jonesboro, where they showed a strong line, holding a good position. The railway buildings were covered by strong works, constructed of bales of cotton, which were manned by a considerable force. I looked for stubborn resistance to our further advance. A well-directed shell from the battery pierced the water-tank, and a few more soon had

THE BUILDINGS AND THE BALES OF COTTON BLAZING.

The effective fire from the battery, and the bold and determined advance of the skirmishers, with the Spencer carbines, soon dislodged the enemy, who rapidly fell back through the town. [*At 5:00 p.m. on August 19 Kilpatrick's force occupied Jonesboro.*]

We were somewhat annoyed by a fire from the windows of the houses, so I requested Lieut. Robinson to send a shell through any house from which a gun was fired, and this brought that annoyance to a very abrupt termination.

One of our men, an old telegraph operator, caught a message on the fly, which gave the information that Pat [*Maj. Gen. Patrick R.*] Cleburne's Division of infantry and [*Maj. Gen. William T.*] Martin's Division of cavalry were en route to reinforce Ross and Ferguson. [*Not true: Cleburne's infantry was in the Atlanta trenches, and Martin's cavalry was off raiding in Tennessee with Joe Wheeler (Evans,* Sherman's Horsemen, *473)*].

My horses having been brought forward, the division was mounted and moved into position to meet this new force.

Kilpatrick now came forward with the Third Division [*his own*], which was at once turned into a working party to destroy the railroad. The 7th Pa. was also brought forward and rejoined my division.

[*A heavy rain prevented Kilpatrick's men from setting the fires they would have used to heat and bend rails; the Federals could only pry them up and throw them aside.*]

All remained quiet until about 10 o'clock [*p.m.*] when Gen. Kilpatrick notified me that the Third Division had destroyed about two miles of road, and was about to move south, and directed me to fall back upon them and take up a new position. [*The telegram about Cleburne and Martin heading his way caused Kilpatrick at 10 o'clock to order his force to mount up and ride south for Lovejoy's Station, another six miles down the line.*]

[It must be admitted that Colonel Minty's emphasis upon his two brigades—not to mention Northern veteran writers' inattentiveness to the identities of the Rebel forces facing them—obscures the big picture. During the evening of August 19, while many of Kilpatrick's soldiers tore up track, others set fire to the courthouse and other public buildings. Wind spread the fires, and soon most of Jonesboro was in flames.

As a diversion, Kilpatrick had dispatched Lt. Col. Robert Klein's First Brigade of his division off to the southeast to cut the M & W below Lovejoy's Station. The Federals reached Bear Creek Station (five track miles south of Lovejoy's) at 11:00 a.m. on the 19th. Dan Reynolds's Arkansas brigade was heading there when Red Jackson ordered him back toward Jonesboro; Ross's weary troopers had withdrawn south of town and needed assistance.

At daylight on August 20, Reynolds's and Ross's men entered a smoking Jonesboro. Ross's horsemen set off in pursuit; Reynolds's foot soldiers boarded a train for Lovejoy's. By then Kilpatrick's column had ridden some three miles east, where they turned south, heading for Lovejoy's with Ross's riders nipping at their heels. Around 11:00 a.m., when they approached the station, the Federals found Reynolds in their front and Ross in their rear.

We resume with Colonel Minty's article.]

As soon as Col. Murray [*and his division*] attempted to move south, he found Gen. Reynolds, with several regiments of Confederate infantry, strongly posted behind a well-constructed barricade of felled trees, opposing him. After feeling the enemy's position, Kilpatrick decided to make a flank movement towards McDonough, our left, and endeavored to strike the railroad at or near Lovejoy Station, from whence he hoped to be able to

CARRY OUT HIS PROGRAM

for destroying the road. He instructed me to send my own brigade in the advance, and to remain with the Second Brigade to hold Reynolds, Ross and Ferguson in check, and to cover the movement. Lieut. Robinson accompanied the First Brigade with one section, and left Lieut. Bennett and the other section with the Second Brigade.

I left Jonesboro with Long's Brigade at about 4 o'clock in the morning [*August 20*]. About five miles out the column turned to the right and made directly for Lovejoy's. As the Second Brigade turned the enemy's cavalry [*Ross's Texas brigade*], which had followed us from Jonesboro, attacked, but Long very handsomely repulsed them.

I galloped to the front, where I formed the advance of the First Brigade, commanded by Maj. Dart [*Benjamin S. Dartt*], of the 7th Pa., who were skirmishing with the enemy. At this point the road forked—the road to the left leading to Lovejoy and the right crossing the railroad further north. I detached the 4th Mich. to the right with orders to make a break in the road. I sent a staff officer to Gen. Kilpatrick with the request that he would order up my Second Brigade.

When within about a mile of Lovejoy, Col. Long reported to me, and at the same time a courier from Maj. Mix, commanding the 4th Mich., gave me the information that that regiment had reached the railroad, and was at work destroying it.

The enemy again attempted to make a stand, and opened fire from a line extending on both sides of the road. Maj. Dart dismounted his battalion, drove them from their position and remounted; but from the next rise of ground fire was again opened, and a mounted force appeared on the road. I instructed

MAJ. DART TO USE HIS SABERS.

He at once charged and drove the Confederates about half a mile, when they developed too heavy a force for the advance to cope with. The entire line of the 7th Pa. was at once moved to the front, dismounted and deployed as skirmishers. They advanced steadily, driving the enemy's skirmish-line before them, until within 15 or 20 rods of the railroad, where the enemy's fire showed a line extending beyond both flanks of the 7th. I sent a mounted squadron of the 4th U.S. to cover the left flank, and ordered that regiment forward to extend my line to the right.

The regiment formed line on the gallop, and Capt. [*James B.*] McIntyre gave the command, "Prepare to fight on foot," and the men moved forward on the double-quick.

The railroad immediately in our front ran through a long cut from three to four feet deep, and not over 20 rods from the line of the 7th Pa. Before the 4th U.S. could gain their position in line with the 7th, Reynolds' Brigade of seven regiments [*actually four, numbering 700 officers and men*], which had been lying down in the cut, sprang to their feet, fired a withering volley, and with the old rebel yell charged over my skirmish-line. It appeared for a moment as if the two regiments had been annihilated; but the Second Brigade rapidly coming into position, they, with the Chicago Board of Trade Battery, repulsed Reynolds with terrible loss. In the first fire my horse had been shot, but one of my Orderlies galloped to the front with a fresh horse, which enabled me to get back to the Second Brigade.

[*The battle of Lovejoy's Station, late morning of August 20, had begun, and Robert Minty was in the thick of it. Minty's brigade was riding as the advance of Kilpatrick's column. Coming to a road-fork, he sent the 4th Michigan off to the right to damage the railroad track. With the 7th Pennsylvania and 4th U.S. Regulars, he moved forward against the Rebels he suspected were in his front. As our author states, his men were advancing on foot. Reynolds's infantry, now backed by Armstrong's brigade (fighting on foot), were crouching in a railroad cut. When Minty's men got within 50 yards, the Southerners rose up and "poured a devastating volley into the Federals. . . . Surprised and shocked, the Federals recoiled in disorder, having lost heavily" (Hibbard and Castel, 39). The withering volley killed Minty's horse, which had to be replaced by an observant orderly. When Reynolds's and Armstrong's troops rushed forward in pursuit, as Minty states, his two regiments were in danger of annihilation. But Col. Eli Long's three Ohio regiments came to the rescue and stopped the Rebels.*]

Immediately after the repulse of Reynolds, my Adjutant-General, Capt. [*Robert*] Burns, informed me that Gen. Kilpatrick desired to see me at once; that Cleburne's Division of infantry was closing on our Right, Jackson's and Martin's Divisions of cavalry were in rear of our left, and that I knew what was in our front. I instructed Capt. Burns to recall the 4th Mich., galloped to the rear and reported to Gen. Kilpatrick, who repeated what Capt. Burns had already told me, and added: "Our only recourse is

TO CUT OUR WAY OUT.

You will form your division in line on the right of the McDonough road, facing to the rear. Col. Murray will form in the same manner on the left, and you will charge simultaneously."

[*Kilpatrick exaggerated the Rebels' strength (Cleburne and Martin were nowhere nearby, but he correctly gauged his predicament: Reynolds/Armstrong was in his front, and Sul Ross his rear. Prudently he resolved to break through Ross's line, give up the thought of further railroad-wrecking, and make his way back to Sherman's forces near Atlanta.*

Colonel Minty relates what ensued, especially his spectacular saber charge that completely overran Ross's line.]

The ground indicated by Gen. Kilpatrick was a deserted plantation, creased in every direction by rain-gullies, and two rail fences between us and the enemy, who were at work building rail barricades. I said, "General, I would not charge over this ground in line. If we ever strike the enemy it will be a thin, wavering blow that will amount to nothing." He asked, "How then would you charge?" I replied, "In column, sir. Our momentum would be like that of a railroad train, when we strike something has to break." He paused for a moment, and then said, "Form in any way you please."

Reynolds, then repulsed, had taken refuge in the railroad cut, and Gen. Kilpatrick ordered Col. Murray to watch him with one regiment.

I returned to my command. Lieut. Robinson reported to me that one of his guns had been disabled, the trail having been broken by a shell, and that he had been unable to haul it off the ground; that it was in the cornfield to the left of the present position of the 3d Ohio. I found the gun hanging by the trunions, with the muzzle in the air. I took about 20 volunteers from the 3d Ohio, and crouching low, moved through the corn. We placed a piece of fence-rail, with a couple of halters attached to the upper end, in the muzzle of the gun, which was soon pulled down to a horizontal position and [*after being wheeled back through the cornfield was*] given to the happy batterymen, who took it [*the 890-pound metal barrel or tube*] off its wheels and placed it in a wagon.

Maj. Mix having reported with the 4th Mich., I withdrew my division, and formed my own brigade in line of regimental columns of fours at regimental distance—the 7th Pa. on the right, 4th Mich. in the center, 4th U.S. on the left—and instructed Col. Long to form his brigade "in rear of my center, in close column, with regimental front, and to sweep up whatever I broke through."

KILPATRICK WAS ON HORSEBACK

on the McDonough road. As soon as my division was in position I rode over to report to him. Col. Murray came forward about the same moment and said:

"General, my men cannot charge over this ground."

"Why not, sir?" said Kilpatrick.

"They cannot do it, General," replied Murray.

Kilpatrick turning to me, said:

"Col. Minty, are you ready?"

"All ready, sir."

"Then charge when you please."

A four-gun battery on a hill in rear of the rail breastworks was shelling us, and a three-gun battery in front of our left was firing canister.

Having led this charge, I scarcely know how to proceed without appearing egotistical; but justice to the grand and noble body of men of whom I had the honor to be the commander, demands that I do not slur over the account of the great saber charge.

I quote the following from the Cincinnati *Commercial* of August 31, 1864:

> While the various regiments were being manuvered into position, the men had time to comprehend the danger that surrounded them; rebels to the right of them, rebels to the left of them, rebels in the rear of them, rebels in front of them—surrounded. There was no salvation but to cut their way out. Visions of Libby, Andersonville and starvation flitted

through their imaginations, and they saw that the deadly conflict could not be avoided. Placing himself at the head of the 4th Mich., the gallant and fearless Minty drew his saber, and his voice rang out clear and loud: "Attention! Draw sabers! Forward—trot, regulate by the center column! March! Gallop! March!" and away the brigade went, with a cheer that echoed across the valley.

The ground from which the start was made and over which they charged was a plantation of about two square miles, thickly strewn with patches of woods, deep water-cuts, fences and ditches. At the word, away went the bold dragoons at the hight of their speed. Fences were jumped and ditches were no impediment.

CHARGING FOR THEIR LIVES,

and yelling like devils, Minty and his troopers encountered the rebels behind a hastily-constructed barricade of rails. Pressing their rowels deep into their horses' flanks, and raising their sabers aloft, on, on, on, nearer and nearer to the rebels they plunged. The terror-stricken enemy could not withstand the thunderous wave of men and horses that threatened to engulf them. They broke and ran just as Minty and his troopers were urging their horses for the decisive blow. In an instant all was confusion. The yells of the horsemen were drowned in the clashing of steel and the groans of the dying. On pressed Minty in pursuit, his men's sabers striking right and left, and cutting down everything in their path. The rebel horsemen were seen to reel and pitch headlong to the earth, while their frightened steeds rushed pell-mell over their bodies. Many of the rebels defended themselves with almost superhuman strength; yet it was all in vain. The charge of Federal steel was irresistible. The heads and limbs of some of the rebels were actually severed from their bodies.

The individual instances of heroism were many. Not a man flinched, and when the brigade came out, most of the sabers were stained with human blood.

I must ask the reader to bear in mind that when "Minty" is named in the foregoing, it is as the representative of, and means, the noble body of men who made this charge.

The following extract is from the *Memphis-Atlanta Appeal,* published at Macon, Ga., early in September, 1864:

The newspapers have lately been full of accounts of how Martin's Division of Cavalry was

RUN OVER BY THE YANKEES

at Lovejoy, on the 20th ult. The writer was on the field on that occasion, and, in justice to the much-abused cavalry, states the facts in the matter: Martin's Division, supporting

> the battery, was formed on the McDonough road. Ross's and Ferguson's commands, on foot, were in front and on each side of the battery, behind rail breastworks. A brigade of Cleburne's Division was on the left of the road in three lines, the last one in a piece of woods about 100 yards in rear of the position of the battery. On the right of the road the State troops were formed in line. When the Yankees charged they came in a solid column, ten or twelve lines deep, running their horses and yelling like devils. They didn't stop to fire, but each fellow for himself rushed on, swinging his saber over his head. They rode right over Ross's and Ferguson's men in the center, and over and through Cleburne's lines, one after the other, on the left. Cleburne's first line tried to use their bayonets, but the Yankees cut them to pieces. After the Yankees had cut through all the other forces and captured the battery, Martin, seeing the field was lost, retreated in good order. The effort to arouse the people against Martin and his brave division is more disgraceful and demoralizing than the Yankees' charge itself, and should be frowned upon by all who wish well to our cause.

[*It is peculiar that a Confederate newspaper shared Colonel Minty's notion that his troops were fighting a brigade from Pat Cleburne's infantry division. Dan Reynolds's brigade belonged to Major General Edward Walthall's division, Lt. Gen. Peter Stewart's corps.*]

In this charge the First Brigade well maintained its title of the "Saber Brigade." Not less than 800 of the enemy were sabered, and the three-gun battery was captured, together with three stand of colors and about 600 prisoners.

Col. Long, instead of following the First Brigade [*Minty's*] in the formation ordered and sweeping up what we broke through, broke into columns of fours and followed the charging regiments. If he had obeyed orders, there was no earthly reason why we should not have taken several thousand prisoners.

[*Proud of his "Saber Brigade," Minty may be excused for exaggerating Ross's losses at Lovejoy Station. According to one Texan, the entire brigade did not number more than 400. After the battle Ross reported to General Hood: "General, I got my brigade run over yesterday"; Hood tried to console him (Martha L. Crabb,* All Afire to Fight: The Untold Tale of the Civil War's Ninth Texas Cavalry *[New York: William Morrow, 2000], 249).*]

As soon as we had cut our way through the surrounding force, Gen. Kilpatrick, with the Third Division, marched for McDonough, leaving orders for me to

COVER HIS RETREAT.

I instructed my Provost-Marshal, Capt. Dickson, of the 7th Pa., to at once turn over the prisoners to the Third Division, and I sent Lieut. Simpson, of the

4th Mich., a temporary Aid on my staff, to Col. Long with orders to dismount his brigade, form across the McDonough road, and hold the enemy in check as long as possible. When too hard pressed to fall back through the First Brigade. At this moment Capt. McIntyre reported that his regiment was out of ammunition, and I directed him to follow Gen. Kilpatrick.

I dismounted the 7th Pa. and 4th Mich., and placed them in position on rising ground, with an open space in front of them, the 7th Pa. and one section of the battery on the right and the 4th Mich. on the left of the road, and instructed them to construct rail breastworks as quickly as possible. The horses of both brigades were strung out on the road in our rear.

Col. Long was brought to the rear, wounded, and the command of his brigade devolved on Col. [*Beroth B.*] Eggleston, of the 1st Ohio, who soon after reported that Cleburne's infantry was endeavoring to turn both of his flanks. I ordered him to fall back, and as he passed the First Brigade I instructed him to move his men on the double-quick, to mount and follow the Third Division [*Kilpatrick's*], to take position with Lieut. Robinson's guns on the high ground beyond the swamp in front of him.

The enemy followed him closely and made a vigorous assault on the position held by the 4th Mich. and 7th Pa., but were repulsed with heavy loss. The section of artillery was doing

MOST EFFECTIVE WORK WITH CANISTER,

when one of the guns burst, and a few moments later a shell wedged in the other gun, rendering it for the time useless. I therefore directed Mr. Bennett to take it to the rear and join the battery.

A second and a third assault was made on the position held by the two regiments of the First Brigade, and both were handsomely repulsed.

After the repulse of the third assault the Second Brigade being well out of the way, we fell back to our horses and followed the column. I found Col. Eggleston with his brigade and Lieut. Robinson with his two guns in position on the high ground beyond the swamp. Immediately after the charge the rain came down in torrents, and it continued to pour without cessation until about 4 o'clock in the morning.

Cleburne followed us through the swamp, but a few shells checked him, and we saw nothing more of him during the expedition. The night was dark as Erebus, but after a few moments' halt we continued the march. About 2 o'clock in the morning my advance came upon the Third Division halted. By the time my column was closed up we were on the move again, and at 6 a.m. we were on the banks of the Cotton River—usually an insignificant stream, but now flooded, and not fordable at any point [*Cotton Indian Creek was about six miles northeast of McDonough*]. This the entire force (about 5,000 men) had to swim, in doing which we lost one man and about 50 horses and mules. The most difficult and trying work was getting our poor wounded comrades across, but this was done without any casualties; and when I saw my 90 wounded officers and men safely on the north side of that stream, I thanked God that I had my ambulances with me and had not been compelled to leave them in the hands of the enemy.

Kilpatrick ordered the destruction of the wagon containing the dismounted [*Parrott*] gun, which was placed where the enemy could not find it.

About 7 p.m. on the 21st we bivouacked at Lithonia, on the Georgia Railroad, and, oh! how grateful we were for our first sleep since leaving Sandtown on the evening of the 18th.

As I before stated, my Provost-Marshal turned over to the Third Division about 600 prisoners. All of these, except about 70, were allowed to escape before reaching our own lines.

In my official report of the expedition, I find the following closing remarks:

> Every officer and soldier in the command acted so well, so nobly, so gallantly, that under ordinary circumstances they would be entitled to special mention. Day and night from the 18th to the 21st these gallant men were without sleep and almost without food. During that time they marched and skirmished almost incessantly, fought four pitched battles and swam a flooded river without once complaining or murmuring.

Our casualties were: First Brigade, 106, or 11 ½ per cent.; Second Brigade, 94, or nearly seven per cent.; Chicago Board of Trade Battery, 6, or nearly six and a half per cent.

*Minty's report (*OR *38, pt. 2, 826) is more specific: 17 killed, 31 wounded, and 58 missing in his First Brigade; 15 K, 63 W, 16 M in Long's Second; 1 killed, 4 wounded, and 1 missing in the battery.*

*In his campaign report, Kilpatrick wrote, "My entire loss in killed, wounded and missing will not exceed 300. Two hundred of this number were killed and wounded" (*OR *38, pt. 2, 859). David Evans totes Union losses in the raid as 277 (*Sherman's Horsemen, *466-467), but that doesn't include a brigade (Klein's). As we have seen, Minty's men did much of the hard fighting, so Kilpatrick's generalization makes sense.*

Colonel Minty, however, dodges the big picture: how much railroad wreckage had the Federal troopers achieved, and for how long had they knocked out the Macon & Western? Kilpatrick claimed that his men had wrecked three miles of track at Jonesboro *and ten more at other places—"enough to disable the road for ten days," as Sherman wired Halleck on August 22 (*OR *38, pt. 5, 628). Historian Evans calculates Kilpatrick's soldiers tore up about two miles—and that was literally tearing up, not heating and twisting the rails. Little wonder that the Confederates, very energetic in their repair, had the M & W up and running by August 21, two days after the raiders had inflicted their damage (Stephen Davis,* Texas Brigadier to the Fall of Atlanta: John Bell Hood *[Macon: Mercer University Press, 2019] 410).*

*Worse for "Kill-Cavalry," as he boasted of his accomplishment at Sherman's HQ on the evening of August 22, his conversation was interrupted by the distant sound of a shrill whistle as a Rebel train chugged into Atlanta (*Sherman's Horsemen, *467).*

54

The Campaign's Decisive Event

C. V. Gorrell, "Cutting the Macon Road"

(October 28, 1909, p. 7)

After Kilpatrick's failure to decisively break the Atlanta-Macon railroad, Sherman determined to "make the matter certain": he would lead six of his seven infantry corps in a wide swing south of Atlanta, then east, aiming to strike the Macon & Western somewhere well south of East Point, toward Jonesboro. The XX Corps—Maj. Gen. Henry W. Slocum took over on August 27—would withdraw back to the Chattahoochee, guarding the river bridges while threatening Atlanta. (Slocum had been called from Vicksburg.)

Once Sherman's "grand movement by the right flank" got underway, Hood would be dangerously stretched on a wide front, guarding the city while protecting his lifeline to the south.

The Federals' movement began during the night of August 25-26. The next morning Confederate pickets found the Union trenches north of the city empty. To track the enemy's movements Hood sent out his cavalry, under Brig. Gen. William H. ("Red") Jackson—Wheeler, with half the army's horse, was off raiding in Tennessee. Frank Armstrong's and Sul Ross's horsemen kept watch on the enemy's advance. As a precaution, Hood sent infantrymen to East Point (seven track-miles from the downtown depot), Rough and Ready Station (six miles farther south), and Jonesboro (23 miles from downtown). Hood reckoned that Sherman would strike the Macon road, but could not predict precisely where.

As it turned out, around 3:00 p.m. on August 31, the M & W was interdicted below Rough and Ready by troops of Jacob Cox's division, XXIII Corps. Hood had no infantry to repel them, and cavalry there was quickly driven off. General Cox proudly declared that his men "struck the Atlanta and Macon Railroad one mile below Rough and Ready Station at 3:00 p.m., being the first of the army to reach that road" (OR *38, pt. 2, 692).*

Hood had sent out from Atlanta two trains with the army's reserve ordnance—the main ordnance stores had already been sent to Hardee at East Point (Frank E. Vandiver, "General Hood as Logistician," Military Affairs, *vol. 16, no. 1 [Spring 1952], 5 n., 23 ["Hood's regular ordnance train was under Hardee's care at Jonesboro"]).*

As these locomotives chugged south, Southern horsemen hailed them and warned there were Yankees on the track ahead. The trains, in reverse, returned to Atlanta to give Hood's headquarters the bad news. The Confederate commander thus knew by 5:00 p.m. that the railroad had been finally cut by the enemy, and that he would have to evacuate Atlanta.

*The matter was soon made more certain. Around 4 o'clock troops of Maj. Gen. David Stanley's IV Corps reached the railroad a bit south of where the XXIII had gotten to it. "A small break was made in the road," General Stanley reported, one that was widened early the next morning (*OR *38, pt. 1, 214).*

*Then at 6:00 p.m., elements of the IV and XIV Corps struck the Macon & Western farther south at Morrow's Station, four miles above Jonesboro, and began tearing up the track. Brigadier General Jefferson C. Davis, commander of the XIV, reported that troops from Absalom Baird's division were entitled to those honors. Baird wrote that among the men who cut the railroad at Morrow's was Col. C. H. Carlton's 89th Ohio (*OR *38, pt. 1, 748). Carlton added that the force was his regiment, plus the 75th and 82nd Indiana, as well as the 31st Ohio (*OR *vol. 38, pt. 1, 784). Colonel Morton C. Hunter, commander of the 82nd Indiana, wrote that he was in command of the four regiments that set off to cut the Macon road, reaching it at Morrow's Station about 6:00 p.m. (*OR *vol. 38, pt. 1, 770-771).*

Clearly, as shown in the following piece, participants in the rail-wrecking on August 31 knew they had done something important.

Editor National Tribune: I belonged to the 75th Ind., Second Brigade [*Col. Newell Gleason's*], Third Division [*Brig. Gen Absalom Baird's*], Fourteenth Corps [*Brig. Gen. Jefferson C. Davis's*]. Referring to the Atlanta campaign, I wish to tell something which I think deserves favorable mention on history's page that I believe you fail to mention in your history of the campaign.

From memory I would say that about noon of the day before the final charge at Jonesboro [*meaning August 31*] the 75th Ind. was sent forward alone. After advancing about one mile we overtook another regiment, and with them advanced perhaps another mile, and reached the Macon road, the last line of supplies Hood's army in Atlanta had. We were reinforced by two more regiments, and held the road all night tearing up a mile or more of track.

The historian of the 75th Ind. says that the reconnaissance occurred on August 31, 1864. The force was composed of the 89th Ohio, 75th Ind., 31st Ohio and 82d Ind., commanded by Hunter, Colonel of the 82 Ind.; that we advanced two miles beyond our line of battle and reached the Macon road at Morrow's or Chapman's Station, four miles from Jonesboro and seven miles from Rough and Ready Station, where the Fourth and Twenty-third Corps later [*sic: earlier, 3 and*

4:00 p.m.] reached the road. He says this force was the first to cut and hold the road, and sustains this claim from official reports of Gen. Baird and Cols. Hunter and Walker [*"the historian of the 75th Indiana," David B. Floyd, 1893, overlooks the IV and XXIII Corps having cut the M & W hours earlier, farther north*].

To one not immediately concerned this affair, being a bloodless victory, may seem small, but there was a brisk skirmish fire before we reached the road. It was repeated at intervals all night, making us feel that the foe was seeking for our position preparatory to a resistless charge; and well we knew that the mantle of night hid all hope of any friendly arm coming to our rescue. That was the most terrible night to me in the history of my nearly three years' experience.—C. V. Gorrell, Payne, Ohio.

Comrade Gorrell's statement is supported by the campaign report of Colonel Hunter, who wrote that his force tore up a mile of track during the night and on the morning of September 1. Colonel Moses B. Walker was in charge of the 1st Brigade, Baird's 3rd Division; from it were drawn the 82nd Indiana, 31st and 89th Ohio. His report on the action is in the Official Records, *vol. 38, pt.1, 765.*

55

"A chance to visit Andersonville"

A. McNeil, "Cutting the Macon Road"

(May 26, 1910, p. 7)

Editor National Tribune: I desire to congratulate Comrade C. V. Gorrell on his accurate account of "Cutting the Macon Road," as published in The National Tribune. I think it is the first published account of Col. M. C. Hunter's command capturing the Macon Railroad I have read, excepting what is found in the Official Records of the Rebellion. I had forgotten that the 75th Ind. was one of the four regiments, and until I read Comrade Gorrell's letter thought it was the 17th Ohio instead.

To satisfy myself on that point I have just examined a copy of a journal kept by Serg't Harry Allspaugh [*Sgt. Jacob H. Allspaugh, Co. H*], of the 31st Ohio, on the Atlanta campaign. Here is what he wrote under date of August 31, 1864:

"With skirmishers out we move east about two miles and fortify. We are the first Yankees here, and the natives are astonished. We captured a number of prisoners. Our skirmishers reached the Macon Road, and held it one and one-half hours, when they were driven back [*by Confederate cavalry*]. About dark we move forward in line of battle, and again reach the Macon Railroad, and intrench in the form of a square. Our force is composed of the 75th and 82d Ind. and the 31st and 89th Ohio (the 17th Ohio is away on some kind of duty), and commanded by Col. M. C. Hunter, of the 82d Ind., who told us that we must hold the railroad or be captured, as we are two and a half miles in front of our main line. Stragglers from the enemy come in in by squads."

In a footnote Serg't. Allspaugh wrote: "Hardee's Corps passed along almost within gunshot of us during the night, and had they known of our detached position on the railroad they doubtless would have given our four regiments a chance to visit Andersonville—that is, those they did not kill."

The survivors of the 31st Ohio often refer to that exciting night attack and the capture of the railroad.

The fortified position was in the form of a square, thru which the railroad extended the length of one regiment front. The earthworks were ever afterwards designated by the members of the 31st Ohio as the "bullpen," and all agreed that somebody took chances on the capture of the entire force by leaving us there all night.

I, too, think this affair "deserves favorable mention on history's pages," as Col. Hunter, with the four named regiments, was the first Union force to capture and hold the Macon road.—S. A. McNeil, Richwood, O.

Comrade McNeil's article introduces a concept heretofore not mulled over by historians of the Atlanta Campaign. Four Federal regiments were abreast of the Macon railroad at Morrow's, holding their position during the night of August 31-September 1. Knowing that they were without support and subject to attack, the men nervously waited out the night, which was (as Comrade Gorrell poignantly put it) "the most terrible night to me in the history of my nearly three years' experience."

McNeil takes us further into the night of August 31-September 1. Hood had learned by 5:00 p.m. that the enemy had cut the M & W—even before the onset of the attack by Hardee and Lee against Howard's army at Jonesboro, which did not begin until 6:00 p.m., and whose repulse Hood in Atlanta did not learn of until around midnight (by courier from Hardee, because the Yankees had cut the telegraph wires that afternoon). With his army dangerously split, and with large enemy forces between the two parts (Stewart's Corps and Georgia Militia in Atlanta; Hood and Lee at Jonesboro), Hood ordered Lee's Corps to march back toward town during the night of August 31-September 1. (Hardee, not knowing in Jonesboro what Hood in Atlanta knew about the Macon railroad, wondered why headquarters called Lee back northward.)

Back to McNeil. Lee's infantry marched toward Atlanta from Jonesboro by way of a road less than a quarter-mile to the west of those four stranded regiments of Absalom Baird's division entrenched on the railroad. The Federals were not "almost within gunshot" of Lee's marching infantry; they were actually within effective musket range.

Now, imagine the kind of battle Confederates bemoaned never happened at Spring Hill, Tennessee, three months later, during the night of November 29-30, 1864, when Schofield's army marched stealthily past Hood's troops toward Franklin. Confederates never anguished over why Lee' s infantry did not fall upon Baird's four regiments because they were unaware of the Yankees' presence on the nearby railroad. And for their part, the Federals were not about to let the Rebels in on the fact that they were "almost within gunshot of us."

Counterfactual: in a night battle, Lee's infantry would have destroyed those four blue-coated regiments. The Confederates would not have restored use of the M & W, as Cox's infantry still held the railroad north, near Rough and Ready, so the outcome of the campaign would not have been altered. But the dramatic story of a night-fight at Morrow's Station and decisive, if small-scale Confederate victory, would be another of those Atlanta Campaign stories historians love to tell.

56

"Built breastworks on railroad"

J. C. Nelson, "Cutting the Macon Road"

(January 11, 1911, p. 3)

Editor National Tribune: In the National Tribune of May 26 I notice with some surprise and amusement a communication from Comrade S. A. McNeil, of the 31st Ohio, under the above caption. I can assist comrades McNeil and Gorrell to straighten this matter out. I was in command of the skirmish line sent out by the First Brigade, Third Division, Fourteenth Corps [*Col. Moses Walker's*]. During the day of August 31 we were advancing, under constant apprehension of meeting the rebels, and as a precaution wherever we halted, even for but a few minutes, we would build breastworks as best we could. We met no enemy, however, and about 5 p.m. I was ordered out with a line of skirmishers to advance on the Macon Railroad.

The weather was oppressively warm, and our way led thru woods and underbrush for some two miles, reached the railroad before dark, as I remember it, without a shot being fired. I did not understand that we were supported within a reasonable distance, and was puzzled to know what I had best do with it, now I had it. While standing on the track cogitating, I was startled by two or three shots from the south, and bullets whistled pretty close, knocking up the dust just in front of me.

It didn't take me long to change position to the other side of a freight car standing on the sidetrack. The comrade is in error in saying "the skirmishers held the railroad one and a half hours and were driven back." As I remember it, we only remained there a few minutes, possibly a half hour, and were recalled by order from our own commander. At this time I am not sure whether the order came from Col. M. C. Hunter, commanding the brigade, or Lieut.-Col. Wm. Glenn, of my own regiment, the 89th Ohio. At any rate, we reached the command before dark, hot, tired, and hungry, but before we had time to rest of get anything to eat we were ordered back over the same course again, starting between 6 and 7 p.m.

It soon became quite dark, and I can say for the benefit of those who never tried it, advancing over logs and thru the bushes in the dark is no joke. As we approached the railroad this time we were met by a few straggling shots, but nothing we could magnify into a resistance. In a short time the brigade came up, and proceeded to erect the square fort as related by the comrades.

It is true the situation was precarious. We were some distance in advance of the main force, in the line of the retreating enemy, and were liable to attack and possible capture, but we were not attacked and were enabled to work quietly on the fortification all night. In my diary of that date—not as complete as I would wish it now, but gave what impressed me at the time—I note, under August 31, 1864: "March forward east a mile; built works; moved again one and a half miles; built works; went to railroad on the skirmish line; retreated; advanced again after night; relieved about midnight; built breastworks on railroad; during the day [*September 1*] built three lines of breastworks and two of skirmish pits."

I do not remember any shots fired except the few straggling ones when the skirmishers advanced early in the evening. I deplore the disposition of comrades to make "mountains out of mole hills." The comrades of the 31st Ohio are hard up for excitement when they characterize this as an "exciting night attack." Altho I bore a prominent part, I never considered it of sufficient importance to make special note of.—J. C. Nelson, Captain, Co. D, 89th Ohio, 4622 N. Robey street, Chicago, Ill.

Captain Nelson's writing to the National Tribune *details what Federal troops did late on August 31 once they had reached the Macon railroad. On September 1, they "built breastworks on railroad; during the day built three lines of breastworks and two of skirmish lines."*

Federal fortifications across the Macon & Western Railroad south of Atlanta? No wonder Hood had to evacuate the city!

57

Editor McElroy Covers Howard's March to Jonesboro and the Battle, August 31-September 1

John McElroy, "The Atlanta Campaign Ends in a Fierce Bayonet Rush Over the Enemy's Works at Jonesboro"

(July 1, 1909, p. 2)

This article is both informed (relating military events from the Official Records, *Sherman's* Memoirs, *and other sources) and not.*

It is reflective of the campaign narrative prevalent more than a century ago. First, it claims that "Hood was deceived" by Sherman's grand wheel to the right—leading his six corps away from Atlanta and toward the Macon & Western Railroad. On the morning of August 26, Confederate pickets saw that the Federals had abandoned their trenches north of the city. General Hood for a few hours entertained the hope that Wheeler's raiders had forced Sherman to retreat, but soon he learned that Sherman's troops still held their lines west of Atlanta (Schofield's army was last to set out). A reconnaissance also found Yankees still at the Chattahoochee (Slocum's XX Corps). Sul Ross's cavalry that afternoon reported enemy infantry marching to the southwest.

With Wheeler gone, Red Jackson was the army's cavalry leader, retaining half of its mounted troops. Southern horsemen kept Hood's HQ apprised of the enemy's movements, so that on the morning of August 30 General Hardee could write his wife, "we know that five certain, perhaps six Corps are on the West Point R. Road" (Sherman's men spent August 29 further wrecking the railway linking Atlanta with Montgomery). Hardee even sent a staff officer, Col. William D. Pickett, on a recon that brought in the news that the enemy was marching toward Rough and Ready as well as Jonesboro (Stephen Davis, Atlanta Will Fall: Sherman, Joe Johnston and the Yankee Heavy Battalions *[Wilmington DE: Scholarly Resources, 2001], 182).*

So much for "Hood was deceived."

Until recently historians of the Atlanta Campaign have failed to see that the Macon & Western Railroad, the logistical lifeline for the Army of Tennessee while defending the city, had been seized and was in the process of being wrecked at 3:00 p.m. on August 31.

General Hood had sent troops to Jonesboro well south of Atlanta to defend the railroad at that point. When Oliver O. Howard's Army of the Tennessee (XV, XVI, and XVII Corps) crossed the Flint River and threatened Jonesboro around sundown of

August 30, Hood judged this to be the main threat to his holding Atlanta and planned accordingly. Calling Generals Hardee and Lee to his downtown headquarters, Hood laid it out. This summary comes from Castel's inestimable Decision in the West, *486).*

- *Their two infantry corps, with Hardee in overall command, were to night-march to Jonesboro, deploy as soon as they can on the morning of the 31st and attack the enemy—whom Red Jackson estimated to be just two corps, and thus likely to give way to Hardee's assault;*
- *While cavalry keep watch on the XX Corps at the Chattahoochee, Stewart's Corps, and the Georgia Militia will march south to East Point;*
- *Lee's Corps was to march back to Rough and Ready;*
- *On the morning of September 1, Lee and Stewart were to attack the left of Sherman's forces while Hardee hit them from the front. Together the Confederates could send the Federals packing.*

There was a big if: what if the Yankees were not driven back at Jonesboro? Already they were entrenched a mile from the railroad. A failure of the Confederate attack would ensure the Federals' control of the train line to Atlanta, in which case the city would have to be evacuated. In that event, Lee was to march north to Rough and Ready to cover the army's retreat southward.

Hardee's troops arrived at Jonesboro around sunrise; Lee's got there between 10:00 a.m. and 1:00 p.m. By the time they deployed, it was 3:00 p.m., hours the Union troops used to strengthen their works. The Southerners' assault accordingly failed in less than two hours. As we have seen, the Confederate repulse was tragically inconsequential; Federals had reached and had begun to tear up the Macon road about 3:00 p.m. Hood knew this even before Hardee sent news of his repulse back to Atlanta by courier (the Federals had also cut the telegraph line). The courier arrived around midnight; by then Hood had already begun to issue orders for the evacuation of Atlanta. Lee, as per plan, marched back toward the city. Hardee was left to take defensive position at Jonesboro, dig in, and await the inevitable Union counterattack (which occurred on September 1, and which the Confederates repulsed, but with considerable loss of prisoners).

Dr. Castel devotes more than a dozen pages to the battle of Jonesboro, August 31-September 1, but just seven lines on the IV and XXIII Corps' cutting the railroad to its north. One of the reasons for this imbalance is that the early campaign literature failed to grasp this latter point and instead focused on the battle between Hardee's and Howard's forces.

John McElroy's article is a case in point, barely mentioning that "Thomas's men, as well as Schofield's, were busily engaged in tearing up the railroad from Rough and Ready on toward Jonesboro."

Hood Completely Deceived.

Hood was deceived in the most astonishing manner by Sherman's manuver. He thought that Sherman had made an effort to reach around to his (Hood's) left, which had been foiled by the defensive works which Hood had thrown up across his path. It seemed to him that this was Sherman's last and utmost effort, and when he saw the works in front of him vacated this belief was confirmed. His scouts followed the Twentieth Corps back to where it went into position in the tete-de-pont on the Chattahoochee, and they believed they were following the rear of the whole army. The rest of Sherman's army had disappeared behind the high hills and the dense woods, and was lost to Hood's view and knowledge. There was every reason to believe that Wheeler had been successful in cutting the railroad, and that Sherman had been obliged to fall back in order to avoid starvation. Naturally, Hood, his army and the people of Atlanta exulted at being freed from a terrible anxiety and danger. Apparently Hood sent out scouts to ascertain what had become of that portion of the army which they had found on the left. For this he and all under him were strongly culpable. So certain were they that all danger was past that a great rejoicing was planned, and train loads of people came in over the Macon road to join in the celebration.

Iago says that "trifles light as air are to the joyous confirmations strong as proofs of holy writ." The same remark will apply to commanders in forming their judgments. Trifles almost light as air will confirm them in that which they wish to believe. On the evening of August 27 an old woman who lived between the lines came into Hardee's camps and asked for food on the ground that the [*Union*] troops had not enough for themselves. She was taken to Hardee, who believed her story implicitly and thought it of sufficient importance to communicate at once to Hood. Hood saw in it indisputable evidence that Wheeler's raid upon the railroad had reduced Sherman's army to the stage of starvation.

The Army's Grand Swing.

In the meantime the whole army was marching as nearly as possible by parallel roads with that order, celerity and punctuality which were the wonder of the Atlanta campaign. All the armies of the United States had at last freed themselves from the haltings, the entanglements, the misconceptions of orders and blunderings as to roads, etc. which had marred so many of the earlier campaigns. In the Army of the Potomac and in Sherman's army every regiment, brigade, division and corps inevitably and certainly marched at the hour it was ordered, took the road intended for it, and in a given time was to be found precisely where it was planned it should be. No army ever mustered excelled the perfection to which Sherman's had reached in this respect.

The movement began on Thursday, August 25. Stanley's Fourth Corps, which formed the left flank on the north of Atlanta, marched to the rear of Williams's [*now Slocum's*] Twentieth Corps. The line vacated by Stanley was occupied by Garrard's dismounted cavalry. The next day Stanley reached Utoy Creek, and was massed in the rear of Davis's Fourteenth Corps, which had also abandoned its lines, leaving only skirmishers to hold them. That night Williams marched his corps back to the Chattahoochee, and went into the works there. Gen. Slocum came up and took command of the corps. The Army of the Tennessee marched to the west of the Army of the Cumberland, and went into position near the village of Utoy, facing south, where it formed the right of the army, which was now well in hand and to the southwest of Atlanta. In consequence of Gen. Dodge having been disabled by a wound [*on August 19, Dodge received a bullet wound to the head that caused a severe concussion; he never returned to active service in the field*], the command of the two divisions of the Sixteenth Corps present passed to Gen. T. E. G. Ransom. Garrard's Cavalry was thrown out to the rear to check observation and guard against attack, and the Twenty-third Corps held its position in front of East Point, forming a pivot on which the rest of the army was swinging.

Sherman had all his trains well covered by their following the roads between the Armies of the Cumberland and Ohio.

Thomas encamped the Army of the Cumberland near Red Oak Station in the night of August 28. This point was seven of miles from Mount Gilead Church and four miles southeast [sic: *seven miles southwest*] of East Point. Howard, with the Army of the Tennessee, reached Fairburn that same evening, a point five miles further southwest on the West Point Railroad. August 29 was given to the thoro destruction of the West Point Railroad, burning the ties and twisting the rails. Schofield moved up a mile northeast of Mount Gilead, and came into line with the left flank of the Army of the Cumberland. The next day the Twenty-third Corps pushed forward to threaten the Macon Railroad and cover the movement of the trains, and, separating itself some three miles from the Army of the Cumberland, was in an exposed position, where an attack from Hood might be feared when he waked up from his delusion as to Sherman's army being in retreat.

Hood did not abandon this idea quickly, and began by substituting for it a possible raid of two of Sherman's corps upon his last railroad. He ordered Hardee, with his own and Lee's Corps, to Jonesboro, and also ordered that the rest of the army should make an attack on the flank of the army which Sherman had presented to him.

Advancing on Jonesboro.

Macon, which was a railroad junction of much importance, was 60 miles south of Atlanta. The railroad connecting the two places runs along a ridge separating the waters of the Flint on the west from those of the Ocmulgee on the east. The little station of Jonesboro is about midway between Macon and Atlanta and some 10 miles south of East Point, the left flank of the works surrounding Atlanta [*as Sherman had extended his left flank toward East Point, Confederates had correspondingly extended their "railway defense line"*]. These works covered the junction of the West Point and Macon roads. Jonesboro was surrounded by works, but Hardee was ordered to assume the aggressive at once, and drive Sherman's advance back across the Flint River. Hardee's own corps was under the command of the noted Pat Cleburne, who had the highest reputation for skill and energy of any division commander in the Confederate army of the West. Cleburne pushed forward rapidly [*in his march from East Point*], but found that Howard was on the shortest road and had fortified himself so that Cleburne was forced to open a new road around Howard's flank. Therefore Cleburne did not read Jonesboro until 9 o'clock on the morning of August 31, and Lee did not come up with his corps until two hours later. Fearing that this delay would give Howard still longer to intrench, Hardee telegraphed to Hood to come and take command of the wing himself and deliver the attack [*the author is incorrect here*], but Hood had gotten a new idea, and did not think it prudent to leave Atlanta at that time.

Sherman and Thomas.

In Sherman's "Memoirs" he says of this stage of the operations:

"I was with Gen. Thomas that day, which was hot but otherwise very pleasant. We stopped for a short noon rest near a little church (marked on our maps as Shoal Creek Church, which stood back about 100 yards from the road in a grove of native oaks. [*Shoal Creek Church was about nine miles northwest of Jonesboro, according to the map prepared by the redoubtable Wilbur G. Kurtz for his article, "Last Battle Near Atlanta" (*Atlanta Journal Sunday Magazine, *February 26, 1933.*] The infantry column had halted in the road, stacked their arms and the men were scattered about, some lying in the shade of the trees and others were bringing cornstalks from a large cornfield across the road to feed our horses, while still others had arms full of the roasting ears, then in their prime. Hundreds of fires were soon started with the fence rails, and the men were busy roasting the ears. Thomas and I were walking up and down the road which led to the church, discussing the chances of the movement, which he thought were extrahazardous, and our path carried us by a fire at which a soldier was roasting his corn. The fire was built artistically; the man was stripping the ears of their husks, standing them in front of his fire, watching them carefully and turning each ear little by little, so as to roast it nicely. He was down on his knees intent on his business, paying little heed to the stately and serious deliberations of his leaders. Thomas's mind was running on the fact that we had cut loose from our base of supplies, and that 70,000 men were then dependent for their food on the chance supplies of the country (already impoverished by the requisitions of the enemy) and on the contents of our wagons. Between Thomas and his men there existed a most kindly relation, and he frequently talked with them in the most familiar way. Pausing awhile and watching the operations of this man roasting his corn, he said: 'What are you doing?' The man looked up smilingly; "Why, Genera, I am laying in a supply of provisions.' 'That is right, my man, but don't waste your provisions.' As we resumed our walk the man remarked, in a sort of musing way but loud enough for me to hear: 'There he goes, there goes the old man, economizing as usual.' 'Economizing' with corn which only cost the labor of gathering and roasting."

Howard's Advance.

On August 30 Howard, with the Army of the Tennessee, pushed along the road from Fairburn toward Jonesboro, meeting some bodies of the enemy's cavalry, which fought him with much stubbornness in order to give time for Hardee to reach Jonesboro and form for attack on the hills bordering the Flint River. Sherman had directed that the right wing should be at Renfroe's [*about six miles northwest of Jonesboro*] on the evening of August 30, and he had told Howard that if he saw a chance of seizing Jonesboro to do so. At Renfroe's Howard could find no water for his men. He heard that the Confederates were at Jonesboro, but the reports as to their strength varied him from a division to a corps. Howard, therefore, decided to advance to the Flint River to get water for his men.

The Army of the Tennessee advanced in two columns, with Logan's Fifteenth Corps on the left and Ransom's Sixteenth on the right. Kilpatrick's Cavalry covered the advance. The obstinate Confederate cavalry was swept away, and followed on the gallop to the Flint. There Kilpatrick's men dismounted, lined the bank, and opened a hot fire on the enemy across the river to prevent their destroying the bridge. Immediately Hazen, now commanding M. L Smith's Division [*as of August 17, transferred from IV Corps*], came up on the rush, dashed across the bridge and carried the barricades of the enemy. This shows with what careful continuity all the movements were made, and how prompt the Generals were to take advantage of their opportunity.

This movement took the head of Logan's column over the Flint, and he pushed at once to the hights beyond, when he intrenched as the night [*of August 30*] fell, putting Hazen's Division on the left, [*Brig. Gen. William*] Harrow's on the right and [*Brig. Gen. Peter J.*] Osterhaus's in reserve. Ransom's Sixteenth Corps was close at hand, and went into position west of the river, facing south to protect Logan's right flank. [*Maj. Gen. Francis P.*] Blair's Seventeenth Corps arrived during the night, and took a similar position west of the river to refuse Logan's left. In the early morning bridges were at once built to cross the Flint by Blair's and Ransom's men, to connect with Logan and afford mutual help in the expected attack.

The heavy movement of trains during the night assured them that Hood had at last waked up to the danger and was rushing every man to defend the threatened point. The position of the Army of the Tennessee was a critical one, for Hood was in position to throw his whole army against it. Howard sent orderlies every few minutes to Sherman, apprising him of the situation, but in the tangle of the roads these did not reach Sherman until late in the day. Sherman was at the time with Thomas's column, and Thomas's men, as well as Schofield's, were busily engaged in tearing up the railroad from Rough and Ready on toward Jonesboro.

Hardee Attacks Logan.

Hardee was endeavoring to do his best to carry out Hood's orders to strike the army quick and hard and force it back across the Flint River. It was 3 o'clock, however, before he could advance to the assault. This enveloped the whole of Logan's front, and extended across the river on Logan's right to involve one division of Ransom's. Howard saw the direction of the assault, and sent C. R. Wood's [*Brig. Gen. Charles R. Wood's*] Division from Blair's Corps across to prevent the enemy from turning Logan's flank, and getting behind him and the river. The [*Confederate*] attack was made with the greatest fierceness; but, after all it did not equal in either energy or weight the previous assaults of the campaign. The Confederates were evidently discouraged by the ill-success attending their former efforts in that direction. [*Even one Confederate officers later commented that in their attack "the men seemed possessed of some great horror of charging breast-works, which no power, persuasion or example could dispel."*] The brunt of the attack was borne by Hazen's Division, which repulsed it without much difficulty, and there was an entire failure all along the line to pierce the Union ranks and gain any foothold on the hights. When the Confederates retired they left over 400 dead behind them, mostly from Lee's Corps.

[*Dr. Castel places Southern casualties on August 31 at 2,200, although without breaking them down as K, W, and M. In his memoir, Gen. J. E. Johnston writes of "the* *ordinary proportion of one killed to five wounded (*Narrative of Military Operations *[New York: D. Appleton and Company,1874], 344 n.) Howard's loss of a mere 172 attests to the lopsided advantage held by veteran infantrymen who were dug in and fought on the defensive (*Decision in the West, *503).*]

Gen. Hazen's Report.

Gen. Hazen says of this engagement:

"Early on the morning of the 31st Col. Theodore Jones, commanding the First Brigade, on the left, was directed to seize and fortify a commanding eminence about half a mile to the front of his left. He had just gained it when the enemy came along also to occupy it. He held his ground, however, with a portion of his command, while the remainder fortified the position. It was found to be of the greatest importance, as it overlooked the entire front occupied by the enemy. Columns of rebel troops were now seen to be extending to our left, planting artillery and making all dispositions necessary to attack. As he extended beyond my left, and as my troops were formed in a light line, with considerable intervals, a brigade from the Seventeenth Corps, under the command of Col. George E. Bryant, 12th Wis., and two regiments, under Col. William B. Woods, 76th Ohio, were sent to me, and posted where most needed, where they afterward performed good service. I now had 16 regiments in the line and one in reserve. No point of it could be given up without endangering the entire line. At 2 p.m. the enemy commenced a vigorous fire of artillery all along his line, and was soon after seen advancing his infantry. We had good works, and the attack was met with the most perfect confidence. He came on in two full lines supported by troops in mass, coming in one place quite inside the works, and persisted in the attack for about three-quarts of an hour, when he was completely repulsed at all points, and those who came too near were captured. We lost quite heavily in the trenches before the fight took place, but during the fight we had but 11 killed, 52 wounded and two missing. Of the enemy we buried over 200, captured 99 unhurt and 79 wounded. We also took two stands of colors and over 100 stands of small-arms. I have reason to believe that over 1,000 of the enemy were wounded."

An Hour of Thrilling Work.

The long campaign was now about to close, the fate of Atlanta was to be sealed by an intense hour of wild, savage work. The curtain was to go down in a mad melee of bayonet thrusts and crashing musket blows, upon the drama which had opened just 100 days before and 100 miles away before the scarped natural battlements of Rocky Face Ridge.

The manuvering, the days of skirmishing and the nights of marching and intrenching, the picket's vigil, the sharpshooter's slaughter, the wild charge and the stubborn defense, were all to culminate in one last fierce, mad rush across the cotton fields, straight at the embattled front of the enemy.

The long, ghastly trail of the dead over mountain, dale and river valley was to conclude with the shallow graves on the red clay hills of Flint River, which would receive blue and gray alike, those who had followed the Flag and those who had struck at it.

Sherman came up to Howard as Logan had finished his battle, and the defeated enemy sullenly retreated to the works from which they had emerged. Sherman instantly bent his thoughts upon surrounding, capturing and destroying the force which Logan had repulsed. He sent orders in all haste to Thomas to drop everything and rush forward to Jonesboro. Stanley was hurried forward, and Jeff C. Davis ordered to bring the Fourteenth Corps to Howard's left, and, swinging around to the right, endeavor to envelop Hardee's right. Blair was ordered to make a detour to the right and reach the railroad south of Jonesboro so as to cut off retreat in that direction. Schofield closed up behind the Fourth Corps.

Hardee comprehended the impending storm, and hastened to get into shape to meet it. He hurried his men behind the strong works which ran in front of Jonesboro, with a sharply refused right covering the railroad. On this refused right was Cleburne's Division, [*Brig. Gen. Daniel*] Govan's Brigade holding the angle, Granberry [*Brig. Gen. Hiram Granbury*] on his left and [*Brig. Gen. Joseph*] Lewis's Brigade on his right.

[*McElroy is about to describe the IV and XIV Corps' September 1 afternoon attack against Hardee's right, which had dug in north of town.*]

September 1 was big with events, and everyone in all the regiments so felt it. Gen. Logan says that he saw Gen. Thomas gallop his horse for the only time during the campaign. [*George Thomas was nicknamed "Old Slow Trot."*] All the movements were made with a celerity and certainty astonishing, even, in such veteran soldiers as they were. Davis was marching the Fourteenth Corps straight down toward the north front of the works around Jonesboro, with the Army of the Tennessee advancing on his right and the Fourth Corps coming down on his left followed by the Army of the Ohio. About 4 o'clock of the bright September afternoon Davis had his corps well in hand, with the division in echelon in front of a cotton field, beyond which rose the Confederate intrenchments.

Tense Fighting Pitch.

The spirit of the army was at fighting pitch, and everybody wanted an immediate settlement. The voice of the Generals was that of the men for a swift, hard blow and charge home and an end of the long struggle, man to man and bayonet to bayonet.

The previous history of the war was filled with stories of gallant charges and bloody repulses. In a few ill-omened hours of a short Winter's day 11,000 men of the Army of the Potomac had fallen at Fredericksburg upon hights no more formidable than those now crowned by Hardee's intrenchments. At Gettysburg Pickett had dashed the life out of his magnificent war thunderbolt of 18,000 men against a thin line far less securely intrenched. At Kenesaw the Armies of the Tennessee and Cumberland had shed their best blood at the foot of the enemy's works. Since Hood had taken command he had wasted his army's strength in beating it against the Union, nowhere more than lightly intrenched. This was all well remembered by those who thought, yet in spite of it an attack was determined on, and it was made almost as soon as the resolution was formed. It was a splendid illustration of what in military tactics is known as the "wave manuver;" that is, successive waves of men beat down upon a stronghold, one following another so quickly that the enemy cannot recover from the blow of the first.

The Assault.

Gen. [*James D.*] Morgan's Division formed by brigades in column of regiments in echelon from right to left—[*Col. Charles M.*] Lum's, [*Col. John G.*] Mitchell's and [*Col. Caleb*] Dilworth's—and these were ordered to assault with the bayonet alone. The division would have about 1,000 yards to go, over cotton fields cut with ditches and broken in places by swamps. Gen. [*William P.*] Carlin's two brigades were to move with Morgan, and in their front there was an additional obstacle in the shape of a dense thicket. Baird's Division was held in reserve, in the rear of Carlin's.

The attack had been heralded and prepared for by a fierce cannonade from [*Capt. Mark H.*] Prescott's and [*Capt. George Q.*] Gardner's Batteries, and then the whole line rushed forward in a terrific charge until it reached a portion of the ground where there was slight protection from the heavy fire which the enemy poured from their defenses. Then it moved forward directly in the teeth of this gale of death, which it seemed impossible for mortal men to successfully breast.

[*Maj. John R.*] Edie's Brigade of Baird's Division succeeded in reaching the enemy's works and in carrying a projected angle, but it was burned to pieces by the fire. In spite of this the brave men clung to the edge of the works, upon which some of their men and officers were already lying dead, killed in the attempt to cross. [*Col. George P.*] Este's Brigade was hurried up to the assistance of Edie, and the 10th Ky. and 74th Ind. succeeded in crossing and holding a part of the enemy's lines, but the 14th and 38th Ohio were for the moment repulsed. Este rushed over to their assistance, gained the help of Col. [*William T. C.*] Grower, 17th N.Y., charged gallantly into the thick of the fray, and the three regiments went together over the works, capturing a number of prisoners. Col. Grower paid for his generous assistance by his life, and was struck down in the moment of victory.

Along the whole of Morgan's front the battle raged with a fierceness that was demoniac. On both sides men seemed hungry to kill, and their rushes with the bayonet had the vengeful wickedness of the serpent's fangs. The lust for murder was in the air, and the yells of the combatants seemed like the cries of wild beasts. Morgan's men, in spite of the horrible gaps in their own ranks, forced their way slowly but surely over the well-manned works, and presently the excited watchers in the rear were gratified by seeing a steady stream of prisoners emerge from the woods into which Morgan's men had disappeared.

Most of the enemy behind the works who were not killed were captured. There was a sad tally list of those who had fought their last battle, both in blue and butternut uniforms. The fight was scarcely ended, when the alarm came that Lee's Corps, which Hood had unwisely detached, was hurrying up to take part in the fight, and the weary soldiers at once began reversing the works to meet this new danger. Fortunately Lee did not arrive before nightfall, when the attack had become useless.

The First and Second Brigades of Morgan's Division took two four-gun batteries, 394 prisoners, including Gen. Govan. Among the trophies were 1,000 stands of small-arms and six battle flags. Morgan's Division had in this exploit lost over 500 killed and wounded, among the killed being Maj. [*Henry S.*] Burnett, 10th Mich., who received his wound as he led the regiment across the works.

The Fourteenth Corps lost altogether 14 officers and 208 men killed, 62 officers and 833 men wounded and one officer and 104 men missing, making a total loss of 1,272.

Sherman's whole army was now on Hood's last railroad, and the fate of Atlanta was sealed.

Castel confirms McElroy's numbers. On September 1, Confederates suffered 1,400 casualties, including 900 taken prisoner (among them Brigadier General Govan). He places Union losses at 1,272, which our author carefully breaks down into K, W, and M. Among the Federals' trophies were indeed eight pieces of artillery.

58
The Battle-born Babe of Flint River

"Fifteenth Corps" [Edward O. F. Roler], "Little Shell-Anna"

(July 10, 1884, pp. 1-2)

The following story is so rich in sentiment that McElroy started it on page one of his newspaper. It is set during the August 30-31 march of Maj. Gen. John A. ("Black Jack") Logan's XV Corps toward the Flint River and Jonesboro (23 miles south of Atlanta).

The author refers to both sides' practices of denoting field hospitals with yellow flags.

A "cracker" was a coarse, poor, white Southerner (Ulrich B. Phillips, Life and Labor in the Old South *[Boston: Little, Brown and Company, 1963 (1929)], 350 n.).*

It was the Summer of 1864, and the army under Sherman had fallen back from its position before Atlanta and swept around to Hood's rear, Gen. Logan leading the advance. I remember that the country was densely wooded, and that magnificent forests of pine, oak and chestnut towered on either side of the road over which we marched. We were not molested until we neared Flint River. There the enemy had planted a masked battery and, as we approached, it enfiladed our line. You could scarce encounter more disagreeable travelers on a lonely road than shot and shell, and the boys were not long in taking to the shelter of the timber. But Gen. Logan at once ordered up a field battery of brass "Napoleons," and presently accepted this challenge to an artillery duel. There was nothing to direct the fire of our gunners save the white puffs of smoke that could be seen rising above the foliage and the course of the enemy's shots, but they nevertheless soon silenced the rebel cannon, and once more cleared the way for the column.

We then rode forward again, the writer in company with Dr. Woodward, the medical inspector of Gen. Logan's staff, and until his death, some four years ago, the head of the Marine Hospital Service. Just as we turned a bend in the road we emerged suddenly into a small clearing. A rude log cabin, surrounded by evergreen shrubbery, stood in the clearing, and hanging from one of the bushes we noticed a yellow cloth.

ONLY A CRACKER'S CABIN.

As medical officers, it naturally occurred to us at once that this was an improvised hospital of some sort, and we rode up to inquire. At the door of the cabin, as we approached, an old woman, evidently of the familiar "cracker" type, presented herself, but, on seeing that we were "Yankees," beat a hasty retreat. But we were not disposed to be so easily baffled, and calling her out again, began to ply her with questions.

She told us "there wa'n't no wounded men thar," and when asked why she had put out a yellow flag there, she replied: "Waal, yer see, my gal is sick, and I reckoned ef I put out that yer hsp't'l rag you'ns wouldn't be pesterin' round so much."

"What's the matter with your child?" said I; "we are medical officers, and perhaps we can do something for her." "Waal, now," she quickly responded, "ef you'ns is real doctors, just look in and see what you'ns all done with your shellin'. Time my gal was sickest, two of yourn shells come clar through my cabin, and, I tell you, it was right skeery for a spell."

We accepted the old woman's invitation and walked in. It was as she said. The cabin, built of rough pine logs, afforded but one room, about twelve feet square. A small log meat-house (empty) was the only out-building,--the cow-stable having been knocked to pieces by our shells,--except a small bark-thatched "lean-to" at the rear in which we found a loom of the most primitive sort and constructed in the roughest fashion, containing a partially-completed web of coarse cotton "homespun." Aside from this loom, the only household articles visible were an old skillet, a rather dilapidated bed, two or three chairs without backs, and a queer collection of gourds. The shells had indeed played havoc with the interior. The roof had been badly shattered, and a stray shot had pierced the walls.

A SAD SPECTACLE.

It had cut one of the logs entirely in two, and forcing one jagged end out into the room so far that it hung threateningly over the bed upon which, to our astonishment, we saw lying a young girl, by whose side was a new-born babe with the prints of the Creator's fingers fresh upon it. It was a strange yet touching spectacle. Here, in this lonely cabin, stripped by lawless stragglers of both armies of food and clothing and shattered by the flying shells of our artillery, in the storm and fury of the battle had been born this sweet innocent. The mother, we learned, was the wife of a Confederate soldier whose blood had stained the "sacred soil" of Virginia but a few months after his marriage and conscription into the service, and the child was fatherless. The babe was still clad only in its own innocence, but the writer with his handy jack-knife cut from the unfinished web in the old loom a piece of coarse homespun, in which it was soon deftly swaddled. Fortunately we had our hospital knapsacks with us, and our orderlies carried a little brandy, with a few medicines and a can of beef extract, and we at once did all that our limited stores permitted to relieve the wants of the young mother and child.

A CHRISTENING IN ORDER.

But by this time quite a number of officers and men, attracted by the sight of the yellow flag and our horses waiting at the door, had gathered about the cabin, and, while we were inside, they amused themselves by listening to the old lady's account of this stirring incident. One of the officers had given her some "store terbacker," with which she had filled a cob-pipe, and the fact that she was spitting through her teeth with such accuracy as to hit a fly at ten paces, nine times out of ten, showed that she was enjoying herself after the true "cracker" style. Presently some one suggested that the baby ought to be christened with full military honors, and it being duly explained to her that to "christen" was all the same as to "baptize," she replied with alacrity: "Oh, yes! baptized, I reckon, if you'ns has got any preacher along."

This was all the boys wanted, and an orderly was at once sent back to the general commanding, with the compliments of the Surgeon and a request that a chaplain belonging to one of the regiments in the advance brigade might be allowed to return with the messenger to the cabin.

The general asked the orderly for what purpose a chaplain was wanted, and the orderly replied that the doctors (mentioning our names) were going to have a baptism.

SOME DEVILTRY ON HAND.

Upon this, Gen. Logan (for he it was) significantly remarked, that the names mentioned were in themselves sufficient to satisfy him that some deviltry was on hand, but that, nevertheless, the chaplain might go. Then, inviting the colonel, who happened to be riding with him at the time, he set out himself for the scene, spurring "Old John" to a gallop, and soon had joined the party at the cabin.

"General," said the Doctor, as the former dismounted, "You are just the man we're after."

"For what?"

"For a godfather," replied the Doctor.

"Godfather to what?" demanded the General.

WHAT THE GENERAL SAID AND DID.

The matter was explained to him, and, as the Doctor led the way into the house, the boys, who had gathered around the General in the expectation that the event would furnish an occasion for a display of his characteristic humor, noticed there was something in Black Jack's face that they were not wont to see there, and that in his eyes there was a certain humid tenderness far different from their usual flashing brightness. He stood for a moment silent, gazing at the unhappy mother and fatherless child, and their pitiful surroundings, and then, turning to those about him, said tersely:

"That looks ---- rough."

Then, glancing around at the ruins wrought by our shells, and addressing the men in the cabin, he called out: "I say, boys, can't you straighten this up a little? Fix up that roof. There are plenty of 'stakes' around that old stable—and push back that log into place, and help the old lady to clear out the litter, and—I don't think it would *hurt* you any to leave a part of your rations!"

THE BOYS GO TO WORK.

Prompt to heed the suggestion, the boys leaned their muskets against the logs, and, while some of them cut brush, others swept up the splinters and pine knots that the shot and shell had strewn over the floor, and not one of them forgot to go to the corner of the cabin and empty his haversack! It made a pile of commissary stores, consisting of meat, coffee, sugar, hard-tack and chickens (probably foraged from her next-door neighbor) surpassing any that this poor "cracker" woman had probably ever seen or possessed at one time.

This done, the next thing in order was the christening, and the chaplain now came forward to perform his sacred office.

"What are you going to give her for a name? I want suthin right peart, now," said grandmother.

She was told that the name should be satisfactory, and forthwith she brought out the baptismal bowl—which on this occasion consisted of a gourd-ful of water fresh from the spring.

THE CHRISTENING.

Gen. Logan now took the baby, wrapped in its swaddling clothes of coarse homespun, and held it while the chaplain went through with the ceremony. The latter was brief and characterized with due solemnity, the spectators behaving with becoming reverence, and thus the battle-born babe was christened "Shell-Anna." I like to think that as the chaplain's prayers were winging their way to heaven, the gory goddess who nurses a gorgon at her breast stayed her red hand awhile!

The party now turned to leave the cabin and resume the march, when Gen. Logan, taking a gold coin from his pocket—a coin that he had carried as a pocket-piece for many a day—presented it to the old lady as a "christening gift" for his godchild, and the officers and men, as they had recently drawn their pay, added one by one a "greenback," until the sum was swelled to an amount greater than this brave-hearted "cracker" had ever handled. Before parting, the General cautioned her to put the money in a safe place, lest some "---- bummer should steal it, in spite of everything," and then, ordering a guard to be kept over her cabin until the last straggler had passed by, he rode away. The old lady's good-by was: "Waal! Them thar Yanks is the beatenist critters I ever seen!"

A LAST GOOD-BY.

Ten days or so after this occurrence, the cabin being by that time within the enemy's lines, the General, accompanied by the writer and 10 of his escort, rode back eight miles to see how our protégé was getting on and found both mother and child, in the language of grandma, "quite peart." Whether Gen. Logan's god-daughter is still alive or not I do not know, but five years after that visit word reached me that she then was. Certainly no one who witnessed that scene will ever forget the big-hearted soldier as he stood Sponsor—grim, yet gentle—for that poor little battle-born babe of Flint River. It all came back to me, the other night, as I walked past the front steps of the General's Washington house and saw a squad of little urchins clambering about his knees. FIFTEENTH CORPS.

In his campaign report, General Logan mentions two medical officers on his staff, "Surgeon E. O. F. Roler, medical director, and Surgeon John M. Woodworth, medical inspector" (OR *38, pt. 3, 111). As "Fifteenth Corps" mentions accompanying "Dr. Woodward" in his article, and in his last paragraph states that he was able to ride with Logan on his last visit to look in on Shell-Anna, the author of this piece is almost certainly Dr. Edward Roler.*

59

The Union Assault at Jonesboro, September 1

Lee H. Rudisille, "What One Brigade Did at Jonesboro"

(August 27, 1890, p. 3)

*On September 1, with Lee's Corps departed, Hardee's Corps was left in the Jonesboro works, awaiting a Federal assault that began around 4:00 p.m. The Northerners launched a rarity in the campaign, as Castel writes, "a large-scale frontal assault (*Decision in the West, *518). Hardee's line held, but barely.*

George Scott of the 16th U.S. Infantry wrote the National Tribune *(March 27, 1890, p. 3), recounting his regiment's charge at Jonesboro, along with "the men of one Ohio regiment." He then asked "What was the number of that regiment?"*

In response came this reply.

EDITOR NATIONAL TRIBUNE: While the boys are skirmishing around among their reminiscences, endeavoring to find their several positions and proper alignment in this sharp and fiery battle, so meagerly detailed by historians of the war, I wish to speak a word for the living and the dead of my comrades who helped to win the battle on that September evening almost 26 years ago, and especially for the men of my regiment—the 38th Ohio.

All day long we had been stubbornly crowding Hood's army farther south, the Fourteenth Corps keeping the general direction of the railroad, and the Fifteenth and Seventeenth Corps swinging to the right with the evident intention of striking the Confederate flank or rear, in order to cut off his retreat in the direction of Macon. About 4 o'clock in the afternoon the forces in front met with considerable resistance, and the heavy firing away to our right indicated that Hood had been fought to standstill, and meant to hold his ground until darkness gave him a better opportunity to continue his retreat.

About this time the Third Division, Fourteenth Corps, commanded by Gen. Absalom Baird, emerged from a dense woods, through which it had been fighting its way most of the afternoon, into an open country of nearly a half mile in extent, where the Confederate position could be fairly outlined in front, although partially masked by a belt of timber. This woods, as we afterward learned at fearful cost, was composed principally of post or jack-oak timber, with a heavy undergrowth, that had been slashed and tangled in every conceivable shape, making the ground in front of their works—which were about 10 or 12 rods back from the open—almost impassable.

The division was rapidly advanced across this open country, the left resting on or near the railroad, until it reached a depression in the ground, affording a slight shelter, about 500 yards from the enemy's works. In the meantime a terrible fusillade had been going on a little to our right and front, in which a rebel battery was taking part, but did not seem to be doing much damage, for, as one of the boys said, "they did not elevate their guns low enough." However, a lull soon occurred, and word went along the line that the Regular Brigade had attempted to carry the works in their front but failed. The Third Brigade of Baird's Division, which was at that time in reserve, was now marched to the right until they reached about the same ground where the fighting had occurred, ordered to unsling knapsacks, fix bayonets, and be ready for the order to charge. Instructions also were given to have every gun loaded, but to reserve their fire until the works were reached. This brigade was composed of the 14th and 38th Ohio, 10th and 18th Ky., and the 74th Ind. My recollection is that the 38th and 14th Ohio were in the advance, and the other regiments in close support. If wrong in this, I no doubt will be amply corrected by the comrades of these regiments. I know the 38th Ohio was one of the regiments composing the front line. At the command the brigade went forward at the double-quick up a slight grade, the rebels reserving their fire until the front line of the charging column reached the edge of the timber, and then delivered a volley straight into our faces; but their aim being too high, it did comparatively little execution, and the works no doubt would have been reached before they could reload if it had not been for the scraggy, tangled brush the line here encountered. As it was, before the advance had forced its way more than half the distance through, it received a withering fire from the works that thinned the ranks frightfully, and staggered it a moment, but the second line soon came up and joined the remnant of the first, and together they fought their way through to the rebel works amid a very hell of carnage, the battle-smoke [*had*] become so thick that one could scarcely see anything but the flash of the guns. The color-bearer of the 38th Ohio was killed while clambering over the brush, well in advance of the line; one of the guards picked up the flag, and he too went down a moment later; then another took it, only to leave the impression of his death-grasp upon its staff and moisten its folds with his warm life-blood; then another and still another of the dauntless and devoted color-guard raised the old flag to its place in the hot breath of the battle front, and the fifth man took it onto the works and kept it there until the fight was won. This man was Charlie Donze, who is now crowning the unsullied record of a soldier with that of a blameless citizen at Lima, O. There were two guns of a rebel battery near the right of our regiment, with others still farther to the right, and I think it was near this that the Confederate line was first broken. A portion of our line then swinging to the left took that of the Confederates in the flank and rear, and by this means they were about to be gobbled in, the smoke being so thick they could not see that their lien had been broken. Well to their right they were found steadily firing to the front, and looked somewhat disgusted when the order to surrender was backed up by a nearness and a rear-ness of Federal bayonets. Even after they had been picked out of their works in this manner, and gathered together, one regiment would curse the other for allowing the line to be broken, so much at a loss were they to know how and where it had occurred. Especially were they indignant when they saw the weakness of our own line. They comprised Govan's entire Brigade, one of the best in the Confederate army, and greatly outnumbered our own after the battle, as we had lost over one-third of our number before we reached the works.

Our regiment took only about 300 men into the fight, and of these 152 were either killed or wounded; 20 percent or more of the regiment were buried on the field, as the records will show. Col. Wm. A Choate fell, mortally wounded within 20 feet of the rifle-pits. A better regimental commander and one more beloved never led men into battle. Altogether it did not leave the 38th one commissioned officer to a company, my own being commanded on the "march to the sea" by Orderly Sergt. J. D. Gleason, now at Bryan, O.

As to the comrades who claim the credit of capturing the rebel cannon, the boys who were first over the works that day supposed they would fall into good hands, and so swept on down the line of gray, caring little what regiment would furnish the motive power to draw those guns off the field.

This brigade comprised three of the regiments that in the beginning of the war had formed the nucleus of Gen. Thomas's command in Kentucky; had marched and fought under his watchful eye and fatherly care ever since; had been a part of his forlorn hope at Chickamauga and his cyclone at Mission Ridge; and now in the meantime, having at this brilliant culmination of a summer of battles, he issued a General Order complimenting the troops engaged in this action, in which he stated it was the only instance within his knowledge where a body of troops had charged a superior force behind intrenchments, and not only carried the works but captured those defending them.

This is no doubt what Comrade Scott, of the 16th U.S., saw on that September evening at Jonesboro, Ga., nearly 26 years ago.—LEE H. RUDISILLE, Co. H, 38th Ohio, White Oaks, N. M.

60

An Incident of the Battle of Jonesboro

Henry Tobey, "They Wanted Water. How a Comrade Got It Under Difficulties"

(February 3, 1887, p. 8)

EDITOR NATIONAL TRIBUNE: At Jonesboro, Ga., soon after the battle began, a rebel battery off to our right was shelling us terribly, when one of our batteries came up just to the left of my regiment and opened on them, shooting lengthwise of our line. Then ensued as lively an artillery duel as I ever witnessed. One of the batterymen came running along the line with two buckets, and asked our Orderly to send a man for water to swab the guns with, quick. The Orderly called "Tobey!" I crawled out (for we were lying flat on our faces,) stripped off my accouterments and started down the line on the run with the leather buckets, when Gen. Grose [*Brig. Gen. William Grose, Third Brigade, First Division, Fourth Corps*] rode up and ordered a volley and a yell, that brought back as good a volley as was sent. I knew the bullets were too thick to dodge, so I ran down toward the rebel battery 30 or 40 rods I guess, to a little creek, and began dipping up the water. A fellow, who was hugging a tree near by, yelled out to me:

"Get out of there, you will be riddled. That pond is chock-full of bullets!"

As I ran back with the water I thought I could feel the bullets hit the buckets. I was so sure of it that they seemed to be getting lighter instead of heavier. I got there with the water all right, had set one bucket down and was carrying the other a little farther along, when a shell burst so near that it stunned and knocked me down. The Captain of the battery lifted me up, threw some water in my face, and I revived and went back down the line. I don't know whether I found the company or they found me. The rebel battery was silenced and the Johnnies routed. We camped for the night near where the battery stood. We heard the explosion of Hood's magazines [*during the night of September 1-2*] at Atlanta, 20 miles away. Next morning I could not lift my head.—HENRY TOBEY, Co. D, 75th Ill., Third Brigade, First Division, Fourth Corps, Ulysses, Neb.

61

Wheeler's Raid, August 10-September 17

A. H., "Some of the Vicissitudes of War"

(September 6, 1883, p. 7)

To the Editor of the NATIONAL TRIBUNE:

I was detailed as one of the guards on the train delivering wood along the railroad from Atlanta to Chattanooga. We stopped at Dalton on the afternoon of August 14, 1864, to await orders, but we had not long to wait, as the report came in that the town was surrounded by rebels, and we were ordered on the skirmish-line to hold them back as long as we could, and then to fall back to the fort on the hill east of the town. The rebels charged up the railroad and captured the depot, completely cutting us off from the fort, and thirty-five or forty of us were taken prisoner. We were taken about half a mile south of the town and put to work tearing up and burning the railroad track. Among those captured at Dalton was a deserter from the rebel army, whose family lived at Spring Place, where we made a short halt, and the poor fellow was shot in sight of his family. We marched all day, and at night camped on the farm of a Union woman who killed all her chickens for us, but the rebels being as hungry as we were, got them all. Before the town was captured our train was run to Chattanooga by the engineer alone. The fireman, who was a brave young man, said to the engineer: "Joe, you can run the train, while I will stay and help the boys keep the rebels out of Dalton." He was not a soldier, but took his part in the fight and when he was captured passed himself off as my brother, and said he belonged to company K, One Hundredth Illinois.

If this should come to his notice, I should like to hear from him. While on our march we did not receive a mouthful of anything to eat, except a few apples that we gathered on the road.

A. H., Co. K, 100th Ill.
FAIRFIELD, NEB.

62
The Occupation of Atlanta, September 2

W. H. McIntosh, "Entering Atlanta.
The Gate City Surrenders to Gen. Coburn"

(October 18, 1888, p. 3)

EDITOR NATIONAL TRIBUNE: When the other corps of Sherman's army moved to the right the Twentieth Corps fell back to occupy the crossings of the Chattahoochee. Coburn's Brigade of the "Blue Stars" threw up works to protect Turner's Ferry. The rebels finding our old line abandoned, reconnoitered to the river, where their skirmishers, stumbling upon a big nest of blue-hued hornets, skedaddled on the back track. During the night of September 1, 1864, we heard frequent heavy explosions from the direction of Atlanta, while broad, livid glares upon the sky told of destructive fires raging there.

Gen. John Coburn started from the ferry at 5 o'clock next morning to see what was going on, and took with him details from each of his four regiments (33d and 85th Ind., 19th Mich. and 22d Wis.) to the number of 900 men, together with an ambulance train, to be prepared for possibilities. A heavy skirmish-line was detailed and deployed, moving steadily forward while the column followed after, resting at intervals to give them time to advance. Nearing our abandoned works, shells were heard exploding and light smoke rose from rebel forts on their line, while away to our left we saw another reconnoitering force from troops of our corps. A squad of Confederate cavalry galloped about in our front, and one unlucky wight fell from his horse and was captured. From him we learned that Hood had evacuated the city, after destroying the rolling-mills and other public property, and that his regiment (the 2d Ark. Cav.) were still in the city.

The skirmish-line advanced with caution, while successive reports of shells from the woods on our left suggested a battery in action upon the other party. Again advancing our line, we entered upon the debated ground between our lunet-like rifle-pits and the narrow, continuous trench on the rebel side. Trees and shrubs were torn by bullets, and several small pines had been topped by the flying lead.

Another short advance brought the line upon and through the broad, heavy main defenses of the city, having to make our way through seven lines of chevaux-de-frise to reach the works. From a fort walled by sand-filled bags clouds of white smoke rose slowly, and frequent explosions of shells explained the war-like sounds we had heard. We began our march for the city, when a report prevailed that the enemy was in front in force. The line was halted along the rear works of the enemy, and details made to guard our rear against a dash. Our skirmishers sent back squads of prisoners, and presently a party, among whom was the Mayor of Atlanta, came out and formally surrendered the city to Gen. Coburn. Then we marched down the road into a street, proud, happy and triumphant. Timid faces peered from doors ajar, then flung them open and silently reviewed our rough-and-ready compact ranks. Halting at the depot and stacking arms, the men scattered to forage, returning laden with boxes of plug-tobacco and matches that would not ignite.

A crash was heard from a building a block away; clouds of white smoke belched from its openings, and with loud cries a crowd of pillagers poured into the street. The Stars and Stripes were waved from the courthouse dome amidst a mighty shout of victory. Houses were perforated by shells; earth shelters were seen near by, but the churches were uninjured. Near the depot stood a huge grated building, across whose front was a sign which read, "Slave Mart," the emblem of the Confederacy.

Finally we fell in and marched after our skirmishers, and bivouacked behind the rebel eastern line of defense, to the left of the Augusta Railroad. A sack of cornmeal was our sole resource for rations, as we had left knapsacks and haversacks at the river. In a large iron kettle we put water to boil, stirred in the meal, and this salted mush was our supper, and board lean-to's put up by the Johnnies, our shelter from the falling rain.—W. H. McINTOSH, Co. F, 22d Wis., Auburn, Ind.

After conducting a semi-siege of Atlanta for more than a month, Sherman planned a bold move to cut the Macon & Western Railroad, Hood's last supply line, once and for all. With the XX Corps falling back to the Chattahoochee, he would lead his six other infantry corps in a wide-ranging march west and south of Atlanta, intending to cut the railroad somewhere in the vicinity of Jonesboro. The movement began on the night of August 25-26. As Sherman swung farther south, Hood was unable to stretch his troops far enough to both guard Atlanta and protect the railroad. By mid-afternoon on August 30, 20,000 Union troops were approaching Jonesboro; 35,000 more were to the north, also marching toward the railroad. Around 3:00 p.m. on August 31, when the latter reached the M & W, they began tearing up track. Hood soon learned of this and ordered the evacuation of Atlanta on the night of September 1-2 (Stephen Davis, Atlanta Will Fall: Sherman, Joe Johnston, and the Yankee Heavy Battalions *[Wilmington DE: Scholarly Resources, 2001], 175, 180, 185-187).*

In their hurried evacuation, Confederates burned weaponry and stores they could not carry off. They also torched a train loaded with ordnance and cotton bales, along with the rolling mill building east of town.

The noise of the ammo detonations was what McIntosh, in the XX Corps camps eight miles northwest of the city, heard during the night. His article in the National Tribune, *more than two decades later, proves to be a remarkable instance of reporting (and remembering).*

Early on the morning of the 2nd, alerted by the explosions, XX Corps commander Maj. Gen. Henry Slocum ordered each of his three divisions to send forward a strong scouting force to ascertain what had happened. Brigadier General William T. Ward's division held the right of Slocum's line at Turner's Ferry. Ward directed Col. [not Gen.] John Coburn to lead 900 infantry, with some cavalry, toward the city. As the Federals neared the abandoned Rebel lines, McIntosh's recollection of hearing shells exploding in the fortifications confirms Confederates' torching of ordnance they could not bring away. "Another reconnoitering force" that the author saw off to his left (westward) was the three infantry regiments that Colonel Nirom Crane was leading toward the city.

Marching in from the northwest, the Federals marched past rows of chevaux-de-frise and the big Confederate "fort walled by sand-filled bags" that Southerners had named for General Hood. McIntosh's assumption that a Southern battery contested their advance is mistaken, however. The only Rebels hovering about Atlanta were the cavalrymen Federals had encountered; by late morning they had ridden out of town. The sounds of artillery discharges were therefore the result of Confederates' detonations.

Late in the morning, Mayor James M. Calhoun and a deputation of citizens rode out on Marietta Street to surrender the city to the first Federal officer they encountered—who proved to be Col. John Coburn. His infantry, marching in behind the cavalry, soon secured the city and raised the Stars and Stripes over City Hall (Stephen Davis, What the Yankees Did to Us: Sherman's Bombardment and Wrecking of Atlanta *[Macon: Mercer University Press, 2012], 255-257, 260-265).*

As McIntosh states, Coburn marched his troops through the city, camping east of it near the Augusta Railroad (Coburn report, September 12, 1864, OR *38, pt. 2, 393).*

The "slave mart" that caught McIntosh's eye was the "Auction & Negro Sales" storefront owned by Robert Crawford and Thomas Frazer at 8 Whitehall Street in downtown Atlanta. It was famously photographed by George N. Barnard during the Federal occupation of fall 1864, with an African-American male, dressed in Federal uniform, sitting in front, reading a book and with a musket leaning by his side (Stephen Berry, "The Book or the Gun?" in J. Matthew Gallman and Gary W. Gallagher, eds., Lens of War: Exploring Iconic Photographs of the Civil War *[Athens: University of Georgia Press, 2015], 215).*

63

Lieutenant Colonel Walker Gets Some of the Credit

C. A. Tompkins, "The First to Enter Atlanta"

(June 3, 1886, p. 3)

"I notice lately that there is quite a little dispute as to what troops first entered Atlanta," writes C. A. Tompkins to the National Tribune. *Here he attempts to set the record straight.*

I must claim the honor (partly divided) for the Third Brigade, Second Division, Twentieth Corps [*Col. David Ireland commanding, five New York and two Pennsylvania regiments, including the 102nd New York and the 111th Pennsylvania*]—for we were there if we were formerly from the East—and will substantiate my claim as follows:

In the Report of the Committee on the Conduct of the War, Vol. 1, Part 1, Supplement, Gen. Sherman, in his report, says: "Hood blew up his magazines at Atlanta and left in the night time, when the Twentieth Corps (Gen. Slocum) took possession of the place. So Atlanta is ours, and fairly won." Then in the same report, Gen. Thomas says: "During the night [*of September 2-3*] information reached us that the Mayor and authorities of Atlanta had surrendered the city to a force of the Twentieth Corps, Maj.-Gen. Slocum commanding," etc. Further on Gen. Slocum says: "On the night of September 1 heavy explosions were heard in the direction of Atlanta, and a force was at once ordered from each division to make reconnaissance in this direction. The command from the Third Division, under Col. Coburn, was met by the Mayor, who made a formal surrender of the town to him." Next, Gen. Ward, commanding Third Division, Twentieth Corps, simply says: "On September 2 a reconnaissance was made which resulted in the capture of Atlanta." Then Gen. John W. Geary, commanding Second Division, Twentieth Corps, says: "In obedience to orders from corps headquarters I sent out a reconnoitering party. The reconnaissance was commanded by Lieut.-Col. Thomas M. Walker, 111th Pa., and was composed of the 111th Pa., 60th N.Y., and details from the 102d N.Y. and 29th Pa., and 20 men from the 7th Pa. Cav. * * * [*ellipsis in original*] Lieut.-Col. Walker, accompanied by the cavalry, preceded his infantry and entered the outskirts of the city, where he met Col. Coburn, commanding reconnaissance of the Third Division, who had also preceded his troops. It was agreed that their commands should enter the city at the same time, which was done. Lieut.-Col. Walker's command was the first to reach the City Hall, upon which the colors of the 60th N.Y. and 111th Pa. were immediately hoisted. To these regiments, representing my division, belong the immortal honors of placing upon the rebel stronghold the first Union flags," etc. My records do not state what troops composed Col. Coburn's command, but I consider this reliable.—C. A. TOMPKINS, 137th N.Y., Glen Castle, N.Y.

Comrade Tompkins gets the story right. Major General Henry Slocum, XX Corps commander, heard the explosions as Confederates evacuated Atlanta. Before dawn of September 2, he ordered each of his three divisions to send out a strong party to probe toward the city.

Brigadier General John W. Geary's 2nd Division sent forth Lieutenant Colonel Thomas M. Walker with several infantry regiments and a score of cavalrymen. Brigadier General William T. Ward's division dispatched Col. John Coburn, commanding the 2nd Brigade, with 900 infantry (including the 33rd Indiana) and some cavalry under Captain Henry M. Scott.

It was Scott, riding in the advance, who encountered Mayor James M. Calhoun, riding out with some citizens to yield the city to the first Federals he encountered. This was Scott's column; Scott rode back, found Colonel Coburn, and led him to Calhoun's party. By 11:00 a.m., Atlanta had been surrendered.

Lieutenant Colonel Walker, as Tompkins states, encountered Coburn; the two agreed to ride in together. Walker claimed that it was his two regiments that reached City Hall and raised the Federal colors. For his part, Coburn claimed that the first Union troops to enter Atlanta were his, men of the 33rd Indiana (Stephen Davis, What the Yankees Did to Us: Sherman's Bombardment and Wrecking of Atlanta *[Macon: Mercer University Press, 2012], 264-266).*

The National Tribune *being what it was, offered other veterans to chime in on what unit first entered Atlanta. James F. Walker, Co. F, 101st Illinois, asserted that it was his regiment (Broughton's brigade, Alpheus Williams's division)—a contention hard to sustain as the author, referring to his diary, states that his unit marched in at 2:00 p.m. on September 2—hours after Coburn and Walker had ridden in ("Who Was First in Atlanta?"* National Tribune *[December 13, 1888], 3).*

As late as 1893, other vets were claiming the 5th Connecticut ("Into Atlanta," National Tribune *[June 29, 1893], 3). This caused one of Coburn's soldiers to reassert his brigade was first, though it was the 19th Michigan, not the 33rd Indiana, as the colonel himself had asserted ("First into Atlanta,"* National Tribune *[July 27, 1893], 3).*

64

Federal Campaign Casualties

B. A. Dunn, "Losses in the Atlanta Campaign"

(May 9, 1905, p. 2)

EDITOR NATIONAL TRIBUNE: Gen. Green B. Raum, in his history of the Atlanta Campaign, gives the Federal total losses in that campaign at 34,514. Gen. Sherman in his Memoirs gives his total losses at 31,687. The Official Records of the War of the Rebellion tell a different story from either Gen. Sherman or Gen. Raum. On page 85, vol. 38 of the O.R., in a report signed by Gen. Sherman himself, he gives his total lost at 37,081, and these figures are substantiated by the reports of the different corps commanders.

I think Gen. Raum's mistake lies in the fact that he did not take in consideration the losses of the Army of the Cumberland for the month of September, in which the battles of Jonesboro and Lovejoy were fought. The losses of the Army of the Cumberland during September were 2,567. These figures added to Gen. Raum's figures would give nearly the correct loss.

The total loss of the Army of the Cumberland during the campaign was 22,807, instead of 20,240, as given by Gen. Raum. (See O.R., page 175, vol. 38.)

There is something strange in the fact that not only in Gen. Sherman's Memoirs but in most of the histories or accounts of the Atlanta campaign, the Army of the Cumberland has never received full credit for its losses.

Stranger still, Gen. Sherman in his Memoirs makes no mention, nor does he seem to take into account, the losses of one of the bloodiest battles fought during the campaign—the battle of Pickett's Mill, May 27. This battle was mainly fought by Gen. Wood's Division of the Fourth Corps, and in no other battle during the campaign did any single division suffer as did Gen. Wood's Division in this battle. It suffered almost as great a loss as did both Gen. Jeff. C. Davis's and Gen. Newton's Divisions in their celebrated charge on Kenesaw, just a month later. In this charge Davis's Division lost 824, and Newton's 654; total, 1,478.

Gen. Wood's Division at Pickett's Mill lost 1,457, only 21 less than both Davis and Newton at Kenesaw. Yet Gen. Sherman thought the conflict not worthy of mention.

All the figures I have given are compiled from the Official Records.—B. A. DUNN, Co. C, 9th Ind., Waukegan, Ill.

Dunn is meticulously correct. Sherman's loss of 37,081 is in the Official Records, *vol. 38, pt. 1, 85. Figures for Thomas's army are in vol. 38, pt. 1, 85, and 175. As for Kennesaw Mountain, Davis's division casualties are in vol. 38, pt. 1, 510, and Newton's on p. 296. Wood's casualties at New Hope Church are in vol. 38, pt. 1, 387.*

Dunn was not the only Union veteran who objected in the National Tribune *to Sherman's failure to mention anything about the battle of Pickett's Mill in his* Memoirs *(vol. 2, 44-45). The general's tendency to hide unfavorable topics in his recollections is the subject of Albert Castel's essay, "Prevaricating Through Georgia: Sherman's Memoirs as a Source on the Atlanta Campaign" in Castel,* Winning and Losing in the Civil War: Essays and Stories *(Columbia: University of South Carolina Press, 1996), 89-116.*

65

The Truce, September 12-21

General Green B. Raum, "With the Western Army. After Atlanta Fell. Occupying the Captured City"

(February 5, 1903, p. 2)

Green B. Raum served as colonel of the 56th Illinois, led a brigade in Sherman's army and was promoted brigadier in February 1865. He wrote a long memoir, With the Western Army, *that the* National Tribune *serialized beginning on November 28, 1901. Thereafter, Raum's articles appeared in every weekly issue of the newspaper until, after 96 installments, he ended his narrative with the battle of Nashville. Twenty-nine installments—nearly a third of Raum's text (which he never published as a book)—pertain to the Atlanta Campaign. Here we excerpt portions having to do with the truce arranged by Hood and Sherman after the Union occupation of Atlanta.*

. . . Gen. Sherman rode into Atlanta on September 8....[*he*] occupied with this staff a large, fine house which fronted the Court-House Square, and belonged to Judge Lyons. The General immediately upon establishing his Headquarters in the city, took up the subject of the future operations of his army. Gen. Hood with Confederate army still occupied Lovejoy, only 30 miles away [*to the south*] from the Court-House in Atlanta. . . .

Three important questions pressed upon Gen. Sherman's attention: First, the establishment of a shorter line of defensive works around Atlanta than the Confederate line, so that a division or a corps at most could securely garrison the city; second, to remove the population from Atlanta, so as to make that city simply a military post, and, third, to secure an exchange of prisoners with Gen. Hood. . . .

The proposition to remove the noncombatant population of men, women and children from Atlanta aroused an immense opposition on the part of the Mayor and Council of Atlanta and Gen. Hood, Commander of the Confederate Army. . . . Gen. Sherman gave due consideration to all these representations, but was fixed in his opinion that the exigencies of the war made it necessary for him to convert Atlanta into a strong fortified camp, and that it would be a source of weakness and danger to permit the population to remain and allow Atlanta to become a great center of illicit trade, as Memphis and other cities occupied by the Union forces had become. . . .

Gen. Hood took the initiative upon the question of the exchange of prisoners. Soon after Gen. Sherman entered Atlanta Gen. Hood communicated with him through a flag of truce, offering to make an exchange of prisoners under authority given him by the Confederate Government at Richmond. As result of the conferences under flags of truce a neutral camp was established at Rough and Ready, a railroad station a few miles south of Atlanta. Lieut.-Col. Willard Warner, of Gen. Sherman's staff, with 100 men, represented the National authority, and Maj. William Clare, Assistant Inspector-General upon Gen. Hood's staff, with a similar guard, represented the Confederate authority. This camp was used both for the purpose of the removal of citizens from Atlanta and the exchange of prisoners. The camp was established September 12. Col. Warner and Maj. Clare co-operated in a friendly and earnest manner in making the removal of the citizens from Atlanta as unembarrassing as possible.

It was so arranged that these citizens upon leaving Atlanta were furnished five days' rations each, from the Union Commissary Department; Col. William G. LeDuc, Quartermaster, Twentieth Corps, made the issues.

In regard to the exchange of prisoners only about 2,000 Confederate soldiers remained within Gen. Sherman's jurisdiction, all the others had been sent North, and were beyond his control.

These 2,000 soldiers Gen. Sherman caused to be brought back to Atlanta from Chattanooga, and offered to exchange them for a like number of Union soldiers who had been captured from his army during the campaign. This offer was declined by Gen. Hood. The Confederate soldiers held by Gen. Sherman would immediately on their discharge be returned to their regiments in Gen. Hood's army; this being the case, Gen. Sherman insisted that in exchange for these men he must have returned to him soldiers of his own army, who in turn would be returned to their respective regiments.

General Raum's article summarizes the truce of September 12-21, arranged by Generals Sherman and Hood at Rough and Ready—a railroad "breakfast station" 13 miles by rail south of Atlanta's train depot. It was named in honor of President Zachary Taylor. There were altogether exchanged 1,128 Federal POWs and 1,332 Confederates (the numerical discrepancy had to do with officers' "equivalency" rates to privates). Raum is incorrect in stating that Hood rejected Sherman's insistence that he would only accept soldiers from units in his army. To be sure, Confederates brought to the truce-point 132 Northern POWs who, it turned out, did not belong to Sherman's army. In one of the war's bizarre gestures, Lieutenant Colonel Warner obediently sent the 132 back to Andersonville. Upon learning this, Sherman informed Hood that the least he could do for these unfortunates was to send them combs and scissors (Sherman to Hood, September 29, 1864, OR *2, vol. 7, 891).*

According to Lt. Col. William Le Duc in Atlanta, during the truce, 1,651 individuals were arranged to be carried by U.S. wagons out of the city to Rough and Ready; from there, Confederates hauled them south to Macon (Stephen Davis, What the Yankees Did to Us: Sherman's Bombardment and Wrecking of Atlanta *[Macon: Mercer University Press, 2012], 299, 308).*

For those without means to find shelter there, 60 miles south of Macon, state authorities erected cabins for some 300 women and children. The site was named "Fosterville" for the state's quartermaster general, Ira Foster ("Home for the Exiles," Atlanta Daily Intelligencer, *October 30, 1864).*

66

Playing Cards with the Johnnies

Harvey O. Williams, "Picket Shots. Exchange of Prisoners at Rough and Ready"

(February 26, 1903, p. 9)

Harvey O. Williams, Remus, Mich., referring to Gen. Green B. Raum's statement in the National Tribune of Feb. 5, regarding the exchange of prisoners at Rough and Ready, says that he was one of the 100 men that represented the National authority at that time. Comrade Williams knows of no other man of the hundred now living, but supposes, of course, that there are quite a number, and he would be glad to hear from members of either the Union or Confederate escorts on that duty. The detail was out five days, and camped side by side with the Confederates, visiting, eating, and playing cards with the Johnnies. Comrade Williams was a member of Co. F, 12th Ind., and served from 1861 until 1865, his last battle being Bentonville.

67

Sherman's Expulsion of Atlanta's Citizens

John W. Waite, "After Atlanta's Surrender. Sending Citizens Through the Confederate Lines and the Exchange of Prisoners"

(April 9, 1903, p. 3)

EDITOR NATIONAL TRIBUNE: I find in The National Tribune of Feb. 26 a letter from Harvey O. Williams, of Remus, Mich., saying he was one of the 100 detailed to remove the women and children and exchanged prisoners from Atlanta after the surrender. I also was one of detailed men. I belonged to Co. G, 6th Iowa. Gen. Sherman issued an order that all women and children should leave Atlanta. He could not furnish them with provisions. Those who wanted to go North could do so, and the rest he made go South. One hundred wagons filled with women and children arrived each day from Atlanta, while the truce lasted, and the occupants were loaded into wagons belonging to Hood's army. I think there were 20,000 women and children in Atlanta when it surrendered. In the exchange of prisoners Hood was to send men that had been captured during Sherman's campaign. Instead, he sent men from Andersonville Prison, all belonging to the Army of the Potomac. I think it would have been impossible for them to have marched five miles a day. I did not see one that had on a full suit—that is, pants, coat, vest, and hat; some had pants without anything else; some had coat and shirt. Nearly all were barefooted, and almost starved. But, you ought to have heard them cheer when they saw our flag.

While we were camping there the Johnnies and our men would meet and talk over the campaign. A number from both sides were lying on the ground one day, when an officer from Hood's army ordered his men to return to camp and stay there. We objected, but it did no good—they had to obey orders. I do not remember the officer's name. It was neutral ground for a mile around the camp, and we were allowed o go anywhere in that space. During the truce a rebel soldier told me he was going to desert, and inquired what direction to take to reach our army. I told him to follow where the railroad track had been, and he would reach our pickets in a cut near Atlanta. He promised to write me if he got through. I never heard from him. I think he lived at Galveston, Tex.; do not remember what regiment. I was enrolled at Burlington, Iowa, July18, 1861, and discharged at close of war, at Louisville, Ky., July 21, 1865. Was with my regiment through all its campaigns. Always belonged to the Fifteenth Corps. Was under Sherman at Shiloh when he commanded a division. Was at the Grand Review at Washington.—JOHN W. WAITE, Wellman, Iowa.

68

Sent Back to Andersonville

Harvey O. Williams, "Prisoners Exchanged at Rough and Ready"

(April 9, 1903, p. 3)

EDITOR NATIONAL TRIBUNE: In answer to my request for correspondence with prisoners exchanged at Rough and Ready, I have received several replies. One from Chancey Reynolds, 72d Ohio, Fremont, O., who says he was one of the 104 Union prisoners who were rejected because their regiments did not belong to Sherman's army. To Comrade Reynolds I would say that we realized his feeling of disappointment at the failure to be exchanged. The condition of these men was the most horrible that I saw during the war. To Comrade John W. Waite, 6th Iowa, I would say that I remember his regiment. It was in the same division (First Division, Fifteenth Corps) as the 12th Ind. To A. W. Wintermute, 76th Ohio, I would say that the 12th Ind. did lead the line of march at the Grand Review at Washington. I was left guide of the second platoon. We passed in review about 9 o'clock a.m. We had with us our brass band. I have often thought since that this was the proudest day of my life.—HARVEY O. WILLIAMS, 12th Ind., Remus, Mich.

Williams's letter is notable in confirming the identity of one of those Federal prisoners sent back to Andersonville during the truce—and that he survived. His reply to two other veterans reminds us of a principal function of the National Tribune*: providing a forum for communication and sharing war memories. Finally, nearly four decades after Sherman's 65,000 veterans marched down Pennsylvania Avenue on May 24, 1865, that Harvey Williams should remember the experience as "the proudest day of my life" is touching indeed (Stuart McConnell,* Glorious Contentment: The Grand Army of the Republic, 1865-1900 *[Chapel Hill: University of North Carolina Press, 1992], 3 ["soldiers on parade would remember the national spectacle of the Grand Review"]).*

69

A Monument for General McPherson

John T. Wiesman, "Field of Atlanta. Disgrace of a Monument to Gen. James B. McPherson"

(May 28, 1906, p. 3)

EDITOR NATIONAL TRIBUNE: As I went down here to Atlanta to visit the Cotton Exposition I also visited the battlefield of July 22, 1864. Having been over the field in 1877, 13 years after the battle, before scarcely any changes had been made, and again in 1881 and 1890, I have been able, to a certain extent, to keep track of the positions occupied by the different commands engaged.

Now, after a lapse of 31 years, I thought it might be of interest to the veterans to learn how it looks. A great change has taken place since, and many of the old boys who fought on that bloody field would scarcely be able to recognize the place.

I met some here who were in the battle, who had been out to Leggett's Hill, and they said they were unable to locate the place occupied by their regiment during the battle. A few were not even able to recognize Leggett's Hill. There now stands a three-story brick residence on or very near the spot occupied by Battery D, 1st Ill. Art. (McAllister's battery), and the 3d Ohio battery. This place is owned by a Mr. Koch, who came down here soon after the war. I am indebted to him for much valuable information, as he bought the place not many years after the war, and before many changes had been made, and he was able to show me where the breastworks were located which were erected on the afternoon of the battle.

To the left of Leggett's Hill, commencing at the southeast angle of the breastworks, in a northeast direction along the left of the Third Division, Seventeenth Corps and the Sixteenth Corps, nothing now remains of the breastworks except a small portion of the works occupied by the extreme left of the Third Division, and here and there a patch where the Sixteenth Corps stood.

Along the McDonough road, northwest of the angle on Leggett's Hill, and along that portion of the line occupied by the 45th and 20th Ill., and other commands of the Third Division, Seventeenth Corps, everything has been leveled down and laid out in town lots, and is occupied by residences.

Leaving the McDonough road, turning almost due north, in the direction of the Fifteenth Corps, through a strip of timber where the 17th Wis. stood, the breastworks are in a fair state of preservation. Along the line of the Fifteenth Corps there is here and there a patch left, just barely enough to trace the line-of-battle.

Of the rebel breastworks considerable is left at different places. Especially is this so across the ravine in front of the left of the Third Division and in front of the Sixteenth Corps, to the left of Leggett's Hill. It will be but a few years till all trace of this famous battlefield will be gone.

In walking over the field I found only one bullet, but the natives have quite a stock of relics on hand, and are disposing of them at a fair price. I was surprised to find nailed high up to a pine tree where Gen. McPherson fell, a sign reading, "Gen. John B. McPherson, killed July 22, '64." How or by whom such a blunder was made I cannot understand. One would suppose that anyone who was in the least familiar with the history of the late war and our Generals, especially one so prominent as our beloved McPherson, would know that it was James B., not John B.

The monument erected where Gen. McPherson fell is a disgrace to our Government. It is a condemned cannon inclosed by a cast-iron rail fence about the size of a hen-coop. That is all that marks the sacred spot where the gallant McPherson gave up his precious life for the Nation.

It seems strange that Shiloh battlefield, away from any town or railroad, should be preserved as a national park, and Leggett's Hill and McPherson be neglected and forgotten; especially when one consider its nearness to Atlanta, a city of 100,000, and which is destined at no far distant day to become the city of the South.—JOHN T. WIESMAN, Battery D, 1st Ill. Art. (McAllister's), 515 North Thirteenth street, Lincoln, Neb.

In May 1877, there were still U.S. soldiers stationed in Atlanta at the McPherson Barracks in the city's west end. Captain John R. McGinness, Chief Ordnance Officer of the U.S. Army Department of the South, and his men conceived of the idea for a monument to General McPherson at the site of his death, which was still well marked. McGinness won the sale of a 30 foot-square parcel of land from its owner, James Brown (who gave it up for only a dollar as a patriotic duty). Captain McGinness and his men developed plans for the monument, raised money, and saw the project through: a base of granite from nearby Stone Mountain, a 24-pounder siege gun donated from the Augusta Arsenal, and finally a monument not too far from Atlanta's Flat Shoals Road.

The McPherson monument dedication drew from the Atlanta Constitution *on September 20, 1877, a guide with directions to the site, which the paper advised its readers would find "interesting."*

70
And a Mile Away
"Where Gen. Wm. H. T. Walker Fell"
(August 7, 1902, p. 7)

The spot where Maj.-Gen. Wm. H. T. Walker, C.S.A., met his death in the battle of Atlanta, July 22, 1864, has been marked by a handsome monument which was unveiled on the 38th anniversary of his death. The exercises were attended by many Union and Confederate veterans. The main shaft of the monument is composed by a big 22-pound gun. The gun stands on end, resting on four blocks of marble bearing appropriate inscriptions. An iron fence surrounds the monument and four smaller guns, relics of the civil war, are used as cornerposts.

On July 22, 1902, in the same manner that a big cannon barrel had been mounted on a stone block for General McPherson a quarter-century earlier, a large cannon tube was dedicated near where General Walker had been killed on July 22, 1864. The monument site, though, was actually a fifth of a mile west of General Walker's actual death-site, according to the meticulous local historian Wilbur G. Kurtz; Atlanta's streets at the time did not reach that far east. Thirty years later, urban development allowed historians to move and rededicate the cannon monument at its more correct place, today's Wilkinson Circle and Glenwood Avenue, east of downtown and just off Interstate Highway 20.

Appendix
Origin of Memorial Day

J. M. Hawks, "Origin of Memorial Day. Graves of Union Soldiers at Charleston Decorated in May, 1865"

(May 18, 1899, p. 3)

Editor National Tribune: It is a very common custom, and has been, no doubt, for a long time, for people to decorate the graves of their friends by planting ornamental flowers and shrubs, and also by placing bouquets of cut flowers on the graves. Of course, the graves of soldiers would be honored in the same way. Out of this general custom has grown the special and beautiful and sacred observance of Memorial Day. The following brief account of probably the earliest public observance of a Memorial or Decoration Day, I think, will be of general interest to your widespread circle of readers. I copy from a little book of "Hymns, Poems and Patriotic Selections, compiled for use in the Public Schools, by Harriet L. Mathews and Elizabeth E. Rule, in 1893."

"Although the origin of the day as now observed is credited to several sources, it is generally conceded that the honor of the first observance of the day, in connection with the Union dead, must be given to James Redpath and Dr. Esther H. Hawks, who on May 30, 1865, planned and carried a memorial service over the graves of the prisoners who had been held in the stockade at Charleston, S.C."

In the diary of Dr. Hawks, dated Charleston, May 30, 1865, we find: "We have today celebrated the decoration of the bleak spot where so many of our soldiers are buried. In the long trenches four short rows contain 249 bodies of our men, the dead of less than a week. The colored men, inspired by Mr. Redpath, have built a fence around the spot. A fine monument is to be erected as soon as we have sufficient means. The school children were formed in procession at the Morris-street Schoolhouse and marched to the race-course, where the opening ceremonies were held. On reaching the ground we found a great crowd of people already assembled, comprising all the military notables and many Northern visitors. Mr. Redpath was the animating spirit of the occasion.

At 10 o'clock a.m. the procession was formed again, the school children in advance, each with bouquets or baskets of lovely flowers. As they passed under the flag, which was stretched across the track leading to the soldiers' graves, singing

'My Country, 'Tis of Thee,' it was a beautiful sight. On entering the inclosure every voice was hushed, and with quiet, reverent steps all marched around the yard depositing the flowers on the graves. It was a most pathetic scene, and it would have gladdened the heart of many a poor mother to have seen this beautiful tribute to the memory of her precious dead.

"The ceremonies in the yard consisted of prayer, singing and reading passages of Scripture. None but the colored people joined in the exercises. It was a very solemn and impressive service."

I will here state that some of the invited guests were detained on duty with their commands. Charles Cowley, of Lowell, Judge Advocate-General of the South Atlantic blockading squadron, expected to be present. In his interesting book, "Afloat and Ashore," hie mentions the meeting and his regret at not being able to be with his friend Redpath that day, and gives a hint at the conciliatory spirit of the remarks he intended to make on that occasion. At the time mentioned there were more than a thousand colored children in the Charleston schools, in charge of Northern teachers, mostly young women.—J. M. Hawks, Hawks Park. Fla.

With this article, the National Tribune *joined the historical debate on the origin of Memorial Day in the United States.*

In early May 1868, John A. Logan, commander-in-chief of the recently organized Grand Army of the Republic, designated the forthcoming May 30 as a Decoration Day to memorialize Union soldiers buried in the national cemeteries being established (John R. Neff, Honoring the Civil War Dead: Commemoration and the Problem of Reconciliation *[Lawrence: University Press of Kansas, 2005], 136-137). In the 1870s and '80s, Northern legislatures designated May 30, Memorial Day, as a legal holiday (Paul H. Buck,* The Road to Reunion 1865-1900 *[Boston: Little. Brown, 1937], 117).*

Then, some began to claim that the first Memorial Day service occurred two years before Logan's decree, in Charleston. During the war, the city's Race Course had been turned into a stockade for Union prisoners, and part of the land became a cemetery for deceased soldiers.

Exhibit A is the article, "The Martyrs of the Race Course," that appeared on Tuesday, May 1, 1865—three weeks after Appomattox—in the Charleston Daily Courier. *"The ceremonies of the dedication of the ground where are buried two hundred and fifty-seven Union soldiers, took place in the presence of an immense gathering yesterday," it began; "fully ten thousand persons were present, mostly of the colored population." African Americans, newly freed in Charleston, had organized as "Friends of the Martyrs" and the "Patriotic Association of Colored Men." They worked to improve the burial ground. Then, with the help of James Redpath, General Superintendent of Education in occupied Charleston, they arranged a big public dedication of the cemetery on May 1 (Stephen Davis,* 100 Significant Civil War Photographs: Charleston in the War *[Charleston: Historical Publications, 2019], 140-143).*

A Lowell, Massachusetts, attorney, Charles Cowley, had served as an officer in the Union Navy's South Atlantic Squadron; he was invited by Redpath to speak at the dedication. Later, in his Leaves from a Lawyer's Life Afloat and Ashore *(1879), Crowley credited the Charleston observances of May 1 as the origin of the U.S. Memorial Day holiday. This led some to jump to the conclusion that the Race Course event had taken place on May 30, 1865. Historian Paul H. Buck, for instance, makes this claim in* The Road to Reunion *(116). More recently, David W. Blight, noting that the first Northern postwar memorial services occurred on "'Decoration Day,' known eventually as Memorial Day," has written that "Black South Carolinians and their Northern white abolitionist allies were primarily responsible for founding decoration Day" (Blight, "Decoration Days: The Origins of Memorial Day in North and South" in Alice Fahs and Joan Waugh, eds.,* The Memory of the Civil War in American Culture *[Chapel Hill University of North Carolina Press, 2004], 94-95).*

This is where J. M. Hawks's article fits in; he quotes from his wife's diary, declaring that the Race Course commemoration occurred on May 30. *In this, he apparently fudged the date so that he could claim that Esther helped establish one of the nation's most memorable holidays.*

It should be noted that current scholars deride the notion that the Charleston service of May 1, 1865, was the first Northern Memorial Day, pointing out that the event was a cemetery dedication, a one-time-only occasion, not to be repeated annually. See Daniel Bellware and Richard Gardiner, The Genesis of the Memorial Day Holiday in America *(Columbus, GA: Columbus State University, 2014).*

In 1889, Congress ruled Memorial Day, May 30, as a national holiday (Matthew Denis, Red, White, and Blue Letter Days: An American Calendar *[Ithaca: Cornell University Press, 2002], 230). Today, by act of Congress, Memorial Day is observed on the last Monday in May.*

Bibliography

Printed Original Sources

"The Martyrs of the Race Course," *Charleston Daily Courier*, May 1, 1865.

Abel, E. Lawrence. *Confederate Sheet Music* (Jefferson NC: McFarland, 2004).

Arnold, S. J. "How Gen. Polk Was Killed," *National Tribune*, April 28, 1898.

Bellware, Daniel and Richard Gardiner. *The Genesis of the Memorial Day Holiday in America* (Columbus, GA: Columbus State University, 2014).

Berry, Stephen. "The Book or the Gun?" in J. Matthew Gallman and Gary W. Gallagher, eds., *Lens of War: Exploring Iconic Photographs of the Civil War* (Athens: University of Georgia Press, 2015).

Blanton, Deanne and Lauren Cook, *They Fought Like Demons: Women Soldiers in the American Civil War* (Baton Rouge: Louisiana State University Press, 2002).

Blight, David. "Decoration Days: The Origins of Memorial Day in North and South" in Alice Fahs and Joan Waugh, eds., *The Memory of the Civil War in American Culture* (Chapel Hill University of North Carolina Press, 2004).

Blount, Jr., Russell W. *The Battles of New Hope Church* (Gretna LA: Pelican Publishing Company, 2010).

Buck, Paul H. *The Road to Reunion 1865-1900* (Boston: Little. Brown, 1937).

Burton, E. Milby. *The Siege of Charleston 1861-1865* (Columbia: University of South Carolina Press, 1970).

Butkovich, Brad. *The Battle of Pickett's Mill: Along the Dead-Line* (Charleston, CS: The History Press, 2013).

Castel Albert. "Union Fizzle at Atlanta: The Battle of Utoy Creek," *Civil War Times Illustrated*, (February 1978).

Castel Albert. *Decision in the West: The Atlanta Campaign of 1864* (Lawrence: University Press of Kansas, 1992).

_____. *Winning and Losing in the Civil War: Essays and Stories* (Columbia: University of South Carolina Press, 1996).

Coffin, Charles "Carleton." "Saving the Nation: The Story of the War Retold for Our Boys and Girls," *National Tribune*, December 6, 1883–March 15, 1888.

Committee of the Regiment. *The Story of the Fifty-fifth Regiment Illinois Volunteer Infantry in the Civil War* (n.p., 1887).

Conyngham, David P. *Sherman's March through the South* (New York: Sheldon & Co., 1865).

Cowley, Charles. *Leaves from a Lawyer's Life, Afloat and Ashore* (Boston: Lee & Shepard, 1879).

Cox, Jacob D. *Atlanta* (New York: Scribner's Sons, 1882).

Crabb, Martha L. *All Afire to Fight: The Untold Tale of the Civil War's Ninth Texas Cavalry* (New York: William Morrow, 2000).

Daniel Larry J. *Days of Glory: The Army of the Cumberland, 1861-1865* (Baton Rouge: Louisiana State University Press, 2004).

Davis, Burke. *Sherman's March* (New York: Random House, 1980).

Davis, Stephen. "No Hope of Success," *Civil War Times*, April 2018.

_____. "Sherman in North Georgia: The Battle of Resaca," *Blue & Gray*, vol. 31, issue 4 (Summer 2015).

_____. "Simply Criminal," *America's Civil War*, vol. 32, no. 2 (May 2019).

_____. "The Bugle Was to Blame," *Civil War News*, vol. 45, no. 1 (January 2019).

_____. "The Death of Bishop Polk," *Blue & Gray*, (June 1989).

_____. *100 Significant Civil War Photographs: Charleston in the War* (Charleston: Historical Publications, 2019).

_____. *Atlanta Will Fall: Sherman, Joe Johnston and the Yankee Heavy Battalions* (Wilmington DE: Scholarly Resources, 2001).

_____. *Texas Brigadier to the Fall of Atlanta: John Bell Hood* (Macon: Mercer University Press, 2019).

_____. *What the Yankees Did to Us: Sherman's Bombardment and Wrecking of Atlanta* (Macon: Mercer University Press, 2012).

Dawes, E. C. "The Confederate Strength in the Atlanta Campaign" in Robert U. Johnson and Clarence C. Buel, eds., *Battles and Leaders of the Civil War*, 4 vols. (New York: Century Co., 1888).

DeLand, W. P. "New Hope Church," *National Tribune*, April 21, 1887.

Denis, Matthew. *Red, White, and Blue Letter Days: An American Calendar* (Ithaca: Cornell University Press, 2002).

Ecelbarger, Gary. *Slaughter at the Chapel: The Battle of Ezra Church 1864* (Norman: University of Oklahoma Press, 2016).

_____. *The Day Dixie Died: The Battle of Atlanta* (New York: Thomas Dunne Books, 2010).

Evans, David. *Sherman's Horsemen: Union Cavalry Operations in the Atlanta Campaign* (Bloomington: Indiana University Press, 1996).

Evans, E. Chris, ed., "Report of the Battle of Atlanta by Capt. Francis DeGress Commanding Battery H, 1st Illinois Light Artillery," *Blue & Gray*, vol. 11, no. 4 (April 1994).

Foster, Ira. "Home for the Exiles," *Atlanta Daily Intelligencer*, October 30, 1864.

Grenville M., Dodge. *The Battle of Atlanta and Other Campaign Addresses, Etc.* (Council Bluffs IA: Monarch Printing Company, 1911).

Hagler, Gould. "Crossing the Hooch without a Hitch," *Civil War News*, vol. 45, no. 9 (September 2019).

Hess, Earl J. *Kennesaw Mountain: Sherman, Johnston, and the Atlanta Campaign* (Chapel Hill: University of North Carolina Press, 2013).

_____. *The Battle of Ezra Church and the Struggle for Atlanta* (Chapel Hill: University of North Carolina Press, 2015).

_____. *The Battle of Peach Tree Creek: Hood's First Effort to Save Atlanta* (Chapel Hill: University of North Carolina Press, 2017).

Hibbard, James and Albert Castel, "Kilpatrick's Jonesboro Raid, August 18-22, 1864," *Atlanta Historical Journal*, vol. 29, no. 2 (Summer 1985).

Hogue, J. W. "Disputed Actions of the Twentieth Corps," *National Tribune*, May 31, 1883.

Hood, John B. *Advance and Retreat: Personal Experiences in the United States and Confederate States Armies* (New Orleans, 1880).

Horn, Huston. *Leonidas Polk: Warrior Bishop of the Confederacy* (Lawrence, KS: University Press of Kansas, 2019].

Horn, Stanley F. *The Army of Tennessee: A Military History* (Norman: University of Oklahoma Press, 1953).

Hunter, Robert, ed. *Sketches of War History 1861-1865: Papers Prepared for the Ohio Commandery of the Military Order of the Loyal Legion of the United States 1880-1890*, 6 vols. (Cincinnati: Robert Clarke & Co., 1890).

Jenkins, Sr., Robert D. *The Battle of Peach Tree Creek: Hood's First Sortie, 20 July 1864* (Macon: Mercer University Press, 2013).

_____. *To the Gates of Atlanta: From Kennesaw Mountain to Peach Tree Creek, 1-19 July 1864* (Macon: Mercer University Press, 2015).

John McElroy, *Andersonville: A Story of Rebel Military Prisons, Fifteen Months a Guest of the So-Called Southern Confederacy* (Toledo: D. R. Locke, 1879).

Johnson, R. W. *A Soldier's Reminiscences in Peace and War* (Philadelphia: J. P. Lippincott, 1886).

Johnston, Joseph E. *Narrative of Military Operations During the Civil War* (New York: D. Appleton and Company, 1874).

Kennett, Lee. *Marching Through Georgia: The Story of Soldiers and Civilians During Sherman's Campaign* (New York: HarperCollins, 1995).

Kerksis, Sydney C. *The Atlanta Papers* (Dayton OH: Press of Morningside Bookshop, 1980).

Killian, Lewis C. "Death of Gen. Polk. Shot First by an Indiana Battery of Rodmans," *National Tribune*, October 2, 1902.

Kime, Marlin G. "Sherman's Gordian Knot: Logistical Problems in the Atlanta Campaign," *Georgia Historical Quarterly*, vol. 70, no. 1, Spring 1986.

Kurtz, Wilbur G. "A Federal Spy in Atlanta," *Atlanta Constitution Magazine*, June 8, 1930.

_____. "Last Battle Near Atlanta," *Atlanta Journal Sunday Magazine*, February 26, 1933.

Lemon, George E. , John McElroy, and W. L. Mattocks, eds., *National Tribune*, June 1879-June 25, 1942.

Lewis, Lloyd. *Sherman: Fighting Prophet* (n.p., 1932).

Loop, Myron B, *The Long Road Home: Ten Thousand Miles Through the Confederacy With the 68th Ohio* (Huntington, WV: Blue Acorn Press, 2006).

_____. "Sounding the Alarm: The 68th Ohio's Trying Time at the Battle of Atlanta," *National Tribune*, December 1, 1898.

Marten, James. *Sing Not War: The Lives of Union & Confederate Veterans in Gilded Age America* (Chapel Hill: University of North Carolina Press, 2011).

Marvel, William. *Andersonville: The Last Depot* (Chapel Hill: University of North Carolina Press, 1994).

McAllister, Ruth Hill Fulton, ed. *Co. "Aytch" First Tennessee Regiment or a Side Show of the Big Show* (Franklin TN: Providence House Publishers, 2007).

McConnell, Stuart. *Glorious Contentment: The Grand Army of the Republic, 1865-1900* (Chapel Hill: University of North Carolina Press, 1992).

McKinney, Francis F. *Education in Violence: The Life of George H. Thomas and the History of the Army of the Cumberland* (Chicago: Americana House, 1991).

McMurry, Richard. *John Bell Hood and the War for Southern Independence* (Lexington: University Press of Kentucky, 1982).

Meredith, Roy, ed. *This Was Andersonville* (New York: McDowell, Obolensky, 1957)

Neff, John R. *Honoring the Civil War Dead: Commemoration and the Problem of Reconciliation* (Lawrence: University Press of Kansas, 2005).

Nevins, Allan, James I. Robertson, Jr., and Bell I. Wiley, eds., *Civil War Books: A Critical Bibliography*, 2 vols. (Baton Rouge: Louisiana State University Press, 1967, 1969.

Phillips, Ulrich B. *Life and Labor in the Old South* (Boston: Little, Brown and Company, 1963 (1929)).

Pollard, Edward A. *The Third Year of the War* (New York: Charles Richardson, 1865).

Richardson, Eldon B. *Kolb's Farm: Rehearsal for Atlanta's Doom* (privately printed, 1979).

Sauers, Richard A. "Introduction" in Sauers, ed., *The National Tribune Civil War Index: A Guide to the Weekly Newspaper Dedicated to Civil War Veterans, 1877-1943*, 3 vols. (El Dorado Hills, CA: Savas Beatie, 2018).

Scaife, William R. *The Campaign for Atlanta* (Saline MI: McNaughton and Gunn, 1993).

Scales, John R. *Sherman Invades Georgia: Planning the North Georgia Campaign Using a Modern Perspective* (Annapolis: Naval Institute Press, 2006).

Sherman, William T. *Memoirs of General William T. Sherman By Himself: Planning the Great Campaigns of 1864* (1897).

Simpson, Brooks D. and Jean V. Berlin, eds., *Sherman's War: Selected Correspondence of William T. Sherman, 1860-1865* (Chapel Hill: University of North Carolina Press, 1999).

Stern, Philip Van Doren, ed. *Andersonville: A Story of Rebel Military Prisons* (Greenwich CT: Fawcett Publications, 1962).

Strayer Larry M. and Richard A. Baumgartner, eds., *Echoes of Battle: The Atlanta Campaign* (Huntington WV: Blue Acorn Press, 1991).

The War of the Rebellion: A Compilation of the Official Records of the Union and Confederate Armies, 128 vols. (Washington, D.C., 1880-1901), Series I, vol. 45, part 1. All references are to Series 1 unless otherwise noted.

Travis, Benjamin. *The Story of the Twenty-Fifth Michigan* (n.p., 1897).

Vandiver, Frank E. "General Hood as Logistician," *Military Affairs*, vol. 16, no. 1 (Spring 1952).

Watkins, Sam. "Battle Near Adairsville," *Confederate Veteran*, April 1902.

Welch, Jack D., M.D. *Medical Histories of Union Generals* (Kent OH: Kent State University Press, 1996).

Winters, John D. The Civil War In Louisiana (Baton Rouge: Louisiana State University Press, 1963).

Woodworth, Steven E. *Nothing But Victory: The Army of the Tennessee 1861-1865* (New York: Alfred A. Knopf, 2005).

Younger, Edward, ed. *Inside the Confederate Government: The Diary of Robert Hill Garlick Kean* (New York: Oxford University Press, 1957).

Zinn, John G. *The Mutinous Regiment: The Thirty-Third New Jersey in the Civil War* (Jefferson NC: McFarland, 2005).

Unpublished

Kurtz, Wilbur G. "Why Was Snake Creek Gap Left Unguarded?" ca. 1935, Kurtz Collection, Atlanta History Center, Atlanta, GA., MSS 130, box 49, folder 14, 21.

Index

Acknowledgments

The creation of this collection of essays on the Atlanta Campaign, drawn from the pages of the National Tribune, has been a labor of love and a collaborative effort. Any oversights or errors in curating this collection are mine alone.

My deepest thanks go to the scholars, archivists, and historians whose decades of research and insights into the Atlanta Campaign provided essential context for this project. Their work laid the foundation for this volume.

I am profoundly grateful to my publisher, Theodore P. Savas, for embracing this project and to the dedicated team at Savas Beatie. Special thanks to Production Manager Veronica Kane for keeping me on schedule and for her keen eye in design and editing.

My heartfelt thanks go to my wife, Billy, and to my friends who assisted in ways both large and small as I completed this project. Your support made this work possible.

Thank you all for your contributions to this effort to preserve and share these important historical perspectives. On to Atlanta.

About the Editor

Stephen Davis of Cumming, Georgia, is the author of many books related to the Atlanta Campaign, including a pair for the Emerging Civil War series: *A Long and Bloody Task: The Atlanta Campaign from Dalton through Kennesaw to the Chattahoochee, May 5–July 18, 1864* and *All the Fighting They Want: The Atlanta Campaign from Peachtree Creek to the Surrender, July 18–September 2, 1864* (Savas Beatie, 2016, 2017). He is also the editor, with Theodore P. Savas, of a forthcoming volume of essays on the Georgia Campaign and Sherman's March to the Sea.